ESCROW

PRINCIPLES and PRACTICES

Dept. of Real Estate
original License Section - Broker
P.O. Box 187002
Sacramento, CA, 95818-7000

ASHLEY
CROWN
SYSTEMS, INC.

Sherry Shindler Price

ESCROW
Fifth Edition

This publication is designed to provide accurate and current information regarding the subject matter covered. The principles and conclusions presented are subject to local, state, and federal laws and regulations, court cases, and revisions of same. If legal advice or other expert assistance is required, the reader is urged to consult a competent professional in the field.

Director of Publishing
Lars Jentsch

Real Estate Publisher
Leigh Conway

Writer/Copy Editor
Susan Carlson

Administrative Assistant
Courtney Gonzales

Senior Technical Writer
Nicole Thome

Technical Writer
Ben Hernandez

Technical Writer/Editor
Lisa Schoenle

Creative Editor/ Production Coordinator
Judy Hobbs

Graphic Design
Susan Mackessy
Dria Kasunich, Assistant Manager

©2007 by Ashley Crown Systems, Inc., a division of Allied Business Schools, Inc.

Published by
Ashley Crown Systems, Inc.
22952 Alcalde Drive
Laguna Hills, California 92653

Printed in the United States of America
ISBN: 0-934772-42-8

TABLE OF CONTENTS

Acknowledgments

The author wishes to thank the real estate professionals and editors who contributed to the earlier edition of this textbook. Contributors to the earlier edition include Peter Meade, Joan Thompson, Cynthia Simone, and Norma Hurlick.

The *Escrow Principles and Practices, 5th edition* is the result of teamwork from the publisher, educators, and other professionals to make this textbook the best in real estate escrow. Special thanks are given to those Allied Business School staff members who used their experience and skill to bring together the material content, illustrations, and layout.

Finally, the author acknowledges the California Department of Real Estate and others for the forms and contracts printed throughout the textbook.

Preface

Whether you are reading this book to increase your knowledge about escrow for the purpose of beginning a new career, using it to satisfy a requirement for your real estate license, or simply wanting to learn more about the fascinating subject of escrow, you will find the information presented in this book useful. Although the book is written for beginning students, consumers will also find answers to their questions about escrow.

Anyone interested in escrow will benefit from the information presented here. It covers the entire processing of the transfer of real property by a neutral third party, whether that party is an escrow officer, real estate broker, title insurer, or an attorney.

Chapter
1

What is Escrow?

Learning Objectives

After reading this chapter, you will be able to:

- discuss the basic requirements for real estate transactions.

- summarize the basic requirements for an escrow.

- explain the relationship between the escrow agent and the real estate broker.

- describe the designation of the escrow holder.

- explain general escrow principles, rules, and procedures.

- explain the termination of an escrow.

- describe the rights and obligations of the parties.

Introduction

The term **escrow** describes a temporary trust arrangement between parties wishing to transact business and exchange money or property. Escrow, from the French word for scroll, is the process where a neutral third party collects all the documents to affect that transfer of property and money, and to make sure the buyer and seller agree to the terms.

To **open escrow** means to name an escrow holder, otherwise known as an escrow company, or some other eligible person, such as an attorney, to act as the impartial agent between both buyer and seller. The choice of an escrow agent is always that of the buyer and seller. However, they probably do not have a relationship with an escrow agent, and may rely on the advice of their real estate broker.

Escrow reduces the potential risk of fraud by acting as a trusted third party that collects, holds, and disburses funds according to buyer and seller instructions. Funds and documents are placed in the custody of the escrow officer for delivery to a grantee only after certain conditions are met.

As a trust arrangement between parties, escrow is the final stage in a transaction between buyer and seller, usually exchanging real estate. The seller grants the property to the person, the buyer, who must prove he or she has sufficient funds to pay for it.

When all relevant documents and monies are collected, they are reviewed, and joint escrow instructions are exchanged between the parties to sign. **Escrow instructions** are written directions, signed by a buyer and seller, detailing the procedures necessary to close a transaction and directing the escrow agent how to proceed.

The conditions of the sale are set in writing as directed by the principals within the law. When these conditions are not met, they are said to **fall out of escrow,** or, where one of the parties is unable to satisfy the conditions of the purchase and sale contract. The authority to conduct an escrow is given mutually by the buyer and seller in the escrow instructions. Neither party may end the escrow without the agreement of the other, in writing. In addition, the escrow officer may not return any funds or documents to either party without agreement from all parties.

The escrow instructions reflect the understanding and agreement of the principals, who may not always be the buyer and seller, because transactions involving the sale of real estate are not the

only kind that requires the use of an escrow. Any time a neutral third party is needed to handle documents or money, such as in the transfer of real property, loans, sale of trust deeds, or bulk sales and sales of a business or business opportunities, an escrow might be required.

In this chapter, escrow as it relates to the sale of real estate is covered. No one is required by law to use an escrow for any of the above transactions, including the sale of real property. However, when a buyer and seller reach an agreement about the sale of property, including terms and price, it is advisable for a neutral third party to handle the details of completing the sale.

Misunderstandings, criminal intent, and negligence, on the part of the principals may incur loss to one or both parties if the contract is not handled by an outside escrow professional.

After instructions are signed, the escrow holder reviews and insures they are upheld, by requesting all parties involved to observe the terms and conditions of the contract. The escrow holder coordinates communication between the principals, the agents, and any other professionals—such as the lender or title company whose services are called for in the instructions.

The escrow process has many steps. The offer to buy a property is usually the purchase agreement that is accepted and signed by all parties. Then escrow is opened. The buyer deposits money into the escrow account, which is held in trust by the escrow company. Then, there is a contingency period, when all conditions in the purchase agreement are executed. These typically include approvals, title reports, loan approvals, appraisals, physical inspections, pest and termite reports, and certifications.

Homeowner's insurance, fire insurance, and other local requirements are updated, paid, and renewed. After all conditions are met, the loan documents are signed and the closing costs are paid. The deed is then recorded. Escrow closes when the escrow holder receives confirmation that title was recorded at the county recorder's office and the new owner takes possession of the property.

Parties to the Escrow

A buyer and a seller are known as principals in an escrow. The **escrow holder** is a neutral third party who is an agent for buyer and seller. A real estate agent is not a party to an escrow unless he or she is the buyer or the seller.

A **buyer** is the party purchasing the property and the one who will receive a deed conveying the title.

A **seller** is the owner of record who must deliver the title agreed upon in the contract.

An **escrow agent** is an impartial third party who collects all documents and money, through the escrow, and transfers them to the proper parties at the close of escrow.

An escrow agent may be a bank, savings and loan, title insurance company, attorney, real estate broker, or an escrow company. A real estate broker may act as an escrow agent in the course of a regular transaction for which a real estate license is necessary. The broker conducts the escrow as a service only if he or she is the listing or selling broker to the subject sale.

Relationship between the Escrow Agent and the Real Estate Broker

No transaction can be completed without a good relationship between a broker and an escrow agent. The good will, positive guidance, and technical knowledge of an escrow officer have helped many brokers get through an escrow, especially those new to the business.

During the escrow, the escrow officer is an agent for both buyer and seller, as you recall, and must operate from the original escrow instructions. When they instruct the escrow agent to  prepare an amendment canceling the escrow, a buyer and seller mutually end their agreement after they both sign the amendment.

After the real estate broker negotiates the sale, it is the job of the escrow agent to see that the agreements made by the parties are carried out. The broker and the escrow agent must check with each other regularly to make sure information is correct and to inform each other of how the escrow is progressing.

Agency

An escrow agent holds a **limited agency**, or authority. Any duties to be conducted must be mentioned specifically in escrow instructions or they are not authorized by the buyer and seller. The escrow holder must remain neutral, as the agent of both the buyer and seller, during the course of the escrow. After all conditions of the escrow have been met, the escrow officer is the agent of each of the parties in dealing with their individual needs.

The Escrow Company

The **Commissioner of Corporations** licenses escrow companies, and does not allow individuals to apply. Only a corporation is qualified and must make an application. A $25,000 bond, or more, based upon predicted yearly average transactions and trust fund use must be furnished by an applicant for an escrow office license. A bond must be posted by all parties (officers,  directors, trustees, and employees) having access to money or securities being held by the escrow company as safety against loss.

Audit

An escrow company must keep accounts and records that can be examined by the Commissioner of Corporations. A yearly inspection prepared by an independent certified public accountant, describing operations, must be delivered to the Commissioner.

Requirements for an Escrow

A valid escrow requires a binding contract between buyer and seller, and conditional delivery of transfer documents and funds to a third party.

A real estate transaction usually starts at the time a broker obtains a listing from a property owner. The most common type of listing is an Exclusive Authorization and Right to Sell. With this type of listing, the seller must pay a commission no matter who sells the property—even if the owner makes the sale. The agent promises to use due diligence to find a ready, willing and able buyer under the exact terms of the listing contract, and the seller promises to pay a commission when the agent fulfills the contract.

At some point, either the listing agent or an agent from another brokerage will find a buyer and write an offer. There are certain items the agent must consider carefully when preparing the offer to purchase (also known as a deposit receipt or purchase contract).

Binding Contract

There must be a binding contract between the parties to an escrow. The binding contract can be a deposit receipt, agreement of sale, exchange agreement, an option, or mutual escrow instructions of the buyer and seller.

The following items included in the offer apply only to the most common aspects of a residential purchase. Commercial, industrial, vacant land, farm or ranch development, and other types of properties require different treatment by a real estate agent.

Information Required in Residential Purchase Offers

1. The date and place contract is signed by buyer

2. Correct name and address of the buyer

3. Form of the buyer's deposit: cash, check, cashier's check, promissory note, money order, or other

4. Designee to hold the deposit: broker, seller, or escrow

5. Purchase price of the property

6. Terms under which the property will be purchased: all cash, refinance, loan assumption, or taking title subject to the existing loan. Do any of the existing loans contain acceleration clauses or prepayment penalties? If so, has the buyer approved the terms?

7. Amount of time to be allowed for the seller to consider the buyer's offer to purchase, and to complete the transaction. Is time of the essence?

8. Definite termination date stated in the contract

9. Covenants, Conditions and Restrictions; easements; rights or other conditions of record that affect the property

10. Deed of conveyance: Is it to be executed by the seller to contain any exceptions or reservations? Has the buyer approved of this?

11. Are there any stipulations or agreements regarding any tenancies or rights of persons in possession of the property?

12. Roof and electrical wiring inspections: Who pays for inspections and work, and who orders reports?

13. Are there any stipulations or agreements regarding facts a survey would reveal, such as the existence of a common wall, other encroachments, or easements?

14. Are there any special or unusual costs or charges to be adjusted through escrow? Who will pay for the title policy, escrow services, and other customary charges? Who pays for any unusual charges?

15. Who will select the escrow holder? The parties should reach a mutual agreement on this.

16. Are there any special documents to be drawn in the transaction, and if so, who will prepare them?

17. If prorations are not to be made as of the date escrow closes, what date is to be used?

18. If possession is granted prior to the close of escrow, what type of agreement must be prepared to cover this occupancy and who will prepare it?

19. If structural pest control inspection report and certification are to be furnished, who pays?

20. Are other brokers involved in this transaction? What are their names, addresses, and telephone numbers?

21. Determine the sales commission and when it will be paid. If the deposit receipt initially establishes that a commission will be paid, it must contain the commission negotiability statement, which declares that by law all commissions are negotiable.

22. All parties must sign the contract. Check signatures of all buyers, all sellers, and agents. Certain documents require in-person and notarized signatures. Electronic signatures

such as on a fax, e-mail, or voice mail giving authorization are not allowed on most recorded documents.

23. Every purchase contract prepared or signed by a real estate salesperson must be reviewed, initialed, and dated by the salesperson's broker within five working days after preparation or signing by the salesperson, or before the close of escrow, whichever occurs first.

24. If the transaction is a residential sale of four-or-fewer units and involves seller-assisted financing, and a licensee is the arranger of such credit, a financing disclosure statement must be prepared and provided to both buyer and seller.

25. A specific written disclosure must be made to prospective buyers of one-to-four dwelling units with facts about the particular piece of property that could  materially affect the property's value and desirability.

26. Licensees acting as listing and selling brokers in certain residential real estate transactions must make informational written and oral disclosures concerning who is representing whom.

27. A real estate licensee who acts as the agent for either the buyer or the seller in the sale or transfer of real property, including manufactured housing, must disclose to both parties the form, amount and source of any compensation received or expected to be received from a lender involved in financing related to the transaction.

The signed instructions become an enforceable contract, binding all parties to the escrow. When there is a conflict between the signed instructions and the original agreement of the principals, the instructions, constituting the later contract, usually control.

Amendments to the escrow instructions can change the original agreement if all parties agree. When all instructions are completed, escrow closes, the buyer gets a deed, and the seller gets the money.

> The Clarks put their home on the market, listing it with a local broker. It was competitively priced, and the broker said it would take about two weeks to sell. An agent from another real estate company showed the house to the Lees, and they loved it. After writing up an offer and presenting it to the Clarks, the buyers' agent called them with the news that the sellers had accepted.
>
> The next day, the agent took the buyer's earnest money (usually about one percent of the purchase price) to the escrow office, gave it to the escrow agent, and got a receipt. The escrow holder immediately cashed the check and deposited it in a trust account. The escrow holder then drew up escrow instructions to reflect the terms and conditions of the sale. The sellers signed their copy, the buyers signed theirs, and both were returned to the escrow company. The escrow was now open.

Conditional Delivery of Documents and Funds

The second requirement of a valid escrow is a conditional delivery of transfer documents and funds, and means the seller will deliver a signed grant deed that conveys title to the buyer. The buyer and/or the lender will deliver to escrow the funds that are required to complete the sale.

The escrow agent holds the security for any loan (trust deed) conditionally until directed by the terms of the escrow. The escrow agent keeps all documents and funds until all other terms of the escrow are completed. Then the agent distributes or disburses the money according to the expressed conditions of the escrow.

Sometime before escrow closes, the seller will be asked to sign a grant deed conveying title to the buyer. Because the seller will sign over ownership to the buyer before getting any money, the escrow holder is instructed to hold the signed deed until funds from the buyer are deposited in escrow and all other terms of the escrow have been met. Conditional delivery of the grant deed has been made by the seller.

Toward the end of the escrow period, the buyer will sign a note and trust deed for the loan in the presence of a notary. The buyer is promising to pay back the money, using the property as security for the loan. Escrow has not closed, and the buyer does not yet own the property. Nor, has the seller received the promised money, but the note and trust deed are signed and deposited into escrow, conditionally, until all other terms have been met. Only then will escrow request loan funds.

The escrow is closed when all the terms and conditions of the escrow are met. Upon close of escrow, the buyer gets the grant deed, after it has been recorded, and the seller gets the money.

Items Provided by Seller

As soon as possible following the opening of escrow, the seller should furnish escrow with numerous items.

1. Escrow instructions signed by all sellers.

2. The latest available tax and assessment bills, and any other statements or bills that are to be prorated through escrow.

3. Seller's loan payment books and records.

4. Seller's fire, liability and other insurance policies, if they are to be assigned to the buyer.

5. A beneficiary statement, demand, certificate, or offset statement from the holder of any mortgage or trust deed of record on the property; any items showing the amount due on any loan of record; the payment date; the date to

which interest is paid; and other important information. Consent to the transfer from lenders of record must be given.

6. Any subordination or other agreement required by the purchase contract, to be approved by the parties through escrow.

7. Certificates or releases showing satisfaction of mechanic's liens, security agreements (chattel mortgages), judgments, or mortgages that are to be paid off through escrow.

8. List of tenants' names and the apartments they occupy, together with the amount of rent paid and unpaid, the dates when rents are due, and, if required, an assignment to the buyer of any unpaid rent, as well as details on advance security deposits, if any.

9. Assignment to buyer of all leases affecting the property.

10. Letters from the seller to tenants instructing them to pay all subsequent rent to the buyer and reaffirming the conditions of the tenancy, including notice of the transfer of the security deposit, if any, to the buyer.

11. The seller's executed and acknowledged deed of conveyance to the buyer or a valid authority to execute the deed of the seller by the seller's attorney-in-fact if the seller is acting through an agent.

12. An executed bill of sale covering any personal property to be conveyed to the buyer, together with an inventory of the items for the buyer's approval.

13. A security agreement (chattel mortgage) for execution by the buyer covering any personal property included in the purchase price but not paid for by the buyer in cash.

14. The deed by which the seller acquired title to the property and the seller's policy of title insurance.

15. Any unrecorded instruments affecting the title.

16. Any other documents or instruments that the seller is to prepare or deliver.

17. Any approvals required for documents that the seller is to receive at closing.

18. Information required to be disclosed to the buyer under the seller financing disclosure, if necessary.

Items Provided by Buyer

As soon as possible after opening escrow, the buyer should furnish the escrow holder with certain documents and information. The escrow holder should personally review or inspect all of the items.

1. Review of signed escrow instructions by all purchasers.

2. Review the preliminary title report for the subject property to make sure that there are no items of record affecting the property that have not already been approved by the buyer.

3. Review any Conditions, Covenants, and Restrictions affecting the property, whether of record or not.

4. Confirm terms of any mortgages or deeds of trust to be assumed by the buyer, or that will remain an encumbrance on the property.

5. Examine any beneficiary statements, fire insurance or liability policies if they are to be assigned to the buyer.

6. Examine offset statements on loans to be assumed, or those under which the buyer is taking title to the property subject to existing loan terms; verify the unpaid principal balances owed, the interest rates, dates to which interest is paid and other vital information.

7. Review and approve structural pest control and other reports to be delivered through escrow.

8. Carefully review all new loan documents prior to signing.

9. Compare the terms of the purchase contract, escrow instructions, title report, and deed to make sure there are no discrepancies in the transaction documents.

10 If tenancies are involved, review the names, addresses and telephone numbers of tenants, the rent amounts, rent due dates, copies of rent agreements or leases, letters from the seller to the tenants verifying the terms of occupancy and notifying the tenants of change of ownership, the assignments of any unpaid rent and leases, details on security deposits if any.

11. Examine the bill of sale and inventory covering the items of personal property to be conveyed to the purchaser.

12. Review copies of any bills to be prorated in escrow.

13. Verify all amounts and prorations on the estimated escrow settlement sheet.

14. Re-inspect the property to determine that it is in the same condition as it was when the buyer made the purchase offer. Recheck for any undisclosed items that might affect the use of the property, such as party walls, access roads to other properties, irrigation canals or ditches, common drives or persons in occupancy or possession of the property, which the county records would not disclose.

15. Deposit sufficient cash or clear funds to cover any balance owed on the purchase contract plus buyer's closing costs and expenses, and approvals as required. The parties should always keep copies of any documents and instruments they sign, deliver to, or receive from any party in the real estate transaction.

Review - Items Required For a Valid Escrow
- Binding contract between buyer and seller

- Conditional delivery of transfer documents to a third party

Escrow Principles and Rules

Once instructions have been signed by the buyer and seller and returned to the escrow holder, neither party may unilaterally change escrow instructions. Any changes must be made by mutual

agreement between buyer and seller. The escrow agent does not have the authority to make changes in the contract upon the direction of either the buyer or seller, unless both agree to the change, in the form of an amendment.

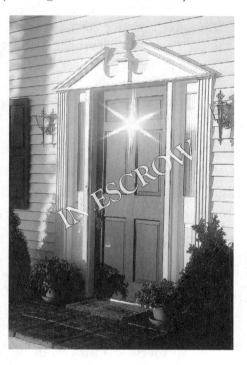

In addition, it should be noted, the broker has no authority whatsoever to amend or change any part of the escrow instructions without the knowledge of the principals. Often, terms of the loan for the buyer are subject to change as complications may appear and include credit problems, liens, or there may be a cloud on the title.

Furthermore, time is of the essence when a buyer tries to lock in a certain interest rate on a mortgage or home loan. These issues can delay and create obstacles for the escrow officer to close the transaction. The obstructions may require an amendment. The written consent of both buyer and seller, in the form of an amendment to the original instructions, must be given before any dates or changes are made.

> The Clarks and the Lees signed escrow instructions on June 9. The agreement reflected a sales price of $450,000, with $90,000 as a down payment. After signing the instructions, however, the buyers decided they only wanted to put $80,000 down, and told the escrow officer to change the instructions. An amendment was written for them to sign, and a copy sent to the sellers to sign.

> The buyers were disappointed when the Clarks did not want to change the contract and refused to sign the amendment. When the Lees wanted to back out, the escrow officer reminded them that they had a mutually binding legal agreement with the sellers. Neither side could change any part of the agreement, including terminating it, without the written agreement of the other.

As agent for both parties to an escrow, the escrow agent is placed in a position of trust. By operating as a dual agent, the escrow holder sits between the buyer and seller as a stakeholder with an obligation to both sides to act as a neutral third party.

Rules Escrow Officers Must Observe

- Escrow instructions must be understood by the principals to the escrow and must be mutually binding. Instructions must be carefully written to be very clear about the agreement between the buyer and seller. Each party must understand his or her obligation to carry out the terms of the contract without assuming the escrow holder has any power to force compliance. The escrow holder may not act unless directed by the principals.

- The escrow holder does not get personally involved in disagreements between the buyer and seller, nor act as a negotiator for the principals. Escrow instructions make each party's obligations and agreements clear, and it is up to the buyer and seller to keep the promises they each made in their agreement with the other. All parties must know that the escrow agent is not an attorney, and must advise anyone seeking legal advice to get counsel from a professional.

- An escrow agent has a limited capacity as agent for buyer and seller, and may only perform acts described in the contents of escrow instructions. While acting as a dual agent, the escrow officer must operate in the best interest of both parties, without special preference to either. The escrow agent serves each principal after escrow closes, in providing them with the  documents and/or funds to which they are entitled.

- All parties must sign escrow instructions for the contract to be binding. An escrow is officially open when both buyer and seller have signed instructions.

- Escrow instructions must be clear and certain in their language.

- All documents to be recorded must be sent to the title company in a timely manner (as quickly as possible), and all interested parties should receive copies of recorded documents.

- Escrow instructions should specify which documents or funds the escrow holder may accept.

- Overdrawn trust accounts (debit balances) are prohibited by law.

- Information regarding any transaction is held in trust by the escrow officer and may not be released to anyone without written permission of the principals.

- An escrow holder has a duty to disclose to the principals any previously undisclosed information that might affect them. An amendment would be drawn at the direction of the buyer and seller to reflect any change as a result of new disclosures.

- A high degree of trust along with good customer service must be provided by an escrow holder.

- An escrow holder must remain strictly neutral regarding the buyer's and the seller's interests.

- Escrow records and files must be maintained daily. A systematic review of open escrow files will make sure no procedure has been overlooked, or time limit ignored.

- Before closing an escrow, all files must be audited carefully.

- All checks or drafts must have cleared before any funds may be released to the seller. Escrow must close in a timely manner, according to the agreement between buyer and seller. A prompt settlement must be made to all principals.

Prohibitions
- Referral fees may not be paid by an escrow company to anyone as a reward for sending business to them.

- Commissions may not be paid to a real estate broker until the closing of an escrow.

- Blank escrow instructions to be filled in after signing are not acceptable. Initials must be placed wherever there is a change or deletion.

- Information regarding an escrow may only be provided to parties to the escrow.

- Copies of escrow instructions must be provided to anyone signing them.

Escrow Procedures

Escrow procedures may vary according to local custom. In some areas, escrow companies or banks conduct escrows. In other areas, title companies or attorneys do the job. However, there are certain procedures that are followed during the regular course of all escrows.

Open Escrow

The person, who opens escrow, if there is a real estate agent involved, is the selling agent. That person usually has an earnest money check that must be deposited into escrow or some other trust account no more than one business day after buyer and seller have signed the deposit receipt. So, at the first opportunity, the real estate agent must take the buyer's check to the escrow officer to put in a trust account. The agent then gives the escrow  officer all the information needed to prepare escrow instructions. Usually within a day or two, computer-generated instructions are ready for buyer and seller to sign. The escrow instructions reflect the agreement between the buyer and seller as seen in the offer to purchase (deposit receipt) and usually include all disclosures required by law. Only the seller's set of escrow instructions include the amount of commission to be paid to the broker, unless, as in some cases, the buyer is paying a commission also.

Direct Escrow

If no real estate agent is involved, the principals may go to escrow directly, and tell the escrow officer to prepare instructions according to their agreement.

Prepare Escrow Instructions

Usually the escrow holder prepares the instructions on a computer-generated form, with details of the particular transaction completed in the blank spaces on the form. All parties sign identical instructions, with the exception of the commission agreement that is prepared for the seller to sign — if the seller is in fact paying the commission. The buyer and seller sign the instructions, which are then returned to the escrow holder who follows the directions in the agreement to complete the escrow. Imagine you are selling your home. Many of the items discussed below will be included in your escrow instructions.

1. **Purchase Price**: This is the amount of money the buyer and seller have agreed upon for the sale of the property.

2. **Terms**: The buyer and seller agree on how the buyer will purchase the property: cash, new loan, loan assumption, VA, or FHA loan, seller to carry a trust deed, trade, or any other special agreements provided in the contract between buyer and seller. This section describes the amount of the down payment and the terms of any loans for which the buyer will apply.

3. **Vesting**: The buyer will take title as sole ownership, joint tenancy, tenants in common, or tenancy in partnership. How the buyer will take title may be important for tax or inheritance purposes and the escrow holder must be directed how to draw the deed to reflect the wishes of the buyer, but may not give advice regarding vesting.

4. **Matters of Record**: Buyer and seller may disagree on a matter of record—some circumstance affecting the property—that is

recorded. It may be an easement, an existing street bond, or a trust deed that must be resolved.

5. **Closing:** Buyer and seller will agree on how long they want the escrow to last. They will mention a specific length of time for the escrow and instruct accordingly.

6. **Inspections:** Buyer and seller will agree on whether or not to have certain inspections of the property before the close of escrow, such as a pest control inspection; property inspection to identify any plumbing, electrical, or structural problems; a soil inspection to check for slippage or unstable compaction. The buyer's approval of the reports will be a contingency of the sale and must be mentioned in the escrow instructions.

7. **Prorations:** The division of expenses and income between the buyer and seller as of the date of closing is known as proration. Some items that are prorated are taxes, rental deposits or income, and insurance premiums. The reason for prorations is that some payments may have been made by the seller for a time period beyond the agreed-upon date for escrow to close. On the other hand, the seller may be in arrears on taxes. The escrow holder debits or credits the seller or buyer, depending on the escrow closing date.

8. **Possession:** The buyer and seller will have agreed on when the buyer can move into the house, and the escrow instructions must reflect their agreement on the date the buyer will take possession of the property. The close of escrow could be the date of possession, or sometimes the seller will rent the property back from the buyer after the close of escrow. In that case, a lease agreement should be signed and handled by the parties outside of escrow.

9. **Documents:** The escrow holder will need to know which documents to prepare, have signed by the proper party, and record at the close of escrow. Usually, these will be a grant deed and a trust deed.

10. **Disbursements**: The escrow holder must settle the accounts of the buyer and seller according to the escrow instructions. In addition, the escrow holder must provide a closing statement of costs and charges to each party and a final distribution of funds at the close of escrow.

Order Title Search

At the time the buyer and seller reach an agreement about the sale of the property, they also select a title company. One of the jobs of the escrow officer, after escrow has been opened, is to order a title search of the subject property.

The title company prepares a preliminary title report, and searches the records for any encumbrances or liens against the property. The company checks to make sure the seller is the owner of record, and inspects the history of ownership, or chain of title, in the preliminary title search.

The purpose is to ensure all transfers of ownership have been recorded correctly, and that there are no unexplained gaps.

The buyer is allowed a certain number of days to approve this preliminary title report. Buyer approval is important to eliminate surprises regarding the title as the escrow progresses. The escrow holder should notify the buyer and seller if there is any difference in the preliminary report and the escrow instruction, by way of an addendum for information only.

As you recall, the escrow agent is a neutral party and only has the authority to do what is described in the escrow instructions. The escrow officer must wait for instructions about what to do next. The preliminary title report is the foundation for the title insurance policy on the buyer's title as instructed by the buyer and seller in the escrow instructions.

The Clarks and the Lees had instructed their escrow officer to order a preliminary title search. The Lees had three days to approve the report, as a contingency of the sale. When they examined it, however, they found there was a bond against the property for street repairs. They had not been aware of it.

The bond was a lien in the amount of $3,500. The buyers could not approve the preliminary title report until the issue was cleared up. An agreement about who would pay the bond had to be reached by the buyers and sellers, then new instructions given to the escrow officer, who would prepare an amendment for both parties' signatures.

Request for Payoff Demands and/or Beneficiary Statements

The escrow officer must also see that existing loans are paid off, or assumed, depending on the agreement of the buyer and seller.

If the existing loan, or the seller's debt, is going to be paid off with proceeds from the sale, a demand from the lender holding the note and trust deed is needed, along with the unpaid principal balance and any other amounts that are due.

The escrow officer requests a demand for payoff of a loan from the lender who holds a loan against the subject property. The exact amount of loans that are to be paid off must be known so the escrow officer's accounting will be correct at the close of escrow.

If an existing loan is going to be assumed, or taken subject to, a beneficiary statement is requested by the escrow holder from the lender.

A statement of the unpaid balance of a loan, the beneficiary statement also describes the condition of the debt. The escrow agent follows instructions about financing the property, and prepares any documents necessary for completing the escrow at the close. These might be a note and trust deed, or assumption papers.

The buyers are obtaining an adjustable loan in the amount of $360,000. The down payment will be $90,000, to make the purchase price of $450,000. The existing $250,000 loan on the property is held by Union Bank. The existing loan will be paid off when the buyer's new loan is funded, and the seller will get the balance of the purchase price, $200,000, less the seller's costs of selling (commissions, termite work, escrow and title fees, etc.).

Union Bank is notified of the expected payoff and asked by the escrow officer to send a statement of the unpaid balance and condition of the existing loan. This is known as a request for demand for payoff.

Order Other Reports

The parties to an escrow may request any number of reports about the condition of the property. The escrow holder is asked in the instructions to accept any reports submitted into escrow. These may include a structural pest control report (termite report), property inspection report, soil condition report, or environmental report. Any approval from the buyer or seller about a report is held in escrow until needed, or given to the appropriate party at the close of escrow.

New Loan Instructions and Documents

Escrow accepts loan documents or instructions about financing the subject property and completes them as directed. The escrow agent gets the buyer's approval of and signature on loan documents, and receives and disburses loan funds as instructed.

Fire Insurance Policies

The parties to an escrow will have agreed on fire insurance policies and will instruct the escrow officer accordingly. The escrow holder will accept, hold and deliver any policies and will follow instructions about transferring them. A lender will require fire insurance, and will expect the escrow holder and the buyer to be accountable for either a new policy or the transfer of an existing one.

Calculate Prorations

The escrow holder will be instructed by the buyer and seller about prorations and other accounting to be done at the close of escrow.

Prorations

- Interest

- Premiums on fire insurance

- Security deposits and rents (if the property is a rental)

- Seller's current property taxes

The buyer and seller will have agreed on impound accounts, and the escrow holder will be guided on how to handle the credit and debit. After the escrow agent completes the accounting, the agent tells the buyer to deliver the down payment (usually in the form of a cashier's check), plus other escrow costs, to the escrow office.

At this time, the principals sign the loan documents, and complete any other paperwork required for the financing. If all is in order, the loan is funded and the money sent to the title company to pay off all encumbrances of record. Then the escrow may close.

Audit the File

At the close of escrow, the escrow officer must **audit** (examine) each file to make sure all accounting has been accurate, and that escrow instructions have been followed. A cash reconciliation statement is completed by the escrow holder and closing statements are prepared for all principals.

Record the Documents

The escrow holder orders the title company to record all transaction documents as instructed by the buyer and seller. This occurs after a final check of the title company records to be sure nothing has changed since the preliminary title search was done. Then the title company issues a policy of title insurance to insure the buyer's title. Documents that might require recording are the grant deed, trust deed, contract of sale, or option.

Close the Escrow

The last job of the escrow holder is to **close the escrow**. The escrow officer gives closing statements to buyer and seller, disburses all money, and delivers all documents to the proper parties after making sure all documents have been recorded by the title company.

The seller gets a check for the proceeds of the sale minus escrow fees, real estate commissions, or any other costs of selling, and any pertinent documents; and the buyer gets a grant deed.

True-False Quiz

Now that you have read all the material in this chapter, take the following self-test and check your knowledge of basic escrow principles and procedures.

True-False

1. *TRUE* An escrow is a short-lived trust arrangement.

2. *False* When there is a conflict between signed instructions and the original agreement, the original contract will prevail.

3. *TRUE* Escrow holds documents, conditionally, until all terms of the escrow are met.

4. *False* A buyer or a seller can change escrow instructions unilaterally.

5. *False* A real estate broker has authority to amend escrow instructions.

6. *TRUE* An escrow agent operates as an agent for buyer and seller.

7. *TRUE* A beneficiary statement is requested if an existing loan is going to be assumed.

8. *False* Prorations usually include principal and interest.

9. *TRUE* The escrow holder gives closing statements to the buyer and seller at the end of the escrow.

10. *False* The escrow holder must return any funds to buyer or seller if requested to do so by either party.

Chapter 2

Parties, Documents, and Real Estate Basics

Learning Objectives

After reading this chapter, you will be able to:

- describe all the parties with whom you are dealing.

- define the common types of deeds.

- understand the use and function of several other documents including Notice of Default, Change of Ownership, Power of Attorney, and Notary Public.

- define real estate basics such as ownership, limitations, and encumbrances.

- understand the system of recording evidence of property title or interest.

Introduction

The business of escrow, like many other professions, has a language all its own, as well as sharing much of the vocabulary of the real estate industry. This chapter will introduce and define the terms you will use to open, complete, and close an escrow. You also will be introduced to the buyers and the sellers, the borrowers and the lenders, and others, as you journey through this introduction to escrow.

Parties to an Escrow

As an escrow agent, you must be knowledgeable about the parties with whom you are dealing. Following is a list of the likely entitities you will meet as you become a practiced escrow professional.

Administrator: a person appointed by the court to handle the affairs of a deceased person when there is no one named in a will to do so.

Assignee: the person to whom a claim, benefit, or right in property is made.

Assignor: the person transferring a claim, benefit, or right in property to another.

Beneficiary: the lender under a deed of trust.

Escrow holder: an independent third party legally bound to carry out the written provisions of an escrow agreement; a neutral, bonded third party who is a dual agent for the principals; sometimes called an escrow agent.

Executor/Executrix: A person named in a will to handle the affairs of a deceased person.

Grantee: the person receiving real property because it has been granted in a deed by another individual.

Grantor: the person who executes or signs a document giving title or ownership of real property to another party. A grantor might sign a grant deed, a quitclaim deed, or a gift deed.

Lessee: Tenant, renter.

Lessor: Landlord, owner.

Principal: the main party to a transaction.

Trustee: Holds bare legal title to property as a neutral third party where there is a deed trust. Only duties are to foreclose or reconvey after a payoff on a loan.

Trustor: the borrower under a deed of trust.

Types of Deeds

When property is transferred by **private grant,** a written instrument is used. An **instrument** is a formal legal document such as a contract, deed, or will. The kinds of deeds commonly used for private grants include: grant deed, quitclaim deed, gift deed, warranty deed, and sheriff's deed. The financing instruments, a deed of trust and a deed of reconveyance, will be seen in financial closings.

Grant Deed

When property is transferred by private grant, the instrument generally used is a **grant deed**. The parties involved are the grantor, or the person conveying the property, and the grantee, the person or group receiving the property.

A grant deed contains two implied warranties by the grantor. One is that the grantor has not already conveyed title to any other person, and the other is that the estate is free from encumbrances other than those disclosed by the grantor.

The grantor also promises to deed any rights he or she might acquire to the property after conveying it to the grantee. For example, oil or mineral rights might revert to the property at some time in the future, after the present owner has sold the property. AFTER ACQUIRED TITLE means any benefits that come to the property after a sale must follow the sale and accrue to the new owner.

A grant deed must contain certain basics in order to be legally binding.

Requirements for a Valid Grant Deed

- According to the Statute of Frauds, a deed must be in writing.

- The parties to the transfer (grantor and grantee) must be sufficiently identified and described.

- The grantor must be competent to convey the property (not a minor or incompetent).

- The grantee must be capable of holding title (must be a real living person, not fictitious).

- The property must be adequately described, but it does not require a legal description.

- Words of granting such as grant or convey must be included.

- The deed must be executed (signed) by the grantor. The deed may be signed by a witnessed mark "X".

- The deed must be delivered to and accepted by the grantee.

A grant deed is not effective until it is delivered. It must be the intention of the grantor that the deed is delivered during his or her lifetime. For example, a deed would not be valid if signed and put in a safe place until the death of the grantor, and then recorded. Recording a deed is considered the same as delivery of the deed.

After a deed has been acknowledged by the grantor, it may be filed with the county recorder, giving constructive notice of the sale. An acknowledgment is a signed statement, made before a notary public, by a named person confirming that the signature on a document is valid and that it was made of free will. A deed does not have to be acknowledged to be valid, but must be acknowledged to be recorded.

The purpose of recording a deed is to protect the chain of title, which is a sequential record of changes in ownership showing the connection from one owner to the next. A complete chain of title is desirable whenever property is transferred and required by title insurance companies if they are writing a policy on a property.

> Example: Donna Rose, a single woman, owned the house in which she lived. After marrying Tom Baker, she decided to sell the house. Because the chain of title showed that Donna owned it under her maiden name, she had to sign the deed as "Donna Baker who acquired title as Donna Rose" when she sold it.

The priority of a deed is determined by the date it is recorded. In other words, recording establishes a claim of ownership which has priority over any deeds recorded after it. The first to record a deed is the first in right.

> Example: Paul sells his house to Kate, and, without telling Kate, sells it also to Sally. Sally records her deed before Kate has a chance to record hers. Sally is the owner of record and gets the house. Kate has definite cause for a lawsuit against Paul.

However, there are some exceptions to the "first to record is first in right" rule. If the same property is sold to two parties, and the second party knows of the first sale and is aware of the fraud intended by the seller, the original sale is valid, even if it was not recorded first.

> Example: Sarah sells her house to Ted, who moves in without recording the deed. Sarah also sells the house to Gary, telling him to record the deed quickly, making him aware that Ted also has an interest in the property. In this case, Ted gets the house because (1) Gary was given knowledge of the prior sale, and (2) Ted had taken possession of the property (he had moved in), which established his right of ownership.

A grantee must accept a deed before it is considered effective. Acceptance is automatic if the grantee is an infant or incompetent person. Acceptance may be shown by the acts of the grantee, such as moving onto the property.

The grant deed need not be signed by the grantee. An undated, unrecorded, and unacknowledged grant deed may be valid as long as it contains the essential items noted below.

Review - Not Necessary for Valid Grant Deed

- Acknowledgment

- Recording

- Competent grantee; may be a minor, felon or incompetent

- Date

- Mention of the consideration

- Signature of grantee

- Habendum clause (to have and to hold)

- Seal or witnesses

- Legal description, an adequate description is sufficient

RECORDING REQUESTED BY

WHEN RECORDED MAIL TO

NAME
ADDRESS
CITY
STATE & ZIP

Title Order No.   Escrow No.

SPACE ABOVE THIS LINE FOR RECORDER'S USE

GRANT DEED

The undersigned declares that the documentary transfer tax is   and is

☐ Computed on the full value of the interest or property conveyed, or is

☐ Computed on the full value less the value of liens or encumbrances remaining at time of sale. The land, tenements realty is located in

☐ Unincorporated area of: ☐ City of: and

FOR A VALUABLE CONSIDERATION, receipt of which is hereby acknowledged.

hereby GRANT(S) to

the following described real property in the

County of: , State of:

Dated:

STATE OF:

COUNTY OF: }ss   _____

On _____ before me, the   _____
undersigned, a Notary Public in and for State,
personally appeared   _____

_____

personally known to me or proved to me on the basis of satisfactory evidence to be the person(s) whose name(s) is/are subscribed to the within instrument and acknowledged to me that he/she/they executed the same in his/her/their authorized capacity(ies), and that by his/her/their signature(s) on the instrument the person(s), or the entity upon behalf of which the person(s) acted, executed the instrument.

WITNESS my hand and official seal

Signature _____   (This area for official notary seal)

MAIL TAX STATEMENTS AS DIRECTED ABOVE

Quitclaim Deed

Another type of deed used to transfer property is a quitclaim deed. This type of deed was commonly used to transfer real property interests between husband and wife. However, an **interspousal grant deed** is now used between spouses instead of a quitclaim deed.

A quitclaim deed is often used to clear a cloud on the title. A cloud on title is any condition that affects the clear title of real property. It also may be used to remove a minor defect in the chain of title or to terminate an easement.

A **quitclaim deed** is a deed conveyance that operates as a release of whatever interest the grantor has in the property, sometimes called a release of a deed. The quitclaim deed contains similar language to a deed, with the important exception that rather than using the words grant and release, it contains language such as remise, release, and quitclaim. Grantors therefore do not warrant title or possession. Grantors only pass on whatever interest they may have, if any. In effect, a grantor forever quits whatever claim he or she had, if in fact any existed.

The quitclaim deed transfers only whatever right, title and interest the grantor had in the land at the time of the execution of the deed and does not pass to the grantee any title or interest subsequently acquired by the grantor. Thus, the grantee cannot claim a right to any "after-acquired title".

Although a quitclaim deed may or may not vest any title in the grantee, it is not inferior to the other types of deeds in what it actually conveys. For example, if a grantor executes and delivers a warranty deed to one person and subsequently executes and delivers a quitclaim deed to the same property to another person, the grantee under the quitclaim deed will prevail over the grantee under the warranty deed, assuming the holder of the quitclaim is first to record the deed.

RECORDING REQUESTED BY

AND WHEN RECORDED MAIL TO

NAME
ADDRESS
CITY
STATE & ZIP

MAIL TAX STATEMENTS TO

NAME
ADDRESS
CITY
STATE & ZIP

Title Order No. _____ Escrow No. _____

SPACE ABOVE THIS LINE FOR RECORDER'S USE

QUITCLAIM DEED

The undersigned grantor(s) declares(s) that the documentary transfer tax is _____ and is

☐ Computed on the full value of the interest or property conveyed, or is

☐ Computed on the full value less the value of liens or encumbrances remaining at time of sale.

☐ Unincorporated area of: _____ ☐ City of: _____ and

FOR A VALUABLE CONSIDERATION, receipt of which is hereby acknowledged.

hereby REMISE(S), RELEASE(S) AND FOREVER QUITCLAIM(S) to

the following described real property in the

County of: _____ , State of: _____

Dated: _____

STATE OF: _____

COUNTY OF: _____ }ss

_____

On _____ before me, the
undersigned, a Notary Public in and for State,
personally appeared

_____

_____

_____

personally known to me or proved to me on the basis of satisfactory evidence to be the person(s) whose name(s) is/are subscribed to the within instrument and acknowledged to me that he/she/they executed the same in his/her/their authorized capacity(ies), and that by his/her/their signature(s) on the instrument the person(s), or the entity upon behalf of which the person(s) acted, executed the instrument.

WITNESS my hand and official seal

Signature _____ (This area for official notary seal)

MAIL TAX STATEMENTS AS DIRECTED ABOVE

Depending on local custom, ordinarily a warranty or bargain and sale deed will be used to transfer a fee simple interest (not in California). A quitclaim deed is not commonly used to convey a fee, but is usually restricted to releasing or conveying minor interests in real estate for the purpose of clearing title defects or clouds on title. It may also be used to convey lesser interests such as life estates and to release such interests as a remainder or reversion.

A title searcher will regard a quitclaim deed in the chain of title as a red flag, and most title companies will not guarantee titles derived out of a quitclaim, at least not without further clarification.

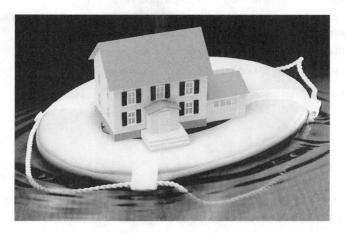

Quitclaim deeds also are often used between close relatives, such as when one heir is buying out the other, or where a seller's finances are so troubled that it is inconsequential to the buyer whether he or she is getting any warranties or not.

Executing a quitclaim deed does not carry even an implied warranty as regards ownership, liens, encumbrances or that the grantor has not previously signed a deed to someone else. It does convey ownership of the property to another person.

Gift Deed

A **gift deed** is used to make a gift of property to a grantee, usually a close friend or relative. The consideration in a gift deed is called love and affection.

DEEDS

- Grant Deed

- Quitclaim Deed

- Warranty Deed

- Deed of trust

- Deed of reconveyance

- Sheriff's Deed

- Gift Deed

Sheriff's Deed

A **sheriff's deed** is given to a buyer when property is sold through court action in order to satisfy a judgment for money or foreclosure of a mortgage. This usually is the result of an execution sale or forced sale of property under a "writ of execution". The proceeds are used to satisfy a money judgment or a mortgage foreclosure.

Warranty Deed

A **warranty deed** is one that contains express covenants of title. In other words, the seller who uses a warranty deed to transfer the property title to a buyer is guaranteeing clear title as well as the right to transfer it. Rarely is it used in California because title companies have taken over the role of insuring title to property.

Financing Instruments

As an escrow holder, you will handle deeds of trust and deeds of reconveyance.

Deed of Trust

A **deed of trust** is a security instrument that conveys title to a trustee to hold as security for the payment of a debt. There are three parties to a deed of trust: the borrower (trustor), lender (beneficiary) and a neutral third party called a trustee. The only interest conveyed to the trustee is bare legal title, and the trustee's only obligation is to foreclose if there is a default on the loan, or reconvey the deed of trust to the borrower when it is paid in full.

WHEN RECORDED MAIL TO:

_____ [Space Above This Line For Recording Data] _____

State of California   **DEED OF TRUST**   FHA Case No.

THIS DEED OF TRUST ("Security Instrument") is made on
The Trustor is

("Borrower").

The trustee is

("Trustee").

The beneficiary is

which is organized and existing under the laws of
and whose address is

("Lender").

Borrower owes Lender the principal sum of

Dollars (U.S. $). This debt is evidenced by Borrower's note
dated the same date as this Security Instrument ("Note"), which provides for monthly payments, with the full debt, if not
paid earlier, due and payable on   . This Security Instrument secures to Lender:
(a) the repayment of the debt evidenced by the Note, with interest, and all renewals, extensions and modifications of the
Note; (b) the payment of all other sums, with interest, advanced under paragraph 7 to protect the security of this Security
Instrument; and (c) the performance of Borrower's covenants and agreements under this Security Instrument and the Note.
For this purpose, Borrower irrevocably grants and conveys to Trustee, in trust, with power of sale, the following described
property located in   County, California:

TOGETHER WITH all the improvements now or hereafter erected on the property, and all easements, appurtenances,
and fixtures now or hereafter a part of the property. All replacements and additions shall also be covered by this Security
Instrument. All of the foregoing is referred to in this Security Instrument as the "Property."

Initials _____
FHA California Deed of Trust 10/95

Deed of Reconveyance

A **deed of reconveyance** conveys title to property from a trustee back to the borrower (trustor) upon payment in full of the debt secured by the deed of trust. When the trustor pays off a loan, a **request for full reconveyance** or a **request for partial reconveyance** is executed by the beneficiary and given to the trustor along with the original note and deed of trust.

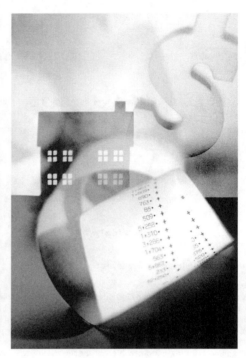

The trustor gives these documents to the trustee, who then issues the deed of reconveyance. Upon recording, it is evidence that the loan has been fully paid and the lien on the deed of trust is extinguished.

The request for full reconveyance generally is found on the backside of a deed of trust (see preceding form). The only time a separate form should be necessary is if the original deed of trust has been lost and a copy is used for reconveyance.

Usually, a partial reconveyance is used with large parcels of property when a portion of the note has been paid and release clauses are part of the deed of trust.

TO: SMS
SETTLEMENT
SERVICES
COMPANY
TRUSTEE

REQUEST FOR FULL RECONVEYANCE

The undersigned is the legal owner and holder of the note or notes, and of all other indebtedness secured by the foregoing Deed of Trust. Said note or notes, together with all other indebtedness secured by said Deed of Trust, have been fully paid and satisfied, and you are hereby requested and directed, on payment to you of any sums owing to you under the terms of said Deed of Trust, to cancel said note or notes above mentioned, and all other evidences of indebtedness secured by said Deed of Trust delivered to you herewith, together with the said Deed of Trust, and to reconvey, without warranty, to the parties designated by the terms of said Deed of Trust, all the estate now held by you under the same.

Dated_____   _____

                                   _____

                                   _____

SIGNATURE MUST BE NOTARIZED

Please mail Deed of Trust,
Note and Reconveyance to_____

Do not lose or destroy this Deed of Trust OR THE NOTE which it secures. Both must be delivered to the Trustee for cancellation before reconveyance will be made.

Other Documents

Request for Notice of Delinquency

By recording a **request for notice of delinquency**, the junior lienholder filing the request will be notified of the delinquency of payments. By the time a lender gets around to foreclosure, the borrower may be many months behind in payments. At the time of notification, the junior lienholder can decide whether to bring pressure on the borrower (in default on the senior loan) before the amount becomes unmanageable, or pay the amount in arrears. Be aware that anyone acquiring the property at a foreclosure sale must bring all payments and fees current for existing senior loans on the property.

Request for Notice of Default

A **request for notice of default** is a recorded document that requires notice to be given if a borrower defaults on a loan. The person most likely to file a request for notice is the holder of the lien junior to the one that is in default.

The request for notice must be filed with the county recorder on the record of the deed of trust. A request for notice must contain the recording data of the deed of trust and the name and address of the person who wants to be notified. Subsequently, if any notice of default or sale is recorded, the person named in the request must be notified. Receipt of a notice of default then may allow the person who requested the notice to take action to protect his or her interest in the property. Some deeds of trust have the request printed on the document and it is not necessary to record a separate request for notice.

> Example: Tim Winter sold his home for $200,000 and carried back a second deed of trust. At the time of the sale, Tim asked escrow to record a request for notice of default on the first deed of trust. Five years went by before the buyer stopped making payments on the first deed of trust. A notice

of default was recorded by the holder of the first deed of trust, starting foreclosure proceedings. During those five years, the value of the property decreased to an amount less than the original price paid by the buyer. In fact, the property is now worth little more than the amount of the first deed of trust. If Tim had not been notified in a timely manner of the trustee's sale, his interest in the property would have been canceled by the sale, with any proceeds going to the foreclosing lender of the first loan. Tim can now file his own notice of default and protect his deed of trust by becoming the new owner, subject to bringing current the first deed of trust.

Substitution of Trustee

The trustee under a deed of trust does not need to accept formally the position of trustee. Forms used by most escrow holders usually name a title company or their own escrow company. Anyone can be a **trustee**, with the only restriction on naming a trustee under a deed of trust being that it cannot be the borrower (trustor).

Because anyone can be a trustee, it is very easy for a named trustee under a deed of trust to be out of business or out of the state. Who then will start foreclosure, and who will reconvey the property to the trustor when the loan is paid off if the trustee is nowhere to be found?

The beneficiary under a deed of trust has the power to change the trustee of his or her deed of trust at any time by completing a "substitution of trustee" which deletes the current trustee and names a new one instead.

Statement of Information

Buyers and sellers must complete a statement of personal information as a necessary and essential part of each escrow opened. The title company needs the correct information regarding places of employment, former residences, former marriages, and social security numbers to identify each party to the escrow as just that party and no other.

SMS

Statement of Information
FILL OUT COMPLETELY AND RETURN TO SIMPLE MORTGAGE SERVICES

ESCROW # 00020-SMS   TRACT#   LOT#

Name_____ Social Security   Driver's
                        #_____   License#_____

Date of birth_____ Place of birth_____ Bus. phone_____ Home phone_____

Resided in USA since_____   Resided in California since_____

If you are married, please complete the following: Date Married_____at_____

Name of Spouse_____ Social Security #_____Driver's License #_____

Resided in USA since_____   Resided in California since_____

Previous Marriage or Marriages (if no previous marriage, write "None"):
Name of former spouse_____ Deceased___Divorced__Where___When____

Name of former spouse_____ Deceased___Divorced____Where___When___

Children by current or previous Marriages:
Name_____ Born_____ Name_____ Born_____
Name_____ Born_____ Name_____ Born_____

Information covering past 10 years:
Residence:

Number/Street	City	From	To
Number/Street	City	From	To

Employment

Firm Name	Location
Firm Name	Location

Spouse Employment:

Firm Name	Location
Firm Name	Location

Have you or your spouse owned or operated a business?
☐Yes   ☐No   If so please list names_____

I have never been adjudged, bankrupt, nor are there any unsatisfied judgments or other matters pending against me which might affect my title to this property except as follows:

_____

The undersigned declare, under penalty of perjury, that the foregoing is true and correct.
Executed on_____ at_____

Preliminary Change of Ownership

This document gives information to the county tax assessor about the property and who now owns it. The assessor can then determine from the sales price the method used to finance the purchase and the reason for the change in ownership, whether or not a change in property tax is required. The **preliminary change of ownership** report allows the assessor to place the appropriate tax on the property, starting on the date of conveyance to the next assessment date. The form must be completed before the close of escrow by the buyer, or the county recorder will impose an extra fee for recording the grant deed.

Even then, the buyer must submit the completed form within 60 days after closing escrow or other penalties will be accrued. The tax assessor then gets to revalue the property and increase the taxes due for the time from the close of escrow to when the next tax bill is issued.

PRELIMINARY CHANGE OF OWNERSHIP REPORT

FOR RECORDER'S USE ONLY

To be completed by transferee (buyer) prior to transfer of subject property in accordance with Section 480.03 of the Revenue and Taxation Code. A Preliminary Change of Ownership Report must be filed with each conveyance in the County Recorder's office for the county where the property is located; this particular form may be used in all 58 counties of California.

THIS REPORT IS NOT A PUBLIC DOCUMENT

SELLER/TRANSFEROR: **Sam Summers and Kate Summers**
BUYER/TRANSFEREE: **Dan Winter and Donna Winter**
ASSESSOR'S PARCEL NUMBER(S) **123-45-6789**
PROPERTY ADDRESS OR LOCATION: **987 Ocean View Drive**
Any City, CA 90000

MAIL TAX INFORMATION TO:

Name **Dan Winter**
Address **25892 Mountain Avenue**
Any Town, CA 90000

NOTICE: A lien for property taxes applies to your property on March 1 of each year for the taxes owing in the following fiscal year, July 1 through June 30. One-half of these taxes is due November 1, and one-half is due February 1. The first installment becomes delinquent on December 10, and the second installment becomes delinquent on April 10. One tax bill is mailed before November 1 to the owner of record. **IF THIS TRANSFER OCCURS AFTER MARCH 1 AND ON OR BEFORE DECEMBER 31, YOU MAY BE RESPONSIBLE FOR THE SECOND INSTALLMENT OF TAXES DUE FEBRUARY 1.**

The property which you acquired may be subject to a supplemental assessment in an amount to be determined by the **Apple County** Assessor. For further information on your supplemental roll obligation, please call the **Apple County Assessor**

PART I: TRANSFER INFORMATION   Please answer all questions.

YES	NO		
☐	☑	A.	Is this transfer solely between husband and wife (Addition of a spouse, death of a spouse, divorce settlement, etc.)?
☐	☑	B.	Is this transaction only a correction of the name(s) of the person(s) holding title to the property (For example, a name change upon marriage)?
☐	☑	C.	Is this document recorded to create, terminate, or reconvey a lender's interest in the property?
☐	☑	D.	Is this transaction recorded only to create, terminate, or reconvey a security interest (e.g. cosigner)?
☐	☑	E.	Is this document recorded to substitute a trustee under a deed of trust, mortgage, or other similar document?
☐	☑	F.	Did this transfer result in the creation of a joint tenancy in which the seller (transferor) remains as one of the joint tenants?
☐	☑	G.	Does this transfer return property to the person who created the joint tenancy (original transferor)?
		H.	Is this transfer of property:
☐	☑		1. to a trust for the benefit of the grantor, or grantor's spouse?
☐	☑		2. to a trust revocable by the transferor?
☐	☑		3. to a trust from which the property reverts to the grantor within 12 years?
☐	☑	I.	If this property is subject to a lease, is the remaining lease term 35 years or more including written options?
☐	☑	J.	Is this a transfer from parents to children or from children to parents?
☐	☑	K.	Is this transaction to replace a principal residence by a person 55 years of age or older?
☐	☑	L.	Is this transaction to replace a principal residence by a person who is severely disabled as defined by Revenue and Code Section 69.5?

If you checked yes to J, K, or L, an applicable claim form must be filed with the County Assessor.
Please provide any other information that would help the Assessors to understand the nature of the transfer.

IF YOU HAVE ANSWERED "YES" TO ANY OF THE ABOVE QUESTIONS EXCEPT J, K, OR L, PLEASE SIGN AND DATE, OTHERWISE COMPLETE BALANCE OF THE FORM.

PART II: OTHER TRANSFER INFORMATION
A. Date of transfer if other than recording date _____.
B. Type of transfer. Please check appropriate box.
☑ Purchase ☐ Foreclosure ☐ Gift ☐ Trade or Exchange ☐ Merger, Stock, or Partnership Acquisition
☐ Contract of Sale - Date of Contract _____
☐ Inheritance - Date of Death _____   ☐ Other: Please explain: _____
☐ Creation of Lease   ☐ Assignment of a Lease   ☐ Termination of a Lease
Date lease began _____
Original term in years (including written options) _____
Remaining term in years (including written options) _____
C. Was only a partial interest in the property transferred? ☐ Yes ☑ No   If yes, indicate the percentage transferred _____%

PRELIMINARY CHANGE OF OWNERSHIP REPORT

Please answer, to the best of your knowledge, all applicable questions, sign and date. If a question does not apply, indicate with "N/A."

PART III: PURCHASE PRICE AND TERMS OF SALE

A. CASH DOWN PAYMENT OR Value of Trade or Exchange (excluding closing costs)　　　　Amount $5,000.00

B. FIRST DEED OF TRUST @ 7.57% interest for 30years. Pymts/Mo.=$857.00(Prin. & Int. only)　　Amount $80,000.00

☐ FHA	☑ Fixed Rate	☑ New Loan
☑ Conventional	☐ Variable Rate	☐ Assumed Existing Loan Balance
☐ VA	☐ All inclusive D.T. ($ _____ Wrapped)	☑ Bank or Savings & Loan
☐ Cal-Vet	☐ Loan Carried by Seller	☐ Finance Company
Balloon Payment　☐ Yes	☑ No　Due Date _____　Amount $ _____	

C. SECOND DEED OF TRUST @ _____% interest for _____years. Pymts/Mo.=$_____(Prin. & Int. only)　　Amount $_____

☐ Bank or Savings & Loan	☐ Fixed Rate	☐ New Loan
☐ Loan Carried by Seller	☐ Variable Rate	☐ Assumed Existing Loan Balance
Balloon Payment　☐ Yes	☐ No　Due Date _____　Amount $ _____	

D. OTHER FINANCING: Is other financing involved not covered in (b) or (c) above? ☐ Yes ☑ No　　Amount $_____

Type_____ @ _____% interest for _____years. Pymts./Mo.=$_____(Prin. & Int. only)

☐ Bank or Savings & Loan	☐ Fixed Rate	☐ New Loan
☐ Loan Carried by Seller	☐ Variable Rate	☐ Assumed Existing Loan Balance
Balloon Payment　☐ Yes	☑ No　Due Date _____　Amount $ _____	

E. IMPROVEMENT BOND　☐ Yes　☑ No　　Outstanding Balance: Amount $_____

F. TOTAL PURCHASE PRICE (or acquisition price, if traded or exchanged, include real estate commission if paid.)

　　　　　　　　　　　　　　　　　　　　Total Items A through E　　$ 100,000.00

G. PROPERTY PURCHASED　☑ Through a broker　☐ Direct from seller　☐ Other (explain)_____

If purchased through a broker, provide broker's name and phone number: Sunshine Real Estate (555) 123-7654

Please explain any special terms or financing and any other information that would help the Assessor understand the purchase price and terms of sale.

PART IV: PROPERTY INFORMATION

A. IS PERSONAL PROPERTY INCLUDED IN PURCHASE PRICE
(other than a mobilehome subject to local property tax)? ☐ Yes　☑ No
If yes, enter the value of the personal property included in the purchase price $_____ (Attach itemized list of personal property).

B. IS THIS PROPERTY INTENDED AS YOUR PRINCIPAL RESIDENCE?　☑ Yes　☐ No
If yes, enter date of occupancy _____ / _____ / _____ or intended occupancy 02/01/20xx
　　　　　　　　　Month　Day　Year　　　　　　　　　　Month Day Year

C. TYPE OF PROPERTY TRANSFERRED:

☑ Single-family residence	☐ Agricultural	☐ Timeshare
☐ Multiple-family residence (no. of units: _____)	☐ Co-op/Own-your-own	☐ Mobilehome
☐ Commercial/Industrial	☐ Condominium	☐ Unimproved lot
☐ Other (Description: _____)		

D. DOES THE PROPERTY PRODUCE INCOME?　☐ Yes　☑ No

E. IF THE ANSWER TO QUESTION D IS YES, IS THE INCOME FROM:
☐ Lease/Rent　☐ Contract　☐ Mineral Rights　☐ Other - Explain: _____

F. WHAT WAS THE CONDITION OF PROPERTY AT THE TIME OF SALE?
☑ Good　☐ Average　☐ Fair　☐ Poor
Enter here, or on an attached sheet, any other information that would assist the Assessor in determining the value of the property such as the physical condition of the property, restrictions, etc.

I certify that the foregoing is true, correct and complete to the best of my knowledge and belief.

Signed _____　　　Dated _____
　　　NEW OWNER/CORPORATE OFFICER

Please Print Name of New Owner/Corporate Officer Bill Sherman and Margaret Sherman _____

Phone Number where you are available from 8:00 a.m. - 5:00 p.m. (555) 123-6754
　　　　　　(NOTE: The Assessor may contact you for further information)

If a document evidencing a change of ownership is presented to the recorder for recordation without the concurrent filing of a preliminary change of ownership report, the recorder may charge an additional recording fee of twenty dollars ($20).

Power of Attorney

A **power of attorney** is used when a principal is not available to sign documents necessary for the conveyance of real property or some other legal act. It is valid for the party named in executing documents, both buying and selling, and has the same force and effect as the principal granting the power would have if he or she signed. The power of attorney must be recorded in the county in which the real property is located.

There are two types of power of attorney that you will become familiar with as an escrow officer – specific and general. The specific power of attorney is used for a specific function such as the sale of real property. It lists the purpose precisely for what it is intended. The purpose of the general power of attorney is broad and may be used by the person empowered to sign anything the principal giving the power would sign or do.

Some lenders, however, will not allow a person with a power of attorney to sign loan documents or grant deeds, so it may be necessary to check with the title company and the lender to see what is accepted.

Notary Public Jurats

A **notary public jurat** is the form attached to a notarized statement or document. It states that the person signing the document appeared before the notary and proved identity. The form makes a notary responsible for identifying the party whose name is to be notarized, and also makes the notary accountable for that determination. The notary does not necessarily need to see the person sign the document, but simply notarizes the document on the basis of the party appearing in person and acknowledging the signatures. A notary public jurat is not, as many believe, affirmation of the truth of a document, but of the truth that this person appearing has signed the document.

Real Estate Basics

Ownership of Real Property

All property has an owner—either the government, a private institution, or an individual. Title is the evidence that the owner of land is in lawful possession. It is the proof of ownership. Separate ownership and concurrent ownership are the two ways real estate may be owned.

Escrow agents can never tell people how to take title. Parties must consult with their attorney, accountant, or anyone they choose and then give the escrow agent instructions regarding vesting.

Separate Ownership

Property owned by one person or entity is known as sole and **separate ownership**, or ownership in severalty. A corporation is known to hold title in severalty, because it is a sole entity.

Concurrent Ownership

When property is owned by two or more persons or entities at the same time, it is known as **concurrent ownership**, or co-ownership.

Concurrent ownership comes in several forms such as joint tenancy, tenancy in common, community property, and tenancy in partnership.

> **Review - Four Types of Concurrent Ownership**
> - Joint Tenancy
> - Tenancy in Common
> - Community Property
> - Tenancy in Partnership

Joint Tenancy

When two or more parties own real property as co-owners, with the right of survivorship, it is called **joint tenancy**. The right of survivorship means that if one of the joint tenants dies, the surviving partner automatically becomes sole owner of the property.

The deceased's share does not go to his or her estate or heirs, but becomes the property of the co-tenant without becoming involved in probate. In addition, the surviving joint tenant is not liable to creditors of the deceased who hold liens on the joint tenancy property.

Example: Fred, Gary, Sam, and Ted are joint tenants. Ted dies and his interest automatically goes to Fred, Gary, and Sam as joint tenants with equal one-third interests.

Example: Donna and Tom own a house as joint tenants. Tom dies and Donna now owns the house as her sole and separate property without probate. Tom's heirs are not entitled to his share because of the right of survivorship. If Donna wishes to convey title after Tom's death, she will need to record an affidavit of "Death of Joint Tenant" and then record a new deed removing Tom from title. This would allow her to convey the title to the property without Tom.

In order to have a joint tenancy, there are four things that must be in agreement—time, title, interest, and possession. If any one of the unities is missing, a tenancy in common is created.

> **The Four Unities of Joint Tenancy**
> **Mnemonic = "T" Tip**
>   Time - All parties must become joint tenants at the same time
>   Title - All parties must take title on the same deed
>   Interest - All parties must have an equal interest in the property
>   Possession - All parties have equal right of possession, known as an undivided interest

All four items must occur to have a joint tenancy. If any one of the unities is broken, the joint tenancy is dissolved.

Co-owners may sell their interest, give it away, or borrow money against it, without consent of the other joint tenants. Because of the right of survivorship, a joint tenant may not will his or her share.

Tenancy in Common

When two or more persons, whose interests are not necessarily equal, are owners of undivided interests in a single estate, a **tenancy in common** exists. Whenever some other form of ownership or vesting is not mentioned specifically, and there are co-owners, title is assumed to be a tenancy in common.

The only requirement of unity for tenants in common is the equal right of possession or undivided interest — as it is called. That means each owner has a certain equitable interest in the property (such as one-half interest, or one-fourth interest), but has the right to use the whole property. None of the owners may exclude any co-owner from the property, nor claim any portion of the property for exclusive use.

The Four Requirements of Tenants in Common
1. Tenants in common may take title at different times
2. Tenants in common may take title on separate deeds
3. Tenants in common may have unequal interests
4. Tenants in common have an undivided interest or equal right of possession

Any tenant in common may sell, encumber, or will his or her interest, with heirs simply becoming a tenant in common among the others. One tenant in common cannot create an easement on the property without the consent of the other co-owners. A tenant in common must pay a proportionate share of any expenses incurred on the property, including money spent for repairs, taxes, loan payments, and insurance. When tenants in common do not agree on matters pertaining to the property, any of the co-owners may file a partition action, which asks the court to decide the fate of the investment.

Example: Pam, Paul, Kate, and Dan are joint tenants. Dan sells his interest to Tara. The joint tenancy has been broken regarding the interest Dan had in the property. The new vesting, after the sale of Dan's interest, is Pam, Paul and Kate as joint tenants with equal interests, and the right of survivorship, with Tara as a tenant in common.

Pam, Paul, Kate, and Tara, in the above property, wish to restore a joint tenancy with each of the four having the right of survivorship. Tara holds a tenancy in common, so she will have to be added to the joint tenancy. Since all joint tenants must take title at the same time, on the same document, Pam, Paul, Kate, and Tara must sign a new deed that lists Pam, Paul and Kate as joint tenants and Tara as a tenant in common. Then the property can be deeded to all four parties as joint tenants. All requirements for a joint tenancy—time, title, interest, and possession—will then be fulfilled.

Community Property

All property acquired by a husband and wife during a valid marriage—except for certain separate property—is called **community property**. **Separate property** includes all property owned before marriage, all property acquired by either of the parties during marriage by gift or inheritance, and all income derived from separate property.

If spouses want to maintain the status of their separate property, they must be very careful not to co-mingle it with their community property. Separate property (such as an apartment building with a negative cash flow) may not be supported with community property funds, nor can the income of either spouse be used in any way to maintain separate property. Any income, including wages from either spouse, is considered community property.

Community property cannot be sold or encumbered by only one of the partners. Either spouse may buy real or personal property without the consent of the other; both are bound by the contract made by either one, unless the new property is bought specifically as separate property, with funds from a separate property account.

Either party may will one-half of the community property. If there is no will, the surviving spouse inherits all community property. This is important to know, particularly with multiple marriages, for estate planning.

Property may be owned with the intention that it go to one's children, only to learn after the parent's death that children of the first marriage are no longer natural heirs. If there is a subsequent husband or wife and no will has been made, the new spouse will become the natural heir to the real property.

Regarding separate property, if there is no will, the surviving spouse gets one-half and one child gets one-half. If there is more than one child, the surviving spouse gets one-third and the children get two-thirds.

Tenancy in Partnership

Ownership by two or more persons who form a partnership for business purposes is known as **tenancy in partnership**. Each partner has an equal right of possession for partnership.

Concurrent Ownership				
	Joint Tenancy	Tenancy in Common	Community Property	Partnership
Parties	Any number	Any number	Spouses only	Any number
Interest	Must be equal	Equal or unequal	Must be equal	Mutual consent
Possession	Equal right	Equal right	Equal right	Equal right
Death	Survivorship	No survivorship	Survivorship (no will)	No survivorship

Encumbrances: Limitations on Real Property

An encumbrance is an interest in real property that is held by someone who is not the owner. Anything that burdens or affects the title or the use of the property is an encumbrance. A property is encumbered when it is burdened with legal obligations against the title. Most buyers purchase encumbered property. Encumbrances fall into two categories: those that affect the title, known as money encumbrances, and those that affect the use of the property, known as non-money encumbrances.

The encumbrances that create a legal obligation to pay (money encumbrances) are known as liens. A lien uses real property as security for the payment of a debt (lien$ - Memory aid: the dollar sign is to show liens involve money). Common types of liens are deeds of trust and mortgages; mechanic's liens; tax liens; and special assessments, attachments and judgments.

Those types of encumbrances that affect the physical use of the property (non-money encumbrances) are easements, building restrictions, and zoning requirements and encroachments.

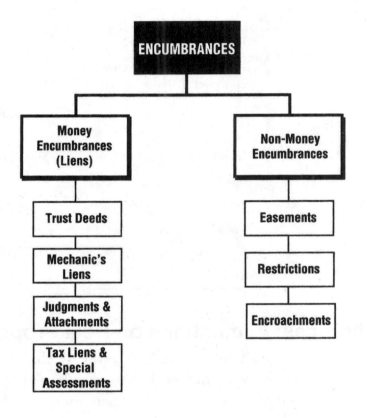

Money Encumbrances (Liens)

A lien is an obligation to pay a money encumbrance that may be voluntary or involuntary. An owner may choose to borrow money, using the property as security for the loan, creating a voluntary lien.

On the other hand, if the owner does not pay taxes or the debt owed, a lien may be placed against his or her property without permission, creating an involuntary lien.

A lien may be specific or general. A specific lien is one that is placed against a certain property, while a general lien affects all property of the owner.

Deeds of trust and mortgages are both instruments used in real estate financing to create voluntary, specific liens against real property. They will be discussed in detail later.

Tax Liens and Special Assessments

If any government taxes, such as income or property taxes are not paid, they become a lien against the property. Special assessments are levied against property owners to pay for local improvements, such as underground utilities, street repair, or water projects. Payment for the projects is secured by a special assessment that becomes a lien against real property.

Attachments and Judgments

An attachment is the process by which the court holds the property of a defendant, pending outcome of a lawsuit. An attachment lien

is valid for three years and may be extended in certain cases.

A judgment is the final determination of the rights of parties in a lawsuit by the court. A judgment does not automatically create a lien. A summary of the court decision, known as an abstract of judgment, must be filed with the county recorder. When the abstract is filed, the judgment becomes a general lien on all property owned or acquired by the judgment debtor for 10 years, in the county in which the abstract is filed.

Lis Pendens

A lis pendens (also called a pendency of action) is a recorded notice that indicates pending litigation affecting the title on a property. It clouds the title preventing the sale or transfer of the property until the lis pendens is removed, the action is dismissed, or final judgment is rendered.

Non-Money Encumbrances

A non-money encumbrance is one that affects the use of property such as an easement, a building restriction, or an encroachment.

Easements

An **easement** is the right to use another's land for a specified purpose, sometimes known as a right-of-way. An interest in an easement is non-possessory. That means the holder of an easement can use it only for the purpose intended and may not exclude anyone else from using it.

Easements are created in various ways—commonly by express grant or reservation in a grant deed or by a written agreement between owners of adjoining land. An easement always should be recorded to assure its continued existence. It is recorded by the party benefiting from the easement as the "dominant tenement".

Five Ways to Create an Easement

1. **Express Grant.** The "servient tenement", or the giver of the easement, grants the easement by deed or express agreement.

2. **Express Reservation.** The seller of a parcel who owns adjoining land reserves an easement or right-of-way over the former property. It is created at the time of the sale with a deed or express agreement.

3. **Implied Grant or Reservation.** The existence of an easement is obvious and necessary at the time a property is conveyed, even though no mention is made of it in the deed.

4. **Necessity.** An easement created when a parcel is completely landlocked and has no access. It is automatically terminated when another way to enter and leave the property becomes available.

5. **Prescription.** The process is that of acquiring an interest, not ownership, in a certain property. An easement by prescription may be created by continuous and uninterrupted use, by a single party, for a period of five years. The use must be known by and against the owner's wishes (open and notorious). The party wishing to obtain the prescriptive easement must have some reasonable claim to the use of the property.

Easements May be Terminated or Extinguished by:

1. **Abandonment.** Obvious and intentional surrender of the easement. Non-Use. When applied to a prescriptive easement for a period of five years, this terminates the easement.

2. **Destruction of the Servient Tenement.** If the government takes the servient tenement for its use, as in eminent domain, the easement is terminated.

3. **Adverse Possession.** The owner of the servient tenement, by his or her own usage, may prevent the dominant tenement from using the easement for a period of five years, thus terminating the easement.

4. **Merger.** If the same person owns both the dominant and servient tenements, the easement is terminated.

5. **Express Release.** The only one who can release an easement is the dominant tenement.

6. **Legal Proceedings.** Quiet title action to terminate the easement brought by the servient tenement against the dominant tenement.

7. **Estoppel.** Unless created by express grant, an easement may be terminated if the property owner has reason to believe that no further use (non-use) is intended.

   Example: Fred is a farmer who owns some land. Tim, the son of a neighboring farmer, cut through Fred's field on the way to high school. Upon graduation, Tim left for college and stopped taking the shortcut through Fred's field. Farmer Fred, seeing that the easement was no longer being used, fenced his field. Fred's action showed that he relied on Tim's conduct (no longer taking the shortcut). Therefore, the easement terminated through the estoppel.

8. **Excessive Use.** Depending upon the terms of the easement, excessive use can terminate the easement.

   Example: Dan Green, the owner of a Victorian style 6-bedroom, 2-story house, has an easement to cross Kate's property to get to his home. When Dan decided to rent out all of the bedrooms in his home to two-three college students per bedroom, he created a boarding house. This increased the traffic across the easement dramatically. Kate, understandably upset, terminated Dan's easement due to excessive use.

The Requirements for Terminating an Easement
Mnemonic = "ADAM E. LEE"

Abandonment

Destruction of the servient tenement

Adverse possession

Merger

Express release

Legal proceedings

Estoppel

Excessive

Restrictions

Another type of encumbrance is a **restriction**, which is a limitation placed on the use of property. It may be placed by a private owner, a developer or the government. It is usually placed on property to assure that land use is consistent and uniform within a certain area.

Restrictions are created in the deed at the time of sale or in the general plan of a subdivision by the developer. For example, a developer may use a height restriction to ensure views from each parcel in a subdivision.

Private restrictions are placed by a present or past owner and affect only a specific property or development, while zoning is an example of government restrictions that benefit the general public.

Restrictions are commonly known as CC&Rs or Covenants, Conditions, and Restrictions. A covenant is a promise to do or not do certain things. The penalty for a breach of a covenant is usually money damages. An example of a covenant might be that the tenant agrees to make some repairs, or that a property may be used only for a specific purpose, such as a church or homeless shelter.

A condition is much the same as a covenant, a promise to do or not do something, except the penalty for breaking a condition is return of the property to the grantor. A condition subsequent is a restriction placed in a deed at the time of conveyance on future use of the property. Upon breach of the condition subsequent, the grantor may take back the property. A condition precedent requires that a certain event, or condition, occur before title can pass to the new owner.

Encroachments

The placement of a permanent improvement such as a fence, wall, driveway, or roof, so that it extends over the lot line into adjacent property owned by another is known as an **encroachment**. This unauthorized intrusion on the adjoining land can limit its use and reduce it in size and value. An owner has three years in which to sue the neighbor to have the unauthorized encroachment removed.

Common Encroachments

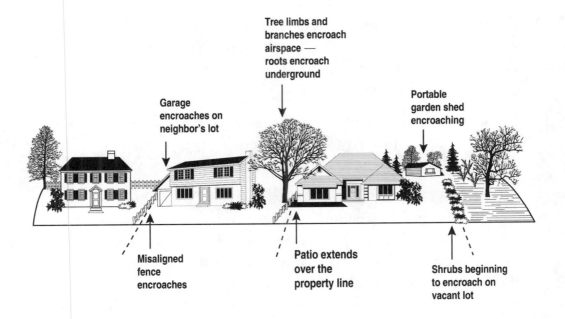

Tree limbs and branches encroach airspace — roots encroach underground

Garage encroaches on neighbor's lot

Portable garden shed encroaching

Misaligned fence encroaches

Patio extends over the property line

Shrubs beginning to encroach on vacant lot

Background of Land Title in California

Ownership of land in California began with Spanish explorers who claimed it for the king of Spain in the early 16th Century. Since the king technically owned everything, all land was granted to private parties by the military representatives of Spanish rule.

Ownership and transfer of land and property rights were determined by local authorities operating under a strict set of civil laws that were given to them by the Spanish king.

This continued until 1822, when Mexico began colonizing California and governing the territory. Mexican governors totally controlled who received grants of land during this time, and recorded the grants, known as expedientes, in the government archives. Even so, the land descriptions were vague and evidence of title may or may not have been in the actual possession of the owner. This led to many disputes over ownership in later years, after California became as state.

In 1848, the Treaty of Guadalupe Hidalgo ended the war with Mexico, and California became a possession of the United States. Land claims that had been granted by Mexico were honored, and confirmed with patents to the land, by the U.S. government, to those with proven ownership. Even though Spain or Mexico granted ownership, according to the Roman Civil Law they followed, the laws changed after California became a state in 1850. England's Common Law principles now governed the title of real property.

Recording Safeguards Ownership

In a move that was strictly an American device for safeguarding the ownership of land, the California legislature adopted a system of **recording** evidence of title or interest. This system meant records could be collected in a convenient and safe public place, so that those purchasing land could be more fully informed about the ownership and condition of the title. Even then, California was a leader in consumer-friendly legislation. Citizens were protected against secret conveyances and liens, and title to real property was freely transferable.

Each county in the state has a County Recorder's office where documents may be recorded. As you recall, a deed does not have to be recorded to be valid. However, recordation maintains the chain of title necessary to create a history of ownership of real property

Acknowledgment

The Recording Act of California provides that, after acknowledgment, any instrument or **judgment** affecting the title to—or possession of—real property may be recorded. **Acknowledgment** is a formal declaration before a notary public or certain public officials, by the person (grantor) who signed (executed) the instrument (deed) that he or she in fact did execute (sign) the document.

A **notary public** (notary) is a licensed public officer who takes or witnesses the acknowledgment. A notary cannot acknowledge any document in which the notary is named a principal. A notary who is an employee of a corporation may notarize a deed involving the corporation so long as he or she does not have a personal interest in the subject matter of the transaction.

Acknowledgment acts as a safeguard against forgery and once acknowledged, a document is accepted as **prima facie** (on its face) evidence in court.

To be recorded, a deed must be acknowledged. Recording permits, rather than requires, all documents that affect title to real property be filed.

Recording Process

The process consists of copying the instrument to be recorded in the proper index, and filing it in alphabetical order, under the names of the parties, without delay. Documents must be recorded by the county recorder in the county within which the property is located to be valid there.

When the recorder receives a document to be filed, he or she notes the time and date of filing and at whose request it was filed. After the contents of the document are copied into the record, the original document is marked "filed for record", stamped with the proper time and date of recording, and returned to the person who requested the recording.

Constructive Notice

Recording a document as well as possession of the property give **constructive notice** of an interest in real property. Recording gives public notice (constructive notice) of the content of any instrument recorded to anyone who cares to look into the records. Possession is also considered constructive notice. Even the act of taking possession of an unrecorded deed gives constructive notice. A buyer should always check to be certain that no one is living on the property who might have a prior claim to ownership. It is the buyer's duty to conduct proper inquiry before purchasing any property. Failure to do so does not relieve the buyer of that responsibility.

> Example: Ann bought a property through her broker, sight unseen. The escrow closed and the deed was recorded. When Ann tried to move into her new home; however, she found George living there. He told her that he bought the property a year ago and had not bothered to record the deed, but had moved in and considered it his home. When she consulted her attorney, Ann found that indeed George—because he was in possession of the property—had given notice to anyone who might inquire. One remedy for the situation would be legal action against the grantor who sold the property to both George and Ann. However, at the moment, George does have legal title because of his possession of the property.

Actual Notice

If a person has direct, express information about the ownership interest of a property, it is called **actual notice**. Actual notice is a fact, such as seeing the grant deed or knowing that a person inherited a property by will.

Priorities in Recording

As we have seen, recording laws are meant to protect citizens against fraud and to give others notification of property ownership. The first valid deed that is recorded determines the owner, unless that person, prior to recording, had either actual or constructive notice of the rights of others. Other information that might influence ownership can be recorded also, such as liens and other encumbrances. **Priority** means the order in which deeds are recorded. Whether or not it is a grant deed, trust deed or some other evidence of a lien or encumbrance, the priority is determined by the date stamped in the upper right-hand corner of the document by the county recorder. To obtain priority through recording, a buyer must be a good faith purchaser, for a valuable **consideration**, and record the deed first.

If there are several grant deeds recorded against the property, the one recorded first is valid. In a case in which there are several deeds of trust recorded against a property, no mention will be made about which one is the first deed of trust, which is the second, and so forth.

A person inquiring about the priority of the deeds should look at the time and date the deed was recorded for that information. You will see, as we proceed in our study, the importance of the date and time of recording. There are certain instruments not affected by the priority of recording rule. Certain liens, such as tax liens and mechanic's liens, take priority even though they are recorded after a deed.

True-False Quiz

Now that you have read all the material in this chapter, take the following self-test and check your knowledge of parties, documents, and real estate basics.

True/False

1. *TRUE* A third party who carries out the written provisions of an escrow agreement is known as an escrow holder.

2. *TRUE* Property is usually transferred with a grant deed.

3. *TRUE* A request for notice of default is a way anyone interested in a particular deed of trust can make sure of being informed if a notice of default has been recorded.

4. *False* A preliminary change of ownership gives a buyer temporary title.

5. *FALSE* Ownership in severalty is the same as concurrent ownership.

6. *TRUE* An encumbrance is a limitation on ownership to real property.

7. *False* A mechanic's lien is an example of a non-money encumbrance.

8. *False* Property acquired by a husband and wife during a marriage, except for certain separate property, is owned by the wife.

9. *TRUE* An encumbrance that creates a legal obligation to pay is known as a lien.

10. *TRUE* A lis pendens indicates pending litigation on a property.

Chapter
3

Real Estate Finance

Learning Objectives

After reading this chapter, you will be able to:

- explain how the real estate financing process works.

- describe promissory notes, trust deeds, and mortgages.

- discuss the common clauses in financing instruments.

- describe the foreclosure process.

- summarize types of real estate loans.

- discuss mandatory lending disclosures.

Introduction

Imagine buying a house and being required to pay the total price in cash. The sweet pleasure of home ownership probably would belong somewhere in the next century for most of us. With the average price of a single-family home being so high, buying a home would be unthinkable without the practical benefit of financing.

By allowing a homebuyer to obtain a loan for the difference between the sales price and the down payment, real estate lenders have provided the solution to the problem of how property can be bought and sold without the requirement of an all-cash sale.

What started out as a simple loan by a local bank—with an agreement that the borrower pay it all back in a timely manner—is now a complex subject. Buyers and sellers need to rely on experts to explain all the choices there are on financing the purchase or sale of property. A real estate licensee is probably one of the experts to whom they will turn.

This chapter on real estate finance is organized with each part building on what you have learned in the earlier sections of this chapter. Try to master each subject— promissory notes, trust deeds, mortgages, special financing clauses, foreclosure, junior trust deeds, other security instruments, miscellaneous provisions of finance, and consumer protection—as you come to it. There is a thread that connects everything you are about to study in this chapter. Read with that in mind.

Now that you know real estate finance is nothing more than lenders loaning money so people can buy property, let us start with an examination of the lending process.

How the Process Works

When a buyer obtains a loan to purchase property, he or she is using the lender's money to finance the sale. This is known as leverage. The use of borrowed capital to buy real estate is a process that permits the buyer to use little of one's own money and large amounts of someone else's.

There are several reasons why leverage is appealing to both the home buyer and the investor. The main advantage is the home buyer does not have to amass the entire purchase price to become a home owner. The investor can use leverage to control several investments, rather than just one, each purchased with a small amount of personal funds, and a large amount of a lender's money. The investor can then earn a return on each property, therefore increasing the amount of yield on investment dollars.

Commonly, financing is secured with a trust deed or mortgage. Under a trust deed, after signing the promissory note, the borrower is required to execute a trust deed at the same time, which is the security guaranteeing loan repayment. This is known as hypothecation, a process that allows a borrower to remain in possession of the property while using it to secure the loan. If the borrower does not make payments per the agreement, he or she then loses the rights of possession and ownership. The lender holds the trust deed, along with the note, until the loan is repaid.

Promissory Notes and Security Instruments

When a loan is made, the borrower signs a promissory note, or note — as it is called, which states that a certain amount of money has been borrowed. The **promissory note** is the evidence of the debt.

When money is loaned for financing real property, some kind of **collateral** (security) is usually required of the borrower, as well as the promise to repay the loan. That means the lender wants some concrete assurance of getting the money back beyond the borrower's written promise to pay. The property being bought or borrowed against is used as the security, or collateral, for the debt. The lender feels more secure about making the loan if assured of the property ownership in case of default, or nonpayment, of the loan. Then the lender can sell it to get the loan money back.

In California, the most common **security instrument** for the note is a trust deed. After signing the promissory note, the borrower is required to **execute** (sign) a trust deed, which is the security guaranteeing loan repayment. The borrower (**trustor**) has possession of the property but transfers naked legal title of the property to a third party to hold as security for the lender in case of default on the loan. This process, known as **hypothecation,** allows a borrower to remain in possession of the property while using it to secure the loan. If the borrower does not make payments according to the terms of the agreement, he or she then loses the rights of possession and ownership. Hypothecation differs from a **pledge** because actual possession of pledged property is given to the lender. For example, in a pledge, personal property (such as stock certificates) is delivered to a lender, or jewelry is delivered to a pawnbroker. Once the loan is repaid, the personal property is returned to the borrower.

The lender holds the original promissory note and the trust deed until the loan is repaid. The trust deed allows the lender, in case of loan default, to order the third party to sell the property described in the deed. Both promissory notes and security instruments will be explained in detail later in this chapter.

Understanding Promissory Notes

A promissory note serves as evidence of the debt and is a written agreement between a lender and a borrower to document a loan. It is a promise to pay back a certain sum of money at specified terms at an agreed-upon time. Sometimes it is called the note, a debt repayment contract, or more informally, it could be called an "IOU".

A promissory note is a negotiable instrument. A **negotiable instrument** is a written unconditional promise or order to pay a certain amount of money at a definite time or on demand. A negotiable instrument is easily transferable from one person to another meaning it can be bought and sold. The most common type of negotiable instrument is an ordinary bank check. A check is an order to the bank to pay money to the person named. A promissory note is the same thing. It can be transferred by

endorsement (signature), just like a check. If correctly prepared, it is considered the same as cash.

The **maker** is the person borrowing the money, or making the note. The note is a personal obligation of the borrower and a complete contract in itself, between the borrower and lender. The **holder** is the person loaning the money, or the one holding the note. A **holder in due course** is an innocent party who purchased a negotiable instrument without knowledge of any defects.

To be considered a negotiable instrument, the document must be consistent with statutory (legal) definition, and include specified requirements.

Requirements for a Valid Promissory Note

A promissory note is:

- an unconditional written promise to pay a certain sum of money.
- made by one person to another, both able to legally enter into a contract.
- signed by the maker (borrower).
- payable on demand or at a definite time.
- paid to bearer or to order.
- voluntarily delivered by the borrower and accepted by the lender.

In addition to showing the amount borrowed, a promissory note sets the terms of the loan, such as the interest rate, the repayment plan, and an acceleration clause in the event of default. With that information, you can calculate the payments using a financial calculator, printed amortization schedule, or software.

Interest Rate

The interest charged on most real estate loans is **simple interest**— interest paid only on the principal owed. The interest rate stated in the note is called the **nominal** or **named rate**. The **effective interest rate** is the rate the borrower is actually paying, commonly called the annual percentage rate (APR). Lenders are compensated for their risk in the form of interest rates. If the lender thinks the borrower is a high risk, the lender will charge a higher interest rate for the privilege of borrowing their money. The lower the risk, the lower the rate.

Some promissory notes have a fixed interest rate, where the interest rate and term do not change over the life of the loan. Others may include a fluctuating interest rate as well as changes in the payment over the life of the loan. Based on this, some loans are called fixed-rate loans and others adjustable rate loans.

Limits on Interest Rates — Usury

The California Usury Law sets limits on the interest rate that can be charged on some types of loans. This is called the usury limit. **Usury** is the charging of an illegal rate of interest. A distinction is made between loans that are exempt from the law and those that are covered under the Usury Law. Exempt loans include loans made by banks, savings and loans, and credit unions; real estate loans  made directly or arranged by a mortgage loan broker; and seller carry-back loans. The Usury Law limits interest rates on hard money real estate loans made directly by private individuals without the services of a real estate broker. The limit is 10% on loans where the funds are used primarily for personal, family, or household purposes. All other loans made by a nonexempt lender are limited to the higher of 10% or 5% plus the discount rate charged by the San Francisco Federal Reserve Bank.

Types of Repayment Plans

A promissory note may stand alone as an unsecured loan or note, or it may be secured by either a trust deed or mortgage. The  promissory note is the primary instrument; and if there are conflicts in the terms of the note and trust deed or mortgage, generally the terms of the note are controlling. The promissory note terms create the basis for the repayment plan. There are several types of repayment plans, each with a different kind of obligation made clear by the terms of the note. The terms of the note include interest rate, repayment plan, and default. Some repayment plans provide that the entire principal be repaid during the term on the loan, whereas others only pay the interest. A systematic payment of principal and interest made to pay off the loan balance by the end of the term is called amortization. **Amortization** is described as the liquidation of a financial obligation.

Typical repayment plans are: (1) a single payment of principal and interest at the end of the loan term, (2) interest-only payments, (3) partially amortized with a balloon payment, and (4) fully amortized payments.

Single Payment of Principal and Interest

Some loans have no regular payments of interest and/or principal. Instead, the loan is paid off all at once, at a specified future date. This payment includes the entire principal amount and the accrued interest.

Interest-Only Payments

An interest-only loan offers consumers greater purchasing power, increased cash flow, and is a very popular alternative to traditional fixed-rate loans. The **interest-only loan** is also called a **straight loan** or **term loan**. It calls for regular interest payments during the term of the note. The interest rate is generally higher on a straight note and the principal does not decrease. A large payment is made at the end of the term to repay the principal and any remaining interest. This type of loan works well for people who only want to stay in a home for just a few years. If the borrower plans to live in the house for three to five years, an interest-only loan may be the right choice. With a conventional 30-year loan, most of the payment is applied directly to the interest of the loan with very little applied to the principal. With an interest-only loan, the borrower will have a lower payment and have almost the same principal balance at the end of three or five years as if a conventional loan had been selected.

INSTALLMENT NOTE
(INTEREST INCLUDED)
(THIS NOTE CONTAINS AN ACCELERATION CLAUSE)

$189,000   **Any City**   , California,   **1/1/20xx**

In installments and at the times hereinafter stated, for value received,   **Dan Winter and Donna Winter**

promise to pay to   **Sam Summers and Kate Summers**

_____   or order

_____ **987 Ocean View Drive, Any City, CA 90000** _____

the principal sum of <u>One Hundred Eighty Thousand</u>   dollars

with interest from <u>January 1, 20xx</u>   on the amounts of

principal remaining from time to time unpaid, until said principal sum is paid, at the rate of _____ 8.9 _____ percent

per annum. Principal and interest due in monthly installments of <u>One Thousand Five Hundred</u> Dollars, $1,500, or more on the 15th day of each and every month, beginning on the 15th day of February, **20xx.**

and continuing until said principal sum has been fully paid. AT ANY TIME, THE PRIVILEGE IS RESERVED TO PAY MORE THAN THE SUM DUE. Should the interest not be so paid, it shall be added to the principal and thereafter bear like interest as the principal, but such unpaid interest so compounded shall not exceed an amount equal to simple interest on the unpaid principal at the maximum rate permitted by law. Should default be made in the payment of any of said installments when due, then the whole sum of principal and interest shall become immediately due and payable at the option of the holder of this note.

If the trustor shall sell, convey, or alienate said property, or any part thereof, or any interest therein, or shall be divested of his title or any interest therein in may manner or way, whether voluntarily or involuntarily, without the written consent of the beneficiary being first had and obtained, beneficiary shall have the right, at its option, to declare any indebtedness or obligations secured hereby, irrespective of the maturity date specified in any note evidencing the same, immediately due and payable.

Should suit be commenced to collect this note or any portion thereof, such sum as the Court may deem reasonable shall be added hereto as attorney's fees. Principal and interest payable for lawful money of the United States of America. This note is secured by a certain DEED OF TRUST to the SMS SETTLEMENT SERVICES, a California corporation, as TRUSTEE.

_____   _____
          Dan Winter   Donna Winter

Promissory Installment Note

RECITATIONS:

Date: _____

Borrower: _____

Borrower's Address: _____

                     _____

Payee: _____

Place for Payment: _____

                     _____

Amortized (Installment) Payments

With installment payments, the loan is repaid in equal payments, typically monthly, until the loan has been repaid in full. The principal and interest are calculated for the term of the loan, and payments are determined by dividing the total by the number of payments in the term of the loan. Regular, periodic payments to include both interest and principal are made, which pay off the debt completely by the end of the term. This type of loan is fully amortized because the loan and interest are fully paid when the last payment is made.

There are loans that are not fully amortized. This occurs when the borrower makes lower payments than what should be made on a fully amortized loan. The difference between what should be paid and what is actually paid is added to the principal balance of the loan. This is called **negative amortization** and the principal increases instead of decreases.

Partially Amortized (Installment) Payments

This type of repayment schedule is used to create lower payments. The **partially amortized installment note** calls for regular, level payments on the principal and interest during the term of the loan. Since the loan does not fully amortize over the original term, there is still a remaining principal loan balance. The last installment, called a **balloon payment**, is much larger than the previous payments because it includes all of the remaining principal and interest. Balloon payments can have extra risks because the borrower may need to refinance the property—possibly at higher interest rates.

Fully Amortized Fixed-Rate Payments

A fully amortized fixed-rate note describes a loan with an interest rate that is fixed and payments that are level for the life of the loan. Because of the level payments, this loan is called a **level-payment** loan and is the most common type with institutional lenders. It is characterized by regular, periodic payments of fixed amounts, to include both interest and principal, which pay off the debt completely by the end of the term.

> **Review - Features of Fixed-Rate Fully Amortized Loans**
> - Interest rate remains fixed for the life of the loan.
> - Payments remain level for the life of the loan. This structure allows payment in full by the end of the loan term.

During the early amortization period, a large percentage of the monthly payment is used to pay the interest. As the loan is paid down, more of the monthly payment is applied to principal. A typical 30-year fixed-rate loan takes 22.5 years of level payments to pay half of the original loan amount. Typically, the longer the term of the loan, the lower the monthly payment. However, the total financing costs over the life of the loan will be higher.

Although fixed-rate loans are available for 30 years, 20 years, 15 years and even 10 years, the most common fixed-rate loans are 15-year and 30-year loans. Bi-weekly loans, which shorten the term by calling for half the monthly payment every two weeks, are also available. (Since there are 52 weeks in a year, the borrower makes 26 payments, or 13 months worth, every year.)

Adjustable Rate Mortgage (ARM)

Lenders have created alternative payment plans, such as the adjustable-rate mortgage, which allow borrowers to qualify for larger loans and at the same time help maintain the lender's investment return. An **adjustable-rate mortgage** (ARM) has an interest rate tied to a movable economic index. The interest rate in the note varies upward or downward over the term of the loan, depending on the agreed-upon index.

Some lenders entice borrowers to ARMs with teaser rates. A **teaser rate** is an unusually low introductory interest rate. Usually the teaser rate reverts to the fully indexed interest rate at the first adjustment date. To protect the borrower from wild swings in interest rates there is usually a limit on how much the interest rate can change on an annual basis, as well as a lifetime cap.

All adjustable rate loans carry **periodic interest-rate caps**. Many ARMs have interest rate caps of six months or a year. There are loans that have interest rate caps of three years. Interest rate caps are beneficial in rising interest rate markets, but can also keep the interest rate higher than the fully indexed rate if rates are falling rapidly. Almost all ARMs have a maximum interest rate or **lifetime interest rate cap**. The lifetime cap varies from company to company and loan to loan. Loans with low lifetime caps usually have higher margins, and the reverse is true. Those loans that carry low margins often have higher lifetime caps.

Some loans have **payment caps** instead of interest rate caps. These loans reduce payment shock in a rising interest rate market, but can also lead to deferred interest or negative amortization. These loans generally cap the annual payment increases to 7.5% of the previous payment.

A lender may offer several choices of interest rates, terms, payments, or adjustment periods to a borrower with an ARM. The initial interest rate, or **qualifying rate**, is determined by the lender. It is often a teaser rate that is below a fully indexed rate. The rate is usually selected to be competitive in the marketplace. A **margin**, which might be anywhere from one-to-three percentage points, is added to the initial interest rate to determine the actual beginning rate the borrower will pay. The margin remains the same for the life of the loan. However, the interest rate may change as the chosen index changes, depending on the economic conditions that lead it.

The borrower's payment will stay the same for a specified time, which might be six months or a year, depending on the agreement with the lender. At the agreed-upon time, the lender re-evaluates the loan to determine if the index has changed upward or downward, and calculates a new payment based on the changed interest rate plus the same margin. That will be the borrower's payment until the next six months or year pass, and the loan will be reviewed again. The annual maximum increase is usually one to two percent while the lifetime cap is usually not allowed to go beyond five or six points above the starting rate.

Generally, adjustable-rate financing benefits the bankers because it allows for an inflow of extra cash during times of higher interest rates. In other words, the borrower's payments will increase because the interest rate will go up; therefore, more money will flow into the financial institution.

Understanding Security Instruments

The rights and duties of lenders and borrowers are described in a document called a security instrument. A **security instrument** creates a security interest in real property and secures a promissory note. A **security interest** is the claim a creditor (lender) has in the property of a debtor (borrower). The security interest allows certain assets of a borrower to be set aside so that a creditor can sell them if the borrower defaults on the loan. Proceeds from the sale of that property can be taken to pay off the debt.

The security instruments used to secure the interest for the lender are the deed of trust, mortgage, and contract for sale. In California and other states, deeds of trust are the principal instruments used to secure loans on real property.

As you will learn, trust deeds and mortgages differ in the number of parties involved, statute of limitations, and transfer of title. In fact, the only thing trust deeds and mortgages have in common is that the property is used as security for the debt. You will hear the term mortgage used loosely in California, as in mortgage company, mortgage broker, and mortgage payment—but the mortgage referenced here usually refers to a deed of trust.

Deed of Trust

In California, the deed of trust (or trust deed) is the most commonly used security instrument in real estate finance. A **trust deed** is a security instrument that conveys title of real property from a trustor to a trustee to hold as security for the beneficiary for payment of a debt. The three parties to a trust deed are the borrower (**trustor**), lender (**beneficiary**), and a neutral third party called a **trustee**.

The trustor (borrower) signs the promissory note and the trust deed and gives them to the beneficiary (lender) who holds them for the term of the loan. Under the trust deed, the trustor has **equitable title** and the trustee has "bare" or "naked" legal title to the property.

Although bare legal title is conveyed using a trust deed, it does not actually convey possession. Possession and equitable title remain with the borrower. **Equitable title** is the interest held by the trustor under a trust deed and gives the borrower the equitable right to obtain absolute ownership to the property when legal title is held by the trustee.

Review - Interests Held Under Equitable Title
- The trustor under a trust deed
- The vendee under a contract for deed
- The buyer of real property from the time the sales contract is signed, and earnest money is paid until the closing

The trustee, who has bare legal title, acts as an agent for the beneficiary and has only two obligations. The first is to foreclose on the property if there is a default on the loan, and the second is to reconvey the title to the borrower when the debt is repaid in full. When the debt is repaid in full, the beneficiary signs a **Request for Full Reconveyance** and sends it to the trustee requesting the trustee to reconvey title to the borrower. The trustee signs and records a **Deed of Reconveyance** to show the debt has been repaid and to clear the lien from the property. The trust deed is recorded at the close of escrow. A **fictitious trust deed** is a recorded trust deed containing details that apply to later loan documents.

Mortgage

Since its introduction in the early 1900s, the deed of trust virtually replaced the use of a note and mortgage when financing real estate. The promissory note shows the obligation of the debt, and the mortgage is a lien against the described property until the debt is repaid.

There are two parties in a mortgage: a **mortgagor** (borrower) and a **mortgagee** (lender). The mortgagor receives loan funds from a mortgagee and signs a promissory note and mortgage. Once signed by the borrower, both the note and mortgage are held by the lender until the loan is paid. Unlike a trust deed, under a mortgage both title and possession remain with the borrower.

Contract of Sale

The **contract of sale** is the financing instrument with many names. It may be called an installment sales contract, a contract of sale, an agreement of sale, a conditional sales contract, a contract for deed, or a land sales contract.

This is a contract in which the seller (**vendor**) becomes the lender to the buyer (**vendee**). The vendor pays off the original financing while receiving payments from the vendee on the contract of sale. The vendor and vendee's relationship is like that of a beneficiary and a trustor in a trust deed.

The vendee (buyer) has possession and use of the property even though legal title is held by the vendor (seller). In a contract of sale, the vendor retains legal ownership of the property, and the vendee holds what is known as equitable title. When all the terms of the contract are met, the vendor will pass title to the vendee.

The vendor in a land contract may not use vendee's impound money for any other purpose without the consent of the payor (**vendee**). Land contracts are used in CalVet loans under the California Veterans Farm and Home Purchase Plan (discussed later in the chapter). The state of California is the vendor who has legal title, and the veteran is the vendee who has equitable title.

Terms Found in Finance Instruments

When a borrower signs a note promising to repay a sum, the lender usually includes some specific requirements in the note regarding repayment. In addition to the terms in the note, the security instrument lists several covenants (promises) regarding the relationship of the borrower and the lender. Some of these special clauses are meant to protect the lender and the lender's interests, while some are meant to protect the borrower.

Prepayment Clauses

Depending on the clauses in the note and mortgage, some loans may be paid early, some loans may be paid off early but are charged a penalty, and other loans cannot be paid before the due date.

A **prepayment clause**, some times called an "**or more**" clause, allows a borrower to pay off a loan early, or make higher payments without penalty.

Occasionally, a trust deed includes a **prepayment penalty clause** in case a borrower pays off a loan early. When lenders make loans, they calculate their return over the term of the loan. If a loan is paid off before that time, the lender gets less interest than planned. Therefore, the return on investment is threatened and the borrower has to make it up by paying a penalty.

For residential property, the prepayment penalty cannot exceed six month's interest. A borrower may prepay up to 20% of the loan amount in any 12-month period without a penalty. A prepayment penalty can then be charged only on the amount in excess of 20% of the original loan amount. A prepayment penalty is not allowed on a loan against the borrower's residence after the loan is seven years old. Other rules apply for non-residential property.

A **lock-in clause** prohibits borrowers from repaying a loan in advance. Sometimes it is in effect for only the first part of the loan. It is not allowed on residential units of less than four units. In a land contract to purchase a home a lock-in clause may be ignored by the vendee (buyer). Do not confuse this lock in clause with a  rate lock. A **rate lock** allows a borrower to lock in an interest rate and points for a specified period of time while the loan application is being processed.

Late Payments

Lenders may not impose a late charge on a payment until after the payment is ten days late.

Acceleration Clause

An **acceleration clause** allows a lender to call the entire note due, on occurrence of a specific event such as default in payment, taxes or insurance, or sale of the property. A lender may use the acceleration clause to call the entire note due if the borrower does not pay the loan payments, the real property taxes or insurance premiums, or if the borrower sells the property. In order to pay off the outstanding loan, a lender will foreclose on the loan.

Alienation Clause

The **alienation** or **due-on-sale clause** is an acceleration clause. A lender may call the entire note due if the original borrower transfers (alienates) ownership of the property to someone else. If the note contains an **acceleration clause** (due on sale), the trust deed must mention this clause in order to enforce the contract. This clause protects the lender from an unqualified, unapproved buyer taking over a loan. Justifiably, the lender fears possible default, with no control over who is making the payments.

Usually a lender will want the existing loan paid off if a property owner transfers the property to someone else. However, under certain circumstances, a property owner may transfer responsibility for the loan to the buyer when he or she sells the property to another party. A buyer may assume an existing loan, or may buy a property subject to an existing loan.

Loan Assumption

An **assumption clause** allows a buyer to assume responsibility for the full payment of the loan with the lender's knowledge and consent. When a property is sold, a buyer may assume the existing loan. Usually with the approval of the lender, the buyer takes over primary liability for the loan, with the original borrower secondarily liable if there is a default. What that means is that even though the original borrower is secondarily responsible, according to the loan assumption agreement, no actual repayment of the loan may be required of that person.

The original borrower (seller) can avoid any responsibility for the loan by asking the lender for a **substitution of liability (novation)**, relieving the seller of all liability for repayment of the loan. In most cases, a buyer assumes an existing loan with the approval of the underlying lender. However, an alienation clause in the note would prevent a buyer from assuming the loan.

Subject To

A buyer may also purchase a property subject to the existing loan, providing the loan document does not include a due-on-sale clause. A **subject to clause** allows a buyer to take over a loan, making the payments without the knowledge or approval of the lender. The original borrower remains responsible for the loan, even though the buyer takes title and makes the payments. In this case, also, the property remains the security for the loan. In the case of default, the property is sold and the proceeds go to the lender, with no recourse to the original buyer other than the foreclosure going against the borrower's credit.

Escrow No. _____   Title Order No. _____

(DUE ON SALE CLAUSE)

$ _____, California _____, 20 _____

_____ after date, for value received

I promise to pay to _____

_____ or order, at

_____

the sum of _____ DOLLARS

with interest from _____ until paid at the

rate of _____ per cent per annum, payable _____

_____

_____

Principal and interest payable in lawful money of the United States of America. should default be made in payment of interest when due the whole sum of principal and interest shall become immediately due at the option of the holder of this note and after said breach, said obligation shall continue to accrue interest at the rate of _____% per annum. If action be instituted on this note I promise to pay such sum as the Court may fix as Attorney's Fees. This note is secured by a Deed of Trust of even date herewith.

In the event the herein described property or any part thereof, or any interest therein which has been given as security for the payment of this obligation is sold, agreed to be sold, conveyed or alienated by the Trustor, or by the operation of the law or otherwise, all obligations secured by this instrument, irrespective of the maturity dates expressed therein, at the option of the holder hereof and without demand or notice shall immediately become due and payable.

_____   _____

_____   _____

_____   _____

DO NOT DESTROY THIS NOTE

When paid, this note, if secured by Deed of Trust, must be surrendered to Trustee for cancellation before reconveyance will be made.

FD-30G (Rev. 2/95)   STRAIGHT NOTE (DUE ON SALE CLAUSE)

When a buyer takes a property subject to the existing loan, the underlying lender may not always be informed. The buyer simply starts making the payments and the seller hopes he or she is diligent and does not default.

The occurrence of subject to sales is relative to economic and market conditions. In a real estate market where there are more buyers than sellers (seller's market) a homeowner does not need to sell subject to his or her loan. When money is tight, interest rates are high, and sellers are wondering where all the buyers are, a subject to sale might be a seller's only option.

Review - Notes, Trust Deeds, and Mortgages
- A note is the evidence of a debt.
- A trust deed or mortgage, even though it is the security for the debt, is still only an incident of the debt.
- A trust deed or mortgage must have a note to secure, but a note does not need a trust deed or mortgage to stand alone.
- If there is a conflict in the terms of a note and the trust deed or mortgage used to secure it, the provisions of the note will control.
- If a note is unenforceable, the presence of a trust deed will not make it valid.

Default and Foreclosure

Default is the nonperformance of a contractual obligation. The default is usually due to failing to make the promised payments, failing to pay property taxes, or insuring the property. **Foreclosure** is the legal procedure used by lenders to terminate all rights, title, and interest of the trustor or mortgagor in real property by selling the property and using the sale proceeds to satisfy the liens of creditors.

There are two ways to foreclose: by trustee's sale and by judicial process. Any trust deed or mortgage with a **power-of-sale clause** may be foreclosed non-judicially by a trustee's sale or judicially by a court procedure. Without the power-of-sale clause, the only remedy a lender has is a judicial foreclosure by a court proceeding. Most trust deeds and mortgages in California include the power-of-sale clause, so the lender may choose either type of foreclosure method.

Foreclosure on Trust Deed by Trustee's Sale (Non-judicial)

Usually the lender will elect to foreclose on the loan using the trustee's sale because it is the quickest and easiest method taking approximately four months. First, the beneficiary (lender) notifies the trustor (borrower) of default and requests the trustee to record a **notice of default**. Anyone who has recorded a **Request for Notice** must be notified of the default. The trustee must wait at least three months after recording the notice of default before advertising the trustee sale. Then the trustee advertises a Notice of Sale once a week for three weeks (21 days) and posts a notice of sale on the property.

RECORDING REQUESTED BY

WHEN RECORDED MAIL TO

NAME

ADDRESS

CITY

STATE&ZIP

Title Order No.   **Escrow No.**

SPACE ABOVE THIS LINE FOR RECORDER'S USE

REQUEST FOR NOTICE OF DELINQUENCIES
UNDER SECTION 2924e CIVIL CODE

In accordance with Section 2924e. California Civil Code. request is hereby made that a written notice of any or all delinquencies of four months or more. in payments of principal or interest on any obligation secured under the Deed of Trust recorded as Instrument Number: on:
Official Records of   County, California, loan number
Wherein   is the trustor, and describing land therein as:

1. The ownership or security interest of the requester, is the beneficial interest under that certain deed of trust recorded as instrument
Number: on   of the Official Records of:
Wherein   County, California.
                                                                                    is the trustor.
2.   is the date on which the interest of the requester will terminate as evidenced by the maturity date of the note of the trustor in favor of the requester.
3.   is the name of the current owner of the security property described above.
4. The street address of the security property as described above is:

5. Said notice of delinquency and the amount thereof shall be sent to:

(Requester Beneficiary)

at

(Address)   (City)

(State)   (Zip)

Dated

(Requester Beneficiary)

CONSENT BY TRUSTOR/OWNER

I _____ AUTHORIZE _____
          (Trustee)   (Senior Lienholder)
TO DISCLOSE IN WRITING TO _____
                              (Requesting Beneficiary)
NOTICE OF ANY AND ALL DELINQUENCIES OF FOUR MONTHS OR MORE, IN PAYMENT OF PRINCIPAL OR INTEREST ON ANY OBLIGATION SECURED BY THAT SENIOR LIEN MORE PARTICULARLY DESCRIBED AS INSTRUMENT NUMBER
_____ RECORDED ON _____
IN OFFICIAL RECORDS OF _____COUNTY. CALIFORNIA.
 DATED _____

As you can see, the minimum time between recording the notice of default and the trustee sale is three months and 21 days. During this time the trustor may **reinstate** (bring current) the loan up to five business days prior to the trustee's sale. The trustee holds the sale and issues a **trustee's deed** to the highest bidder. A trustor has no right of redemption after the trustee sale.

Proceeds from the sale of the property are paid out in the following order:

1. Trustee's fees, costs, and expenses of the sale.
2. Any tax and assessment liens that are due and owing.
3. Trust deeds, mortgages, and mechanic's liens in their order of priority.
4. The defaulting borrower.

Sometimes the proceeds of the sale are not sufficient to satisfy the debt being foreclosed. If that happens, the lender may try to obtain a deficiency judgment against the borrower. A **deficiency judgment** is a personal judgment against a borrower for the balance of a debt owed when the security for the loan is not sufficient to pay the debt. However, the lender cannot obtain a deficiency judgment against the trustor under a trustee sale.

Foreclosure by Court Proceeding (Judicial)

Default on a mortgage, unless the mortgage includes a power-of-sale clause, requires a court foreclosure. The mortgagee (lender) goes to court to start the foreclosure. The court issues a decree of foreclosure and an order of sale. After publication and posting of the sale notice, the court-appointed commissioner sells the property to the highest bidder and gives the buyer a Certification of Sale. After a court

foreclosure sale on a mortgage, the mortgagor (borrower) gets to keep possession of the property and has one year to redeem the property by satisfying the loan in full including court costs and any interest. This process is called **equity of redemption**. If after one year, the mortgagor does not redeem the property, a **sheriff's deed** is issued to the new buyer.

If a trust deed is foreclosed in court, it is treated like a mortgage and the trustor (borrower) may keep possession during the redemption period. Sometimes a lender with a trust deed may elect to foreclose by a court foreclosure because it is the only way the beneficiary can obtain a deficiency judgment against the borrower.

Deficiency Judgments

As mentioned earlier, a deficiency judgment is a personal judgment against a borrower for the difference between the unpaid amount of the loan, plus interest, costs and fees of the sale, and the amount of the actual proceeds of the foreclosure sale. This means if the property sells for less than what is owed to the lender, the borrower will be personally responsible for repayment after the deficiency judgment is filed.

Deficiency Judgment Not Allowed

If a lender (beneficiary or mortgagee) chooses to foreclose a trust deed or mortgage with a power of sale using a trustee sale, no deficiency judgment is allowed if the proceeds do not satisfy the debt and all costs. Since trust deeds are used almost exclusively in California to secure loans, the only security for a beneficiary is the property itself. Any other personal assets of the borrower in default are protected from judgment under a trust deed.

Additionally, a lender cannot get a deficiency judgment against a borrower if the loan is a purchase money loan secured by either a trust deed or a mortgage. Any loan made at the time of a sale, as part of that sale, is known as a **purchase-money loan**. This includes first trust deeds, junior loans used to purchase the property, and seller carry-back financing. A seller is said to **carry back** when the seller extends credit to a buyer by taking a promissory note executed by the buyer and secured by a trust deed on the property being purchased as a part of the purchase price.

Deficiency Judgment Permitted

A deficiency judgment is allowed on hard money loans. A **hard money loan** is one made in exchange for cash, as opposed to a loan made to finance the purchase of a home. Typically, a hard money loan refers to junior loans used to take money out for consumer purchases, home equity loans, debt consolidation, and even a refinance.

Trust Deed	Mortgage Contract
1. Number of Parties (3) **Trustor**: Borrower who conveys title to trustee who holds as security for debt. **Beneficiary**: Lender who holds original note and trust deed during life of the debt. **Trustee**: Receiver of naked legal title who conveys it when debt is paid or will sell if foreclosure is necessary.	**1. Number of Parties (2)** **Mortgager**: Borrower retains title but gives lender a lien on the property as security. **Mortgagee**: Lender who holds the mortgage.
2. Title: Conveyed to trustee with trustor retaining equitable possession of the property.	**2. Title:** Held by mortgagor together with possession.
3. Statute of Limitations: The security for debt is held by trustee, rights of creditor are not ended when statute runs out on the note.	**3. Statute of Limitations:** Foreclosure is barred if no action is taken within four (4) years of delinquency on the note.
4. Remedy for Default: Foreclosure can be instituted through trustee's sale or court foreclosure. (Court foreclosure follows mortgage foreclosure procedure #7.)	**4. Remedy for Default:** Court foreclosure is usually the only remedy.
5. Right of Redemption: When title has been sold by trustee at trustee's sale no right or equity of redemption exists.	**5. Right of Redemption:** Mortgagor has up to one (1) year to redeem the property after court foreclosure called "equity of redemption."
6. Satisfaction: The beneficiary sends a request for full reconveyance to the trustee with the original note and trust deed. Upon payment of fees, the trustee issues a reconveyance deed which must be recorded.	**6. Satisfaction:** Upon final payment and on demand, the mortgagee signs the certificate that the debt is satisfied. Then the certificate or release is recorded.

7. Foreclosure by Trustee's Sale:	**7. Foreclosure by Court:**
Beneficiary notifies the trustee of default. The trustee notifies the trustor and records the notice. Anyone who has recorded the "Request for Notice for Default" must also be notified. The trustee waits at least three (3) months. During the three (3) month period, the trustor can reinstate the loan. Then the trustee advertises a "notice of sale" once a week for three weeks (21 days) and posts a notice on the property. Trustor can now invade the three (3) week advertising period and can reinstate the loan up to five (5) days prior to the trustee's sale. The trustee conducts the sale and issues a trustee's deed to the highest bidder.	Court action is commenced by the mortgagee. The court issues a decree of foreclosure and an order of sale. A court appointed commissioner sells to the highest bidder after the publication and posting of the sale notice. The Certificate of Sale is issued. Mortgagor has one (1) year to redeem the property and remains in possession for that year. If sale proceeds satisfy the debt, court costs and interest then the mortgagor has only three (3) months to redeem the property. If a trust deed is foreclosed in court, it is treated like a mortgage contract, and trustor remains in possession during the redemption period. A sheriff's deed is issued after one (1) year.
8. Deficiency Judgment: No deficiency judgment is available if the foreclosure is by trustee's sale.	**8. Deficiency Judgment** A deficiency judgment is available in a court foreclosure.
9. No deficiency judgment is available on a "purchase-money" trust deed or mortgage.	

Conventional and Government-Backed Loans

All loans can be classified according to their loan terms and whether they have government backing. First, all of the various loans are classified by their terms—fixed rate loans, adjustable-rate loans, and their combinations. Second, loans are classified by whether they have government backing—conventional or government loans. Some lenders specialize in only conventional conforming loans, whereas full service lenders offer a wide selection of loan programs including conventional, government-sponsored FHA and VA loans, and non-conforming loans.

Conventional Loans

A **conventional loan** is any loan made by lenders without any governmental guarantees. The basic protection for a lender making conventional loans is the borrower's equity in the property. A low down payment will mean greater risk for the lender and a higher interest charged to the borrower. Conventional loans may be conforming or non-conforming.

Conforming Loans

Conforming loans have terms and conditions that follow the guidelines set forth by Fannie Mae and Freddie Mac. These loans are called "A" paper loans, or prime loans, and can be made to purchase or refinance homes (one-to-four residential units). Fannie Mae and Freddie Mac guidelines establish the maximum loan amount, borrower credit and income requirements, down payment, and suitable properties. Fannie Mae and Freddie Mac announce new loan limits every year. To get the current loan limits, go to the Fannie Mae website at www.fanniemae.com or the Freddie Mac website at www.freddiemac.com.

Private Mortgage Insurance (PMI)

Conventional lenders usually require private mortgage insurance (PMI) on low down payment loans. This is done for the lender's protection in the event the homeowner fails to make his or her payments. **Private mortgage insurance** protects the lender against financial loss if a homeowner stops making mortgage payments. When the loan exceeds 80% of the value of the property, lenders usually require private mortgage insurance on conventional loans. Usually borrowers pay for this insurance as part of the monthly payment. A few companies provide this insurance.

Non-Conforming Loans

Sometimes the borrower's credit worthiness or the size of the loan does not meet conventional lending standards. In that case, a **non-conforming loan** is used. Non-conforming loans include jumbo and subprime loans.

Jumbo Loans

Loans that exceed the maximum loan limit set by Fannie Mae and Freddie Mac are called **jumbo loans**. Because jumbo loans are not funded by these government-sponsored entities, they usually carry a higher interest rate and some additional underwriting requirements.

Subprime Loans

Loans that do not meet the borrower credit requirements of Fannie Mae and Freddie Mac are called **subprime loans** or "B" and "C" paper loans as opposed to "A" paper conforming loans. Subprime loans were developed to help higher risk borrowers obtain a mortgage. These loans are offered to borrowers who may have recently filed for bankruptcy or foreclosure, or have had late payments on their credit reports. The purpose is to offer temporary financing to these applicants until they can qualify for conforming "A" financing. Due to the higher risk associated with lending to borrowers who have a poor credit history, subprime loans typically require a larger down payment and a higher interest rate.

Subprime loans were developed to help higher risk borrowers obtain a loan. Prior to 1990, it was very difficult for anyone to obtain a mortgage if he or she did not qualify for a conventional FHA or VA loan. Many borrowers with bad credit are good people who honestly intended to pay their bills on time. Catastrophic events such as the loss of a job or a family illness can lead to missed or late payments, or even foreclosure and bankruptcy.

Government Participation in Real Estate Finance

There are two federal agencies and one state agency that help make it possible for people to buy homes they would never be able to purchase without government involvement.

The two federal agencies that participate in real estate financing are the Federal Housing Administration (FHA) and the Veterans Administration (VA). The California Farm and Home Purchase Program, or CalVet loan, is a state program that helps eligible veterans.

Federal Housing Administration (FHA)

The FHA program, a part of HUD (U.S. Department of Housing and Urban Development) since 1934, has caused the greatest change in home mortgage lending in the history of real estate finance. The FHA was established to improve the construction and financing of housing. The main purpose of the FHA program has been to promote home ownership. Secondary results include setting minimum property requirements and systemizing appraisals. An appraiser would be reprimanded if he or she did not use FHA guidelines when preparing appraisals for FHA loans. Additionally, an appraiser who intentionally misrepresents the value on FHA loan appraisals, which subsequently cause a loss, could be fined and face legal action.

The FHA does not make loans; rather, it insures lenders against loss. Loans are made by authorized lending institutions such as banks, savings banks, and independent mortgage companies. As long as FHA guidelines are used in funding the loan, the FHA, upon default by the borrower, insures the lender against loss. If the borrower does default, the lender may foreclose and the FHA will pay cash up to the established limit of the insurance.

The lender is protected, in case of foreclosure, by charging the borrower a fee for an insurance policy called **Mutual Mortgage Insurance** (MMI). This insurance requirement is how the FHA finances its program. The premium may be financed as part of the loan or paid in cash at the close of escrow.

The borrower applies directly to the FHA-approved lender (mortgagee), not the FHA, for a loan. FHA does not make loans, build homes, or insure the property. A buyer who would like to purchase a home with FHA financing would apply to an FHA-approved mortgagee (lender) who would then request a **conditional commitment** from FHA. The conditional commitment is good for six months. A firm commitment is requested when the FHA approves the borrower (mortgagor).

The FHA guidelines encourage home ownership by allowing 100% of the down payment to be a gift from family or friends and by allowing closing costs to be financed to reduce the up-front cost of buying a home. The down payment on FHA loans varies with the amount of the loan.

Interest rates are determined by mutual agreement between the borrower and the lender—they are not set by the Federal Reserve Board. Sometimes a borrower will pay points to the lender to increase the lender's yield and compensate the lender for the difference between FHA interest rates (which tend to be low) and conventional interest rates. **Points** are a percentage of the loan amount paid to the lender when negotiating a loan. One point is equal to 1% of the loan amount. Points increase the lenders real yield by 1/8 of one percent per point charged. The borrower must make monthly payments. The FHA does not allow a borrower to make semi-monthly or semi-annual payments.

The FHA maximum loan amounts vary from one county to another. It is important that the total loan amount, including financed closing costs, not exceed the maximum limit set by the FHA for the county in which the property is located. FHA loans do not have income limits. FHA loans are based on the selling price if it is lower than the appraisal.

There are no alienation and prepayment penalty clauses allowed in FHA loans. Any qualified resident of the United States may obtain an FHA loan as long as the property will be the borrower's principal residence and is located in the United States.

The FHA insures a variety of types of loans. For example, borrowers can get qualified for an FHA loan before a builder starts construction, enabling both borrower and builder to count on the completion of the transaction.

Popular FHA Loan Programs

Section 203(b)

The FHA 203(b) loan offers financing on the purchase or construction of owner-occupied residences of one-to-four units. This program offers 30-year, fixed-rate, fully amortized, mortgages with a down payment requirement as low as 3%, allowing financing of up to 97% of the value of the home. FHA has mortgage limits that vary from county to county. Their website, https://entp.hud.gov/idapp/html/hicostlook.cfm, provides the current FHA mortgage limits for several areas.

Section 203(k)

A purchase rehabilitation loan (purchase rehab) is a great option for buyers who are looking to improve their property immediately upon purchase. This mortgage loan provides the funds to purchase your home and the funds to complete your improvement project all in one loan, one application, one set of fees, one closing, and one convenient monthly payment.

A purchase rehab loan could be used for a variety of improvements such as adding a family room or bedroom, remodeling a kitchen or bathroom, making general upgrades to an older property, or even completing a total teardown and rebuild.

Section 245 Graduated Payment Mortgage

A **graduated payment mortgage** (GPM) has a monthly payment that starts out at the lowest level and increases at a specific rate. Payments for the first five years are low, and cover only part of the interest due, with the unpaid amount added to the principal balance. After that time, the loan is recalculated with the new payments staying the same from that point on. In this loan, the interest rate is not adjustable and does not change during the term of the loan. What actually changes is the amount of the monthly mortgage payment.

A GPM is offered by the FHA to borrowers who might have trouble qualifying for regular loan payments, but who expect their income to increase. This loan is for the buyer who expects to be earning more after a few years and can make a higher payment at that time. GPMs are available in 30-year and 15-year amortization and for both conforming and jumbo loans. The interest rate for a GPM is traditionally .5% to .75% higher than the interest rate for a straight fixed-rate mortgage. The higher note rate and scheduled negative amortization of the GPM makes the cost of the mortgage more expensive to the borrower.

Energy Efficient Mortgage

The Energy Efficient Mortgages Program (EEM) helps homebuyers or homeowners save money on utility bills by enabling them to finance the cost of adding energy-efficiency features to new or existing housing. The program provides mortgage insurance for the purchase or refinance of a principal residence that incorporates the cost of energy efficient improvements into the loan.

Section 255 Reverse Annuity Mortgages

Reverse Annuity Mortgages are also called Home Equity Conversion Mortgages (HECM). It is a program for homeowners (62 years and older), who have paid off their mortgages or have only small mortgage balances remaining. The program has three options for homeowners: (1) borrow against the equity in their homes in a lump sum, (2) borrow on a monthly basis for a fixed term or for as long as they live in the home, or (3) borrow as a line of credit.

The borrower is not required to make payments as long as the borrower lives in the home. The loan is paid off when the property is sold. FHA collects an insurance premium from all borrowers to provide mortgage coverage that will cover any shortfall if the proceeds from the sale of the property are not sufficient to cover the loan amount. Senior citizens are charged 2% of the home's value as an up-front payment plus 1/2% on the loan balance each year. These amounts are usually paid by the mortgage company and charged to the borrower's principal balance. FHA's reverse mortgage insurance makes this program less expensive to borrowers than the smaller reverse mortgage programs run by private companies without FHA insurance.

VA Loan

The Department of Veterans Affairs (DVA) does not make loans. It guarantees loans made by an approved institutional lender, much like the FHA. Both programs were created to assist people in buying homes when conventional loan programs did not fit their needs. There are two main differences between the two government programs: (1) only an eligible veteran may obtain a VA loan, and (2) the DVA does not require a down payment up to a certain loan amount, which means qualified veterans, could get 100% financing. As with FHA loans, alienation and prepayment penalty clauses are not allowed in VA loans.

VA loans are made by a lender, such as a mortgage company, savings and loan, or bank. The DVA's guaranty on the loan protects the lender against loss if the payments are not made, and is intended to encourage lenders to offer veterans loans with more favorable terms. To determine the amount of guaranty on the loan, the loan amount and any previous entitlement must be taken into consideration.

VA Loan Process

A veteran must possess a **Certificate of Eligibility**, which is available from the Veterans Administration, before applying for a VA loan. The certificate will show the veteran's entitlement or right to obtain the loan.

When a veteran finds a house to purchase, a VA-approved conventional lender will take the loan application and the

veteran's Certificate of Eligibility and process the loan according to VA guidelines. The lender will request the VA to assign a licensed appraiser to determine the reasonable value for the property. A **Certificate of Reasonable Value** (CRV) will be issued. A loan may not exceed the value established by the CRV appraisal. After the loan closes, it is sent to the VA for guaranty. The Certificate of Eligibility is annotated to show how much of the entitlement has been used and will be returned to the veteran.

A veteran may get another VA loan, if the prior VA loan is paid off and the property sold. A VA loan may be assumed by a non-veteran buyer, upon approval by the VA. If a veteran sells his or her property and allows the buyer to assume the existing VA loan, he or she cannot get another VA loan until the buyer who assumed the VA loan has paid it off. If a VA loan is foreclosed and there is a loss, the veteran cannot have eligibility restored until the loss has been repaid in full.

Fees and Closing Costs

Although a veteran can get 100% financing, he or she will be required to pay a 2.0% funding fee. The funding fee charged for loans to refinance an existing VA home loan with a new VA home loan is 0.5%. The funding fee can be paid in cash or included in the loan.

VA Department of Veterans Affairs

VA LOAN SUMMARY SHEET

1. VA'S 12-DIGIT LOAN NUMBER

2. VETERAN'S NAME *(First, middle, last)*

3. VETERAN'S SOCIAL SECURITY NUMBER	4. GENDER OF VETERAN *(Check one)* ☐ MALE ☐ FEMALE	5. VETERAN'S DATE OF BIRTH *(mm/dd/yyyy)*

6A. ETHNICITY

☐ NOT HISPANIC OR LATINO
☐ HISPANIC OR LATINO

6B. RACE *(May select more than one)*

☐ AMERICAN INDIAN OR ALASKAN NATIVE   ☐ ASIAN   ☐ BLACK OR AFRICAN AMERICAN
☐ NATIVE HAWAIIAN OR PACIFIC ISLANDER ☐ WHITE   ☐ UNKNOWN

7. ENTITLEMENT CODE *(01 to 11, from VA Certificate of Eligibility)*	8. AMOUNT OF ENTITLEMENT AVAILABLE *(from VA Certificate of Eligibility)*

9. BRANCH OF SERVICE *(Check one)*

☐ 1. ARMY   ☐ 2. NAVY   ☐ 3. AIR FORCE   ☐ 4. MARINE CORPS   ☐ 5. COAST GUARD   ☐ 6. OTHER

10. MILITARY STATUS *(Check one)*

☐ 1. SEPARATED FROM SERVICE   ☐ 2. IN SERVICE

11. FIRST TIME HOME BUYER *(Check one)*

☐ YES   ☐ NO

> This means a veteran who has not previously purchased a home, either by cash, assumption, or new financing.

12. LOAN PROCEDURE *(Check one)*

☐ AUTOMATIC   ☐ AUTO-IRRRL   ☐ VA PRIOR APPROVAL

13. PURPOSE OF LOAN *(Check one)*

☐ 1. HOME (INCLUDES MH ON PERMANENT FOUNDATION)   ☐ 2. MANUFACTURED HOME   ☐ 3. CONDOMINIUM
☐ 4. ALTERATIONS/IMPROVEMENTS   ☐ 5. REFINANCE

14. LOAN CODE *(Check one)*

☐ 1. PURCHASE   ☐ 2. IRRRL (STREAMLINE REFINANCE)   ☐ 3. CASH OUT REFINANCE (MAX 90% LTV)
☐ 4. MANUFACTURED HOME REFI   ☐ 5. REFINANCING OVER 90% OF RV

15. TYPE OF MORTGAGE *(Check one)*

☐ 0. REGULAR FIXED PAYMENT   ☐ 1. GPM-NEVER TO EXCEED CRV   ☐ 2. OTHER GPMs   ☐ 3. GEM
☐ 4. TEMPORARY BUYDOWN   ☐ 5. HYBRID ARM   ☐ 6. ARM

16. TYPE OF HYBRID-ARM *(NOTE: Must be completed if Hybrid Arm selected in Item 15.)*

☐ 3/1   ☐ 5/1   ☐ 7/1   ☐ 10/1

17. TYPE OF OWNERSHIP *(Check one)*	18. CLOSING DATE *(mm/dd/yyyy)*
☐ 1. SOLE OWNERSHIP (VETERAN & SPOUSE OR VETERAN ONLY) ☐ 2. JOINT - 2 OR MORE VETERANS ☐ 3. JOINT - VETERAN/NON-VETERAN	

19. PURCHASE PRICE *(N/A for Refinance Loans)*	$
20. REASONABLE VALUE *(For IRRRLs - If appraisal has not been done, loan amount of prior VA loan)*	$

21. ENERGY IMPROVEMENTS *(Check all applicable boxes)* $

☐ NONE   ☐ INSTALLATION OF SOLAR HEATING/COOLING
☐ REPLACEMENT OF A MAJOR SYSTEM   ☐ ADDITION OF A NEW FEATURE
☐ INSULATION, CAULKING, WEATHER-STRIPPING, ETC.   ☐ OTHER IMPROVEMENTS

22. LOAN AMOUNT	(Purchase - Purchase Price or RV (lesser) + Funding Fee) (Refi - Max 90% LTV + Funding Fee) (IRRRL - Old Loan Payoff + All Closing Costs)	$

23. PROPERTY TYPE *(Check one)*

☐ NEITHER   ☐ PUD   ☐ CONDOMINIUM

24. APPRAISAL TYPE *(Check one)*

☐ IND - SINGLE PROPERTY-IND APPRAISAL   ☐ ONE - MASTER CRV CASE (MCRV)   ☐ LAPP - LENDER APPRAISAL
☐ MBL - MANUFACTURED HOME   ☐ HUD - CONVERSION   ☐ PMC - PROP. MGMT. CASE

VA FORM
AUG 2006   **26-0286**   SUPERSEDES VA FORM 26-0286, OCT 2003, WHICH WILL NOT BE USED.

25. TYPE OF STRUCTURE *(Check one)*
- ☐ 1. CONVENTIONAL CONSTRUCTION
- ☐ 2. SINGLEWIDE M/H
- ☐ 3. DOUBLEWIDE M/H
- ☐ 4. M/H LOT ONLY
- ☐ 5. PREFABRICATED HOME
- ☐ 6. CONDOMINIUM CONVERSION

26. PROPERTY DESIGNATION *(Check one)*
- ☐ 1. EXISTING OR USED HOME, CONDO, M/H
- ☐ 2. APPRAISED AS PROPOSED CONSTRUCTION
- ☐ 3. NEW EXISTING - NEVER OCCUPIED
- ☐ 4. ENERGY IMPROVEMENTS

27. NO. OF UNITS *(Check one)*	**28. MCRV NO.**
☐ SINGLE ☐ TWO UNITS ☐ THREE UNITS ☐ FOUR OR MORE	

29. MANUFACTURED HOME CATEGORY *(Check one)*
- ☐ 0. OTHER - NOT M/H
- ☐ 1. M/H ONLY (RENTED SPACE)
- ☐ 2. M/H ONLY (VETERAN-OWNED LOT)
- ☐ 7. M/H ON PERMANENT FOUNDATION

30. PROPERTY ADDRESS

31. CITY	**32. STATE**	**33. ZIP CODE**	**34. COUNTY**

35. LENDER VA ID NUMBER	**36. AGENT VA ID NUMBER** *(If applicable)*	**37. LENDER LOAN NUMBER**

FOR LAPP CASES ONLY

38. LENDER SAR ID NUMBER

39. GROSS LIVING AREA *(Square Feet)*	**40. AGE OF PROPERTY** *(Yrs.)*	**41. DATE SAR ISSUED NOTIFICATION OF VALUE** *(mm/dd/yyyy)*

42. TOTAL ROOM COUNT	**43. BATHS** *(No.)*	**44. BEDROOMS** *(No.)*

45. IF PROCESSED UNDER LAPP, WAS THE FEE APPRAISER'S ORIGINAL VALUE ESTIMATE CHANGED OR REPAIR RECOMMENDATIONS REVISED, OR DID THE SAR OTHERWISE MAKE SIGNIFICANT ADJUSTMENTS?
☐ YES *(If "Yes," there must be written justification by fee appraiser and/or SAR)*   ☐ NO

INCOME INFORMATION *(Not Applicable for IRRRLs)*

46A. LOAN PROCESSED UNDER VA RECOGNIZED AUTOMATED UNDERWRITING SYSTEM
☐ YES ☐ NO   *(If "Yes," Complete Item 46B and 46C)*

46B. WHICH SYSTEM WAS USED?	**46C. RISK CLASSIFICATION**
☐ 01. LP ☐ 02. DU ☐ 03. PMI AURA ☐ 04. CLUES ☐ 05 ZIPPY	☐ 1. APPROVE ☐ 2. REFER

47. CREDIT SCORE *(Enter the median credit score for the veteran only)*	
48. LIQUID ASSETS	$
49. TOTAL MONTHLY GROSS INCOME *(Item 32 + Item 39 from VA Form 26-6393)*	$
50. RESIDUAL INCOME	$
51. RESIDUAL INCOME GUIDELINE	$

52. DEBT-INCOME RATIO *(If Income Ratio is over 41% and Residual Income is not 120% of guideline, statement of justification signed by underwriter's supervisor must be included on or with VA Form 26-6393)*   %

53. SPOUSE INCOME CONSIDERED	**54. SPOUSE'S INCOME AMOUNT** *(If considered)*
☐ YES ☐ NO *(If "Yes," Complete Item 54)*	$

DISCOUNT INFORMATION *(Applicable for All Loans)*

55. DISCOUNT POINTS CHARGED	% OR	$
56. DISCOUNT POINTS PAID BY VETERAN	% OR	$

57. TERM *(Months)*	**58. INTEREST RATE**	**59. FUNDING FEE EXEMPT**
	%	☐ Y - EXEMPT ☐ N - NOT EXEMPT

FOR IRRRLS ONLY

60. PAID IN FULL VA LOAN NUMBER

61. ORIGINAL LOAN AMOUNT	**62. ORIGINAL INTEREST RATE**
$	%

63. REMARKS

VA FORM 26-0286, AUG 2006

The lender may charge reasonable closing costs that may not be included in the loan. The closing costs may be paid by the buyer (veteran) or the seller. Typical closing costs include Certificate of Reasonable Value, credit report, loan origination fee, discount points, title insurance, and recording fees. The VA allows the veteran to pay reasonable discount points on a refinance or a purchase. No commissions, brokerage fees, or buyer broker fees may be charged to the veteran.

California Veteran Loans (CalVet)

The California Department of Veterans Affairs administers the CalVet loan program to assist California veterans in buying a home or farm. Unlike other government financing, the CalVet program funds and services its own loans. Funds are obtained through the sale of State General Obligation Bonds. The CA DVA sells bonds to purchase homes and then sells the homes to qualified California veterans using a land sale contract.

An eligible California veteran (includes a 17-year old veteran) applies for the loan and makes loan payments directly to the Department of Veterans Affairs. Upon application for a CalVet loan and approval of the borrower and property, the Department of Veterans Affairs purchases the property from the seller, takes title to the property, and sells to the veteran on a contract of sale. Discount points are not charged on a CalVet loan. The department holds legal title, with the veteran holding equitable title, until the loan is paid off. The veteran has an obligation to apply for life insurance, with the Department of Veterans Affairs as beneficiary, to pay off the debt in case of the veteran's death.

Priority of Recording

Priority is the order in which documents are recorded and is determined by the date stamped in the upper right-hand corner of the document by the county recorder. If there are several liens recorded against a property, no mention will be made about which one is the first, second, third, or fourth. A person inquiring about the priority should look at the time and date each was recorded.

First and Junior Trust Deeds

The trust deed recorded first against a property is called a **first trust deed**. All others are junior loans. A junior trust deed is any loan recorded after the first trust deed, secured by a second, third or subsequent trust deed. Secondary or junior financing is another way to finance a property, either at the time of a sale, or afterward. The interest rates are usually higher because there is a greater risk of default on a junior loan. The beneficiary of a junior loan should record a Request for Notice of Default in order to be notified if the borrower defaults on a prior loan.

Subordination Clause

A **subordination clause** is used to change the priority of a financial instrument. A lender agrees to give up priority to later loans. The priority of a trust deed is fixed by the date it is recorded: the earlier the date, the greater the advantage. When a note and trust deed includes a subordination clause, a new, later loan may be recorded, and because of the subordination clause, assume a higher priority. This clause is used mainly when land is purchased for future purposes of construction that will require financing. The lender on the new financing would want to be in first position to secure his or her interest, so the existing trust deed on the land would become subordinate to a new loan on the structure when the new loan was funded and recorded. Typically, the subordination clause benefits the trustor (borrower).

Loan Programs

Traditionally, fixed-rate loans were the only choice offered by commercial banks and savings and loans for a home buyer. Over the past few years, lending institutions have been deregulated allowing them to offer consumers new solutions to credit demands.

Deregulation is a process where financial institutions that formerly had been restrained in their lending activities by the law, are allowed to compete freely for profits in the marketplace. Controls on lending practices still exist, but loans can now be marketed competitively by all lending institutions. As a result of deregulation, the distinction between commercial and savings banks has practically been eliminated.

No single type of financing fits everyone, because borrowers have different credit profiles and borrowing needs. In an attempt to offer alternatives to consumers, and renew their faith in their ability to borrow money for homes, lenders found new ways to make loans consumer friendly.

Secondary Financing (Junior Loans)

Secondary financing or a **junior loan** is a loan secured by a trust deed or mortgage on a property, other than first-trust deed. One way to get the needed financing is for the buyer to obtain a secondary loan through an outside source, such as a mortgage lender, private investor, or even the seller of the property. Junior loans take advantage of built-up equity in a property. **Equity** is defined as the difference between the value of the property and any outstanding loans or the initial down payment. Assuming there is enough equity, a homeowner can apply for a cash loan for any purpose. It can be advantageous to be a homeowner, especially if there is built up equity in a house, townhouse, duplex, or condominium. The equity can pay for home improvements, bill consolidation, or college tuition. Typical junior loans include home equity loans, home equity lines of credit, and seller financing.

Home Equity Loan

With a **home equity loan,** the borrower is credited with the entire loan balance at one time. It is a fixed-rate second mortgage with principal and interest payments remaining the same over the life of the loan. The priority of the loan will depend on what other instruments are recorded ahead of it. Home equity loans are **hard money loans** because the proceeds are not used to purchase the property.

A lender uses strict standards about the amount of equity required in a property before loaning money, particularly for a junior loan. All a lender wants is to get his or her money back in a timely manner, along with the calculated return on the investment. Care must be taken in case of a decrease in the value of the subject property, to be certain that there is enough of a margin between the total amount owed and the value of the property. If the lender has to sell the property at a foreclosure sale, he or she will be assured of getting the money back. By only loaning up to 75%-90% of the property value, the lender leaves some room for loss.

> Example: Michael's home was appraised at $400,000, with a $250,000 first trust deed recorded against it. Michael wants a $65,000 home equity loan. To determine whether to make the loan, the lender adds the amount owed to the amount desired in the loan to determine the percentage that would be encumbered by the existing first trust deed, and the desired second trust deed. If the lender would only loan up to 80% of the appraised value of the property, would Michael get his loan? Of course, Michael does get his loan because he has enough equity in the property to qualify.

Home Equity Line of Credit

With a **home equity line of credit** (HELOC), the borrower takes money as it is needed——up to the credit limit. It has a low starting interest rate, with a variable monthly rate based on outstanding balance. Many lenders offer home equity lines of credit. By using the equity in their home, borrowers may qualify for a sizable amount of credit, available for use when and how they please, and at a relatively low interest rate. Furthermore, under the California tax law——depending on the borrower's specific situation——he or she may be allowed to deduct the interest because the debt is secured by their home.

What is a home equity line of credit?

A home equity line of credit is a type of revolving credit in which a borrower's home serves as the collateral. Many homeowners use their credit lines only for major items such as education, home improvements, or medical bills, and not for day-to-day expenses.

With a home equity line, a borrower will be approved for a specific amount of credit—the credit limit—meaning the maximum amount, he or she can borrow at any one time.

Many lenders set the credit limit on a home equity line by taking a percentage (75%-90%) of the appraised value of the home and subtracting the balance owed on the existing mortgage. In determining the borrower's actual credit line, the lender also will consider his or her ability to repay, by looking at income, debts, and other financial obligations, as well as the borrower's credit history.

Home equity plans often set a fixed time during which a homeowner can borrow money, such as 10 years. When this period is up, the plan may allow the borrower to renew the credit line. However, in a plan that does not allow renewals, a borrower will not be able to borrow additional money once the time has expired. Some plans may call for payment in full of any outstanding balance. Others may permit a borrower to repay over a fixed time, for example 10 years.

Once approved for the home equity plan, a borrower usually will be able to borrow up to the credit limit whenever he or she wants. Typically, a borrower will be able to draw on the credit line by using special checks, or under some plans, borrowers can use a credit card.

What are the plan features?

Home equity plans typically involve variable interest rates rather than fixed rates. A variable rate must be based on a publicly available index (such as the prime rate published in some major daily newspapers or a U.S. Treasury bill rate); the interest rate will change, mirroring fluctuations in the index. To figure the interest rate that the borrower will pay, most lenders add a margin of one or two percentage points to the index value. Because the cost of borrowing is tied directly to the index rate, it is important to find out what index and margin each lender uses, how often the index changes, and how high it has risen in the past.

How will the borrower repay the home equity loan?

Before entering into a plan, borrowers must consider how they will repay any money that is borrowed. Some plans set minimum payments that cover a portion of the principal (the amount borrowed) plus accrued interest. However, unlike the typical installment loan, the portion that goes toward principal may not be enough to repay the debt by the end of the term. Other plans may allow payments of interest alone during the life of the plan, which means that the borrower pays nothing toward the principal. If the homeowner borrows $10,000, he or she will owe that entire sum when the plan ends.

Whatever the payment arrangements during the life of the plan—whether the borrower pays some, a little, or none of the principal amount of the loan—when the plan ends the borrower may have to pay the entire balance owed, all at once. He or she must be prepared to make this balloon payment by refinancing it with the lender, by obtaining a loan from another lender, or by some other means.

If a homeowner is thinking about a home equity line of credit, he or she also might want to consider a more traditional second mortgage loan. This type of loan provides a fixed amount of money repayable over a fixed period. Usually the payment schedule calls for equal payments that will pay off the entire loan within that time.

Seller Financing — Second Trust Deed

Another common source for secondary financing of a sale is the seller. If the seller is going to lend money to the buyer, he or she agrees to **carry back** part of the purchase price as junior loan. That loan is secured by a trust deed, in favor of the seller, recorded after the first trust deed. In a seller carryback loan, the seller acts as the beneficiary and the buyer is the trustor.

When a seller carries the paper on the sale of his or her home, it is also called a **purchase-money loan**, just like the loan made by an outside lender. If a seller receives a substantial amount from the proceeds of a first loan, plus the buyer's down payment, it may be in the seller's interest to carry a second trust deed—possibly for income or to reduce tax liability by accepting installment payments.

> Example: Pat made an offer on a house owned by Dan, who accepted an offer of $375,000 with $37,500 as the down payment. The buyer qualified for a new first loan in the amount of $318,750, and asked Dan to carry a second loan for $18,750 to complete the purchase price.

When the seller extends credit in the form of a loan secured by a second deed of trust, the note may be written as a straight note, with interest-only payments, or even no payments. It could be an installment note with a balloon payment at the end, or fully amortized note with equal payments until it is paid off. The term of the loan is decided by the buyer and seller. The instructions of the buyer and seller regarding the seller financing are usually carried out through escrow.

If a trust deed held by the seller is sold to an outside party, usually a mortgage broker, the note will be discounted. **Discounting a note** is selling a note for less than the face amount or the current balance. Even though the seller receives a reduction in value by the mortgage broker, it is one way a seller can get cash out of a note that was carried back.

> Example: Fred and Tom owned a house together as investors. After several years, they put the house on the market for $550,000 and hoped to get a full-price offer so they could go their separate ways with the profit from the house.

After a short time, they did get a full-price offer. The buyer offered to put $110,000 down, get a $385,000 new first loan and asked Fred and Tom to carry a loan $55,000 for five years, as a second. Fred and Tom would have turned the offer down if their broker had not suggested they accept and sell the second after the close of escrow. Even though it would be discounted, it was one way they could get most of the cash out of their investment.

If the second loan were sold at a discounted 20%, or $11,000, Fred and Tom would end up with $55,000, less $11,000, or $44,000. In that way they would get the cash out of the sale, though they would be netting less than they originally planned because of the discount. They followed their sales associate's suggestion, and were satisfied with the result.

Whenever there is seller financing in a real estate transaction, the law requires the buyer and seller to complete a **Seller Financing Disclosure Statement**. It gives both the seller and buyer all the information needed to make an informed decision about using seller financing to complete the sale.

The seller can see from the disclosure whether the buyer has the ability to pay off the loan by looking at the buyer's income, and whether the buyer has a good credit history. The buyer can see what the existing loans are, as well as such things as due dates and payments on existing loans that would be senior to the loan in question.

Seller Financing — All-Inclusive Trust Deed (AITD)

The **all-inclusive trust deed (AITD)**, or **wrap-around mortgage**, is a type of seller financing. It is used in a transaction between the buyer and seller to make the financing attractive to the buyer and beneficial to the seller as well. Instead of the buyer assuming an existing loan and the seller carrying back a second trust deed, the AITD can accomplish the same purpose with greater benefit to both parties. At the closing the buyer receives title to the property.

An AITD (wrap-around mortgage) combines an existing loan with a new loan, and the borrower makes one payment for both. In other words, the new trust deed (the AITD) includes the present encumbrances, such as first, second, third, or more trust deeds, plus the amount to be financed by the seller.

Before trying to buy property using an AITD, it is important to be sure the existing loan can be legally combined with (or wrapped by) the new AITD. Many loans contain alienation (due on sale) clauses as part of the promissory note, which prohibit the transfer of the property to a new owner without the approval of the underlying lender.

The AITD is a junior loan and subordinate to existing encumbrances because the AITD is created at a later date. This means any existing encumbrances have priority over the AITD, even though they are included, or wrapped, by the new all-inclusive trust deed.

The AITD does not disturb any existing loan(s). The seller, as the new lender, makes the payments while giving a new increased loan at a higher rate of interest to the borrower. The amount of the AITD includes the unpaid principal balance of the existing (underlying) loan, plus the amount of the new loan being made by the seller. The borrower makes payment on the new larger loan to the seller, who in turn makes payment to the holder of the existing underlying loan. The new loan wraps around the existing loan.

A seller usually will carry back a wrap-around trust deed at a higher rate of interest than the underlying note, thereby increasing the yield. The seller continues to pay off the original note from the payments on the wrap-around, while keeping the difference. This type of financing works best when the underlying interest rate is low and the seller can then charge a higher rate on the wrapped loan.

> Example: Tom wanted to sell his house, and listed it for $300,000. The existing first trust deed was for $90,000 at 6%, payable at $540 monthly. He thought about carrying a second trust deed at 7%, counting on the income from the

note. However, Kate, his listing agent, explained he could get a greater return from carrying an all-inclusive trust deed (AITD) instead of just a note and second trust deed from a buyer. She also told him any offer that included an AITD should be referred to an attorney. Tom, with his attorney's approval, accepted the following offer soon after listing the house:

The Buyer's Offer

Sales price	$300,000
Less buyer's 20% cash down payment	- $60,000
Wrap-around in favor of Tom	$240,000

The buyer would make payments to Tom on the new wrap-around of $240,000 at 7% or $1,597 monthly. Tom would continue to make payments on the underlying first mortgage of $90,000 at 6% or $540 monthly.

Tom's Cash Flow

Wrap-around payment to Tom	$1,597
Less payment on existing mortgage	- $540
Monthly difference to Tom	$1,057

Other Types of Loans

Several loan programs are currently available and borrowers should consider many different factors before choosing a loan.

Factors to Consider When Selecting a Loan

- Current financial picture
- Future financial expectations
- Length of time expected to own the home
- Comfort level of changing mortgage payments
- Ability to qualify for a conventional loan
- Amount of down payment
- Ability to qualify for a VA loan

- Desire to take advantage of FHA-insured loans
- Credit rating of the borrower
- Purpose of the loan (home purchase, refinance, equity loan)

Loan programs are differentiated by the terms in the promissory note—primarily interest rate and repayment schedule. The borrower's credit worthiness affects the interest rate quoted by the lender.

Unsecured Loan

People who need a small loan to fix the car, buy a new appliance, or take a trip might choose a closed-end, unsecured loan instead of using their credit cards or getting a home equity loan. An **unsecured loan** is one in which the lender receives a promissory note from the borrower, without any security for payment of the debt, such as a trust deed or mortgage. The only recourse is a lengthy court action to force payment. This is truly the traditional IOU.

Open-End Loan

An **open-end loan** is essentially a revolving line of credit. An additional amount of money may be loaned to a borrower in the future under the same note. The effect is to preserve the original loan's priority claim against the property with this open-end loan.

Package Loan

A loan on real property secured by more than the land and structure is known as a **package loan**. It includes fixtures attached to the building (appliances, carpeting, drapes, air conditioning) and other personal property.

Blanket Loan

A loan that covers more than one parcel of property may be secured by a **blanket mortgage**. This type of loan is commonly used in connection with new development of housing tracts, or with construction loans. A blanket loan usually contains a **partial release clause** that provides for the release of any particular parcel upon the repayment of a specified part of the loan. When a house is sold in a subdivision, the partial release clause is signed, releasing that parcel from the blanket construction loan. A **deed of partial reconveyance** is recorded to show that the obligation has been met.

Another use of a blanket loan is for a homeowner to buy or build a new home, even if the current home still needs to be sold. In this instance, a blanket loan would cover both homes, the current property, as well as the property being built or purchased. The result is making one monthly payment instead of two and eliminating the uncertainty of buying or building a home and selling a home at the same time. A blanket loan will save money and eliminate the inconvenience of obtaining a swing loan.

WRAP AROUND MORTGAGE RIDER

Rider and addendum to Security Instrument dated_____, _____

The attached security instrument is a "wrap-around" mortgage/deed of trust subordinate to a certain mortgage/deed of trust dated _____, _____, executed in favor of _____ and currently held by_____ in the original principal amount of $_____, which was recorded on the _____day of _____,_____ in the county records of _____ County, State_____ as follows:

Book:_____
Page: _____
Libor: _____
Reception: _____
Date: _____

Borrower agrees to comply with all the terms and conditions of the above described mortgage including, but not limited to, those concerning taxes and insurance, other than with respect to the payment of principal or interest due under said mortgage. If Borrower herein shall fail to comply with all the terms, provisions and conditions of said mortgage so as to result in a default thereunder (other than with respect to payments of principal or interest due), that failure on the part of Borrower herein shall constitute a default under this security instrument and shall entitle the lender, at its options, to exercise any and all rights and remedies given this security instrument in the event of a default under this security instrument.

If the lender hereunder shall default in making any required payment of principal or interest under the above described mortgage or deed of trust, the Borrower shall have the right to advance funds necessary to cure that default and all funds so advanced by Borrower shall be credited against the next installment of principal and interest due under the Note secured by this security instrument.

_____   _____
Borrower   Borrower

Swing (Bridge) Loan

A **swing loan** (also called interim or bridge loan) is a temporary loan made on a borrower's equity in his or her home. It is usually a short-term loan due in six months or when the borrower's home sells, whichever occurs first. It is used when the borrower has purchased another property, with the present home unsold, and needs the cash to close the sale of the new home. The new loan is secured by a trust deed or mortgage against the borrower's home. Usually there are no payments, with interest accruing during the term of the loan. When the borrower's home sells, the swing loan plus interest is repaid, through escrow, from the proceeds of the sale.

Swing loans can be risky depending on the current real estate market. In a fast-paced real estate market, it is usually safe to assume that the home will sell within several months if it is priced right. However, if the market is stagnant, it could take longer than six (6) months to sell and the borrower would have to pay the carrying costs on two homes.

Pledged Account Mortgage

A **pledged account mortgage** (PAM) is a loan made against security, such as money held in a savings account or a certificate of deposit. When a borrower has a large amount of money in a savings or thrift account, one way he or she can use that to an advantage is to **pledge** the account as security for a lender. Another version enables the borrower to get 100% financing if a relative (or more than one relative) agrees to pledge a savings account or Certificate of Deposit as collateral for the loan. A benefit of this loan program is that the person who pledges the money continues to earn interest. When the borrower has sufficient equity in the property, the pledge money is returned.

The lender will require a certain ratio of the loan amount to the balance in the account, and the borrower must keep that amount in the account for a specified length of time. The lender may release the pledge account when the property has acquired enough equity to qualify under normal loan-to-value ratios.

Shared Appreciation Mortgage

A **shared appreciation mortgage** (SAM) is a loan in which the lender offers a below-market interest rate in return for a portion of the profits made by the homeowner when the property is sold. The holding period (usually three to five years) and the percentage of shared equity are spelled out in the loan agreements.

Rollover Mortgage

The **rollover mortgage** (ROM) is a loan in which the unpaid balance is refinanced typically every five years at current rates. This is good for the borrower and bad for the lender if interest rates are falling, and bad for the borrower and good for the lender if interest rates are rising.

Renegotiable Rate Mortgage

A **renegotiable rate mortgage** is a loan in which the interest rate is renegotiated periodically. The loan may be either a long-term loan with periodic interest rate adjustments, or a short-term loan that is renewed periodically at new interest rates, but based on a long-term loan. There is a maximum interest rate fluctuation during the term of the loan.

Construction Loans

Construction financing comprises two phases— the construction phase and completion. An **interim loan** is a short-term loan to finance construction costs, such as the building of a new home. The lender advances funds to the borrower as needed while construction progresses. Since it is a high-risk loan it has a higher interest rate. Upon completion of the construction, the borrower must obtain permanent financing or pay the construction loan in full. The permanent loan that pays off a construction loan is called a **takeout loan**.

Interim construction loans are usually made by commercial banks, whereas standby commitments and takeout loans are arranged by mortgage companies for large investors such as insurance companies.

Do not confuse a takeout loan with a forward-takeout commitment (also called a standby commitment). A **forward-takeout commitment** is an expensive letter promising to deliver a takeout loan in the future if the property is built according to plans and specifications and leased at the target rental rate. A forward-takeout commitment typically costs a developer one-to-two points, plus a minimum of one additional point if the loan eventually funds. However, the borrower does not have to take the loan.

Truth-in-Lending Act (Regulation Z)

The Truth-in-Lending Act, known as Regulation Z, requires a lender to inform the borrower how much he or she is paying for credit. The lender must reflect all financing costs as a percentage, called the Annual Percentage Rate (APR).

Equal Credit Opportunity Act

This federal law, the Equal Credit Opportunity Act, protects borrowers from discrimination based on race, sex, color, religion, national origin, age, or marital status.

Soldiers' and Sailors' Civil Relief Act

Persons in the military, under this law known as the Soldiers' and Sailors' Civil Relief Act, are protected from foreclosure on their homes while serving time in the military service.

True-False Quiz

Now that you have read all the material in this chapter, take the following self-test and check your knowledge of real estate finance.

True/False

1. _True_ Hypothecation is when an owner uses a property as security for a loan, but does not give up possession.

2. _True_ A trustee is a neutral third party in a trust deed.

3. _False_ In a trust deed, the borrower is the same as the beneficiary.

4. _False_ The beneficiary holds bare legal title to a property encumbered by a trust deed.

5. _True_ A reconveyance deed is used to deed a property to the trustor after the deed of trust has been paid in full.

6. _True_ An "or more" clause allows a borrower to pay off a loan early with no penalty.

7. _True_ A promissory note, if prepared correctly, is the same as cash.

8. _False_ Foreclosure is the cure for a tenant's default on monthly rental payments.

9. _True_ A trustee must sign a reconveyance deed.

10. _True_ A land sales contract and a contract of sale are alike.

Chapter
4

Escrow, Title, and Other Professions

Learning Objectives

After reading this chapter, you will be able to:

- describe the duties and functions of escrow professions.

- describe the duties and functions of title insurance professionals.

- define escrow associations.

- discuss types of insurers.

- explain the functions of real estate brokers, builders, attorneys, and independent escrow companies.

Introduction

The jobs of escrow and title officer have developed throughout the years into professions requiring much more than simply searching a title or gathering documents. Both have grown into independent industries, with special designations and codes of ethics that guide their professional conduct, just like those followed by other real estate professionals.

Escrow Professionals

Escrow professionals provide service either as a separate company, as part of a title company, or as a department within banks or other financial institutions. An escrow career track can emphasize sale escrows, loan escrows, or a combination of both. Learning the business of escrow requires a personality suited to details, some instructional escrow classes and, most important of all, practical hands-on experience.

Clerk

As an entry level position, the job of clerk, whether it is known as secretary, receptionist, or general office worker, is where most escrow professionals start their career. An awareness of office functions as well as word and data processing are basic to being successful. In addition, for a beginner in  the escrow business, a background in finance or real estate is a valuable asset.

After working in an escrow office for some time, an ambitious escrow secretary may eventually function as a junior escrow officer or escrow officer in training.

Escrow Officer

Escrow officer is the next natural progression after working with escrows and becoming familiar with the many tasks required to complete an escrow.

Duties of an Escrow Officer

- Gathering information, examining and organizing it into accurate escrow instructions.

- Preparing documents for various escrows.

- Being aware of aspects which are parallel to escrow, such as title and legal requirements.

- Having knowledge of real estate financing to the extent of being able to answer clients' questions and prepare financing documents appropriate to the acquisition and sale of real property.

- Being aware of the productivity and its relationship to the cost of doing business as an escrow holder.

An escrow officer must possess certain personal talents and gifts in order to be successful in the complicated, fast-paced world of escrow. Efficiency, organization and a systematic approach are primary skills an escrow officer must exercise during the orderly process of each unique escrow, to be thorough in processing all details.

Qualifications of an Escrow Officer

- Organization is essential in coordinating documents and other instruments.

- A systematic and logical perception of all processes, as well as the ability to gather information and to produce properly drawn instructions is a primary qualification. Because of an escrow's many legal requirements.

- A background in law is an extra, welcome, qualification. Laws affecting real estate transfers are constantly changing

and an escrow officer must be aware of his or her impact on current escrows.

- A competent escrow officer rarely wastes time or money. Mistakes usually cost someone, and an efficient officer can save time and money by conducting business in an orderly, capable manner.

- Prorations, closing statements, computation of demands, financial statements and balances all require mathematical proficiency. An escrow officer must be skillful with numbers and have the ability to calculate accurately.

A serene, patient personality is well suited to the career of escrow officer. Good judgment and a sense of humor under difficult conditions are basic requirements for a successful career in escrow.

Loan Escrow Officer

A loan escrow professional specializes in closing loan escrows or as a loan underwriter. An escrow officer and a loan escrow officer have many of the same duties.

Duties of a Loan Escrow Officer

- Supervise the process of closing a loan, from the beginning when the loan committee gives the loan file to the loan officer through the final funding of the loan.

- Follow lender directions for supplying support documents, credit requirements, title provisions and other information.

- Act as a go-between for lenders and borrowers.

- Acknowledge differences in requirements of lenders for loan processing.

- Know how loans are structured, from technical provisions of consumer protection laws and requirements of the many regulatory agencies, to the complications of construction loans and income property loans. The loan officer must work closely with the escrow officer to assure all legal aspects are in order for the closing.

Personal Attributes of a Loan Escrow Officer

A loan escrow officer must be capable of adjusting to more changes and having more contact with the customer than a general escrow officer who primarily closes sale escrows.

Outstanding communication skills are necessary when explaining the various steps in the loan escrow process because of the  complexities of the lending process. Because of the greater possibility of conflict and surprise in the lending process, a loan officer must be adept at coping with upset and emotional customers.

A loan officer must be skilled at mathematics in order to calculate loan payoffs and payment schedules.

All escrow officers must be efficient and organized, and a loan escrow officer is no different. The use of computer technology has speeded up loan processing and allowed the loan officer greater flexibility and organization in less time than in the past.

Training

Generally, a loan officer has worked in some part of the loan industry before coming to escrow as a professional. Former employment often includes savings banks, commercial banks, mortgage bankers, insurance companies, mortgage brokers, credit unions, and finance companies. Formal training is available from professional groups and private schools.

Manager

As an escrow manager, a career professional must possess greater technical knowledge and have more practical experience than an escrow officer has.

A manager must be able to coordinate the various concurrent jobs in a timely and efficient way in an escrow office. He or she must balance technical competence with knowledge of how to make a profit for the company. The manager must be profit oriented as well as service oriented. A successful manager must be able to communicate ideas both written and verbal. The effectiveness of management will be impaired if communication is not free flowing within the organization and between the organization and other real estate professionals. As always, when dealing with fellow workers, respect for their ideas and position is basic to good relations.

The ability to train new escrow professionals is a necessary quality for an escrow manager. Communicating ideas and concepts as well as guiding new workers through the confusing maze of balancing existing escrows while opening new ones is a challenging task for a manager. As we have mentioned before, escrow is learned through doing, and a manager must be able to teach the practical lessons of the business as well as supervise the office.

Another important task for the escrow manager is marketing the business. Customers are necessary if there is to be a business, and constant, aggressive representation in the community of the escrow company is the only way to assure a large market share of the customers.

Finally, an ongoing objective as a manager is the evaluation of staff, allowing for the identification of problem areas and training development to strengthen weaknesses in the product.

Administrator

All the relationships in a multi-office escrow business are the responsibility of the escrow administrator. The position does require a highly developed technical knowledge of escrow, but most importantly requires excellent management skills.

The administrator is responsible for recognizing staff potential, as well as effectively utilizing that potential for a greater return on the company dollar. One of the major prerequisites of an administrator is skill with problem solving. The administrator who has the ability to resolve uncertainty and to settle disputes is essential to handling of any problems that may occur.

Desirable Traits of an Administrator

- Dependability, loyalty, and confidentiality

- Exceptional communication skills

- Flexibility and a good work ethic

- Personal organization and courtesy

- Ability to delegate tasks

- Fair and unprejudiced dealings with personnel

- Skilled coordination of all aspects of escrow

Title Insurance Professionals

Job descriptions in the business of title insurance range from research and interpretation of title information to underwriting insurance, to administering and marketing the title company's services.

Searcher

Individuals often enter the title business as a title searcher. When a title order is opened, the searcher must evaluate the instructions for the type of search required. Normally, tracing the chain of title or  history of sales on the property is included in the search. There may also be a request in the instructions for information on loans, ownership of minerals, easements, reversionary rights under a recorded deed restriction, leasehold interest, or special title requirements. Particular policy coverages like condemnation, trust deed foreclosure, subdivision, and litigation guarantees require special searches. Maps or copies of documents are ordered as requested.

After reviewing the instructions for the title order, the searcher prepares a chain of title, starting from the policy date of the latest title policy issued on the property under search, to the present time. The chain of title includes the types of documents, parties involved and other recorded data on the property in question.

A general index search is the next order of business for the searcher. After the chain of title has been prepared and the title search completed, a search of recorded documents by alphabetical index is done to discover any judgments, divorces, tax liens, bankruptcies, probates, incompetencies, and other general matters affecting the parties involved with the property.

Researched documents such as deeds, reconveyances, judgments, and other liens are placed on microfilm or microfiche and copies are made for the title search. The searcher's job is easier in sparsely populated counties where the recordings are few. It is more complicated in densely populated areas like Los Angeles County where thousands of documents are recorded daily.

Historically, the searcher has had to look through lot books in which documents have been posted by hand and classified by legal description. Today, however, the general index or name search has been automated along with the lot book. Information is now searched from computerized files in a title plant.

After all recorded documents have been found and assembled by date order into a non-interrupted chain of title, the searcher submits the package to the opinion department for legal review. If all is in order, the search is returned to the title department.

Before a sale is recorded, but after the initial or preliminary title search, new documents on the property in question may be recorded. The searcher must complete a final screening manually or by computer before the title order is closed.

The title searcher must be accurate. Missed documents in the chain of title can cause significant damage to the title company that is guaranteeing that all past title matters have been researched and exposed for examination. It is desirable for a searcher to be detail-oriented and to have a high degree of skill in clerical matters.

As the searcher compiles a history of property ownership, decisions must be made about whether a document in the chain should be included and whether, in fact, the document even affects the property. An orderly and logical method must be used to sift through the myriad data found and present it for the issuance of the policy of title insurance.

After entering the title business as a searcher, a capable worker can advance to the position of senior searcher, or long-order searcher. This position requires knowledge and skill in dealing with such complex matters as property resurveys, street abandonments, railroad title reversions, tideland and wetland matters, and oil searches.

Examiner

A policy of title insurance is written based upon interpretation. The main person responsible for the interpretation is the title examiner or title officer. The title examiner orders the search and examines the information compiled from the search.

During the course of the title examination, the title officer works closely with the escrow officer who has placed the title order, based on instructions for the transaction in question.

After examination and inquiry, the title examiner submits a written opinion about the clear title of the property, known as a preliminary title report. This report, also known as an interim binder, is a commitment to issue title insurance on the property.

If there is a question about interpretation of the condition of the title of the property in question, the examiner may seek the advice of a title advisor, attorney, or reference sources.

Another job of the examiner is to check the accuracy of the preliminary title report regarding the legal description, vesting of title and encumbrances on the land.

All legal documents required by the transaction must be examined by the title officer prior to recording to make sure escrow instructions have been followed and the documentation is adequate for closing.

The most skilled and capable title officers in the company are asked to deal with specialized and complicated title matters where the greatest degree of risk exists for title insurers.

Advisory Title Officers

Many times senior title examiners operate in the capacity of advisor title officers. They solve complicated issues and make underwriting decisions about whether a property is an acceptable insurance risk for the company. A separately staffed underwriting department may exist in the larger title companies.

Title Analyst

The job of title analyst involves research and development, particularly on complex projects. When title insurers are asked to deal with complicated underwriting tasks, the title research analyst complements the work of advisory title officers. The title analyst might deal with questions of Native American lands, tidelands and submerged lands, lake and river boundaries, or land resurvey problems. In addition, a title analyst might develop new underwriting procedures for the company or expand procedures already in place.

Title Marketer

Title companies rely on "title reps" to market their product in specific geographical areas, much like any other sales oriented company. Title representatives call on existing customers and new prospects to promote their title company.

The high tech end of title marketing is usually handled by experienced marketers with technical background in the various fields. Wholesale customers of title insurance might be developers, franchisers, or hotel chains.

Branch Manager

The duties of a title company branch manager include hiring, setting an example, training and development, expanding market share, reporting results, and assessing personnel. A manager must be skilled at interviewing, leadership, teaching, sales, and communication.

Executive Management

As financial services companies combine their offerings to bring greater opportunity to the public, more administrators are required to manage various locations and to deal with newly developed duties. The title industry requires its executives to develop and understand the big picture as far as planning, market share, future growth, and profit.

An executive administrator must possess superior communication skills and be able to project and promote the company image both internally and to the outside business community.

Escrow Associations

The escrow industry, dedicated to professionalism, has advanced various goals through several local and national organizations.

Escrow Association Goals

"The objects and purposes of an escrow association shall be to promote sound and ethical business practices among its members; to provide for the collection, study and dissemination of information relating to problems of and improvements in land title evidence; to promote and encourage sound legislation affecting land titles; to encourage practices which will best serve the public interest; to educate and inform the public of the integrity and stability of its members and the advantages and desirability of their services."

Under the education arm of state organizations, training programs and continuing education are offered. Seminars, workshops, and annual educational conferences are designed to bring escrow professionals current information regarding changes in the industry.

Local and state organizations publish newsletters outlining trends, new legislation, timely topics, and recent court decisions. New education opportunities for escrow professionals are provided by *Escrow Update* and *A.E.A. News* (American Escrow Association).

Public recognition and ethical standards of the escrow industry are enhanced by professional organizations. By monitoring laws that affect the industry and advocating legislation which will benefit the industry and the public, escrow organizations educate and strengthen the growth of the industry.

The escrow industry is also empowered by the establishment of career designations for escrow professionals by the CEA, as well as a Code of Ethics.

Professional Escrow Designations

- Certified Escrow Officer (CEO)

- Certified Senior Escrow Officer (CSEO)

Insurers

Title Companies

Escrow holders use both title insurers and general insurance companies in conducting their business.

There are two kinds of title companies: those directly responsible for their own financial risk, or underwriting, and those indirectly responsible for underwriting policies.

The Insurance Commissioner is the supervisor for title insurers in the state where the home office is located, and is aided by insurance commissioners in states where branch offices are used. The criteria for financial responsibility (bonding and reserve requirements) are regulated by the Insurance Code and are different from those fixed by the Corporations Commissioner, Banking Commissioner, and the Real Estate Commissioner.

In some states, many title insurers offer escrow benefits along with their title business. In Northern California, title companies do most of the sale escrow work. Escrow holders are responsible for most of the escrows in Southern California.

Insurance Companies

In the 1920s and 1930s, insurance companies were major investors in housing. After World War II, the need for housing was so great and the capital to build was so inadequate, insurance companies from the eastern United States moved west to fill the need for capital. Insurance companies became commonplace loan processors and helped maintain the housing boom.

By the 1960s, insurance companies began to move their interest from investing in single-family home loans to loans on large, income-producing projects. Loan underwriting and escrow practices have had to modify with the changing needs of the insurance industry.

Insurance companies, regulated by the Insurance Commissioner, must comply with the legal and financial requirements and regulations of that department. The Insurance Commissioner is also responsible for audits of financial procedures used by insurance companies.

Commonly, insurance companies make their loans through mortgage bankers or other money brokers. Some companies, however, deal directly with the public and use escrow holders to complete their loans or sales.

Because many insurance companies have large real estate portfolios, they act as principals as well as lenders with real estate as security. In this capacity, they must be very specific about their title insurance needs, usually requiring extended coverage.

Real Estate Brokers

Depending on each situation, real estate brokers can be escrow holders themselves, or customers of escrow services.

A real estate broker operating in the capacity of escrow holder is exempt from the requirements of the Corporations Commissioner and is not under supervision of the Department of Corporations. Any company, broker, or agent licensed by the Real Estate Commissioner, while performing acts in the course of or incidental to the real estate business, may hold escrows in connection with any transaction. A broker, however, may not hold escrows for separate individuals or entities, for compensation, unless he or she is representing either the buyer or seller, or both in a particular transaction.

In order for a broker to advertise escrow services, it must be mentioned in any promotion that the services are only in connection with real estate brokerage. Because the escrow business is so unpredictable, many broker-owned escrows have been converted to independent escrow companies so those businesses can expand their possible markets.

When a broker does act as an escrow holder, he or she must maintain all escrow funds in a trust account. That account, along with all required records, remains subject to inspection by the Real Estate Commissioner's investigative staff and auditors.

The business of an escrow holder cannot be taken up as a second job, or sideline. The broker is responsible for accurate record keeping and detailed organization of all aspects of escrow, even though only in-house brokerage transactions are being handled.

As the primary practitioners of the residential resale industry, real estate brokers are the main source of business for escrow holders. One of the jobs of escrow companies is marketing their product. By cooperating and offering special services such as pick up and delivery of documents an escrow company can count certain real estate brokers as steady customers. Other real estate professionals, such as title companies, seek business from brokers directly because of the broker's close association with the escrow company. Generally, when a title order on a particular transaction is opened, the title company will get the order.

Builders

Many large developers and builders have established their own escrow companies in an effort to control the various parts of their business, and to get a greater return on their investment dollar. These escrow companies are licensed by the Corporations Commissioner, and fall under the guidelines and requirements of that department.

Subdivision escrows are highly specialized. Extensive knowledge of the many different legal requirements is required. The legal requirements for subdivisions require that the escrow holder must:

- know about the correct creation of protective restrictions for a development.

- make sure that the preliminary public report has been delivered to all prospective purchasers.

- be knowledgeable about the formation of homeowners' associations.

- be aware that a legal percentage of parcels in the new development must be sold before the first one can close.

In some states, builders are licensed by the State Contractors Licensing Board, in addition to the Corporations Commissioner overseeing their escrow procedures. Builders are also lightly supervised by the Federal Housing Administration or Veterans Administration or other secondary lenders if they build under government sponsored programs. Developers then may use an escrow company of their choice for the loan processing in connection with their sales.

Many title insurance companies have developed special subdivision departments that have trained personnel to quicken the submission of subdivisions' paperwork throughout the Department of Real Estate. Designated title professionals work specifically with builders and developers to meet their special needs.

Attorneys

The escrow activities of lawyers are monitored by the State Bar Association. Attorneys have the authority to hold escrows for their clients. They are exempt from licensing and other requirements as long as the escrow is held in connection  with the business of law. Money must be deposited in trust accounts and must be separated by individual files.

Independent Escrow Companies

Closing sale and loan transactions are the principal means of business for independent escrow companies. Additionally, an independent escrow company may act as a corporate trustee on outstanding deeds of trust or as a collection service for customer's accounts as a special service.

Independent escrows are tightly supervised and regulated by the Corporations Commissioner to assure consumer protection. The Commissioner's rules require someone at each escrow company location to have at least five years experience in the escrow field whenever the company is open for business.

An auditing and liaison staff is maintained by the Corporations Commissioner who oversees financial responsibility, ethics and bonding requirements. Frequent audits are held, with the escrow company under examination responsible for the cost of the audit. Each escrow company must maintain orderly files and records in accordance with the Commissioner's rules.

In California, the Escrow Agents Fidelity Corporation (created by the state legislature, governed by industry members and a casualty insurance administrator) provides employee fidelity bonds for independent escrow holders. The Escrow Agents Fidelity Corporation holds a fidelity bond from independent escrows within California. In addition, a trust balance is required of each member escrow company, depending on the amounts of trust funds held.

True-False Quiz

Now that you have read all the material in this chapter, take the following self-test and check your knowledge of escrow and title professions.

True/False

1. _TRUE_ The job of escrow clerk requires a four-year college degree.

2. _TRUE_ Mathematical ability is a primary requirement of an escrow officer.

3. _TRUE_ A loan escrow officer specializes in loan escrows.

4. _TRUE_ An escrow administrator manages a multi-office escrow business.

5. _False_ A title clerk is the main person responsible for interpretation of the condition of title.

6. _TRUE_ A title analyst might deal with tidelands and submerged lands.

7. _TRUE_ Another name for a "title rep" is title marketer.

8. _TRUE_ In order to conduct escrows, a real estate broker must be licensed by the Real Estate Commissioner.

9. _FALSE_ A real estate broker must keep all escrow funds in a personal account.

10. _FALSE_ The Corporations Commissioner monitors the escrow activities of layers.

Chapter 5

Contracts

Learning Objectives

After reading this chapter, you will be able to:

- define contracts—general and real estate.

- summarize essential contract elements, including performance and discharge of real estate contracts.

- describe Statute of Frauds.

- define the Statute of Limitations.

- explain common remedies for Breach of Contract.

- describe an Option (to purchase).

Introduction

So far, we have studied the nature of escrow, who needs an escrow, the documents needed with some real estate basics, finance, and who the professionals are that carry out escrows. This chapter explains what a contract is and how contracts are used to assure the understanding and approval of all parties to an agreement.

In every real estate transaction, some kind of contract that transfers or indicates an interest in the property is used. It is important that you, as a student of escrow, understand the nature of legal agreements so you can prepare instructions that accurately and legally reflect the agreement between the principals.

Contracts in General

A contract is an agreement, enforceable by law, to do or not to do a certain thing. There are five types of contracts: (1) express contracts, (2) implied contracts, (3) bilateral contracts, (4) unilateral contracts, and (5) executory contracts.

An **express contract** is one in which the parties declare the terms and put their intentions in words, either oral or written. A lease or rental agreement, for example, is an express contract. The landlord agrees to allow the tenant to live in the dwelling and the renter agrees to pay rent in return.

An **implied contract** is one where agreement is shown by act and conduct rather than words. This type of contract is found every day when we go into a restaurant and order food, go to a movie, or have a daily newspaper delivered. By showing a desire to use a service, we imply that we will pay for it.

A **bilateral contract** is one in which the promise of one party is given in exchange for the promise of the other party. In other words, both parties must keep their agreement for the contract to be completed. An example might be a promise from a would-be aviatrix to pay $2,500 for flying lessons, and a return promise from the instructor to teach her to fly.

A **unilateral contract** is one where a promise is given by one party with the expectation of performance by the other party. The second party is not bound to act, but if he or she does, the first party is obligated to keep the promise. An example would be an option. (See Options - final section of this chapter.)

A contract may be executory or executed. In an **executory contract,** something remains to be done by one or both parties. An escrow that is not yet closed or a contract that is not signed by the parties are examples of an executory contract. In an executed contract, all parties have performed completely.

One of the meanings of execute is to sign, or complete in some way. An **executed contract** may be a sales agreement that has been signed by all parties.

In addition, contracts may be void, voidable, unenforceable, or valid. A **void contract** is not a contract at all. It has no legal effect. For example, due to *lack of capacity* or *illegal subject matter* the contract is invalid.

A contract that is valid and enforceable on its face, but may be rejected by one or more of the parties is known as a **voidable contract.** Examples of a voidable contract include those induced by fraud, menace or duress, or by an elderly party who is no longer competent.

An **unenforceable contract** may be valid, but for some reason it cannot be proved by one or both of the parties. For example, if a contract is made based on an oral agreement, it may be unenforceable because there is no written confirmation of the oral agreement (reference: the Statute of Frauds).

A contract that has all the basic elements required by law, and is binding and enforceable is a **valid contract**.

Essential Elements of a Contract

For a contract to be legally binding and enforceable, the following requirements must be met.

- Legally competent parties

- Mutual consent

- Lawful objective

- Sufficient consideration

- Contract in writing (when required by law)

Legally Competent Parties

Parties entering into a contract must have legal capacity to do so. Almost anyone is capable, with a few exceptions. A person must be at least 18 years of age, unless married, in the military or emancipated.

A minor is not capable of appointing an agent, or entering into an agency agreement with a broker to buy or sell. A broker could represent an informed adult in dealing with a minor, but the client must be willing to take a chance that the contract may be voidable. Brokers dealing with minors should proceed cautiously and should seek an attorney's advice.

When it has been determined judicially that a person is not of sound mind, no contract can be made with that incompetent person. In addition, if it is obvious that a person is completely without understanding, even without declaration, there can be no contract. In the case of an incompetent, a court appointed guardian would have legal capacity to contract.

Both minors and incompetents may acquire title to real property by gift or inheritance. Any conveyance of acquired property, however, must be court approved. A contract made by a person who is intoxicated or under the influence of legal or illegal drugs may be canceled when the individual sobers up. However, it also may be ratified or approved, depending on the parties.

Any person may give another the authority to act on his or her behalf. The document that does this is called a **power of attorney**. The person holding the power of attorney is called an **Attorney-in-Fact**. When dealing with real property, a power of attorney must be recorded to be valid, and is good for as long as the principal is competent. A power of attorney can be canceled by the principal at any time by recording a revocation and a title company will only honor a power of attorney for one year. After that time, a new one must be signed and recorded. A power of attorney is useful, for example, when a buyer or seller is out of town and has full trust in that agent to operate in his or her behalf.

Mutual Consent

In a valid contract, all parties must mutually agree. **Mutual consent**, or mutual assent, is sometimes called a meeting of the minds. It is an offer by one party and acceptance by the other party.

Offer

One party must offer and another accept, without condition. An **offer** shows the contractual intent of the offeror, or the person making the offer, to enter into a contract. That offer must be communicated to the offeree, or the person to whom the offer is being made. Unconditional acceptance of the offer is necessary for all parties to be legally bound. The offer must be definite and certain in its terms, and the agreement must be genuine or the contract may be voidable by one or both parties.

Acceptance

An **acceptance** is an unqualified agreement to the terms of an offer. The offeree must agree to every item of the offer for the acceptance to be complete. If the original terms are changed in any way in the acceptance, the offer becomes a counteroffer, and the first offer is terminated. The person making the original offer is no longer bound by that offer, and may accept the counteroffer or not. The counteroffer becomes a new offer, made by the original offeree.

Acceptance of an offer must be communicated to the offeror, in the manner specified, before a contract becomes binding between the parties. Silence is not considered an acceptance.

Termination

An offeror is hopeful that his or her offer will be accepted in a timely manner and a contract will be formed. An offer is specific, however, and an offeror does not have to wait indefinitely for an answer. An offer is revoked if the offeree fails to accept it within a prescribed period. An offer can be terminated by the offeror if notice of revocation is given anytime prior to the other party communicating acceptance.

Ways to Terminate an Offer

- Lapse of time

- Communication of notice of revocation

- Failure of offeree to fulfill a condition of acceptance prescribed by the offeror

- A qualified acceptance, or counteroffer by the offeree

- Rejection by the offeree

- Death or insanity of the offeror or offeree

- Unlawful object of the proposed contract

Genuine Assent

A final requirement for mutual consent is that the offer and acceptance be genuine and freely made by all parties. Genuine assent does not exist if there is *fraud, misrepresentation, mistake, duress, menace,* or *undue influence* involved in reaching an agreement.

Fraud is an act meant to deceive in order to get someone to part with something of value. An outright lie, or making a promise with no intention of carrying it out, can be fraud. Lack of disclosure—causing someone to make or accept an offer—is also fraud. An example of fraud would be failing to inform the prospective buyer that the roof leaks when he or she happens to make an offer to purchase on a sunny day. Fraud can make the contract voidable.

Innocent misrepresentation occurs when the person providing the wrong information is not doing it to deceive, but for reaching an agreement. Even though no dishonesty is involved, a contract may be rescinded or revoked by the party who feels misled.

Mistake, in contract law, means negotiations were clouded or there was a misunderstanding in the material facts. It does not include ignorance, inability, or poor judgment. For example, if you accepted an offer to purchase your home based on what you thought was an all cash offer, and later found that you had agreed to carry a second trust deed, you would be expected to carry through with the agreement. Even though you made a mistake in reading the sales contract, you now have a binding agreement.

There are times when you could be credited with a **misunderstanding**, and ultimately get out of the contract. For instance, what if you were given directions to a friend's beach house, went there on your own, and fell in love with it. You immediately made an offer, which was accepted, only to discover you had gone to the wrong house. Because you thought you were purchasing a different property than the one the seller was selling, this could be considered a "major misunderstanding of a material fact", and there would be no mutual agreement, voiding any contract that was signed.

Use of force, known as **duress**, or menace, which is the threat of violence, may not be used to get agreement. **Undue influence** or using unfair advantage is also unacceptable. All can cause a contract to be voidable by the injured party.

Review - These Conditions Prohibit Genuine Assent
- Fraud
- Misrepresentation
- Mistake
- Duress
- Undue Influence

Lawful Objective

Even though the parties are capable, and mutually agreeable, the object of the contract must be lawful. A contract requiring the performance of an illegal act would not be valid, nor would one where the consideration was stolen.

The contract also must be legal in its formation and operation. For example, a note bearing an interest rate in excess of that allowed by law would be void. Contracts contrary to good morals and general public policy are also unenforceable.

Sufficient Consideration

All contracts require consideration. There are several types of consideration in a contract. Generally, **consideration** is something of value such as a promise of future payment, money, property, or personal services. For example, there can be an exchange of a promise for a promise, money for a promise, money for property, or goods for services.

Forbearance, or forgiving a debt or obligation, also qualifies as consideration. As a group, the above qualify as valuable consideration. Gifts such as those of real property that is given based solely on love and affection are acknowledged as good consideration. They meet the legal requirement that consideration be present in a contract.

In an option, the promise of the offeror is the consideration for the forbearance desired from the offeree. In other words, the person wanting the option promises to give something of value in return for being able to exercise the option to purchase at some specifically named time in the future.

In a bilateral contract, a promise of one party is consideration for the promise of another. For example, in the sale of real property, the buyer promises to pay a certain amount and the seller promises to transfer title.

It should be noted that the **earnest money** given at the time of an offer is not the consideration for the sale. It is simply an indication of the buyer's intent to perform the contract, and may be used for damages, even if the buyer backs out of the sale.

Contract In Writing

In California, the Statute of Frauds requires that certain contracts be in writing to prevent fraud in the sale of land, or an interest in land. Included in this are offers, acceptances, loan assumptions, land contracts, deeds, escrows, and options to purchase. Trust deeds, promissory notes, and leases for more than one year also must be in writing to be enforceable.

Statute of Frauds

Most contracts required by law to be in writing are found under the **Statute of Frauds**. The statute, adopted first in England in 1677, became part of English common law. Later it was introduced to this country, and it is now part of California's law.

The statute's primary purpose is to prevent forgery, perjury and dishonest conduct on the part of scoundrels and crooks against citizens. Thus, it improves the existence and terms of certain important types of contracts.

The law provides that certain contracts are invalid unless they are in writing and signed by either the parties involved or their agents.

Contracts That Must Be In Writing
- Any agreement where the terms are not to be performed within a year from making the contract
- A special promise to answer for the debt, default or no performance of another, except in cases covered by the Civil Code
- An agreement made upon the consideration of marriage, other than a mutual promise to marry
- An agreement to lease real property for a period longer than one year, or to sell real property or an interest therein; also, any agreement authorizing an agent to perform the above acts
- An agreement employing an agent, broker or any other person to purchase, sell or lease real estate for one year; or find a buyer, seller, lessee or lessor for more than one year in return for compensation
- An agreement, which by its terms is not to be performed during the lifetime of the promissor, or an agreement that devises or bequeaths any property, or makes provisions for any reason by will
- An agreement by a purchaser of real estate to pay a debt secured by a trust deed or mortgage on the property purchased, unless assumption of that debt by the purchaser is specifically designated in the conveyance of such property

Personal property is also affected by the Statute of Frauds. The sale of personal property with a value of more than $500 must be accompanied by a bill of sale in writing.

Parol Evidence Rule

When two parties make oral promises to each other, and then write and sign a contract promising something different, the written contract will be considered the valid one. Parol means "oral", or by "word of mouth". The **parol evidence rule** extends this meaning and prohibits introducing any kind of outside evidence to vary or add to the terms of deeds, contracts or other writings once executed. Under the parol evidence rule, when a contract is intended to be the parties' complete and final agreement, no further outside promises, oral or written, are allowed. Occasionally a contract is ambiguous or vague. Then the courts will allow use of prior agreements to clarify an existing disputed contract.

One of a real estate agent's major duties is to make sure all contract language conveys the parties' wishes and agreements. Oral agreements have caused much confusion and bad feelings over the years, particularly in real estate. Even a lease for less than one year should be in writing, though it is not required by the Statute of Frauds. It is easy to forget verbal agreements. A written contract is the most reasonable way to ensure mutual assent.

Preprinted Forms

What about using and changing preprinted real estate forms such as a deposit receipt or a counteroffer form? If the parties involved want to make handwritten changes and initial them, those changes control the document. However, escrow instructions reflect the real estate contract between the parties. If changes are made, they should be in the form of amendments to the escrow instructions after opening the escrow.

Generally, when using preprinted forms:

- specific information takes precedence over general information.

- typed clauses and insertions take precedence over the preprinted material.

- handwritten clauses and insertions take precedence over the typed and preprinted material.

Performance of Contracts

A principal has several choices when considering the performance of a contract. One is by the assignment of the contract to an assignee. The effect of assignment is to transfer to the **assignee** all the interests of the assignor, with the assignee taking over the assignor's rights, remedies, benefits, and duties.

For example, the original renter assigns rental interest to a new tenant, who is then responsible for the lease. The assignor is still liable in case the assignee does not perform, but the assignee is now primarily responsible for the contract.

If the assignor wants to be released entirely from any obligation for the contract, it may be done by **novation**. That is the substitution, by agreement, of a new obligation for an existing one, with the intent to extinguish the original contract. For example, novation occurs when a buyer assumes a seller's loan, and the lender releases the seller from the loan contract by substituting the buyer's name on the loan.

Time is often significant in a contract; indeed, its performance may be measured by the passage of time. Real estate contract and escrow instructions must have closing dates, or they are unenforceable.

Discharge of Contracts

The **discharge of a contract** occurs when the contract has been terminated. Contracts are discharged by performance, release, assignment, novation, and breach. Most contracts are discharged by full performance on the part of the contracting parties in accordance with the agreed-upon terms. Occasionally, the end-result is a breach of contract, where someone does not fulfill part of the agreement. In that case, the injured party has several remedies available.

Remedies for Breach of Contract

A **breach of contract** is a failure to perform on part or all of the terms and conditions of a contract. A person harmed by non-performance can accept the failure to perform, or has a choice of three remedies: unilateral rescission, lawsuit for money damages, or lawsuit for specific performance.

Unilateral Rescission

Unilateral rescission is available to a person who enters a contract without genuine assent because of fraud, mistake, duress, menace, undue influence, or faulty consideration. Rescission may be used as a means of discharging a contract by agreement, as we have mentioned.

However, once escrow is opened, rescission is not available—no unilateral instruction is acceptable. Occasionally, a buyer may call right after the close of escrow and order the escrow agent to "rescind" the sale. This is not possible except through court order. Some buyers think it is like buying a car where you can change your mind within three days. This is not the case once escrow instructions have been signed, and certainly not so after the escrow closes.

If one of the parties has been wronged by a breach of contract, however, that innocent party can stop performing all obligations as well, therefore unilaterally rescinding the contract. It must be done promptly, restoring to the other party everything of value received as a result of the breached contract, on condition that the other party shall do the same.

Lawsuit for Money Damages

When a party is a breach-of-contract victim, a second remedy is a **lawsuit for money damages**. If damages to an injured party can be reasonably expressed in a dollar amount, the innocent party

could sue for money damages including: the price paid by the buyer, the difference between the contract price and the value of the property, title and document expenses, consequential damages, and interest.

Lawsuit for Specific Performance

A third remedy for breach of contract is a **lawsuit for specific performance**. This is an action in court by the injured party to force the breaching party to carry out the remainder of the contract according to the precise terms, price, and conditions agreed upon in the contract. Generally, this remedy is used when money cannot restore an injured party's position. This is often the case in real estate because of the difficulty in finding a similar property.

Review - Discharge of Contracts
- Acceptance of a breach of the contract
- Agreement between the parties
- Impossibility of performance
- Operation of law
- Part performance
- Release of one or all of the parties
- Substantial performance

Statute of Limitations

Under California law, any person seeking relief for a breach of contract must do so within the guidelines of the Statute of Limitations. This set of laws determines that civil actions can be started only within the time periods prescribed by law. An **action** is a civil or criminal judicial proceeding. Civil actions, or lawsuits, must be brought within the allowed time or the right to do so will expire. Here are some actions of special interest to real estate agents, with the time frames required:

- Actions Which Must Be Brought **Within 90 Days**:
  Civil actions to recover personal property such as suitcases, clothing or jewelry alleged to have been left at a hotel or in an apartment; must begin within 90 days after the owners depart from the personal property.

- Actions Which Must Be Brought **Within Six Months**:
  An action against an officer to recover property seized in an official capacity—such as by a tax collector.

- Actions Which Must Be Brought **Within One Year**:
  Libel or slander, injury or death caused by wrongful act, or loss to depositor against a bank for the payment of a forged check.

- Actions Which Must Be Brought **Within Two Years**: Action on a contract, not in writing; action based on a policy of title insurance.

- Actions Which Must Be Brought **Within Three Years**: Action on a liability created by statute; action for trespass on or injury to real property, such as encroachment; action for relief on the grounds of fraud or mistake; attachment.

- Actions Which Must Be Brought **Within Four Years**: An action on any written contract; includes most real estate contracts.

- Actions Which Must Be Brought **Within 10 Years**. Action on a judgment or decree of any court in the United States.

Real Estate Contracts

Every sale escrow has two basic requirements to be valid: a binding contract between the buyer and seller and conditional delivery of transfer documents to a third party. The binding contract can be an offer to purchase (deposit receipt) or an option.

Real Estate Contracts, contracts for the sale of real property, or of an interest therein, must be in writing, according to the Statute of Frauds, and must be signed by the parties.

Offer to Purchase

In California, most real estate agents use the Residential Purchase Agreement and Joint Escrow Instructions, commonly known as a **deposit receipt** or **purchase offer** because it is an offer to purchase real property. The deposit receipt acts as the receipt for earnest money given by the buyer to secure an offer, as well as being the basic contract, or agreement, between the buyer and seller. Once the seller agrees to the offer and the buyer is informed of the seller's acceptance, the deposit receipt is a legally binding contract. Once all parties **execute**, or sign, the deposit receipt it becomes a bilateral contract.

Upon writing an offer to purchase real property, a buyer may give some consideration such as a personal check, commonly for 1% of the purchase price, as a sign that he or she is serious about making the offer. The check is made out to an escrow company or the listing broker. The real estate agent holds the check. If the seller refuses the offer, the check is returned to the buyer. If the seller accepts the offer, the buyer's check is deposited into an escrow account or into the broker's trust account within three business days after receiving it.

The deposit receipt includes all terms of the sale, including agreements about financing. The buyer and seller are bound by the contract when the buyer receives notification of the seller's acceptance of the offer, without any changes. The deposit receipt, as the original agreement between the buyer and seller, may become the actual escrow instructions or simply the basic agreement for escrow instructions that will follow when escrow is opened. Usually there are terms in the contract that must be met during the escrow period; therefore, the contract is considered executory until all the terms are completed and escrow closes.

Option

An **option** is a right, given for consideration, to a party (optionee) by a property owner (optionor), to purchase or lease property within a specified time at a specified price and terms. It is a written agreement between the owner of real property (**optionor**, seller, lessor) and a prospective buyer (**optionee**, lessee), stating the right to purchase, a fixed price, and specific time period. The price and all other terms should be stated clearly, as the option will become the sales agreement when the optionee exercises the right to purchase.

The optionee is the only one who has a choice, once the contract is signed and the consideration given. The option does not bind the optionee to any performance. It merely provides the right to demand performance from the optionor, who must sell if the optionee decides to buy the property during the course of the option. If the optionee decides not to buy the property during the term of the option, the consideration remains with the optionor.

The option may be assigned or sold without permission of the optionor during the course of the term, or the optionee may find another buyer for the property to exercise the option.

Normally, a real estate agent earns commission on an option only when it is exercised.

The Main Clauses Included in the Deposit Receipt

The escrow officer should be aware that the contract covers more than just the purchase price and closing date. It covers not only the escrow instructions, but also contingencies, various inspections, mandatory disclosures, the buyer's rights to investigate the property, how the buyer will take title, damages and dispute resolution, compensation to the brokers, and acceptance of the offer. The escrow officer should pay particular attention to the following terms:

Offer. This paragraph shows the name of the buyer, describes the property to be purchased, the offered purchase price, and the closing date for escrow.

Finance Terms. This section addresses whether the purchase will be an all cash offer or an offer based on obtaining financing. If the buyer must obtain financing to complete the transaction, the finance terms should state if the purchase of the property is contingent upon the buyer's ability to get financing. The amounts of the **initial deposit**, any **increased deposit,** and the loans are listed and added to total the amount of the purchase price. Remember, any earnest money or deposits received by an agent are trust funds and handled as prescribed by the Commissioner's Real Estate Law and Regulations.

Closing and Occupancy. This section covers the intent of the buyer to occupy the property as a primary residence, the date the seller (or tenant) will turn over possession of the property to the buyer, and if the buyer is allowed to take possession of the property prior to close of escrow. In order to protect the rights and obligations of both seller and buyer, an **Interim Occupancy Agreement** should be used if a buyer wants early possession of the property. The new C.A.R. form contains wording that prohibits a landlord from demanding that rent be paid in cash.

Allocation of Costs. Since there are many inspections, reports, and tests associated with purchasing a property, it is important for both buyer and seller to agree about who will be responsible for their payment. In addition, the buyer and seller select the escrow and title provider and allocate the payment responsibility.

Prorations. Since most real estate offices use the C.A.R. *Purchase Agreement and Joint Escrow Instruction* contract, this clause tells escrow the buyers' and sellers' wishes regarding the prorations (allocation) of property tax, interest, assessments, and any other charge normally prorated in escrow.

Title and Vesting. Explain the importance of reviewing the preliminary title report with the buyer. Check for any undisclosed liens or easements that may affect the use of the property. Because the property is still owned by the seller, any existing trust deeds will be shown with the seller as the trustor. Once the property is sold, the new title insurance policy will show the buyer's loan. The manner in which a buyer takes title to real property (**vesting**) can have unforeseen legal and tax ramifications. Always direct the buyer to an attorney and/or tax professional for advice on vesting.

Contingencies. Buyers and sellers are given specific amounts of time to meet the various conditions written in the contract.

Time is of the Essence. Time is often significant in a contract; indeed, its performance may be measured by the passage of time. By law, if no time is required by the contract, a reasonable time is allowed. If the act can be done instantly—as in the payment of money—it must be done at once.

Expiration of the Offer. If the offer is not accepted by the seller within the time frame, the offer is revoked and any deposit is returned to the buyer. A deposit may be refunded by agreement, judgment, or arbitration.

Liquidated Damages. Parties to a contract may decide in advance the amount of damages to be paid, should either party breach the contract. In fact, the offer to purchase, or sales contract, contains a printed clause that says the seller may keep the deposit as **liquidated damages** if the buyer backs out without good reason.

True-False Quiz

Now that you have read all the material in this chapter, take the following self-test and check your knowledge of contracts.

True/False

1. _TRUE_ An option is an example of a unilateral contract.

2. _FALSE_ A written contract does not take precedence over oral agreements.

3. _TRUE_ A contract is an agreement to do or not to do a certain act.

4. _False_ A promise given by one party with the expectation of performance by the other party is known as a bilateral contract.

5. _FALSE_ A contract that has been approved is said to be rescinded.

6. _FALSE_ Another name for mutual consent is implied agreement.

7. _FALSE_ Parties to a contract may be unemancipated minors.

8. _TRUE_ Mutual consent is sometimes called a meeting of the minds.

9. _False_ In an option, the buyer must perform.

10. _TRUE_ The failure to perform a contract is called breach of contract.

Chapter 6

Escrow Basics

Learning Objectives

After reading this chapter, you will be able to:

- explain the basic regional differences of escrow instructions.

- define the general principles followed by all escrow officers.

- discuss the escrow instructions (bilateral) prevalent in Southern California.

- describe the escrow instructions (unilateral) that are prevalent in Northern California.

Introduction

Every real estate transaction is unique, and **escrow instructions** differ greatly from transaction to transaction. The transaction can be effectively completed when the escrow officer gathers together the purchase agreement and other important documents, and creates detailed instructions to handle the transaction.

These instructions are written authorization to the escrow holder or title company to carry out the directions of the parties involved in the transaction.

All conditions, which must be met before the close of escrow, are specifically mentioned in the escrow instructions. Who will pay for what costs, how money is to be disbursed, and what documents are to be recorded at the close of escrow are some questions that are answered in the instructions. When an escrow is opened, it remains open until it is terminated according to the agreement of the parties.

Escrow instructions must be in writing and signed by all parties involved as principals in the transaction. The instructions are legally binding, and are revocable only by mutual consent.

Most escrow companies have standard, computer-generated forms, which the escrow officer uses for individual transactions. The forms can be altered for different kinds of transactions such as a simple sale of real property or a more complex exchange. If there is an attorney involved, he or she may want to draw up specific escrow instructions to reflect a more complicated transaction.

The format for escrow instructions is not set by law, and as long as all parties approve, escrow officers may receive and follow specially drawn instructions from a qualified outside party just as if they were drawn on their own company forms.

The escrow officer must know all facts of the purchase in order to carry out the expectations of all the parties to the transaction. All agreements between the principals should be made BEFORE signing escrow instructions, and those agreements must be reflected in the instructions exactly. All information given to the escrow officer should reflect the agreement by the principals in the purchase contract.

Escrow Instruction Information Given to the Escrow Holder

- A list of all documents, money, or any other items of value to be deposited into escrow and by whom they are to be deposited.

- Conditions to be met before the close of escrow, such as financing, pest control work, property inspections, or repairs.

- A list of all items to be prorated, such as rents, deposits, insurance, interest and property taxes.

- An explanation of all fees to be paid by the principals to the escrow.

If any changes in the original instructions are required, the escrow officer must draw up an amendment for each change. Maybe the seller wants to close later than the original date agreed upon, or the buyer wants to get an adjustable loan rather than a fixed rate as previously stated in the offer to purchase. No matter how small the detail, if it differs from the original agreement, ALL parties to the escrow must agree to the change by signing an amendment.

Escrow instructions are divided into two types. They can be bilateral, where the buyer and the seller sign identical sets of instructions, or unilateral, where the buyer signs one set of instructions and the seller signs another set.

Generally, custom dictates which type is used. In areas which use unilateral instructions, the real estate agent is responsible for getting information to the escrow company and making sure requirements of the escrow are met where the principal is involved. The instructions are usually drawn after all the information has been given to the escrow officer, just before the escrow is to close.

When the instructions are bilateral, the escrow instructions generally are drawn up and signed when escrow is first opened.

Review - Escrow Instructions
- Bilateral. The buyer and the seller sign identical sets of instructions

- Unilateral. The buyer signs one set of instructions and the seller signs another

Basic Regional Differences

The forms used for escrow instructions vary almost as much as the number of escrow holders. Each escrow holder (escrow officer) uses the type of instructions that he or she prefers, according to custom. In addition, instructions vary widely from one part of the country to another.

However, regardless of geographical area, escrow is interested in gathering the required information and carrying out the closing process in order to transfer real property and provide the accounting to the principals.

General Principles

There are some basic principles that all escrow officers follow, whether they are in Southern, Central or Northern California, or in some other state, in order to complete an escrow.

Prepare Escrow Instruction

The contractual intent and agreement of the parties is stated here. Since escrow is a limited agency, the escrow officer may only perform those duties identified as being necessary to the well-being of the escrow and delegated by the parties to the transaction.

An escrow officer is only responsible for carrying out the duties specified in the escrow instructions and is not obligated to fulfill the full disclosure requirement of a general agency.

Gather Documentation

Grant deeds, trust deeds, quitclaim deeds, notes, bills of sale, security agreements, Uniform Commercial Code forms (financing statements, information requests, termination statements, assignments) must all be collected and prepared.

Order Title Report

The title report gives the escrow holder information about liens such as existing trust deeds, unpaid taxes, judgments or tax liens. Generally, the buyer has the right to approve or disapprove the preliminary title report as a contingency of the sale. The preliminary title report gives all the information included in the final title report that is usually insured in favor of the buyer, the seller and/or the lender.

Complete Escrow Instructions

Escrow instructions are for the purpose of communicating the intentions of the principals in a transaction to the escrow officer. The escrow officer has a stated time period to accomplish all the necessary tasks delegated by the instructions so the escrow will close in a timely manner according to the wishes of the parties. Commissions must be calculated if there is a broker involved, charges must be listed and made to the correct party, and all contingencies must be completed.

In Southern California, instructions are likely to be prepared as soon as escrow is opened and amended as ordered by the parties during the escrow. These are known as bilateral instructions.

In Northern California, the instructions are drawn at the end of the escrow period.

Prepare to Record

Upon completion of all terms of the agreement between the parties, the escrow officer will authorize the recording of documents necessary to the transfer. (All documents, signed instructions, and amendments have been deposited and are in the possession of the escrow holder. Good funds have been received and are in the possession of the escrow holder. All conditions of the contract have been satisfied.)

Recordation

Upon recordation of grant deed, trust deed, or other documents required for the transfer, the sale is complete. The seller gets the money, the broker gets the commission and the buyer gets the property, with the grant deed to follow as soon as it is mailed to him or her by the county recorder. Information about the transfer of ownership is forwarded to the fire insurance company and existing lenders or any other interested parties. A closing statement summarizing the disbursement of funds and costs of the escrow is prepared by the escrow officer and given to each of the parties.

The major differences in escrow procedures between Northern and Southern California are the way duties and responsibilities between the real estate agent and the escrow officer are divided, the form of the escrow instructions, the role of bank or title company, and the apportionment of fees.

Joint (Bilateral) Escrow Instructions

In Southern California, the escrow officer gets involved at the very beginning of the transaction, or immediately after the buyer and the seller have reached an agreement and signed the offer to purchase.

A connection with the lender begins at the same time as other early stages of the escrow.

The joint or bilateral escrow instructions are more complex than in those drawn in Northern California and are likely to be laden with statements absolving all parties of any innocent wrongdoing or negligent failure to disclose all issues.

Sometimes when instructions are *PREPARED AT THE BEGINNING OF ESCROW*, they may be amended frequently. As we have seen, there are basic steps to be taken by the escrow officer. They are taken in somewhat different order than in the north, however.

Bilateral Escrow Instructions

Broker opens escrow

Prepare escrow instructions and required documents
Obtain signatures of all parties

Order title search
Receive and review preliminary report
Request demands
Request explanation of liens
Review taxes as reported
Receive demands and enter into file

Process financing
Request beneficiary statement
Review terms of transfer and
current payment status
Request copy of new loan application
Obtain loan approval
Request loan documents

Review escrow file for:
Completion of all requirements of escrow
Documents correct and ready for signature
Good funds received

Figure prorations and all other costs as of the closing

Request signatures on all remaining documents

Forward documents to title company

Obtain funds from the buyer

Return loan documents

Request loan funds sent to title company

Order recording

Close file, prepare statements, disburse funds

Close file

Draw Instructions

The bilateral escrow instructions, along with required deeds, purchase money encumbrances and notes are prepared and delivered to the appropriate parties for signatures as soon as possible after opening escrow. Copies of the same document are sent to both the buyer and the seller (bilateral instructions) or may be delivered by their respective real estate agents. Once the instructions are signed by both sides, a valid contract exists and the escrow officer starts preparing the title for closing and following financing instructions.

Review Title

A preliminary title report is ordered from the title company agreed upon by the buyer and the seller in the offer to purchase. After reviewing the preliminary report to discover items which must be made to conform with the conditions of the transfer, the escrow officer proceeds to follow the instructions regarding loan payoffs, liens, or any other matters necessary to present the title at the closing as agreed upon by the parties.

From the preliminary title report, the escrow agent examines any existing liens and reviews taxes to make sure both conform to the agreement of the parties. If instructed to pay off any liens, the escrow agent requests a demand for payment and supportive documents from the holder of the lien. If a new lender has specific requirements regarding taxes, the escrow agent must satisfy those conditions.

When the escrow agent receives any demands for payoff of loans, he or she puts the demands into the open escrow file to be paid at the closing. The payoff amounts shown in the demands must match with the understanding of the parties. Any amounts that seem unreasonable or out of the ordinary, such as a large prepayment penalty, extreme late charges or a surprise principal balance owed, should be questioned by the escrow agent and approved by the party responsible for payment, usually the seller, before the closing.

Financing

At the same time the title review is going on, the escrow agent prepares documents for any assumption of an existing loan on the property or any other special financing, such as an all-inclusive trust deed, contract of sale or any trust deeds required by the escrow. Some of the necessary documents may need to be prepared by an attorney and submitted to the escrow.

If the buyer is to assume an existing loan, a formal agreement, which might change the existing loan terms, must be prepared by the escrow agent and signed by the parties as part of the closing.

In order for a loan to be assumed, the escrow officer requests a beneficiary statement from the lender describing the condition of the loan. Principal, interest rate payment amount, payment status, and any special terms of the loan are specified. If there is a "due on sale" clause in the loan, this request for a beneficiary statement will notify the existing lender of the pending sale, who will then demand the loan be paid in full upon the closing of the escrow. If the loan is assumable, the lender will submit documents and most likely a credit application for the buyer to complete.

The escrow agent will determine, from the information provided, if the lender's prior approval of the loan assumption is required before recording the sale. If the lender requests documentation on the sale, the escrow officer will provide what is needed as instructed in the escrow instructions.

While the escrow holder is getting information about existing liens, new financing is being processed. The lender will require cooperation and complete information from the escrow officer in order to give loan approval and fund the loan without unnecessary delays.

If the buyer is applying for a new conventional loan, chances are he or she will complete a Federal Home Loan Mortgage Corporation (Freddie Mac/Fannie Mae) loan application form. VA and FHA forms ask for similar information from the buyer.

After the buyer completes the loan application, the credit history is verified, and the property appraised, the loan package is ready to be approved by the loan committee. Once the loan, along with the preliminary title report, is approved, the lender issues a loan commitment letter.

After receiving the lender's approval or qualified approval, the escrow officer will review the loan terms to make sure they conform to the desires of the buyer as expressed in the escrow instructions. The escrow agent then must get the buyer's approval and acceptance of the terms of the loan, including any lender-required changes in the original terms of the loan.

> Example: Ken and Sally applied for a loan of $250,000 at an interest rate not to exceed 8%, due in 30 years, with points not to exceed 2%. They might be offered only $225,000 because the property did not appraise as high as the buyer expected. At this point, they must decide whether to accept the reduced loan and put a larger amount down, renegotiate with the seller, or simply cancel the sale because the loan contingency was not met according to the agreement in the offer to purchase.

Review Before Closing

When all conditions of the escrow have been met, and all documents have been drawn correctly and are ready for signing by the parties, the escrow officer calculates prorations and other costs as per the closing date.

The required documents such as the grant deed, any trust deeds or other matters to be recorded are sent to the title company for review and recording upon further instructions.

The escrow officer then calls the buyer and asks him or her to come to the escrow office and bring the down payment and other funds necessary to close the escrow.

The buyer signs the loan documents and any disclosures not already signed, and the items are returned to the lender. The signed trust deed is sent with the other documents to the title company to be recorded.

Funds Requested by Escrow Officer

If all goes smoothly during the review and signing of documents, the escrow agent requests the loan funds from the lender. When the money is received by the escrow holder or the title company the transaction is ready to record.

The differences between the type of escrow instructions used in Southern California and Northern California are few from here on. Procedures for auditing, recording, disbursement of funds and closing are conducted by escrow officers in a similar fashion. Any differences have to do with the fact that procedures in the north combine with the title insurance process to a greater degree, and the escrow officer might perform certain title company functions that would not be required in the south.

Both regions conduct competent escrows; and neither method is superior to the other. Bilateral instructions used in Southern California reduce the possibility of disputes between the parties about the terms of the escrow. In the north, since escrow instructions are not drawn until the end of the escrow period, the need for unending amendments is reduced.

Northern California
Unilateral Escrow Instructions

Southern California
Bilateral Escrow Instructions

Unilateral Escrow Instructions

Broker opens escrow

Request preliminary title report from title department
Receive and review   Order statements of
preliminary report   the buyer/seller identity

Order demands   Order beneficiary statement
Review, inform client   Review terms, inform client

Collect bills from pest control company, property inspection, home warranty, contractors, and any other special demands to be paid at closing

Receive loan documents from lender
Prepare the buyer/seller instructions and all other required documents
Execute and return the buyer/seller instructions and documents

Review escrow file for:
Completion of all requirements of escrow
Documents correctly executed and notarized
Good funds received

Request loan funds from lender

Forward documents to recording desk in title department to be held until recording is ordered

Complete title policy write-up

Receive loan funds

Order recording   Closing statements
Audit escrow   Disburse funds

Close file

Unilateral Escrows

In Northern California where unilateral escrow procedures are prevalent, there are three major differences.

1. The title insurance process is connected to the escrow procedure much more closely.

2. The escrow agent relies on the real estate broker far more than in joint (bilateral) escrows.

3. Escrow instructions are prepared by the escrow agent *at the end* of the escrow period. Joint instructions precede the escrow process and are often amended.

Opening the Order

With unilateral instructions, the real estate broker begins the escrow process. After a buyer and a seller have reached an agreement, the title company chosen by the principals is contacted by the real estate broker who orders a preliminary title report.

This is done through the escrow department of the title company.

Before the escrow officer can ask the title department to conduct a title search on the subject property, certain information must be on hand.

Required Title Search Information

- Legal description—usually assessor's block and parcel number.

- The buyers and the sellers each complete an identity statement so the title company can obtain complete information about who currently owns the property in question and how title is currently held.

- The type of title insurance desired—a standard policy or extended policy.

- Name and address of new lender if any.

- Any particular information required about copies of CC&Rs, any special endorsements or inspections requested in the original offer to purchase between the buyer and the seller.

Preliminary Title Report

After receiving a copy of the preliminary title report, the real estate broker carefully reviews it to make sure the title is in the condition it is believed to be in by the buyer and the seller as shown in the offer to purchase.

Title/Interests Held

The broker looks at how title is held (joint tenants, community property, tenants in common, and so on), or whether any life estates, leaseholds, easements, or other interests affecting title exist.

Current Ownership

Vesting must match the name of the seller on the original offer to purchase. If not, the real estate broker must determine if there has been a misrepresentation by the seller or if some other mistake has occurred. In any case, at this early point, vesting must be researched and any discrepancy discovered and corrected.

Parcel Description

The legal description must match the description of the subject property as described in the original offer to purchase document. Measurements of the parcel as shown in the preliminary report are compared with those on the listing to make sure they are accurate. The parcel is usually referred by an APN number or Assessor's Parcel Number, on the tax record.

Exceptions or Encumbrances

The preliminary report will show any money liens, judgments, easements, taxes owed, or any restrictions affecting title or use of the property in question. The lender will then give loan approval based on his or her evaluation of the report. Some items may be named as exceptions to getting the loan, or as items that must be paid prior to the closing.

If an existing loan is to be paid off, a demand for payoff must be sent to the holder of the loan. If the present loan is to be assumed, a beneficiary statement is required from the current lien holder. The real estate broker relays information to the escrow agent regarding financing as agreed upon in the offer to purchase.

Statement of Information

All parties in a transaction are asked by the title company to complete a statement relating to information that might affect their capacity to close the escrow. There are certain matters that might be found in the general index of the recorder's office that must be researched by the escrow officer such as judgments, tax liens, insanities, paroles, attorneys in fact, guardianship proceedings, bankruptcies, probates or other legal matters relating to the financial responsibility of the principals. Since guarding against forgery is one of the assurances given by the title policy, a signature is required from each of the principals.

Demand

A demand states the balance owed on an existing loan. It is sent to the escrow holder by the lender after a written request is made, asking for a letter disclosing the total amount owed and any supportive documents necessary for the payoff.

After receiving the demand from the lender of record, the escrow officer must verify the payoff information with the seller to determine its accuracy according to the seller's records. Occasionally, a prepayment penalty of six months' interest on the unpaid balance will be part of the payoff, and the seller must be made aware of the amount and be in agreement. If there is an alienation (due-on-sale) clause in the existing note, the lender will be notified of the pending sale by the demand for payoff.

Beneficiary Statement

When the buyer wants to assume or take "subject to" an existing loan, a written request for the current status of the loan is made to the lender (beneficiary). Information about the balance of the loan, the terms of payment, any insurance data and requirements of the lender for loan assumption is included in the request.

Some notes simply state that the note is assumable but the lender has the right to approve the buyer, who must submit a loan assumption application. The lender usually has the right to adjust the terms of the loan to the new borrower after giving approval of the assumption.

Neutral Depository

The escrow holder is a neutral party for the forwarding of any bills accumulated as a result of work done to complete the terms of the escrow. Pest controllers, roofers, property inspectors, or any other professionals who have completed work on the property may submit bills to the escrow holder, who will pay them at the closing from the proceeds of the sale, as directed by the principals.

Opening of Escrow

The way escrow is opened is the main difference between unilateral (Northern) and bilateral (Southern) California escrows. After receiving loan approval and the terms of the loan

being approved by the buyer, the documentation is sent to the escrow officer who holds them for the buyer's signature just prior to the closing. Then escrow instructions are drawn and the closing process starts.

Escrow Instructions

Unilateral instructions are prepared for the buyer and the seller to sign. Any other documents required by the escrow are prepared at this time also. The seller's instructions show money received and a deed being given. In the buyer's instructions, money is given in return for the deed. Prorations and other fees are charged to the appropriate party and specific terms of the transaction are carried out to close the escrow.

Just prior to recording, the escrow officer conducts a final review of the escrow file to make sure all documents have been properly signed and notarized, and good funds received.

If the file is complete, documents are sent to the title officer who holds them until instructed to record. At the same time, loan funds are requested if there is a new loan involved.

Collecting Funds

The final act of the escrow officer is to collect funds from the buyer and the lender, if a new loan is involved. The buyer is contacted and asked to bring in the remainder of the down payment and the amount needed to close the escrow. After all money is deposited with the escrow officer, including closing costs, the escrow file is reconciled one more time to make sure all conditions have been met.

Closing

After the final audit, documents are ordered to be recorded and final settlement begins. The buyer and the seller receive closing statements describing their costs. The buyer gets a deed and the seller gets a check.

True-False Quiz

Now that you have read all the material in this chapter, take the following self-test and check your knowledge of escrow basics and local variations.

True/False

1. _False_ The format for escrow instructions is set by law.

2. _True_ Escrow instructions can be bilateral or unilateral.

3. _True_ With bilateral instructions, the buyer and the seller sign identical sets of instructions.

4. _False_ Unilateral instructions are not used in Northern California.

5. _False_ Instructions are drawn at the beginning of the escrow period in Northern California.

6. _True_ In Southern California, both parties sign an identical set of instructions.

7. _True_ One of the main differences between Northern and Southern California escrows is the way duties and responsibilities between the broker and escrow officer are divided.

8. _False_ The title insurance process is more closely connected to the escrow procedure in Southern California.

9. _False_ In Northern California, the escrow agent begins the escrow process.

10. _False_ Unilateral instructions are more complex than bilateral instructions.

Chapter
7

Escrow Instructions

Learning Objectives

After reading this chapter, you will be able to:

- collect information for an escrow.

- explain the use of a Take Sheet.

- define the three documents that comprise a sale or loan escrow.

- describe how to prepare a Note.

- summarize the Real Estate Settlement Procedures Act Disclosures.

- define General Escrow Instructions.

Introduction

A buyer and a seller have come to an agreement and want to complete the sale of real property. To make sure all the items they have agreed upon are carried out or executed, they need a neutral third party to conduct an escrow to carry out their wishes. An escrow agent will probably conduct the escrow. As agent for both parties to an escrow, the escrow agent is in a position of trust. By operating as a dual agent, the escrow holder sits between the buyer and the seller as a stakeholder with an obligation to both sides.

Escrow instructions are written, as we have seen, from the agreement between the principals. The escrow agent does not direct the transaction; the principals do. The escrow agent reacts to instructions that represent the mutual agreement of the parties.

The instructions are carefully drawn after the escrow agent gathers all the necessary information from the original agreement and the parties connected with the transaction. It is the escrow instructions that reflect, exactly, the intention of the parties to complete the transaction, and describe in detail how that will be accomplished. Once the instructions are prepared, the buyer, the seller, and real estate agent all get copies either to be signed and returned to the closing agent, or to be filed and kept as required by law. The remainder of this chapter explains how escrow instructions are assembled.

Collecting the Information

Most of the time, the real estate agent brings the deposit check from the buyer and is the initial contact for the escrow holder. The process of information gathering takes place before the escrow agent prepares the instructions for the parties to sign.

Collecting the information needed to provide accurate and complete instructions is the first step for an escrow agent. It is important to be specific and well organized in using the information gathered to produce instructions that reflect the agreement of the parties correctly.

In producing complete, error-free instructions, the escrow agent must be sure of the mechanics of the transaction, including the time frame in which the escrow is to be carried out according to the agreement of the principals, the number and types of documents needed, an inclusive description of consideration and other agreements relating to cash, and allocation of charges to the proper parties.

A timeline and a checklist are essential for the smooth progress of the escrow. The escrow agent must know when certain transactions should be completed to assure a timely closing. There is a priority of documentation so that the file is in order for closing. If, for example, a payoff demand is not in place and documented in the file, the loan documents cannot be finalized or signed. A payoff can be authorized verbally by phone, but there must be an official document enclosed in the file by the time the loan documents are signed by the buyers. One missing document can delay or cancel the signing. The closing agent must proceed in an orderly manner toward the end-result, which is the transfer of real or personal property and the hypothecation or pledging of real or personal property.

Escrow concerns

- Title. Who owns the property now and to whom and how is it being transferred?

- Consideration. How much is being paid, borrowed, traded, or given? How is it to be allocated?

Deposit Receipt

At the first contact with the real estate agent who is opening the escrow, the escrow holder makes a copy of the deposit receipt to keep in the transaction file. It may be used for reference if confusion or conflict arises as the escrow progresses.

Take Sheet

The escrow agent will use a "take sheet" as the framework for the instructions, making sure the escrow contract accurately reflects the understanding and intent of the parties as stated in the original deposit receipt.

This information sheet is used to list the important data without itemizing the terms of the transaction. Each of the conditions of this transaction must be evaluated correctly so the escrow or title agent can reduce them to instructions that satisfy all parties.

Take Sheet

Escrow #_____

Date opened_____

Deposit receipt on file ( )_____

Seller/Lender_____

Buyer/Borrower_____

Mailing address_____

Mailing address_____

Home address_____

Home address_____

Telephone (home)_____

Telephone(home)_____

      (work)_____

      (work)_____

Address after close of escrow_____

Address after close of escrow_____

_____

_____

Property address_____

Legal description_____

_____

_____

_____

Proration as of close of escrow or:_____

Buyer will deposit_____

Deposit by buyer_____

      Property taxes ( )

Cash to be added_____

      Homeowners dues ( )

1st Trust Deed_____

      Rents ( )

2nd Trust Deed_____

      Interest-1st trust deed ( )

Total consideration_____

      Impound account ( )

_____ARM/fixed_____Years

Points_____

Commission_____%_____Split

Close of escrow_____

Seller's agent_____

Buyer's agent_____

Real estate company_____

Real estate company_____

Address_____

Address_____

_____

_____

Telephone_____Fax_____

Telephone_____Fax_____

Title Company_____

Credit_____

Address_____

Payoff_____

Telephone_____

Address_____

Title order #_____

Loan #_____

Payoff_____

Address_____

Loan #_____

Subject to buyer/property qualifying for:

( ) All cash

( ) Escrow instructions signed_____days

( ) Preliminary title_____days

( ) Verbal approval_____days

( ) Homeowner's Protection Plan/seller

( ) Written loan approval_____days

( ) Homeowner's Protection Plan/buyer

( ) Walk through_____days, not a contingency

( ) Homeowner's Protection-Broker to pay from

( ) Possession COE

      commission

( ) Possession_____days after COE

( ) Supplemental taxes

( ) Buyer acting as principal

( ) Bonds paid current

( ) Seller acting as principal

( ) HOA transfer paid-buyer/seller

( ) Geological_____days

( ) Memo items

( ) Purchase price includes_____

( ) Property inspection_____days

_____

( ) Condo unit#___Space___Dues_____Days_____

( ) Buyer to occupy

Framework of Transaction

The escrow agent must have a clear understanding of whom the parties are and what they want to achieve.

An experienced escrow agent will create a summary of the proposed transaction before preparing or ordering any documents.

Transaction Summary

Amount of deposit

Balance of down payment owed

Listing of all loan amounts

Type of transaction

Length of escrow

Legal description

Property address

Seller's name

Buyer's name

Buyer's address

Terms of financing

Any payoffs

Items to be prorated

Transaction Summary

Dan and Donna Winter are buying a house from Sam and Kate Summers for $400,000. The Summers are putting $160,000 down and getting a new first loan in the amount of $240,000.

$ 4,000	Good faith deposit
156,000	Balance of down payment
240,000	New first loan
$400,000	Total consideration

Type of transaction	Sale
Length of escrow	45 days
Legal description	Lot 6, Blk 6, tract 785 Any City County of Apple Map book page 36, page 12
Property address	987 Ocean View Drive Any City, CA 90000
Seller	Sam/Kate Summers 987 Ocean View Drive Any City, CA 90000
Buyer	Dan/Donna Winter 25892 Mountain Avenue Any Town, CA 90000
Financing	$240,000 @ 8.5%-new first loan Lender-First Savings
Payoff	Any Town Bank $244,000 @ 7.5%-current balance payable monthly @ $1,800 loan #050650
Prorations	$5,000 annually-taxes $1,200 annually-hazard insurance

Gathering the Data

- Legal name, current address, and telephone number of principals, brokers, and lenders must be listed and kept on hand for use during the term of the escrow.

- Financial information about the transaction must be collected, such as the sales price, trust deeds to remain and those to be paid off, any new loans to be obtained, or the price of any personal property included.

- An accurate legal description is needed to assure that the buyer is getting the right parcel. A street address is also included if there is one.

- The type of property (single-family residence, income property, etc.) must be noted in case there are local requirements to be met when there is a sale, such as retrofit or zoning limitations.

- The seller must provide existing loan information, and the buyer or the buyer's agent must provide the name of any new lender.

- The closing agent must have the proper names of the parties to the transaction (buyer/seller, borrower/lender, vendor/vendee, lessor/lessee).

- Exact terms of the escrow must be indicated, including any time limitations and date of closing.

- Prorations include such items as interest on existing loans, taxes, assessments, bonds, insurance, homeowner's association dues, maintenance fees, and rental deposits. The expectations of the parties regarding prorations must be defined clearly, especially if the principals have agreed mutually on non-traditional proration time frames, such as using an actual "day month" instead of the 30-day month, or have decided not to prorate some normal items.

- Identification of the title company indicated by the buyer and the seller must be noted.

- Conditions of fire, liability, and lender's insurance must be defined.

- Requirements are noted for pest control inspection, time frame for work to be done, and an account of who will pay for the inspection and/or any work required.

- Distribution of charges is made based on the agreement of the parties to the transaction, as long as the charges are not in conflict with laws or rules regulating legal matters.

- Information must be collected, usually from the listing broker, as to how commissions are to be paid and how they are to be split between brokers.

- Any particular agreements made by the principals must be noted, such as leaseback instructions, an all-inclusive trust deed (AITD) agreement to be drawn, or instruction for attorney involvement (to be sent copies of all documents, etc.).

Documents

An escrow holder generally is able to prepare, or order from the proper source, all documents relating to an escrow. As long as the documents do not include the shaping of a contract requiring legal judgments or other acts that would indicate the escrow holder is practicing law, the services of an attorney usually are not necessary in normal transactions.

There are three documents that serve as the heart of a sale or loan escrow: the grant deed, promissory note, and deed of trust. Other documents, such as a quitclaim deed, security agreement, financing statement, bill of sale, and additional disclosure forms, also may be required by the escrow.

Grant Deed

Deeds may be used to convey any type of interest, burden or encumbrance, as well as fee simple transfers in property.

Special Interests Conveyed on Deeds
- Rights reserved by the grantor
- General plan restrictions (covenants, conditions and restrictions)
- Rights incidental or appurtenant to the parcel being transferred
- Riparian rights
- Mineral rights
- Stock rights in a mutually owned water company
- Leasehold rights of the grantor created by prior arrangement

When property is transferred by private grant or by one private party to another, the instrument generally used is a grant deed. The parties involved are the grantor, or the person conveying the property, and the grantee, the person or group receiving the property. At the closing, the buyer gets the grant deed, which  has been signed by the seller, as evidence of the transfer of ownership. Each time the property transfers from one party to another, a new grant deed must be prepared by the escrow officer.

A Valid Grant Deed Must

- Be in writing, according to the Statute of Frauds

- Have the parties to the transfer (grantor and grantee) sufficiently described

- Have a grantor who is competent to convey the property (not a minor or incompetent)

- Have a grantee who is capable of holding title (a real living person, not fictitious)

- Be adequately described

- Have the "granting clause"—the act of granting (grant, convey) must be included

- Be signed by the grantor

- Be delivered to and accepted by the grantee

A grant deed carries with it two specific warranties: that the grantor has not previously conveyed the same property or an interest in it to someone else, and that the estate is free from encumbrances that have not been disclosed by the grantor.

In addition, if a grantor subsequently acquires any title or interest in the property that he or she has granted as a fee simple estate, that *after-acquired title* passes to the grantee.

A grant deed does not have to be recorded to be valid. In order for the parties' rights to be protected, however, the deed must be recorded. The deed must be acknowledged before it can be recorded.

Each county, upon the transfer of property, may charge a documentary transfer tax. The amount of the transfer tax is stamped in the upper right-hand corner of a recorded deed and sent to the buyer after the closing. The amount of the tax is based on $1.10 per $1,000 or $.55 per $500 of transferred value. The deed is sent to the buyer after the closing by the County Recorder.

How to Calculate Documentary Transfer Tax

- When a sale is all cash, or a new loan is obtained by the buyer, the tax is calculated on the entire sales price.

- When an existing loan is assumed by a buyer, the tax is calculated on the difference between the assumed loan and the sales price.

Promissory Note

As previously discussed in Chapter 3, a promissory note is a written promise to pay back a certain sum of money with specified terms at an agreed upon time. It is a personal obligation of the borrower, and in itself, a complete contract between the borrower and lender.

According to the Uniform Commercial Code, a promissory note must meet certain requirements to be valid or enforceable.

Review - A Promissory Note is:

- an unconditional written promise to pay a certain sum.

- made by one person to another.

- signed by the maker or borrower.

- payable at a definite time.

- paid to bearer or to order.

- voluntarily delivered by the borrower.

Normally, in a transaction where the buyer is financing the sale (borrowing money) through an institutional lender, loan documents that include a promissory note are signed by the buyer/borrower in the presence of the closing agent just before the closing. If the sale is being financed by the seller, loan documents would not be available or necessary and a promissory note is prepared by the closing agent, according to the instructions of the principals.

Preparing the Note

There are certain items regarding the note of which a closing agent must be aware and must include in preparing the escrow instructions.

Lender

- Name of lender?

- Institution or individual?

- Is it a loan regulated by the Business and Professions Code involving real estate licensees?

- Is it a loan regulated by the state usury law or is it a purchase money loan to a seller or other private-party loan?

Terms

- What is the amount being borrowed?

- How many notes are required for the principal amount?

- What is the interest rate?

- Is the interest rate fixed or variable? If variable, what is the index, time period for rate changes, how is interest to be treated (deferred or added to principal payment)? Are there any unusual interest terms?

- How are payments to be made? Are they fixed or variable or a combination of both (graduated payment loans)? If payment does not cover monthly interest, how is deferred interest to be accrued, and how are future payments to be applied?

- Is there a balloon payment? Note should be made if the loan is arranged under the Business and Professions Code sections applying to licensee-arranged loans. The regulations specify that no balloon payment be allowed until the 73rd month on a single-family, owner-occupied residence. Holders of notes containing a balloon payment must remind borrowers no sooner than 150 days nor later than 90 days from maturity of when the loan is due.

- Where will payment be made or sent? If the location is outside California, usury laws of that state may apply.

- Will there be late charges?

- Is there a pre-payment penalty?

- If there is a due-on-sale clause, it must be contained in both the note and trust deed. The make-up of the acceleration clause usually will be supplied by the lender.

- What type of note is it? Payment should reflect whether the note is a straight note (interest only), installment note (principal amortized), or some other type of note.

- What is the collateral for the note? If more than one property is being used to secure the loan (blanket mortgage), it should be noted that two trust deeds are being utilized for the note.

Special Requirements of the Note

- Are there restrictions on principal reductions?

- Is there a pre-payment penalty?

- If the transaction deals with a subdivision, is there a partial release clause? Is the subdivision regulated by the Subdivision Map Act, and have the proper steps been taken to comply with laws regarding creation of a trust deed dividing an existing lot?

- Will the note specify whether there can be loan advances, extension of the loan, future subordination, or renegotiation of rate at any time?

Deed of Trust

As we have mentioned, a trust deed is used to secure a loan on real property. It describes the property being used as security, or collateral, for a debt, and usually includes a power of sale and assignment of rents clause.

Trust Deeds Usually Include:

Power of Sale Clause. Gives trustee the right to foreclose, sell and convey ownership to a purchaser of the property if the borrower defaults on the loan

Assignment of Rents Clause. Upon default by the borrower, the lender can take possession of the property and collect any rents being paid

The process of borrowing money, secured by a trust deed, where the buyer remains in possession of the property during the payoff of the loan or note, is called hypothecation.

A certain uniformity is required by FNMA/FHLMC in trust deeds securing loans bought by those agencies. The following is a list of inclusions necessary to describe the rights and obligations of parties to a trust deed.

Rights and Obligations of Parties to a Trust Deed

1. Payment of principal and interest

2. Payment of taxes and insurance

3. Statement of how payments are to be made relating to the note

4. Charges to be made to borrower (if required to pay taxes and insurance without an impound account by lender) and liens to be placed for non-payment

5. Requirements for hazard insurance coverage and application of insurance proceeds

6. Obligations to comply with the provisions of a lease (optional)

7. Statement of lender's right to take action if borrower defaults

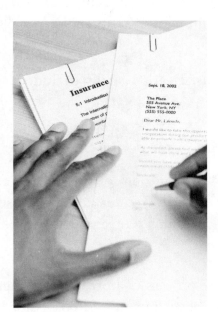

8. Property inspection by lender before action is taken upon the default of borrower

9. Settlement agreement in case of eminent domain proceedings

10. Lender's right to give forbearance in certain cases, but no obligation in all cases

11. Description of liability for parties including joint, several, and co-signers, as well as all successors of interest.

12. Charges given for the loan

13. Provision for an acceleration clause if not all terms are met

14. Address of borrower and lender listed

15. Copy of document to borrower

16. Requirements of lender with transfer of ownership (due on sale, assumption)

17. Methods of curing default

18. Description of lender's right to foreclose upon default of borrower, and of default

19. Rents from property occupants, collected by lender or an appointed receiver, in case of default

20. Conditions for reconveyance after loan paid in full

21. Substitution of trustee allowed

22. Requirement for notification of default to be mailed to borrower at the property address (request for notice)

23. List of any special conditions of the loan

24. Possible fee by the lender for preparing a beneficiary's statement

Trust Deed as a Lien

A trust deed becomes a lien on the real property being conveyed when the buyer borrows money to buy the property. The escrow agent prepares the trust deed and it is then added to the loan document package supplied by the lender for the buyer's signature. The trust deed does not have to be recorded to be valid, but ordering recordation of the signed trust deed is normally part of the closing agent's responsibility.

Quitclaim Deed

Another type of deed that may be prepared by the closing agent is a quitclaim deed. In the past, this type of deed was commonly used to transfer real property interests between husband and wife.

However, an inter-spousal grant deed is now used between spouses instead of a quitclaim deed.

A quitclaim deed is a deed of conveyance that operates as a release of whatever interest the grantor has in the property. The quitclaim deed contains similar language to a deed, with the important exception that rather than using the words *grant and release*, it contains language such as *remise, release, and quitclaim*. Grantors therefore do not warrant title or possession. Grantors only pass on whatever interest they may have, if any. In effect, a grantor forever quits whatever claim he or she had, if in fact any existed.

Executing a quitclaim deed does not carry even an implied warranty as regards ownership, liens, encumbrances, or the possibility that the grantor has not previously signed a deed to someone else. It does convey ownership of the property to another person.

A quitclaim deed is not commonly used to convey a fee, but is usually restricted to releasing or conveying minor interests in real estate. The purpose of this is usually to clear title defects or clouds on title. It may also be used to convey lesser interests such as life estates and to release such interests as a remainder or reversion.

Quitclaim deeds also are often used between close relatives, such as when one heir is buying out the other, or where a seller's finances are so troubled that it is inconsequential to the buyer whether he or she is getting any warranties or not.

Although a quitclaim deed may or may not vest any title in the grantee, it is not inferior to the other types of deeds in what it actually conveys. For example, if a grantor executes and delivers a grant deed to one person and subsequently executes and delivers a quitclaim deed to the same property to another person, the grantee under the quitclaim deed will prevail over the grantee under the grant deed, assuming the holder of the quitclaim is first to record the deed.

A title searcher will regard a quitclaim deed in the chain of title as a red flag, and most title companies will not guarantee titles derived out of a quitclaim, at least not without further clarification.

Bill of Sale

A bill of sale is a written agreement by which one person sells, assigns, or transfers to another his or her interest in personal property. A bill of sale sometimes is used by a seller of real estate to show the transfer of personal property, such as when the owner of a store sells the building and includes the store equipment and trade fixtures. The transfer of the personal property can be affected by mentioning in the deed, or more commonly, by a separate bill-of-sale document, which is prepared by the closing agent for signature by the seller.

Security Agreement

A security agreement is a document that creates a lien on personal property, including possessions that are attached to land as fixtures after the sale closes. Rather than recording the security agreement to give notice of the lien, however, the law provides for filing a financing statement to perfect the security interest. A closing agent usually will be required to prepare a security agreement in the sale of a business opportunity.

Financing Statement

A financing statement is a written notice (of credit given and ensuing terms in a security agreement) to be filed in the public records. A closing agent will prepare a financing statement and order it to be recorded at the request of a seller who has given credit for the purchase of personal property. The purpose of recording the statement is to establish the creditor's interest in the personal property (separate from the real property being conveyed in the transaction) which is the security for the debt. The financing statement is the document that is recorded to show evidence of a security agreement.

Truth in Lending Documents

The main purpose of the Truth-in-Lending Law or Regulation Z, as it is commonly known, is to assure that borrowers in need of consumer credit are given accurate and meaningful information about the cost of the credit being extended. Most escrow agents are involved in these lender disclosures, and, as required by law, give them to the borrower.

Real Estate Settlement Procedures Act Disclosures

The **Real Estate Settlement Procedures Act (RESPA)** is a federal loan disclosure law applicable to first mortgage loans on residential property. It requires certain disclosures to borrowers and provides the consumer with information on loan settlement costs. Information contained in these disclosures usually is provided by the closing agent. A **Special Information Booklet** and **Good Faith Estimate (GFE)** of the amount or range of closing costs must be given to a borrower when he or she applies for a loan. The Good Faith Estimate (*Uniform Settlement Statement*) provides detailed information on escrow costs so that the borrower can shop around for escrow services. Additionally, the buyers and borrowers will be able to make informed decisions during the loan/sale transaction and the settlement/escrow process. One day before the scheduled closing, the borrower has the right under RESPA to inspect the *Uniform Settlement Statement* that gives an itemized account of all fees charged by the lender. A lender may not charge anyone in connection with the preparation of the Good Faith Estimate or distribution of the Special Information Booklet.

Consideration/Cash Agreements

At the beginning of the printed escrow instructions there is a listing of the consideration included in the transaction. This listing describes the source and use of all funds in the transaction.

Any money required by the transaction is noted, with its source, whether it is a cash deposit or new financing. This amount, plus or minus any fees, adjustments, or prorations, represents the true cash that passes through the escrow.

Any other consideration that is not to be given as cash is accounted for in the instructions. Items of value such as personal or other real property to be added to the transaction are listed, as well as the equities to be transferred if the transaction is a tax-deferred exchange.

Other Information

Certain basic information must be available to answer questions that may be asked about:

- the escrow instructions.

- title and transfer documents.

- new financing being obtained to complete the transfer.

- any liens being paid off through the transaction.

After all necessary information has been gathered and noted in the take sheet, the closing agent is ready to utilize the data in preparing instructions.

Prepare Escrow Instructions

The escrow is officially opened when the escrow holder accepts the purchase agreement that has been signed by all parties to the escrow. When escrow instructions are drawn, the escrow holder prepares them on a computer-generated form, with details of the particular transaction completed in the blank spaces on the form. All parties sign identical instructions, with the exception of the commission agreement that is prepared for the seller to sign—if the seller in fact is paying the commission.

The buyer and the seller sign the instructions, which are then returned to the escrow holder who follows the directions in the agreement to complete the escrow. By signing the instructions, the buyer and the seller agree to the general provisions of the instructions that disclose various elements of the transaction general to most escrows.

The following would probably be included in the escrow instructions or purchase agreement. In California, the purchase agreement becomes the escrow instructions.

> **Purchase Price**. The **purchase price** is the amount of consideration the buyer and the seller have agreed upon for the sale of the property. The consideration in dollar amounts, including the amount of good faith deposit, additional cash to be added for down payment, any deeds of trust to be recorded, and sales price, term of escrow, title insurance policy liability, legal description of property, street address of property, and vesting are listed at the beginning of the instructions.

> **Terms**. The buyer and the seller agree on how the buyer will purchase the property: cash, new loan, loan assumption, VA, or FHA loan, the seller to carry a trust deed, trade, or any other special agreements provided in the contract between the buyer and the seller. This section describes the amount of the

down payment and the terms of any loans for which the buyer will apply. This section also states that the closing and costs allocated to the parties are subject to payment of taxes, liens, or other restrictions on financing.

Vesting. The way title will be taken is called **vesting**. The buyer will take title in one of the following ways: sole ownership, joint tenancy, tenants in common, or tenancy in partnership. How the buyer will take title may be important for tax or inheritance purposes and the escrow holder must be directed how to draw the deed to reflect the wishes of the buyer.

Matters of Record. The buyer and the seller may agree on some matter of record or, in other words, some matter that is recorded, affecting the property. It may be an easement, an existing street bond, or a trust deed. An agreement may be made about who will be responsible for whatever exists as a recorded encumbrance on the title at the time of the sale.

Closing. The buyer and the seller will agree on how long they want the escrow to last. They will mention a specific length of time for the escrow and instruct the escrow holder accordingly.

Inspections. The buyer and the seller will agree on whether to have certain inspections of the property before the close of escrow, such as a pest control inspection, property inspection to identify any plumbing, electrical, or structural problems, and a soil inspection to check for slippage or unstable compaction. The buyer's approval of the reports will be a contingency of the sale and must be mentioned in the escrow instructions.

Prorations. The division of expenses and income between the buyer and the seller as of the date of closing is known as proration. Items to be prorated as of close of escrow may include taxes, rental deposits or income, and insurance premiums. The reason for proration is that some payments may have been made by the seller for a time beyond the agreed-upon date of closing of escrow, or the seller may be in arrears on taxes or insurance. The escrow holder debits or credits the seller or the buyer, depending on the escrow closing date. Normally, proration is based on a 30-day month and a 360-day year.

Possession. The time and date of property possession by the buyer is listed, even though it may not be essential to the transaction. The buyer and the seller will have agreed on when the buyer can move into the house, and the escrow instructions must reflect their agreement of the date on which the buyer will take possession of the property. The close of escrow could be the date of possession, or sometimes the seller will rent the property back from the buyer after the close of escrow. In that case, a lease agreement should be signed and deposited in escrow.

Documents. The escrow holder will need to know which documents to prepare, have signed by the proper party, and record at the close of escrow. Usually, these will be a grant deed and a trust deed.

Disbursements. The escrow holder must settle the accounts of the buyer and the seller according to the escrow instructions. At the close of escrow, each party receives a closing statement of costs and charges along with a final distribution of funds.

Local Differences. As discussed in Chapter 6, there are differences in the closing practices within California. There are two main differences between the locales. The first is the timing of the signing of closing documents. The second is the type of instructions prepared for the principals to sign. In Northern California, the instructions are unilateral, where the buyer and the seller sign different sets of instructions. Bilateral instructions are those used in Southern California in which the buyer and the seller each sign identical sets of instructions.

In Northern California, an estimated closing statement is issued as part of the instructions, showing, for example, the proceeds going to the seller and the estimated cash needed to close for the buyer. In Southern California, the broker's net sheet serves the same purpose, except the closing statement is provided at the settlement.

Third Party Instructions

When third parties are involved in the transaction, such as lenders or other lien holders, special instructions are required that give the escrow holder authority to deal with parties other than the principals. These might include documents, demands or the deposit of funds into escrow.

Parties other than the principals, typically, may execute a third-party instruction to claim or discard a financial interest in the transaction. All parties must accept the additional instruction and sign any amendments affecting a third party.

Review - Third Party Instructions are required:

- for fire insurance authorization.

- for commission payment authorization.

- for an interspousal transfer grant deed between spouses.

- to lender regarding payoff or assumption of an existing loan.

- for release of mechanic's and other liens.

- for release of a judgment.

General Instructions

The general instructions are usually the pre-printed part of any set of instructions. As important as the contract items of agreement between the buyer and the seller, this part of the escrow contract describes the procedures that will be used to accomplish the task required of the escrow officer.

Every escrow holder has a different concept of how many and which of the protective and disclosure clauses are required in the general instructions. Included below are an extended number of these protective and disclosure clauses. The general instructions also deal with practically every aspect of the escrow, explaining each item of the escrow process.

These instructions authorize the escrow holder to carry out the general procedures needed to complete the escrow.

Instructions Signed

The escrow holder's duty does not commence until mutual escrow instructions signed by all parties are received by the escrow holder. Until that time, either party may unilaterally revoke these instructions. In addition, upon written request delivered to escrow holder, either party may withdraw any funds, instruments, documents, or items that they have previously handed to the escrow holder.

Purchase Agreement

In the event any Offer to Purchase, Deposit Receipt or any other form of Purchase Agreement, amendment or supplement is deposited in this escrow, it is understood that such document shall be effective only as between the parties signing the document. The escrow holder is not to be concerned with the terms of such Purchase Agreement and is relieved of all responsibility and/or liability for the enforcement of such terms. The only duty is to comply with the instructions set forth in this escrow.

The escrow holder is not responsible for knowing or interpreting any provisions of any Purchase Agreement on which these instructions may be based. The escrow holder shall not rely on any knowledge or understanding of the Purchase Agreement in performing the duties required by this escrow. In connection with any loan transaction, the escrow holder is authorized to deliver a copy of any such Purchase Agreement, along with any supplement or amendment to that document to the lender.

Deposit of Funds

The escrow holder is authorized and directed to deposit any and all funds placed in this escrow with any state or national bank or savings bank in a trust account in the name of the escrow holder without any liability for interest to be withdrawn by the escrow holder and disbursed in accordance with the instructions of the parties.

Title Company

The escrow holder is to immediately open an order with the title company and request a preliminary title report concerning the subject property, regardless of the consummation of this escrow.

Title

The escrow holder is instructed to clear title to the subject real property according to the beneficiary demands and/or beneficiary statements delivered to the escrow holder by the existing lienholders. The escrow holder is not responsible for the correctness of the above. The escrow holder is not required to submit any such beneficiary statement and/or beneficiary demand to the parties for approval prior to the close of escrow unless expressly instructed to do so, in writing, by the parties. The escrow holder will not conduct a lien or title search of chattels or personal property in connection with this escrow.

Statement of Information

Each principal agrees to give the escrow holder a fully completed and executed "Statement of Information". In turn, the escrow holder will send it to the title company as required. If the principals refuse to deliver the "Statement of Information" in a timely manner, this may delay the closing.

Change of Ownership Form

The buyer acknowledges that a Change of Ownership form is required by the county recorder to be completed and affixed to any documents submitted for recording which indicate a conveyance of title. The Change of Ownership form shall be furnished to the buyer by the escrow holder, and the buyer is informed that if he or she does not complete the form in full, sign, and return it to the escrow holder prior to closing, a penalty will be assessed by the county recorder.

If the Change of Ownership form is not filed after the close of escrow within the time limits set forth by the county recorder, additional penalties will be assessed against the buyer. For information or assistance in completing the Change of Ownership form, the buyer may contact the county assessor's office in the county in which the subject property is located.

Physical Inspection

The escrow holder shall make no physical inspection of the real and/or personal property described in any instrument deposited in this escrow. The escrow holder shall not make any representations and/or guarantees concerning any real and/or personal property, and is not to be concerned with or liable for the condition of such properties.

Disclosures

The escrow holder is not to be concerned with the giving of any disclosures required by federal or state law, including, but not limited to, RESPA (Real Estate Settlement Procedures Act), Regulation Z (Truth-In-Lending Disclosures), FIRPTA (Foreign Investment Real Property Tax Act), or other warnings, or any other warranties, expressed or implied.

The escrow holder shall not be responsible in any way and is released from any liability, obligation, or responsibility with respect to withholding of funds in response to FIRPTA regulations. The escrow holder is not responsible in determining whether the transferor is a foreign person, or for obtaining a non-foreign affidavit or exemption from withholding under FIRPTA.

Liability for Disclosure

The parties agree that as far as the responsibilities and liabilities of the escrow holder are concerned, this transaction is an escrow, and does not create any other legal relationship except that of an escrow holder upon the terms and conditions expressly set forth in these instructions.

The escrow holder shall have no duty or responsibility to disclose any profit realized by any person, firm, or corporation including, but not limited to, any real estate broker, real estate sales agent, and/or a party. However, if the escrow holder is instructed by any party to this escrow, in writing, to disclose any sale, resale, loan, exchange, or other transaction involving any real or personal property described herein or any profit realized by any person, firm, or corporation as set forth herein, the escrow holder should do so without incurring any liability to any party.

The escrow holder shall not be liable for any acts or omissions done in good faith, nor for any claims, demands, losses, or damages made, or claims suffered by any party to this escrow. The only exceptions would be those that may arise through, or be caused by, willful neglect or gross misconduct on the part of the escrow holder.

Subdivision

The parties to this escrow have satisfied themselves outside of escrow that the transaction covered is not in violation of the Subdivision Map Act, any law regulating land division, zoning ordinances or building restrictions. The escrow

holder is relieved of all responsibility and/or liability in connection with the above-mentioned regulations and is not to be concerned with the enforcement of any laws, restrictions, ordinances, or regulations.

Prorations

All prorations and adjustments are to be made based on a thirty (30) day month unless otherwise instructed in writing by all parties. For proration purposes, the buyer will have ownership of the real property, which is the subject of this escrow for the entire day, regardless of the hour of recording. The "close of escrow" with reference to said prorations and adjustments of all purposes for this escrow shall be the day instruments of conveyance called for are recorded or filed with the county recorder.

The escrow holder is instructed to prorate taxes for the current fiscal year based on the most recent information furnished to you by title insurer herein. Prorations are made on the basis of a 360 day year. In view of the change of ownership of the subject property that will take place on the close of this escrow, it is to be expected that the taxing authorities will re-assess the property and issue a supplemental tax bill. The seller and the buyer acknowledge their awareness of the foregoing and hereby release and relieve the escrow holder of all liability in connection with same, and the escrow holder shall not be further concerned with the above re-assessment in any manner.

The escrow holder is authorized to obtain a Statement of Fees from Homeowners' Association affecting subject property and to charge account of the seller to bring account current, if necessary, and to use said statement to determine amounts required for proration purposes. The seller has furnished or will furnish, prior to close of escrow, to the buyer outside of this escrow a copy of CC&Rs, By-Laws, Budget and Articles of Incorporation for said Association.

The escrow holder has no duty or responsibility regarding those documents. The escrow holder is instructed to charge to the account of the buyer any transfer fee as charged by the Homeowners' Association and to split any "move-in/move-out" fee 1/2 to the seller and 1/2 to the buyer.

In the event rents are to be prorated, the escrow holder is instructed to prorate and charge the seller and credit the buyer with any deposits paid in advance on the basis of a statement furnished by the seller. The seller represents that he or she will collect all rents that fall due prior to the close of escrow. The escrow holder is to make all adjustments on the basis that all rents are current.

Charges

In addition to other costs and charges set forth in the escrow instructions, the seller agrees to pay on demand, whether or not the escrow closes, any and all charges incurred by the escrow holder on the seller's behalf, including but not limited to charges for owner's policy of title insurance, beneficiary statements and/or demands, offset statements, documentary transfer tax, preparation of, notarizing and recording of documents necessary on the seller's behalf, the seller's portion of sub-escrow fee, the seller's escrow fee, and other costs as charged.

The escrow holder is authorized to deduct from the seller's net proceeds, or the buyer's net proceeds, any amount that the seller or the buyer, as the case may be, may owe in any other matter or transaction. The escrow holder is authorized to charge and the parties agree to pay additional escrow fees for extraordinary services not within the range of customary escrow processing.

Third Party Claims

The parties expressly indemnify and hold the escrow holder harmless against third party claims for any fees, costs, or expenses where the escrow holder has acted in good faith, with reasonable care and prudence and/or in compliance with escrow instructions.

Insurance

The closing agent must make arrangements for new fire and hazard coverage or the transfer of coverage from the seller to the buyer. New documents reflecting the change must be gathered or prepared for signature by all parties.

When the seller assigns an insurance policy to the buyer, the seller guarantees that each policy is in force, has not been hypothecated, and all necessary premiums have been paid. The escrow holder has the authorization to execute assignments of interest in any insurance policy (other than title insurance policies) called for in this escrow. He or she is also authorized to work with the insurance agent to make sure the assignment is handled correctly.

The insurance policy will be forwarded to the lender and party entitled to it. The escrow holder is not responsible for verifying the acceptance of the request for assignment and the policy of insurance by the insurance company. Many escrow instructions contain similar words.

> "The parties mutually agree that you will make no attempt to verify the receipt of the request for assignment by the insurance company. The parties are placed on notice that if

the insurance company should fail to receive said assignment, the insuring company may deny coverage for any loss suffered by the buyer. It is the obligation of the insured or a representative to verify the acceptance of the policy's assignment by the issuing company."

Tax Information

In connection with the Federal Tax Reform Act of 1986 and the California Revenue and Taxation Code, certain transactions must be reported to the Internal Revenue Service and the California State Franchise Tax Board. For those transactions that must be reported, the seller will furnish a correct tax identification number to the escrow holder as required by law. The seller must understand that he or she may be subject to civil or criminal penalties for failure to do so.

Personal Property Tax

The escrow holder is not responsible for any personal property tax that may be assessed against the property described in the escrow instructions.

Documents

The escrow holder shall not be responsible in any way for the sufficiency or correctness as to form, manner of execution, or validity of any documents deposited in this escrow, nor as to the identity, authority, or right of any person executing the same to documents of record or to those handled in this escrow.

Nor shall the escrow holder be responsible in any way whatsoever for the failure of any party to comply with any of the provisions of any agreement, contract or other instrument filed or deposited in the escrow or referred to in the escrow instructions. The escrow holder duties shall be limited to the safekeeping of such money and documents received and for the disposition of the same in accordance with the written instructions.

The escrow holder shall not be required to take any action in connection with the collection, maturity, or apparent outlaw of any obligations deposited in this escrow unless otherwise instructed in writing.

Delivery of Documents

The parties agree to deliver to the escrow holder all documents, instruments, escrow instructions, and funds required to process and close this escrow in accordance with these instructions.

Copies Delivered

The escrow holder is authorized to deliver copies of all escrow instructions, supplements and amendments, estimated and final closing statements, preliminary title reports and notices of cancellation, if any, to the real estate broker, real estate agent, lender, lender's agent and/or attorney for the parties, upon their oral or written request. The escrow holder shall not incur any liability in doing so.

Recording, Delivery of Instruments or Funds

The parties to this escrow authorize the recordation of any instrument necessary or proper for the issuance of the policy of title insurance calling for or affecting the closing of this escrow. Funds, instructions or instruments received in this escrow may be delivered to, or deposited with, any title insurance company or title company for the purpose of complying with the terms and conditions of this escrow. The escrow holder is not responsible for the sufficiency, correctness of form or authority of person signing of any documents drawn outside of escrow and deposited with the escrow holder.

Terms of New Loan

The escrow holder is not to be responsible in any way nor to be concerned with the terms of any new loan or the content of any

loan documents obtained by the buyer or the seller in connection with the escrow except to order such loan documents into the escrow file and to transmit the same to the buyer for execution and transmit the executed loan documents to lender. The parties understand and agree that the escrow holder is not involved or concerned with the processing of any loan and cannot advise or give an opinion regarding the processing of any loan.

Usury

The escrow holder shall not be responsible for or concerned with any question of usury in any loan or encumbrance, whether new or of record, which may arise during the processing of this escrow.

Pest Control Report

If a structural pest control report and/or notice of work completed are handed to the escrow holder, a copy shall be mailed to the buyer as soon as is practicable after receipt.

Forms

The escrow holder is to use the usual instrument forms such as notes, deeds, or deeds of trust, or the usual forms of any title insurance company. Dates and terms are to be inserted on the usual instruments if they are incomplete in such particulars, provided the insertions comply with the instructions contained in these escrow instructions.

Sub-Escrow

In the event it may be necessary, proper, or convenient for the completion of this escrow, you are authorized to deposit or have deposited funds or documents or both, handed you under these escrow instructions, with any duly authorized sub-escrow agent. These may include, but are not limited to, any bank, trust company, title insurance company, title company, or licensed escrow agent. The above described sub-escrow agent is to be subject to the escrow holder's order at or prior to close of that sub-escrow in the course of carrying out the close of this escrow. Any such deposit shall be considered as one in accordance with the meaning of these escrow instructions.

Hold Open Fee

Notwithstanding any other provisions contained in escrow instructions, and in addition to such other fees and costs to which the escrow holder may be entitled, the parties, jointly and severally, agree that in the event the escrow is not consummated within ninety (90) days of the date set for closing, the escrow holder is instructed to withhold the escrow hold open fee of $25.00 per month from the funds on deposit with you regardless of the depositor.

Agency

The agency between the principals to this escrow and the escrow holder shall automatically terminate six (6) months following the date set for the close of escrow. It shall be subject to earlier termination if the parties to the escrow submit mutually executed cancellation instructions. In the event the conditions of this escrow have not been complied with at the expiration provided, the escrow holder is instructed to complete the termination at the earliest possible date, unless any of the parties have made written demand upon the escrow holder for the return of funds and/or instruments deposited by either of the parties.

If there are funds or instruments to be disbursed, the escrow holder is instructed to stop proceedings, without liability for interest on funds held, until mutual cancellation instructions are received from the parties. The parties, jointly and severally, agree that in the event of cancellation or other termination of this escrow prior to closing to pay for any expenses that the escrow holder has incurred while following these instructions.

The principals agree, if this escrow is mutually terminated prior to the closing date, to pay a reasonable escrow fee for services contracted by them and to deposit such funds into escrow prior to cancellation. The buyer and the seller agree that any cancellation charges or fees for services shall be divided fairly between the parties in a manner the escrow holder considers equitable. The escrow holder's decision regarding the distribution of fees will be considered binding and conclusive upon the parties.

Upon receipt of mutual cancellation instructions or a final order or judgment of a court, the escrow holder is instructed to disburse any funds and instruments in accordance with such instructions, order, or judgment. This escrow, without further notice, will then be considered terminated and canceled.

Cooperation of Parties

The parties shall cooperate with the escrow holder in carrying out the instructions and completing the escrow. In the interest of following the instructions, the parties shall deposit into escrow any additional funds, instruments, documents, or authorizations as requested. These additions shall be reasonably necessary to enable the escrow holder to comply with demands made by third parties, to secure policies of title insurance, or otherwise carry out the terms of the instructions and close this escrow.

In the event conflicting demands are made upon the escrow holder or controversy arises between the parties or with any third person arising out of this escrow, the escrow holder shall have the absolute right to withhold and stop any further proceedings in the performance of this escrow until receiving written notification of the dispute's settlement.

All parties to this escrow promise to compensate the escrow holder for specific, unexpected costs connected with the escrow. These might be litigation costs, judgments, attorney's fees, expenses, obligations, and liabilities of any kind, which, in good faith, the escrow holder may incur in connection with carrying out this escrow.

As a safeguard, the escrow holder is given a lien on all rights, titles, and interests of parties to this escrow as well as all escrow papers, other property and money deposited in case there is a need for the escrow holder to be reimbursed. In the event of failure to pay fees or expenses due the escrow holder or for costs and attorneys fees incurred in any litigation or interpleader, the parties agree to pay a reasonable fee for any attorney services which may be required to collect such fees or expenses, whether such attorney's fees are incurred prior to trial, at trial or on appeal.

Dishonored Checks

If any check submitted to the escrow holder is dishonored upon presentment for payment for any reason, the escrow holder is authorized to notify all parties to the escrow and/or their respective real estate broker or real estate sales agent.

In Writing

All notices, demands, and instructions must be in writing. No notice, demand, instruction, amendment, supplement or modification of these instructions shall be of any effect in this escrow until delivered in writing to the escrow holder. All documents must be executed by all parties affected.

Any purported oral instruction, amendment, supplement, modification, notice, or demand deposited with the escrow holder by the parties shall be invalid. The escrow holder is to be concerned only with the directives expressly set forth in the escrow instructions, supplements, and amendments. The escrow holder is not concerned with or liable for items designated as "memorandum items" in the escrow instructions.

Oral Instructions

The escrow holder is authorized to accept oral instructions from the parties' real estate broker, real estate agent, lender, or lender's agent concerning the preparation of escrow instructions, amendments, or supplements. However, the escrow holder may not act upon any instruction delivered orally until receiving written authorization signed by all parties to this escrow.

Counterparts

These instructions may be executed in counterparts, each of which shall be considered an original regardless of the date of its execution and delivery. All such counterparts together shall constitute one and the same document. Together they make up the entire contract.

Gender

In these escrow instructions, wherever the context so requires, the masculine includes the feminine and/or neuter and the singular number includes the plural.

Legal Limitations

The parties acknowledge that the escrow holder is not authorized to practice law or to give legal advice. Each of the parties is advised to seek legal or financial counsel and advice concerning the effect of these escrow instructions. Further, the parties acknowledge that no representations are made by the escrow holder as to the legal sufficiency, legal consequences, financial effects, or tax consequences of this transaction.

Authorization to Dispose of Escrow Paperwork

The escrow holder is authorized to destroy or otherwise dispose of all documents, papers, instructions, correspondence and records or other material in this escrow file AFTER five (5) years from the date of close of escrow or cancellation. The escrow holder shall have no liability for disposing of the above without further notice to the parties.

Disbursements

All disbursements of funds and/or delivery of other documents or instruments concerning this escrow will be mailed to parties entitled thereto by regular first-class mail, postage prepaid to their respective addresses shown on the escrow file.

Signatures

The parties' signatures on all escrow instructions and instruments indicate their unconditional acceptance and approval. The escrow holder is entitled to rely on the signatures contained in these instructions.

Electronic Signatures

Due to federal legislation enacted in 2000, electronic contracts and electronic signatures are just as legal and enforceable as traditional paper contracts signed in ink. The law is known as The Electronic Signatures in Global and (Inter) National Commerce Act, (E-SIGN). It allows for certain transactions to be confirmed electronically.

However, for purposes of real estate, escrow, and banking, electronic signatures are not allowed for signatures required under the Uniform Commercial Code. It also includes Notice of Default, Acceleration, Repossession, Foreclosure, Eviction, Right to Cure (when individual's residence is used to secure a loan).

Parties to a transaction or contract are allowed to negotiate document integrity and electronic signing, but there are specific standards regarding promissory notes, pertaining to photocopies, faxes, and electronic transmissions of original documents, and does not include voice or audio transmissions. Documents that are notarized and recorded cannot be signed electronically.

Any City Escrow, Inc.

24321 Riverfront Rd., Suite B, Any City, CA 90000
(555) 123-4567 telephone-(555) 321-5476 fax

BUYER AND SELLER ESCROW INSTRUCTIONS
Escrow No: 1-4035-J
Kelly Rose: Escrow Officer
Date: January 17, 20xx
Page: 1 of 5

THIS COMPANY IS LICENSED BY DEPT. OF CORPORATIONS

BROKER WILL HAND YOU FOR BUYER	$5,000.00
BUYER WILL HAND YOU PRIOR TO CLOSE OF ESCROW	$11,050.00
DEED OF TRUST TO RECORD	$304,950.00
TOTAL SALES PRICE	$321,000.00

Buyer to deliver to you any instruments and/or funds required from Buyer to enable you to comply with these instructions, all of which you are authorized to use and/or deliver on or before March 6, 20xx, and when you are in a position to obtain a standard Policy of Title Insurance through HOMETOWN TITLE, provided that said policy has a liability of at least the amount of the above total consideration, (new title policy to be delivered to lien holder), covering the following described property in ANY CITY, County of APPLE, State of CALIFORNIA:

SEE LEGAL DESCRIPTION ATTACHED HERETO AND MADE A PART HEREOF AS EXHIBIT
"A"
SELLER STATES PROPERTY ADDRESS IS:
987 OCEAN VIEW DRIVE, ANY CITY, CALIFORNIA 90000
INSURING TITLE VESTED IN:

DAN AND DONNA WINTER, HUSBAND AND WIFE AS COMMUNITY PROPERTY

SUBJECT ONLY TO:
CURRENT installment(s) of the General and special county, and city (if any) Taxes, including any special district levies, payments which are included therein and collected therewith, for current fiscal year, not delinquent, including taxes for ensuing year, if any, a lien not yet due or payable; personal property taxes, if any; covenants, conditions, reservations (including exceptions of oil, gas, minerals, and hydrocarbons, without right of surface entry), restrictions, rights, rights of way and easements for public utilities, districts, water companies, alley and streets, and any gas and oil leases.

INITIAL HERE: **SELLER ( ) ( )   BUYER ( ) ( )**

Any City Escrow, Inc.

24321 Riverfront Rd., Suite B, Any City, CA 90000
(555) 123-4567 telephone-(555) 321-5476 fax

BUYER AND SELLER ESCROW INSTRUCTIONS
Escrow No: 1-4035-J
Kelly Rose: Escrow Officer
Date: January 17, 20xx
Page: 2 of 5

THIS COMPANY IS LICENSED BY DEPT. OF CORPORATIONS

DEED OF TRUST to file, as obtained by the BUYER herein securing a Note in the amount of $304,950.00, in favor of Lender of BUYERS choice. Exact terms of loan to follow with loan documents and BUYERS execution of same shall indicate their full approval of all terms and conditions contained therein. Escrow Holder is authorized and instructed to comply with lenders instructions and requirements.

CLOSE OF ESCROW is subject to BUYER and PROPERTY qualifying for above financing with 6.5% initial adjustable rate with a maximum lifetime interest rate cap of 11% for 30 years, points not to exceed 1%. BUYER to provide verification of down payment funds within 48 hours of 1/17/20xx.

SELLER agrees to pay a maximum of $6,000.00 towards BUYERS non-recurring closing costs.

CLOSE OF ESCROW subject to Buyers approval of Preliminary Title Report within 7 days of receipt of same. In the event Escrow Holder is not in receipt of written disapproval within time period stated, Escrow Holder shall deem this contingency waived.

Seller to furnish Buyer with a One Year Home Protection Policy issued by SUNSHINE HOME WARRANTY CO., the cost of which is not to exceed $400.00 and is to be paid from Sellers Net Proceeds upon Close of Escrow.

BUYER shall hand you, prior to the close of escrow, completed, executed preliminary change of ownership to be attached to deed for recording per section 480.30 of revenue and taxation code and in the absence of said report or in the event the recorder deems said report to be incomplete, recorder shall impose $20.00 fee to BUYER.

INITIAL HERE: **SELLER (   ) (   )   BUYER (   ) (   )**

Any City Escrow, Inc.

24321 Riverfront Rd., Suite B, Any City, CA 90000
(555) 123-4567 telephone-(555) 321-5476 fax

BUYER AND SELLER ESCROW INSTRUCTIONS
Escrow No: 1-4035-J
Kelly Rose: Escrow Officer
Date: January 17, 20xx
Page: 3 of 5

THIS COMPANY IS LICENSED BY DEPT. OF CORPORATIONS

BUYER is made aware that the tax assessor has the right to impose a supplemental tax on subject property after the close of escrow, and in such event, said tax shall be the BUYER'S responsibility. BROKER, ESCROW HOLDER, and SELLER are relieved of any liability with regard to same. If the SELLER receives a supplemental tax bill prior to the close of escrow, escrow holder is to be notified, and same shall be paid accordingly.

CONDOMINIUM PLAN/P.U.D.: The subject of this transaction is a condominium/planned unit development (P.U.D.) designated as unit specified and specified parking space and an undivided interest in community areas, and _____.
The current monthly assessment charge by the homeowner's association or other governing body is $43 approx. As soon as practicable, Seller shall provide Buyer with copies of covenants conditions and restrictions, articles of incorporation, by-laws, current rules and regulations, most current financial statements, and any other documents as required by law. Seller shall disclose in writing any known pending special assessment, claims, or litigation to buyer. Buyer shall be allowed 7 calendar days from receipt to review these documents. If such documents disclose conditions or information unsatisfactory to Buyer, Buyer may cancel this agreement. BUYER'S FAILURE TO NOTIFY SELLER IN WRITING SHALL CONCLUSIVELY BE CONSIDERED APPROVAL.

BUYER to pay Homeowners Association transfer fee at close of escrow.

A pest control report per item 20 of the Real Estate Purchase Contract and Receipt for Deposit is a requirement of this escrow. Seller to pay for report and any corrective work required for a Notice of Completion. Buyer to pay for work in Section 2, if any.

INITIAL HERE: **BUYER (   ) (   )   SELLER (   ) (   )**

Any City Escrow, Inc.

24321 Riverfront Rd., Suite B, Any City, CA 90000
(555) 123-4567 telephone-(555) 321-5476 fax

BUYER AND SELLER ESCROW INSTRUCTIONS
Escrow No: 1-4035-J
Kelly Rose: Escrow Officer
Date: January 17, 20xx
Page: 4 of 5

THIS COMPANY IS LICENSED BY DEPT. OF CORPORATIONS

ESCROW HOLDER is specifically instructed by the undersigned Buyer and Seller to request that the new loan proceeds be deposited directly in the Any City Escrow, Inc. Trust Account for payoff of existing encumbrances and disbursement in accordance with these escrow instructions without the use of the title company sub-escrow. In the event the new Lender refuses to fund to Any City Escrow, Inc. and instead should direct funds to the title company in this transaction, Buyer and Seller herein instruct Escrow Holder to authorize recordation, regardless and agree to hold Any City Escrow, Inc. harmless and without liability in connection with funds on deposit with the title company.

CANCELLATION FEE: In the event of cancellation of this escrow, all parties are aware and agree that escrow holders is hereby authorized and instructed to charge a cancellation fee. Said Fee shall be determined upon the stage in the escrow and work done to date.

SELLER, BUYER, or BORROWER shall each pay their own respective closing costs, including their own portion of escrow fees, in connection with this transaction, unless otherwise stated herein.

AS A MEMORANDUM ITEM ONLY WITH WHICH ESCROW HOLDER IS NOT TO BE CONCERNED, it is agreed between BUYER AND SELLER outside of escrow that: BUYERS do intend to occupy subject property.

Possession of subject property is to be granted to BUYER 72 hours after close of escrow.

****

In accordance with the manner specified under the "General Provisions" attached hereto, you are authorized and instructed to adjust or prorate the following to CLOSE OF ESCROW: **PROPERTY TAXES AND HOMEOWNERS DUES.**

INITIAL HERE: **BUYER ( ) ( )   SELLER ( ) ( )**

Any City Escrow, Inc.

24321 Riverfront Rd., Suite B, Any City, CA 90000
(555) 123-4567 telephone-(555) 321-5476 fax

BUYER AND SELLER ESCROW INSTRUCTIONS
Escrow No: 1-4035-J
Kelly Rose: Escrow Officer
Date: January 17, 20xx
Page: 5 of 5

THIS COMPANY IS LICENSED BY DEPT. OF CORPORATIONS

THE FOREGOING TERMS, CONDITIONS AND INSTRUCTIONS, INCLUDING THE "GENERAL PROVISIONS" ATTACHED HERETO, (AS IF FULLY SET FORTH HEREIN), HAVE BEEN READ AND ARE UNDERSTOOD BY EACH OF THE UNDERSIGNED, WHO HEREBY AGREE TO, CONCUR WITH, APPROVE AND ACCEPT THE SAME IN THEIR ENTIRETY.

SELLER'S SIGNATURE: BUYER'S SIGNATURE:

_____   _____
SAM SUMMERS   DAN WINTER

_____   _____
KATE SUMMERS   DONNA WINTER

True False Quiz

Now that you have read all the material in this chapter, take the following self-test and check your knowledge of escrow instructions.

True/False

1. _TRUE_ A take sheet is the framework for the escrow instructions.

2. _TRUE_ Collecting the information needed to provide complete escrow instructions is the first step for an escrow agent.

3. _FALSE_ The three documents that serve as the heart of a sale escrow are the grant deed, promissory note, and bill of sale.

4. _FALSE_ A promissory note is the security for a debt.

5. _TRUE_ General instructions authorize the escrow holder to carry out general procedures needed to complete the escrow.

6. _FALSE_ General instructions are special instructions given by a buyer or a seller to the escrow holder.

7. _TRUE_ Third party instructions may include a demand or claim from a person not involved in the escrow as a principal.

8. _FALSE_ The escrow holder's obligation to the parties starts as soon as escrow instructions are written.

9. _FALSE_ Prorations are made based on a 25- day month.

10. _TRUE_ If rents are to be prorated, the escrow holder should prorate and debit the seller and credit the buyer with any deposits paid in advance to the seller by the tenants.

Chapter

8

Record Keeping and Prorations

Learning Objectives

After reading this chapter, you will be able to:

- define a Closing Statement.

- explain the escrow checklist for a selling broker.

- explain the escrow checklist for listing broker.

- describe Prorations.

Introduction

One of the closing agent's main jobs is to represent the obligations of each party in a personalized closing statement. The flow of consideration through escrow is outlined in the closing statement, as well as adjustments and disbursements reflecting the prior agreement of the parties.

The Closing Statement

The **closing statement** is where the accounting for the escrow is set down for the buyer and seller. It is a reflection of the parties' agreements and matches their wishes exactly. Both the seller and buyer are credited and debited for their agreed upon share of costs on the closing statement for the transaction.

The debit-credit columns shown on the closing statement are marked either *seller/lender* or *buyer/borrower*, depending on whether it describes a sale or loan escrow. The information from this statement will be used at the closing to conform to the Real Estate Settlement Procedures Act (RESPA).

If you recall from Chapter 7 (the Transaction Summary and the Any City Escrow, Inc. instructions), Dan and Donna Winter are buying a house from Sam and Kate Summers for $400,000. The transaction is due to close and all parties expect to be informed of the costs incurred during the escrow, as well as receive an accounting of the process.

The Seller's Statement

This represents the accounting the Summers will receive upon the transaction's closing.

Credits

The total consideration in the transaction is $400,000.00 as specified in the escrow instructions. CREDIT THE SELLER, DEBIT THE BUYER.

The first installment of taxes for the tax year was paid by the seller. A credit in the amount of $77.34, representing 15 days of prepaid property tax, is given to the seller. CREDIT THE SELLER, DEBIT THE BUYER.

The seller has prepaid 15 days of monthly homeowners' association dues at the rate of $50.00 per month, or 25.00. CREDIT THE SELLER, DEBIT THE BUYER.

Debits

The escrow holder was instructed to calculate rent from 12/16 to 12/31, or $400.00. DEBIT THE SELLER, CREDIT THE BUYER.

The payoff on the existing loan plus interest charges is a DEBIT TO THE SELLER.

The commission paid to the real estate broker, $24,000, is a DEBIT TO THE SELLER.

The seller has agreed to pay the $200.00 cost for the termite report. DEBIT THE SELLER.

It is the job of the title company to transfer the insured title to the buyer. DEBIT THE SELLER for the following items:

Title policy premium	$579.00
Reconveyance fee	60.00
Documentary transfer tax	440.00
Recording fee (reconveyance)	3.00
Total	$1,082.00

Balance

This figure represents the proceeds the seller can expect to receive.

Total Debits to the Seller

The end debits must balance with the corresponding credits.

Checklist of the Seller's Costs and Credits

Costs

Selling Commission	Title Insurance
Escrow Fee	Legal Fees
Prepayment Penalty	State or Local Transfer Tax
Pest Control Inspection Fee	Pest Control Work
Recording Fee	FHA or VA points
Reconveyance Fees	Notary Fee
Prorated Taxes	Personal Property Tax
Interest if paid in arrears	Prorated Rents
Security Deposits on hand	

Credits

Interest if paid in advance (from recordation to date of next loan payment)

Refund existing Trust Fund (Impound Account), if any

Prorated Taxes (if paid beyond recordation)

The Buyer's Statement

This statement represents the accounting the Winters will receive upon the closing of the transaction.

Credits

The money deposited by the buyer to open the escrow is noted as a CREDIT TO THE BUYER.

The amount of the new loan, $240,000.00, is a CREDIT TO THE BUYER.

The rental credit of $400, noted as a debit to the seller, is a CREDIT TO THE BUYER (for seller rent back).

The total amount CREDITED TO THE BUYER includes the remainder of the down payment that is due at the closing.

Debits

Items that have been credited to the seller are noted as debits to the buyer, such as the amount of total consideration, tax prorations, and association dues.

Charges made by the lender in connection with the new loan may be loan fees or advance collections for taxes or insurance. In this case, one month's interest is charged to the buyer. In addition, a tax service charge, credit report, appraisal fee, impound account deposit for taxes, two months' insurance, document fee and mortgage insurance are all listed as DEBITS TO THE BUYER.

Fees related to title company charges are DEBITED TO THE BUYER (lender's title policy premium and recording fees for deed and trust deed). The end debits must balance with the corresponding credits.

Checklist of the Buyer's Closing Costs and Credits

Non-Recurring Costs

- Title Insurance
- Legal Fees
- Appraisal Fee
- Credit Report
- Recording Fee
- Document Preparation Fee
- Underwriting Fee
- Verification Fee
- Escrow Fee
- Loan Fee
- Tax Service
- Notary Fee
- Pest Control Inspection
- Review/Application Fee
- Courier Fee
- Warehousing Fee

Recurring Costs
- Hazard Insurance
- Trust Fund or Impound Account
- Prorated Taxes (if paid beyond recordation)
- Prorated Interest (if charged in arrears: to end of month/if charged in advance: to date of first payment)

Credits
- Prorated Taxes
- Prorated Rents
- Security Deposits on hand

Escrow Checklist for the Selling Broker

As we have seen, in some areas the real estate broker handles many of the details of collecting information for the escrow and making sure all contingencies are met. In varying degrees, then, the real estate agent is important to the closing process. The following is a list of functions that may be performed by the selling broker.

The Selling Broker Functions

- Obtain increase of deposit

- Open the escrow

- Order credit report on the buyer (if required)

- Order pest control inspection

- Order other inspections (roof, etc., if required)

- Check on any contingencies to be eliminated

- Check occupancy permit

- Order loan commitment

- Assist the buyer with loan application and submit to the lender

- Arrange for hazard insurance

- Have closing instructions prepared and signed by the buyer

Escrow Checklist for the Listing Broker

Once again, in different areas, a real estate agent performs particular duties. The listing broker has a special list of jobs to perform in completing his or her commitment to the seller.

Duties of the Listing Broker

- Give notice of sale to the multiple listing service

- Check on increase of deposit

- Examine preliminary title report and assist in eliminating clouds on the title, if any

- Check on any contingencies to be eliminated

- Request title company or escrow company to order pay-off demand, or statement of condition and assumption papers from lender

- Check with selling broker on the buyer's loan

- If income property, obtain rent schedule, rent due dates, Security deposits, copies of leases, names and phone numbers of tenants

- Have the seller's instructions prepared and signed

- If the seller carries a second loan, have the escrow holder record a "Request for copy of Notice of Default" and subscribe to a tax agency

- Obtain the seller's future address and phone number

Prorations

Items to be prorated by the closing agent such as taxes and insurance and rents may be calculated using proration tables, financial calculators, or software created specifically for that purpose. In addition to understanding the principles used to determine the percentages or dollar figures shown on the proration tables, the closing agent must be able to calculate simple prorations.

The proper time period in which to prorate items must be established first. The day of closing is not included for proration purposes. In completing the prorations for a transaction, time is converted to a day factor, either as an amount per day or as a percentage of the total time period for the transaction. Prorations are typically based on a 30-day month and a 360-day year.

Time Periods for Prorations
- **Taxes:** based on 180 days or six months
- **Insurance:** usually based on a 360-day year
- **Rents:** based on a 30-day month

Taxes

Tax prorations are based on due dates for taxes. Real property tax becomes a lien on the property assessed on March 1 preceding the tax year for which the taxes are due. Remember, the tax, or fiscal year is from July 1 through the following June 30.

Regardless of the time other liens are created, real property taxes have priority over any other liens on the property. The payment of property tax is enforced by the sale of the subject property in a manner dictated by statute.

Taxes are due twice yearly. The first half is due on November 1 and becomes delinquent December 10. The second half is due February 1 and becomes delinquent April 10.

Memory Aid for Tax Due Dates	
No	Nov 1
Darn	December 10
Fooling	February 1
Around	April 10

Each year, after April 10, a delinquent roll is prepared showing all property upon which taxes are due.

In addition, each year, before June 8, a delinquency list of real property taxes is published in local newspapers describing a date upon which the delinquent property will be "sold to the state". The property is not really "sold to the state", with the state taking possession or ownership. The taxpayer retains legal title to the

property and enjoys possession during the five-year redemption period.

The term "sold to the state" refers to a bookkeeping transaction that starts a five-year period during which the owner may pay all delinquent taxes, cost, penalties, and interest, and return the property to its former lien-free status. At the end of the five-year redemption period, if the delinquency has not been cured, the property is sold at a tax sale, with no recourse by the former owner allowed.

Additional taxes may be levied at the time of a sale to reflect the sales price. These are called supplemental taxes and should be expected by the parties to an escrow. The buyer completes a *Preliminary Change of Ownership* form, which informs the tax assessor of the possible change in value. At that time, the tax assessor may levy a supplemental tax for that tax year based on the sales price, and send it to the buyer. This usually occurs outside of escrow and is not a matter for the closing agent.

A supplemental tax may also be assessed if an improvement to the real property is completed during the tax-billing period (before November 1). After the improvement has been assessed, the tax collector will calculate the new taxes on a prorated basis, depending on the improvement's date of completion. The new tax generally is based on 1% of the market value or sales price, plus a part of a percentage for local or county taxes or special assessments. The tax is prorated based on the closing date of the transaction.

Taxes on a property may decrease if the value of the property has declined, and the supplemental tax will reflect the change.

Calculation of Prorated Taxes

The close of escrow is 10/25/20xx, and the seller has not paid the first installment of property taxes of $980.00, which is due 11/01/20xx. Both the buyer and the seller must pay a portion of the taxes. To calculate the amounts owed, prorate the tax according to the number of days in the tax year each party owned the property.

To Prorate Taxes:

1. First, calculate the cost of taxes per day for the six- month period in question.

    $980 = taxes for 180 days (six months)

    $980 divided by 180 = $5.44 /day

2. Count the number of days during the tax period in question when the seller owned the property.

    July 1 to September 30 = 90 days

    October 1 to October 24 = 24 days

    90 days plus 24 days = 114 days

3. The seller owned the property 114 days of current tax period

    114 (days) x $5.44 (taxes/day) = $620.16 (amount owed by the seller)

4. Subtract $620.16 from the total tax charged to the seller. The buyer owes the difference.

    $980.00 less $620.16 = $359.84 (amount owed by the buyer)

Insurance

Traditionally, the type of insurance required by lenders and expected by the buyers was fire insurance. Today, there are several types of policies covering various types of damage, such as earthquake or flood destruction. In any case, the closing agent may prorate some of the policies and some might be done by the insurer. If calculations are required for insurance prorations, the following example will be helpful:

The buyer is taking over a three-year policy with a premium of $1,200, which the seller had prepaid. It was effective May 13, 2005, to be prorated as of the closing, October 25, 2007, using a 30-day month and a 360-day year:

1. Determine number of days to be prorated:

	Year	Month	Day	Total
10/25/2007	2007	10	25	
5/13/2005	-2005	-5	-13	
	2	5	12	
	x360	x30	x1	
	720	150	12	882

2. Then calculate the cost per day for the term of the policy by dividing $1,200 by 1,080 (the number of days in the three-year policy) to arrive at $1.11.

3. Finally, multiply the total number of days to be prorated, or 882, by $1.11 to arrive at $979.00, or the dollar amount of the premium that has been used.

4. Subtracting $979.00 from the cost of the policy, or $1,200, the seller would be credited $221, and the buyer debited the same amount.

Rents

Normally, a 30-day month is used to prorate rents. The closing agent must be aware that rents are collected in advance and should be prorated accordingly.

A triplex with the following rents is in escrow with the transaction to close on September 25, 20xx.

> Apartment A = $780 paid through 12/30/20xx
> Apartment B = $780 paid through 12/30/20xx
> Apartment C = $780 paid through 12/30/20xx

Prorating Rents

1. The closing agent must first calculate the amount of daily rent by dividing the monthly rent of $780 by 30, or $26 a day.

2. The buyer will be taking title on the 25th day of September, and should be credited for 6 days of rent (the total days between September 25 and September 30).

3. By multiplying 6 (days) x $26 (the daily rental cost) to get $156 per unit, the closing agent can multiply that amount by 3 (apartments), and credit the buyer with $468.00.

The seller must provide information about when the rents are collected, as well as the amounts of security deposits, cleaning deposits, and any other funds that are to be transferred at the closing. An accounting is done at the closing to reflect funds to be transferred to the buyer or remain with the seller.

Loan Assumptions/Loan Payoffs

The escrow holder must be very careful in calculating the amounts when loans are involved. Terms of a beneficiary statement in the case of a loan assumption, or the demand statement in the case of a loan payoff, must be observed carefully by the closing agent.

There are certain items of which the closing agent must be especially aware.

Loan Assumption/Loan Payoff

- A beneficiary statement is a statement of the unpaid balance of a loan and the condition of the indebtedness and is requested from the lender when a buyer is assuming an existing loan or purchasing the property subject to that loan. A demand statement or demand for pay-off is requested from an existing lender when a buyer is obtaining a new loan.

- **Payment Date** - Most loans are paid monthly. Even though this is usually the case, payments on some loans are due quarterly, semi-annually, or annually.

- **Payment Status** - The closing agent must be aware of whether or not all current loan payments are being made in a timely manner. In case the payments are not kept current, any statements of loan condition should not be ordered until the very last part of the escrow period.

- **Impounds** - In the case where existing impounds must be credited to the correct party, the closing agent must receive instructions about the amount and to whom it is entitled.

  If the buyer is obtaining a new loan with an impound account, the lender determines the amount of additional funds required from the buyer to establish the account and includes the amount in the loan documents.

- **How is the Loan Paid?** Are the payments interest only, partially amortized with a balloon payment or fully amortized?

- **Calculating Loan Payoff or Assumptions** - In the typical loan payoff, the payment is being made in arrears. It also must be determined whether the lender requires payment to the date of closing or to the date the lender receives the payoff funds. Because of this requirement, the money required for closing could change. Interest between the buyer and seller must be allocated carefully by the closing agent.

Miscellaneous Prorations

In addition to property taxes and interest, closing agents may have other items to be prorated. Homeowners' association assessments or other items that may have been prepaid by the seller or assumed by the buyer must be calculated and prorated to the close of escrow.

SMS SETTLEMENT SERVICES
THE SELLER'S ESTIMATED CLOSING STATEMENT

Seller: Sam Summers
        Kate Summers

Escrow No: 004860-999 DW
Close Date: 01-01-20xx
Proration Date: 12-31-20xx
Date Prepared: 11/22/20xx

Property: 987 Ocean View Drive
            Any City, CA 90000

Description	Debit	Credit
TOTAL CONSIDERATION:		189,900.00
NEW AND EXISTING ENCUMBRANCES:		
County Taxes from 1-20-20xx to 1/31-20xx		238.33
Based on the annual amount of $7,800.00		
Assessments from 1-01-20xx to 1-01-20xx		100.00
County Taxes 1-01-20xx to 3-31-20xx	293.33	
Based on the annual amount of $1,200.00		
PAYOFFS:		
Payoff to Any City Bank	68,045.63	
67,595.00 Principal balance		
450.63 Interest from 12-01-20xx to 1-31-20xx		
ESCROW AND TITLE CHARGES:		
Settlement/Closing Fee to SMS SETTLEMENT SERVICES	175.00	
Title Examination to SMS SETTLEMENT SERVICES	250.00	
Attorney's Fees to Rose and Green	85.00	
Title Insurance to SMS SETTLEMENT SERVICES	813.00	
RECORDING FEES:		
City/County Tax Stamps to SMS SETTLEMENT SERVICES	36.00	
COMMISSIONS:	11,394.00	
5,697.00 to Sunshine Real Estate		
5,697.00 to ABC Realty Company		
Sub Totals	261,184.29	190,238.33
Balance Due from Seller		70,945.96
Totals	261,184.29	261,184.29

_____

Sam Summers

Trustor of the First Street Trust

_____

Kate Summers

BUYER'S ESTIMATED CLOSING STATEMENT

Buyer: Dan Winter
        Donna Winter

Escrow No: 004860-999 DW
Close Date: 01-01-20xx
Proration Date: 12-31-20xx
Date Prepared: 11/22/20xx

Property: 987 Ocean View Drive
        Any City, CA 90000

Description	Debit	Credit
TOTAL CONSIDERATION:		
Total Consideration	189,900	
Deposit/Earnest Money		5,000
NEW AND EXISTING ENCUMBRANCES:		
Existing Loan Amount from Any City Bank		180,000
NEW LOAN CHARGES		
Loan Origination Fee to Any City Bank	180,000	
Loan Discount to Any City Bank	180,000	
Appraisal Fee to Any City Bank	350.00	
Credit Report to XYZ Credit Services	15.00	
Servicing/Document Prep. to Any City Bank	250.00	
Credit Line to Any City Bank	200.00	
Tax Service to Any City Bank	68.50	
Underwriting Fee to Any City Bank	75.00	
Hazard Insurance Premium to Any City Bank	1,200.00	
Hazard Insurance to Any City Bank	100.00	
City Property Taxes to Any City Bank	600.00	
County Property Taxes to Any City Bank	400.00	
PRORATIONS AND ADJUSTMENTS:		
County Taxes from 1-20-20xx to 1-31-20xx	238.33	
Based on annual amount of $7,800.00		
County Taxes 1-01-20xx to 3-29-20xx		293.33
Based on the annual amount of $1,200.00		
ESCROW AND TITLE CHARGES:		
Settlement/Closing Fee to SMS SETTLEMENT SERVICES	176.00	
Title Insurance to SMS SETTLEMENT SERVICES	60.00	
Credit line Endorsement to SMS SETTLEMENT SERVICES	75.00	
Transfer Fee to SMS SETTLEMENT SERVICES	25.00	
RECORDING FEES		
Recording Fees to SMS SETTLEMENT SERVICES	20.50	
ADDITIONAL CHARGES		
Survey to Hillcrest Surveying	350.00	
Pest Inspection to D.I. Green Exterminating Co.	200.00	
Overnight Delivery Fee to First Lenders Mortgage	75.00	
Sub Totals	194,727.33	185,386.66
Balance Due From Buyer		9,340.67
Totals	194,727.33	194,727.33

True-False Quiz

Now that you have read all the material in this chapter, take the following self-test and check your knowledge of record keeping and prorations.

True/False

1. _____ *False* Items that are credits to the seller are debits to the buyer.

2. _____ *True* Taxes and rents are usually prorated.

3. _____ *False* The day of closing is included for proration purposes.

4. _____ *True* Prorations are based on a 30-day month.

5. _____ *True* Proration of taxes is based on 180 days or six months.

6. _____ *False* The first installment of property tax is due on December 1.

7. _____ *False* Supplementary taxes are paid by the seller.

8. _____ *True* The buyer's new taxes are generally calculated on 1% of the purchase price plus part of a percentage for local or county taxes or special assessments.

9. _____ *False* Life insurance is required by most lenders.

10. _____ *True* Property taxes are due twice yearly.

Chapter 9

Processing and Closing

Learning Objectives

After reading this chapter, you will be able to:

- explain escrow instructions.

- discuss the requirements for closing and the closing statement

- define transfer, financing, and other documents needed for closing.

- summarize document conveyance.

- explain the final closing review, and the processes of closing and recording.

Introduction

The major commitment of an escrow holder is to complete all the terms of the agreement between the principals. Both in the manner desired and in the time period specified, the escrow holder must perform the appointed tasks. Upon satisfaction of all requirements of the escrow, including loan approval and removal of contingencies, then, and only then, can the escrow close. One of the major tasks, as the closing nears, is to make sure all requirements of the escrow have been met. As we have seen, the escrow holder has the original take sheet to use as a guide to assure a smooth closing. Each part of the transaction must be evaluated and double-checked for accuracy. The following is a list of items that have been ongoing throughout the processing of the escrow. This list can be used as a guide for review just prior to closing.

Items to be Reviewed

- Legal description of property as well as street address if applicable

- Current ownership information

- Any particular conditions or contingencies of the sale, such as the escrow being subject to the sale of the buyer's current home, or subject to loan approval

- Deeds of trust to be created, along with terms, conditions and responsibilities imposed by lender

- Loans to be assumed/impounds involved

- If the loan is current

- If the assumption is subject to lender approval

- Hazard and other insurance provisions

- Charges to the buyer and the seller

- Commission instructions

- Separate loan escrow instructions required for loans other than purchase money

- Legal name of buyer and method of taking title

- Personal property included in the sale (only personal property for identification purposes)

- Pest control inspection

- Prorations

- Other requirements particular to the transaction

Joint Escrow Instructions

Currently, the approach to conducting escrow is to use the Purchase Agreement as escrow instructions. The California Association of REALTORS® (C.A.R.) updates their forms regularly, so it is critical to stay current with all documentation. The Residential Purchase Agreement and Joint Escrow Instructions initiate both the sale and escrow process, and allows for conformity in escrow practices throughout the state.

The purchase agreement combines the original contract between the buyer and the seller with the joint escrow instructions into one form. This should reflect the mutual and agreed upon desires of the parties when it becomes the actual escrow instructions. Any mutual changes are made using an addendum to the original contract rather than amendment to escrow instructions.

An escrow is opened when a real estate agent brings the signed purchase agreement to the escrow holder, who makes a copy and accepts it by signing off in the required box in the document. The escrow holder should be concerned with whether or not the contract is complete, fully signed and

initialed before accepting it. The contract must be valid before it can become instructions for the escrow.

In addition to the purchase agreement as escrow instructions, an escrow holder will submit an acceptance or additional escrow instructions for the buyer's and the seller's signatures. These instructions will include any other terms that need to be agreed upon by the buyer and the seller to complete the escrow.

Local Variations

As we have seen, processing is done differently in the northern and southern parts of California. In Northern California, an estimated closing statement is issued as part of the instructions, showing, for example, the proceeds going to the seller and the estimated cash needed to close for the buyer. In Southern California, the broker's net sheet serves the same purpose, except the closing statement is provided at the settlement.

Northern California

The buyers and the sellers in Northern California each sign separate instructions at the end of the escrow period. These unilateral instructions represent the end of the transfer process and describe the agreement between the parties to the escrow. The closing agent, however, has been carrying out specific duties, as ordered by the principals, since the opening of  the escrow, even though no instructions have been signed. The instructions also apportion closing costs to the appropriate parties. After signing the instructions, all that remains to be completed is the provision of funds from the buyer and the lender.

The contents of the buyer and the seller's instructions differ in requirements for closing. The buyer's instructions call for consideration to be given by the buyer when all documents of title transfer have been signed and the escrow is in a position to close. The seller's instructions provide for the necessary documents of transfer in exchange for consideration (either money, or money and debt obligation) by the buyer.

A complication that may arise out of having separate instructions is a breakdown of communication between the buyer and the seller.

The buyer or the seller may have changed some part of the transaction without getting the approval of the other party, and at the closing, everyone is surprised. The buyer might decide to change financing arrangements, or one party could change his or her mind about the time of closing or possession. Any number of items could require amendments for all parties to sign before the closing can occur. In Northern California, the real estate broker produces the amendments to the purchase contract and gives copies to the closer.

When the buyer and the seller sign unilateral escrow instructions, they are approving the previously ordered actions of the escrow holder. They are acknowledging that demands have been satisfied, title reports completed, the amount of pest control work determined and any new loans approved. The unilateral instructions act principally as a closing statement. Closing costs for the buyer and the seller are disclosed separately in each of their instructions.

Southern California

In the bilateral escrow instructions of the southern part of California, the shared promises of the buyer and the seller are joined into one document. That instruction contains conditions of the buyer's purchase as well as general (boilerplate) instructions for both parties about requirements of the escrow. The seller agrees to the necessary steps to place title in the name of the buyer.

When bilateral instructions are used, amendments are common as a transaction progresses. Because escrow instructions are a binding contract between the buyer and the seller, any changes in the original instructions require the signature of both the buyer and the seller on an amendment stating the desired changes. No changes may be made without the agreement of all parties to the escrow.

Requirements for Closing

Certain protective or disclosure clauses may be included in escrow instructions that go beyond the personal, original agreements of the parties. These clauses limit the closing agent's responsibility and liability regarding the conformity to tax codes and other legal requirements.

Supplemental Tax Roll: All parties must be made aware that tax bills sent after the closing may increase or decrease the tax level imposed on the property being transferred.

Preliminary Change of Ownership Report: The buyer is required to complete this change of ownership form before closing. The purpose is to inform the county tax assessor of the change in ownership so new taxes can be calculated from the date of closing and the new owner billed appropriately.

FIRPTA. Both federal and state tax laws are affected by the **Foreign Investment in Real Property Tax Act** (FIRPTA). In both cases, the buyer is responsible for making sure either the proper disclosures have been made and/or the proper funds have been set aside. Generally, the broker and escrow agent make sure this is done. All documents must be kept by the broker and the buyer for five years. Federal law requires that a buyer of real property must withhold and send to the Internal Revenue Service (IRS) 10% of the gross sales price if the seller of the real property is a foreign person.

Due to the number of exceptions and other requirements relating to this law, it is recommended that the IRS be consulted. Sellers, buyers, and the real estate agents involved who desire further advice should consult an attorney, CPA, or other qualified tax advisor.

Exceptions from the FIRPTA Withholding Requirement

- The buyer must sign a Buyer's Affidavit of Residency, stating whether he or she is a resident or citizen, that the sales price of the property does not exceed $300,000, and that the property will be used as a residence.

- The seller, under penalty of perjury, must sign a Seller's Affidavit of Non-foreign Status, stating that he or she is not a foreigner.

- The seller gives the buyer a qualifying statement obtained through the IRS saying arrangements have been made for the collection of or exemption from the tax.

Health and Safety Code Provisions

Retrofit Requirements: Smoke detectors must be installed in all sold residential properties and a disclosure must be given to the buyer as a result of state law.

The Closing Statement

An escrow has been completed when all documents have been signed, all contingencies have been met, all requirements fulfilled, all money (and other consideration) has been collected and deposited with the closing agent. The closing agent can now request recordation of documents and distribute the proceeds to the proper parties. A closing statement is then prepared by the closing agent for the buyer and the seller, explaining the disposition of funds, and credits and debits made to their account.

When all is in order, the closing agent must determine the charges and account for the following items:

Sales price

Was the final sales price the same as it was originally?

Deposits

Have all moneys been disbursed or used according to instructions from all parties?

Trust deeds

Have all trust deeds of record been verified as to balance, interest rate and terms?

Payoff of existing debt

Did the seller approve a payoff of existing debt against the property, including any pre-payment penalty?

Impound account

How are existing impound accounts to be transferred to buyer?

New loan

Are all terms of the new loan agreeable to buyer (amount, interest rate, charges)?

Prorations

Have prorations been made according to instruction regarding interest on any existing debt, homeowners' association fees, taxes, insurance, and rents?

Association transfer fee

Were instructions given regarding payment of association transfer fee (who pays it)?

Supplemental tax provisions

How is the supplemental tax bill to be paid?

Commission

Has the seller approved payment of commission to real estate broker?

Fees

Have the buyer and the seller agreed, in the instructions, to fees incurred during the escrow?

Incidental charges

Have instructions been given by the buyer and the seller regarding supplementary charges such as judgments, tax liens, credit card payoffs, private note payments, or purchase of personal property?

Outside of escrow

Are there any special agreements between the buyer and the seller about money being disbursed outside of escrow?

Remaining balance

There may be a balance due to the seller or a refund to the buyer. If the buyer has not deposited enough money, the escrow is short and may not close.

Transfer Documents

A contract is formed between the parties as soon as the instructions are complete and signed by the principals. At the same time the escrow instructions are being prepared, the escrow holder is preparing documents needed for the transfer of ownership from the seller to the buyer.

In most cases, the document of transfer will be a grant deed. As you recall, a grant deed is a statement granting title, prepared according to written instruction from the parties. It must be signed and notarized by the seller and returned to the escrow holder with the signed escrow instructions.

An important job of the escrow holder at this point, when preparing to close, is to verify that the grant deed and the instructions conform exactly and to make sure the grant deed is completed as required by the county recorder.

The assessor's parcel number ("APN") must be identified correctly on the grant deed in order for the county recorder to accept the document for recording.

The documentary transfer tax must be computed by the escrow holder and the information added to the grant deed in the space provided. As you recall, the transfer tax is calculated based on $1.10 per thousand of the purchase price. It is computed on the consideration or purchase price or on the consideration or purchase price less remaining encumbrances if the buyer is assuming the existing loan.

The grant deed must be prepared exactly to the specifications of the county recorder or it will be rejected and sent back to the escrow holder. Some common mistakes made by the escrow holders, requiring a new deed to be drawn, signed by the seller, notarized and submitted for recording, are:

Common Mistakes in Grant Deeds

- Notary seal unclear or incomplete

- Notarization incorrect or notary commissions expired

- Signatures not clear, missing or questionable

- Legal description of property not clearly visible in photocopy attached to deed

- Property in question in another county

Other documents of transfer might be a patent deed if the transfer is between the government and a private individual, a gift deed or a tax deed.

Financing Documents

When a property is sold, usually some form of financing is involved. Commonly the buyer applies for a new loan, and that, along with the buyer's down payment, constitutes the financing.

Other types of financing may be involved in a sale as well. The seller could carry back a note secured by a deed of trust, or a Contract of Sale could be used to secure the financing.

Types of Financing

- Note and Trust Deed

- Contract of Sale

Whatever the case, the escrow holder must be certain that all the documents are in order regarding the financing of the sale before the transaction can close.

The most common document used in a sale is a promissory note. The promissory note is the evidence of the debt created by a loan. It indicates the exact terms of the loan, including any special clauses agreed upon by the borrower and the lender. The note is included for the borrower's signature in the loan documents.

Loan documents are usually prepared by the lender and ordered in a timely manner by the escrow holder when the escrow is ready to close. Commonly, the borrower (buyer) brings in the remainder of the down payment and signs the loan documents, including the note and trust deed in the presence of the escrow holder.

The trust deed is the security for the loan and is also included in the loan documents. This document creates a lien on the buyer's new property once it is recorded. The trust deed includes the name of the borrower, the trustee, the beneficiary (lender), the amount owed, along with the legal description of the property. It does not have to be recorded to be valid, but should be recorded to preserve the lender's priority in case of default. In almost all cases, recording is a requirement of the lender.

Upon the close of the escrow, the escrow holder sends the trust deed, along with the grant deed and any other documents requiring filing, to the county recorder's office for recording.

Other Documents Needed for Closing

Escrow instructions are reviewed by the escrow holder to determine what documents other than a grant deed and financing instruments are needed for the closing.

The preliminary title report, which most likely was ordered at the start of the escrow, is reviewed by the escrow holder for liens or other complications or disagreement with the escrow instructions.

If any surprises show up, such as a lien for delinquent taxes or a trust deed not previously mentioned by the seller, the escrow holder must contact the principals for direction in the matter. Any changes must be approved, in writing, by all parties.

If any lien holders are to be paid off at the close, a demand must be ordered by the escrow holder. A demand is simply a statement of condition of a loan, including the amount owed along with a request for payment in full.

Document Conveyance

Certain documents require review and processing by the title company issuing the policy of title insurance as well as the tax assessor.

Prior to the close, the properly notarized deed is sent to the title insurance company. The title officer of the title insurance company will examine the deed to verify its acceptability for recording. Correct name and vesting for the buyer are verified, as well as the uninterrupted chain of title.

In Northern California, this requires little more than sending the documents to another department within the title company conducting the escrow. After the notarized trust deed has been signed by the buyer, it is sent to the title company for examination and held for further instruction from the escrow holder. Certain confidential information about the buyer and the seller is required by the title company to assure certain identity of the parties. Also, the general index at the title company is checked for judgments against either party that might affect the closing.

A preliminary change of ownership report is required by the tax assessor as a result of the sale. It must be prepared at the closing and sent to the assessor.

Final Closing Review

Most escrow holders will use a checklist to make sure all parties have complied with the terms of the instructions. Often, the escrow folder is printed with this checklist. As the escrow progresses, the agent notes each item as it is completed. Some of the more important items to be reviewed are emphasized below.

Instructions

Have escrow instructions been signed by all parties and returned to the escrow holder? Have all parties with a vested interest in the transaction been included in the instructions?

Supplemental Instructions

Have there been amendments or modifications in the original instructions? Have all changes been reflected in writing and signed by all parties?

Disbursements

Has instruction been given to the escrow holder regarding disbursements? Typically, disbursements include:

- real estate broker commissions.

- existing loan payoffs.

- loan escrow approval.

- title fees.

- pest control work.

- withholding funds for work to be done after escrow closes.

- bills to be presented.

Legal Description

A mistake in the legal description could cause the wrong property to be transferred and incur liability by the parties responsible for the error.

Fire Insurance

The escrow holder must be sure the fire insurance coverage is sufficient, and the insurance company is approved by the lender.

Correct Names on Documents

The name of the buyer on the preliminary title report must agree with the name of the person taking title to the property. Has the buyer's name and vesting been correctly copied to the appropriate documents?

Sufficient Funds

The escrow file cannot be closed unless there are sufficient funds from the seller and the buyer.

Checks Cleared

Both the buyer and the seller should be notified prior to the closing that only cashiers' or certified checks may be used to close the escrow. If personal checks are used, time must be allowed for them to clear prior to closing.

Taxes

Have funds been withheld or exemption filed to comply with the Foreign Investment in Real Property Tax Act (FIRPTA)? If the seller is not a citizen, the escrow holder must hold a percentage of the sale proceeds for the IRS in single-family residential sales of more than $300,000 and in transactions other than residential of more than $50,000, unless parties qualify for exemption.

Has Form 1099-S been filed by the escrow holder? The escrow holder must prepare a 1099-S with the seller's name, the seller's tax identification number, and the amount of consideration passing in the transaction.

Pest Control

Has all required work been completed? If not, has escrow been instructed to withhold funds for work to be completed after the close of escrow?

Closing/Recording

Upon completion of all steps required in the escrow instructions, and after final escrow costs and prorations are computed as of the date of closing, the escrow holder arranges for the buyer to bring in a cashier's check for the amount needed to close the escrow. That would usually include the remainder of the down payment and closing costs.

At that point, depending on the locale of the escrow, the buyer might sign escrow instructions along with loan documents. If escrow instructions have already been signed and returned to escrow, only the promissory note and trust deed still need to be signed by the buyer and notarized.

If the seller has not signed escrow instructions, or the grant deed, he or she must do so before the transaction can be completed.

If all is ready, the grant deed, trust deed or deeds, and any other documents that need to be recorded are sent to the title company for final examination and recording upon closing.

Upon notification from the escrow holder, funds are sent, by wire, to the title company from the lender with the request that the title company ensure that the title is clear (all liens have been paid). The title company must have sufficient funds from the lender to pay the loan of record, any tax liens, problems that show up on the preliminary title report, and other necessary payoffs before title insurance is issued.

When the title company has received all the necessary documents and has received the money from the lender, the escrow may close.

Before releasing any funds or recording any documents, the title company clears any existing loans, taxes, and any recorded liens against the property. However, the title company is only concerned with paying off matters affecting the title. All other charges relating to the transaction are prorated and/or paid through the sale escrow.

Requirements for Closing
- All contingencies and requirements of escrow are met
- Escrow instructions are signed by all parties
- Grant deed is signed by the seller and notarized
- The escrow holder orders loan documents
- The buyer brings in closing funds
- Loan documents are signed by the borrower and notarized
- The escrow holder sends original signed promissory note and copy of signed trust deed back to the lender
- The escrow holder funds are sent from the lender to the title company

- The title company records original deed, trust deed or deeds in order of priority, as required by the transaction

- The title company pays off all liens and other amounts due to clear the title after a final review of documents

- Any surplus funds are sent to the escrow holder for disbursement

After the title company records all documents and pays all existing loans and encumbrances of record, the balance of funds, if any, are sent by the title company to the escrow holder for disbursement and proration to the parties according to escrow instructions.

The escrow holder makes all payments to the buyer, the seller, real estate agents, termite company, insurance company, construction company, and any other demands on the escrow that may have accumulated.

The escrow holder prepares the closing statements for the buyer and the seller. All deposits and other prorations are either debited or credited to the buyer or the seller, and the seller gets a check for the amount due after selling expenses.

True-False Quiz

Now that you have read all the material in this chapter, take the following self-test and check your knowledge of processing and closing escrow.

True/False

1. _FALSE_ Buyers and sellers in Northern California do not sign separate escrow instructions.

2. _TRUE_ Unilateral instructions are used in Northern California.

3. _TRUE_ Bilateral instructions are used in Southern California.

4. _TRUE_ Disclosure clauses limit the closing agent's responsibility and liability regarding the conformity to tax codes and other legal requirements.

5. _TRUE_ Both federal and state tax laws are affected by the Foreign Investment in Real Estate Property Tax Act (FIRPTA).

6. _TRUE_ Smoke detectors must be installed in all sold residential properties.

7. _TRUE_ In most cases, the document of transfer will be a grant deed.

8. _FALSE_ Loan documents are usually prepared by the title company.

9. _FALSE_ A demand is a statement of loan default.

10. _FALSE_ A grant deed does not HAVE to be notarized to be recorded.

Chapter
10

Contingencies

Learning Objectives

After reading this chapter, you will be able to:

- discuss working with contingencies.

- summarize the processes of cancellation.

- explain the variations on the sale escrow including contract of sale, subject to sale, and loan assumption sales.

Introduction

Escrows are opened, in the majority of cases, with the hopes and expectation that the agreement of the parties will prevail and the transaction will close. That, however, is not always the case. An escrow can fail to close, or "fall out" for many reasons. As a matter of fact, it is a miracle so many escrows manage to close considering all the contingencies that must be removed before the contract can be completed.

Along with contingencies, an escrow holder must deal with special types of transactions as well. While most escrows are typical, the escrow holder must be aware of all unusual factors and be able to provide instructions for escrows that vary from those commonly opened by both buyers and sellers. We shall see here what an escrow holder can expect when special circumstances prevail. Instructions must reflect any uncommon or unusual meeting of the minds between the parties, as well as the familiar agreements.

Contingencies

A contingency requires the completion of a certain act or the happening of a certain event before a contract is binding. The parties themselves, by imposing contingencies, may cause obstacles to the closing process. In some cases, the contingencies are so abundant that it seems there can never be a meeting of the minds close enough for the transaction to be completed.

As you know, once escrow instructions have been signed by all parties, neither party may unilaterally change the content of the contract. All parties to the escrow may instruct the escrow holder to change the instructions, by mutual agreement.

At the opening of the escrow, the parties already have agreed, in the original deposit receipt, that certain items will be resolved during the process of the escrow. If one party decides that certain contingencies are no longer valid, or wants to add contingencies to the agreement, both must agree.

The problem is, people dislike rethinking decisions. Given another chance to decide, one party may balk at any change. Now we have a situation where someone must renegotiate between the parties or the escrow is at a stalemate. That person is *not* the escrow holder.

The escrow agent is considered a neutral party and is only required to provide written instructions reflecting the mutual thinking of the parties to the escrow. Joining the parties in their controversies or settling them is not part of the job. Keeping the escrow moving along and following the written instructions *is* the job, however.

No matter how carefully everyone tries to escape the possibility of new contingencies being created, it happens more times than not. One of the benefits to the deposit receipt commonly used is that the document includes just about every item that both the buyers and sellers need to agree on at the start of the transaction. Even so, parties to any escrow must confirm or deny their acceptance of contingency removals, according to their prior agreement.

The unilateral instructions used in Northern California also offer a benefit. Between the time escrow instructions are drawn and the end of the escrow process, changes have been arranged by the broker as amendments to the original deposit receipt. The escrow holder is presented with the finished agreement in writing.

In the southern part of the state, however, many times amendment after amendment to the escrow instruction is drawn to keep up with the demanding progression of the escrow. At the end, sometimes the demand overwhelms the ability of the parties to come to a decision and the escrow falls-out.

In reality, then, the deposit receipt is nothing more than an executory contract, with the parties waiting in suspense for the outcome of each contingency removal during the escrow period.

As stated in the deposit receipt, time is of the essence, especially regarding contingencies. This means each contingency must be met in a timely manner, exactly as described in the contract. If the contingency is not accepted or rejected in the manner specified, within the stated restriction of time, the contract is voidable.

There are certain parts of the deposit receipt that contain matters which must be resolved during the escrow and upon which the transaction depends. Escrow instructions will reflect these items also. If all contingencies are not met in a timely manner, the escrow is voidable by the injured party. In other words, the party waiting for satisfaction from the contingency being met has the right to cancel the escrow if the time period is not observed. Once again, the escrow holder must receive signed cancellation orders from all parties for the escrow to be terminated.

Financing

Financing must be obtained, obviously, before the buyer can complete the sale. Terms and conditions of financing are described in the deposit receipt as well as a time period for the buyer and property to qualify for any loans. The escrow also is contingent on agreements about existing and/or seller financing being executed.

Escrow Instructions

Escrow instructions must be signed within the time frame specified in the original deposit receipt.

Condominium

The buyer must receive and approve a copy of CC&Rs as well as any pertinent information on the condition of the homeowners' association within a certain number of days after receiving them.

The Buyer's Investigation of Property Condition

The buyer has the right to inspect and approve of the property within a specified time frame. The seller must be given copies of all reports from inspections.

The buyer is advised to investigate the condition and suitability of all aspects of the property, as well as all matters affecting its value, including the following items:

- built-in appliances, structural, foundation, roof, plumbing, heating, air conditioning, electrical, mechanical, security, pool/spa systems and components, and any personal property included in the sale.

- square footage, room dimensions, lot size, and age of improvements to the property.

- property lines and boundaries.

- sewer, septic and well systems and components. (Property may not be connected to sewer, and applicable fees may not have been paid. Septic tank may need to be pumped and each field may need to be inspected.)

- limitations, restrictions and requirements regarding property use, future development, zoning, building, size, government permits, and inspections.

- water and utility availability and use restrictions.

- potential environmental hazards including asbestos, formaldehyde, radon gas, lead-based paint, or other lead contamination, fuel or chemical storage tanks, contaminated soil or water.

- geologic/seismic conditions, soil and terrain stability, suitability and drainage.

- neighborhood or property conditions including schools; proximity and adequacy of law enforcement; proximity to commercial, industrial or agricultural activities; crime statistics; fire protection; other government services; existing and proposed transportation; construction and development; airport noise, noise or odor from any source; other nuisances, hazards or circumstances; and any conditions or influences of significance to certain cultures and/or religions.

Transfer Disclosure Statement

The buyer must approve the TDS (Transfer Disclosure Statement) which has been completed by the seller within three days after delivery. All parties, including the seller, the buyer, the seller's agent, and the buyer's agent, must sign the disclosure. Buyer may terminate the agreement if the TDS is not received in a timely manner.

Property Disclosures

When applicable to the property and required by law, the seller shall provide to the buyer, at the seller's expense, the following disclosures and information. The buyer shall then, within the time specified, investigate the disclosures and provide notice of disapproval (Southern California) or written notice of approval (Northern California).

- Geologic/Seismic Hazard Zones Disclosure

- Special Flood Hazard Areas Disclosure

- State Fire Responsibility Areas Disclosure

- Mello-Roos Disclosure

- Earthquake Safety Disclosure

- Smoke Detector Disclosure

- Environmental Hazards Booklet

- Lead-Based Paint Disclosure

Governmental Compliance

The seller shall disclose to the buyer any improvements, additions, alterations, or repairs made without the required permits, final inspections, or government approval (local or state). The buyer shall, within the time specified, either disapprove or approve in writing, depending on the custom and requirement of the escrow.

Pest Control

The buyer has the right to disapprove or approve the pest control report within a stated number of days after receiving it.

Sale of the Buyer's Property

The escrow may be canceled if the contingency regarding the sale of the buyer's property is not removed in a timely and correct manner. Depending on the agreement between the buyer and seller, several variations on this contingency may be included in the instructions. The seller can continue to market the property or not, by agreement with the buyer. If a new buyer is found, the buyer in this escrow has an agreed-upon time period to remove this contingency or the escrow is terminated.

The buyer can continue to market his or her property for a specified time period. If that time period comes and goes, the escrow may be terminated if the buyer does not remove the contingency for the sale of his or her property.

Cancellation of Prior Sale/Back-up Offer

The escrow may be contingent on the cancellation of one entered into by the seller, prior to the current buyer's offer. This escrow is contingent on the successful cancellation of the earlier escrow.

Court Confirmation

Court confirmation may be required in a probate, conservatorship, guardianship, receivership, bankruptcy, or other proceeding. The buyer understands that the property may continue to be marketed by a broker or others, and that others may represent different competitive bidders prior to and at the court confirmation. If court confirmation is not obtained by the date shown in the instructions, the buyer may cancel this agreement by giving written notice of cancellation to the seller.

Cancellations

As we have seen, an escrow may be canceled with the mutual consent of all parties. The dissolution of the escrow must be concerned with the mutuality of everyone involved as well as the rights of third parties who are affected by the termination of the escrow.

Often, the parties cannot come to a mutual agreement about cancellation and the disposal of funds on deposit with the escrow holder or fees to be paid to the escrow holder. There are three options for funds being held by the escrow holder:

1. The funds may remain on deposit for three years, after which time they escheat to the state if there are no valid claims.
2. A court may determine the rightful owner of funds on deposit with the escrow holder. Either party may initiate an action for the funds through the court system or an arbitrator.
3. The parties can come to an agreement about the funds and direct escrow to disburse them accordingly.

Variations on the Sale Escrow

As you know, an escrow holder is obligated to produce and follow a set of escrow instructions that exactly mirrors the agreement of the parties in the deposit receipt.

The majority of sale escrows will be either a cash sale, with the buyer to qualify for a new loan sale, or seller financed.

Occasionally, however, certain situations arise where the buyer and seller have agreed to a variation on commonly used financing to achieve the desired result.

All-Inclusive Deed of Trust

Also known as an all-inclusive trust deed (AITD), or a wrap-around trust deed, this type of loan wraps an existing trust deed with a new trust deed, and the borrower makes one payment for both. In other words, the new trust deed (the AITD) includes the present encumbrances, such as first, second, third or more trust deeds, plus the amount to be financed by the seller.

The AITD is subordinate to existing encumbrances because the AITD is created at a later date. This means any existing encumbrances have priority over the AITD, even though they are included, or wrapped, by the new all-inclusive trust deed. At the close of escrow, the buyer receives title to the property.

Typically, an AITD is used in a transaction between the buyer and seller to make the financing attractive to the buyer and beneficial to the seller as well. Instead of the buyer assuming an existing loan and the seller carrying back a second trust deed, the AITD can accomplish the same purpose with greater benefit to both parties in some instances.

AITDs are popular when interest rates are high and the underlying loans are not adjustable or have a low interest rate. When interest rates are low and a buyer can obtain a loan from an institution, it does not make sense to wrap an underlying loan, therefore paying a higher rate of interest to the seller than if an outside loan were obtained.

Benefits of an All-Inclusive Trust Deed
The Seller:
      Usually gets full-price offer
      Higher interest rate on amount carried
The Buyer:
      Low down payment
      No qualifying for a loan or payment of loan fees

The AITD does not disturb the existing loan. The seller, as the new lender, keeps making the payments while giving a new increased loan at a higher rate of interest to the borrower. The amount of the AITD includes the unpaid principal balance of the existing (underlying) loan, plus the amount of the new loan being made by the seller. The borrower makes payment on the new larger loan to the seller, who in turn makes payment to the holder of the existing underlying loan. The new loan "wraps around" the existing loan.

A seller usually will carry back a wrap-around trust deed at a higher rate of interest than the underlying trust deed, thereby increasing the yield. The seller continues to pay off the original trust deed from the payments on the wrap-around, while keeping the difference. This type of financing works best when the underlying interest rate is low and the seller can then charge a higher rate on the wrapped loan.

A wrap-around loan is not for everyone. If a seller needs to cash out, it will not work. In addition, most loans contain a due-on-sale clause, and cannot be wrapped without the lender's knowledge and approval. Depending on the buyer and seller's motivation, sometimes an AITD will be created, with full knowledge of the risk. This is how the term "creative financing" came into being.

Generally, these payments are collected by a professional collection company and sent on to the appropriate parties. This assures the maker (borrower) of the AITD that all underlying payments are being forwarded and are kept current by a neutral party.

In some instances, a rider containing additional agreements between a buyer and seller will be attached to an all-inclusive deed of trust.

Additions to an AITD

The AITD may be placed on contract collection with a professional collection company authorized to do business. Money is collected and disbursed for current installments, payments of taxes and insurance if necessary. Any amount then remaining is disbursed to the holder of the note secured by the AITD.

If the trustor (borrower) defaults, beneficiary obligations (lender) will be suspended until the default is cured. If the trustor is delinquent in making any payments due under the note, and the beneficiary incurs any penalties or other expenses on account of the underlying obligations during the period of trustor delinquency, the amount of any penalties and expenses will be added to the amount of the note and will be payable by the trustor with the next payment due under the note.

In the event of foreclosure of the all-inclusive deed of trust, the beneficiary agrees that he or she will, at the trustee's sale, bid an

amount representing that due under the AITD, less the total balance due on the underlying notes, plus any advances or other disbursements that the beneficiary is allowed by law to include in the bid.

When the note secured by the AITD becomes due or the trustor requests a demand for payoff of the note, the main amount payable to the beneficiary will be reduced by the unpaid balances of the underlying obligations.

If any installment payment under the note secured by the AITD is not paid within 15 days after the due date, a late charge may be incurred by the trustor and be due and payable upon the beneficiary's demand.

Adequate funds for the payment of taxes and fire insurance will be deposited and held by the collection account holder. Monthly, an amount equal to one-twelfth of the annual tax amount and one-twelfth the amount of the annual fire insurance billing will be deposited by the trustor. Taxes and insurance reserves have been provided by the trustor to the beneficiary for the initial reserve fund.

If the trustor makes any additional payments or added increments beyond the required monthly amount, the beneficiary, upon a request by the trustor in writing, will forward any extra funds to the holders of the underlying notes for application to the unpaid principal balances.

Wrap-Around Loans (AITDs)
Secured by a trust deed that "wraps," or includes existing financing plus the amount to be financed by the seller

Contract of Sale = OPION

The contract of sale is the financing instrument with many names. It may be called an installment sales contract, a contract of sale, an agreement of sale, a conditional sales contract, or a land contract.

In this type of agreement, the seller retains legal ownership of the property until the buyer has made the last payment, much like buying a car. This is a contract between a buyer and seller, and can be used during times when usual financing is difficult.

The buyer, or vendee, holds what is known as equitable title. The vendee may enjoy possession and use of the property even though legal title is held by the seller, or vendor. Like the holder of an AITD, the vendor pays off the original financing while receiving payments from the vendee on the contract of sale. Indeed, a contract of sale and an AITD are very similar. The most important distinction is that with the AITD, title passes to the buyer; under a contract of sale, title stays with the seller until the contract is paid off.

> **Difference between AITD and Contract of Sale**
> - AITD: the buyer gets title to property
> - Contract of Sale: the seller keeps title until loan is paid off

Contracts of sale are not commonly used except in special circumstances and under the guidance of an attorney, who will draw the document. They were heavily used in the 1980s, but fell out of favor because of the risk involved and the difficulty of foreclosure in many cases.

Deed in Lieu of Foreclosure

Normally, when a trustor (borrower) defaults on a loan, the property in question is sold at a trustee's sale or title is conveyed to the beneficiary as a result of the foreclosure. The borrower has a ding on his or her credit as a result of the default and subsequent foreclosure and the lender must pick up any costs accrued by the sale.

Occasionally, however, the lender is willing to forgo the trustee's sale and allow the borrower to deed the property back to them voluntarily. This is most likely to happen if the lender is the former owner. The unpaid debt is then canceled, removing the lien against the property and in the process, saves the borrower's credit. If the beneficiary were an institutional lender, the property would be accepted and become one more unloved and difficult REO (Real Estate Owned) property needing a new owner. This is known as a "deed in lieu of foreclosure".

The escrow holder considers the deed in lieu as the principal instrument of conveyance in a transaction where this is the agreement between the parties. The consideration in this sale escrow is the satisfaction of the debt to the lender in return for a deed from the borrower, who executes a grant deed in favor of the beneficiary.

In order to guarantee the insurability of the deed, a disclaimer is added to the deed or a separate affidavit is prepared for the trustor to sign.

The note holder should always get a policy of title insurance with a deed in lieu of foreclosure so that any liens or judgments against the former owner (party in default) will not attach to the note holder.

"Subject to" Sale

A buyer may also purchase a property "subject to" the existing loan. The original borrower remains responsible for the loan, even though the buyer takes title and makes the payments. In this case, also, the property remains the security for the loan. In the case of default, it is sold and the proceeds go to the lender, with no recourse to the original buyer other than the foreclosure going against the buyer's credit.

However, a deficiency judgment is allowed if the loan was not a purchase money loan, or one made specifically upon purchase of the property. If the loan was a hard money loan, or a loan made to get cash, the original borrower could be held personally liable until the loan is paid off.

> Example: Sam bought his home 20 years ago, and refinanced it after 10 years for money to add on a room. His first deed of trust was a purchase money loan in the amount of $10,000, and the second loan was a hard money loan, secured by the property.
>
> Sam sold the property to Sally, who bought the property "subject to" his two loans. When she defaulted on the loans and the property went into foreclosure, Sam was responsible for the second loan, even though he no longer owned the property.
>
> What Sam should have done, in this case, was to ask the lender, upon sale of the property, for a substitution of liability and agreement to pay (novation), relieving himself of any liability.

Many times a property will be sold "subject to" existing loans because there is a due-on-sale clause in the present note. It may be the buyer's desire to take over the loan without triggering the due-on-sale clause.

When escrow deals with an existing institutional lender, there is rarely any contact with the lender. Escrow instructions are written to include the appropriate exculpatory language relative to the transfer. They are not compliant with normal lender requirements, such as the buyer qualifying for the loan, or paying loan fees.

> Example: The escrow holder is authorized and instructed not to order a beneficiary statement on existing trust deed of record and both the buyer and seller herein releases Any City Escrow, as the escrow holder, from any liability in any manner or way in connection herewith. The seller shall furnish the escrow holder with an offset statement and a copy of promissory note setting forth the exact unpaid balance, terms, and conditions of said loan for the buyer's approval prior to close of escrow. The seller herein shall keep all payments current during the escrow period. In the event offset statement reflects the balance to be more or less than the amount stated herein, the

escrow holder is instructed to adjust any differences in the buyer's cash down payment.

The buyer herein acknowledges that the within loan of record does contain a "due on sale" clause in the note which may cause an acceleration of maturity upon transfer of title. Regardless of this matter, the escrow holder is authorized and instructed to close this escrow at the earliest possible date. All parties hold Any City Escrow, as escrow holder, from any liability in any manner or way in connection herewith.

Loan Assumption Sale

When a property is sold, a buyer may assume the existing loan. With the approval of the lender, the buyer takes over primary liability for the loan, with the original borrower secondarily liable if there is a default.

What this means is that even though the original borrower is secondarily responsible, according to the loan assumption agreement, no actual repayment of the loan may be required of that person. If the new owner defaults, the property is foreclosed, and no deficiency judgment is allowed beyond the amount received at the trustee's sale, even though the original borrower's credit is affected by the foreclosure.

An escrow involving an assumption is similar to an escrow involving new financing. The escrow is contingent on the buyer qualifying with the existing lender. The buyer completes a loan package and escrow submits the loan package to the lender with a request for a beneficiary statement. When the lender approves, the escrow holder is sent a set of assumption documents for the buyer's signature.

True-False Quiz

Now that you have read all the material in this chapter, take the following self-test and check your knowledge of escrow contingencies.

True/False

1. _False_ A contract is binding even though all contingencies have not been met.

2. _True_ All principals to an escrow must be in agreement for contingencies to be added or changed.

3. _True_ A deposit receipt is an executory instrument.

4. _False_ Time is of the essence means that all parties can take their time in meeting any contingencies.

5. _False_ Escrow instructions may be signed by one or all parties to the transaction.

6. _True_ Buyers must receive and approve a copy of CC&Rs within a certain number of days after receiving them.

7. _False_ The sale of the buyer's property may not be a contingency.

8. _False_ If parties to an escrow cannot agree about the disposition of funds when an escrow is cancelled, the escrow holder must release them to the seller.

9. _True_ If the escrow is cancelled, either party may initiate an action for funds—through the courts or by arbitration.

10. _True_ A wrap around trust deed is also known as an All-Inclusive Trust Deed. (AITD)

Chapter 11

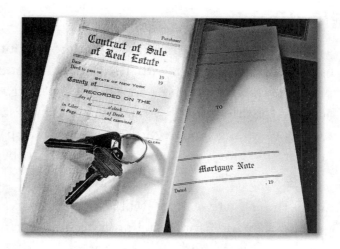

Title Insurance

Learning Objectives

After reading this chapter, you will be able to:

- define title insurance.

- explain the history of title insurance.

- describe types of title insurance policies.

- explain special endorsements and guarantees.

Introduction

The business of title insurance has grown out of increased real estate activity together with the need to process the sale of real property quickly, safely, and effectively. Early guarantees of the accuracy of title started with abstractors who established a chain of title by checking land records from the old Spanish and Mexican land grants, along with any records that had been kept from land sales to early settlers.

With the growth of the real estate industry, consumers began making demands for a guarantee of the accuracy of these early searches. Buyers and sellers wanted the title searchers to take responsibility for their comprehensive conclusions about all matters of record. Meeting this demand evolved into the title industry we know today.

What Is Title Insurance?

Title is the foundation of property ownership. It means that the owner has a legal right to possess that property and to use it within the restrictions or limitations imposed by authorities.

No other property has a useful life that compares with the life of land. Owners die, new ones succeed, but land goes on forever. Owners of goods may change their locations at will, but land is immovable. Being both permanent and immovable, it lends itself to the absorption of innumerable rights. Over the ages, this so impressed lawyers and jurists that they formed a separate body of laws for land. These laws, creating many types of rights in land, are so numerous and so complex it is impossible for there to be a mathematical certainty of ownership.

Title insurance is a contract to protect against losses arising through defects in title to real estate. In other words, the insurer guarantees the title to be free of liens or other encumbrances that would cause title to be unclear or clouded for the new owner. Title insurance is the application of insurance principles to hazards inherent in real estate titles.

The basic function of a title insurance company is to take positive steps that will minimize the risk that a policyholder will suffer any loss or be subject to any adverse claim, as well as to safeguard his or her ownership of or claim in the property.

The primary purpose of title insurance is to eliminate risks and prevent losses caused by defects in title arising out of events that have happened in the past.

A title defect is anything in the entire history of ownership of a piece of real estate which may encumber the owner's right to the "peaceful enjoyment" of the property or which may cause the owner to lose any portion of the property.

Many title risks cannot be revealed by even the most thorough search. Some examples of these risks are listed below.

Title Risks

- Mistakes in interpretation of wills or other legal documents

- Impersonation of the real owner

- Forged deeds or reconveyances

- Instruments executed under a fabricated or an expired power of attorney

- Deed delivered after the death of the grantor or grantee or without the consent of the grantor

- Undisclosed or missing heirs

- Wills not probated

- Deeds signed by persons of unsound mind, by minors, or by persons supposedly single but actually married

- Birth or adoption of children after the date of a will

- Mistakes in recording of legal documents

- Want of jurisdiction over persons in judicial proceedings affecting the title

- Errors in indexing of public records

- Falsification of records

- Confusion arising from similarity of names

- Title passing through a foreclosure sale where compliance of the requirements of the applicable foreclosure statutes have not been strictly met

Title insurance, however, is not always used in property transfers. It is not required by law and is usually a matter of agreement between the buyer and seller. A lender's policy usually is required by a lender as a requisite for obtaining new financing.

An abstract of title is one way to research the title to a property and is good as far as it goes. But an abstract is simply a condensed version of the recorded documents affecting title to the property. The limitations on the liability of an abstracter who issues an abstract are the same as those of an attorney who issues an opinion of title.

Sometimes an abstract of title is considered sufficient by the buyer or an attorney will offer an opinion or certificate of title, which a purchaser might accept as sufficient protection. However, there are many title defects that even the most careful title examination will not reveal or uncover. In this case, the chance of recovery in the event of a title loss depends entirely upon the solvency of the attorney examining the title.

The attorney's liability is limited to errors and oversights that would not be made by a diligent attorney. The attorney is not liable for loss caused by hidden defects.

Every attorney knows that there are hazards in real estate title that cannot possibly be discovered with even a diligent search of the public records. For instance, the attorney cannot be sure that:

- the marital rights of all previous owners have been properly relinquished.

- all mortgages, judgments, and other liens affecting the property have been properly indexed in the record room.

- all signatures on all recorded documents are genuine.

- no unknown heir of a former owner can appear to assert his or her claim.

These are but a few of the matters that can defeat real estate titles. Among others are such circumstances as fraud, duress, insanity, or false impersonations.

An attorney is not liable if the buyer should suffer loss because of any of the "hidden defects" in a real estate title. Liability extends only to losses caused by oversights or carelessness in the attorney's work. In addition, liability is limited by the attorney's ability to pay, as well as by his or her life span.

Title insurance is usually required by a lender before funding a new loan. While the title insurance coverage afforded the lender and owner is somewhat the same, it is also substantially different in important areas. Because of the diminishing debt of the mortgage and the increasing equity of the owner as payments are made, it is apparent that there could be a complete title failure with the lender suffering no loss because of title insurance coverage and the owner suffering substantial loss because he or she had no title insurance.

Many buyers think that the purchase contract they signed makes the sale subject to their getting clear title. While that generally is true, there are cases where the seller cannot be absolutely certain the title is good. The seller knows about the title during his or her property ownership, but what about previous owners? Even a perfect looking title can be seriously unsound because of hidden defects. If anything would happen to defeat the title after escrow has closed and the buyer is the new owner, the chance of recovery of damages would depend upon finding and suing the seller, winning the suit and, finally, on whether or not the seller was able to pay the judgment. In any event, the attorney's fees and expenses would be the buyer's loss.

Title insurance services are designed to give homeowners, lenders, and others with interests in real estate the maximum degree of protection from adverse title claims or risks. The financial assurance offered by a title insurance policy—by not only satisfying any valid claims against the title as insured, but also by defraying the expenses of defending against any attacks on the insured title—is, of course, a key aspect of this title protection.

The risk elimination aspects of the title search and examination, performed as a prerequisite to the issuance of a title insurance policy, are equally important, since they ensure that all parties have a clear understanding of their interests BEFORE the transaction is consummated. The parties then are able to resolve potential title claims before those claims result in losses.

History of Title Insurance

Historically, the need for title insurance arose from the fact that traditional methods of conveying real property did not provide adequate safety to the parties involved. Until a century ago, transferring title to real property was handled primarily by conveyancers, who were responsible for all aspects of the transaction. The conveyancer conducted a title search to determine the ownership rights of the seller and any other rights, interest, liens, or encumbrances that might exist with respect to the property. Based on that search, the conveyancer provided a signed abstract (or description) of the status of the title.

Although the conveyancer generally was not a lawyer, he or she was recognized as an authority on real estate law. The origin of title insurance is directly traceable to the limited protection that the work of such a conveyancer provided the buyer of real property.

In 1868, the famous lawsuit of *Watson* v. *Muirhead* was filed in Pennsylvania. In that case, Muirhead, a conveyancer, had searched and abstracted a title for Watson, the buyer of a parcel of real estate. In good faith and after consulting an attorney, Muirhead chose to ignore certain recorded judgments and to report the title was good and unencumbered.

Based on Muirhead's abstract, Watson went ahead with the purchase, but subsequently was presented with, and required to satisfy, the liens that Muirhead had concluded were not impairments of title. Watson sued Muirhead to recover his losses, but the Pennsylvania Supreme Court ruled that there was no negligence on the conveyancer's part and dismissed the case. Watson, an innocent buyer who had suffered financial damages because of the encumbrances on his title, had no recourse.

The decision in *Watson* v. *Muirhead* showed clearly that the existing conveyancing system could not provide total assurance to purchasers of real property that they would be safe and secure in their ownership. Because of that decision, the Pennsylvania legislature shortly thereafter passed an act "to provide for the incorporation and regulation of title insurance companies". On March 28, 1876, the first land title insurance company, The Real Estate Title Insurance Company was founded in Philadelphia.

During the next few years, title insurance companies were organized in other cities throughout the country, including New York, Chicago, Minneapolis, San Francisco, and Los Angeles.

The nature and complexity of real estate titles and transfers have increased immeasurably since that time (as a result, in part, of the greater amount of interest and rights that are now recognized in real property). Services provided by title insurance companies also have expanded and adapted to the changing needs of our society. However, the same goals are still sought by title insurance companies today.

Types of Policies

Title requirements vary between transactions, depending on the complexity of the sale. This requires the escrow holder to have a complete understanding of title insurance and the specific coverage that is available with each kind of policy.

In matching the title insurance coverage to the transaction, the elements to be considered include the type of coverage— standard coverage, extended coverage, coverage modified by special endorsements; the type of estate—fee, leasehold, equitable interest; and the parties insured—owner, lender, lessee, vendee, vendor.

Standard Coverage

A Standard Coverage or CLTA (California Land Title Association) policy of title insurance is designed especially for the homebuyer. It may be used, however, to insure a lender as well.

The title company insures the buyer, as of the date of the policy, against loss or damage not exceeding the amount of insurance stated in the policy, and any costs, attorneys' fees, and expenses which the title company may be obligated to pay in satisfying the buyer in case of a loss.

The Standard Coverage Policy is limited because it will insure against only those matters disclosed in public records and will not cover any defects that are concealed from the title company. Off-record items such as an encroachment, an unrecorded easement, a discrepancy in boundary lines or an interest of parties in possession of the property, which are discovered only by a survey or inspection of the property, are not covered by a CLTA Standard Policy.

The CLTA policy, when issued to insure a lender, provides coverage against a loss suffered because of an invalid trust deed, if the trust deed proved to be in a lessor position than shown or if an assignment in the policy was shown to be invalid.

Review - A CLTA policy may be issued:
- as an owner's policy.

- as a lender's policy (either private or institutional).

- as a joint protection policy for both the owner and lender (commonly used when the seller acts as the lender and carries back a trust deed).

If a policyholder wants coverage against items not included in the standard policy, endorsements may be added to the Standard Coverage policy. Most title companies add an inflation endorsement, at no charge, which, in case of a claim against the title, requires them to cover the appreciated or inflated value of the property rather than the original sales price. Another endorsement usually available is the homeowner's endorsement. This coverage is issued only on owner-occupied dwellings with four or

less units. It insures against limited off-record risks involving certain matters related to access, encroachments, restrictions, zoning, taxes, and mechanics' liens.

While a standard title policy offers only limited coverage of off-record matters, an extended policy offers comprehensive protection for a much broader coverage. A standard policy normally is purchased by buyers of single-family residences, for whom it is usually adequate. In some cases, however, it may not be enough.

Some common extensions of Standard Coverage

- Expanded encroachment coverage

- Expanded access to a public street coverage

- Unrecorded taxes or assessments — limited coverage

- Unrecorded mechanics' liens

- Violation of covenants, conditions and restrictions

- Violation of zoning ordinances

- Damage from a holder of mineral rights searching for or removing minerals from the insured property

- An inflation endorsement which can increase policy coverage up to 150% of the original policy amount

Standard Coverage Policy (CLTA)
Insured Risks

- Most matters revealed by public records

- Some off-record risks, such as forgery or incompetence

Limited coverage

Non-insured Risks

- Matters not disclosed by public records

- Environmental laws, zoning, and laws regarding the use of the property

- Defects known to the insured before the property was purchased and not revealed to the title company before the sale

Extended Coverage

While a standard title policy offers only limited coverage of off-record matters, an extended policy offers comprehensive protection for much broader coverage.

Extended Coverage Policy (ALTA)

- Matters disclosed by a physical inspection of the property

- Off-record matters disclosed by asking the occupants of the premises

- Matters disclosed by a current survey

- Violations of recorded covenants, conditions and restrictions

- Encroachments of improvements onto existing easements

- Any unrecorded easement rights disclosed by inspection

- The right of other parties, possessory or otherwise

- Unrecorded leases of tenants occupying the land

- Unrecorded assessments and inspection of tax office records

- Unrecorded claims resulting from work performed or materials supplied for improvement of the property

In the 1920s, the American Title Association, now called the American Land Title Association (ALTA), and lenders from the East formed a partnership that resulted in the ALTA lender's policy of title insurance being offered. The extended coverage, provided at a higher price than standard coverage, protects against many risks which are not a matter of record. A lender's title requirements include any problems that affect the value of the loan security. Today, in almost all transactions where there is a new institutional lender, an ALTA extended coverage policy is required. Some of the risks covered by an ALTA extended coverage lender's policy have been listed below.

Extended coverage surveys may reveal information not shown on record. An ordinary survey confirms matters of record and shows where improvements are with regard to lot lines.

Items an Extended Coverage Survey May Show

- Shortages or overages in lot dimensions

- Natural watercourses crossing the property

- Unrecorded easements above or below the surface of the property

- Encroachments of existing improvements from adjoining property onto the property to be insured

- Anything existing on the surface or subsurface of the land from which a title claim may arise from other than the owner

- Claims to the title that are not a matter of record by asking the current owner about the occupancy of the land or whether there has been any work done recently on the property

Special Endorsements

A basic policy of title insurance may be expanded or modified by special endorsements. These endorsements are needed because the parties want special coverage for the amount of consideration, the type of property being insured, the complexity of the transaction, or any title exceptions or encumbrances affecting the property.

Guarantees

Specific limited-use coverages for special situations are called guarantees in the title insurance industry. They may include:

1. **Subdivision guarantee:** When only a *preliminary* subdivision report has been filed with the Real Estate Commissioner on the property in question, this special coverage guarantees a final report will be filed.

2. **Chain of title guarantee:** A chain of title is researched in every transaction and a preliminary title report is produced prior to issuing the policy of title insurance. Occasionally, a chain of title guarantee is required, however. The preliminary title report, as you know, contains the legal description of the property to be insured, title vesting, and all encumbrances against the property. The encumbrances show what exceptions will be in the title insurance policy desired and will allow the insured to choose what exceptions he or she can live with and which ones will have to be removed before the close of escrow.

Non Liability

Title insurance does not cover any defect that was known by the parties prior to the transfer. So, if anyone, such as the real estate broker, escrow agent or seller, lies or knows of an untrue statement that would affect the quality of the title, the insurance is not valid. The title company must prove that the defect was known and misstated and is then not liable.

Policy of Title Insurance

RIVERFRONT TITLE COMPANY

Policy No._____

Subject to the Exclusions from Coverage, the exceptions contained in schedule B and the conditions and stipulations hereof, Riverfront Title Company, a California Corporation, herein called the Company, insures the insured, as of Date of Policy shown in Schedule A, against loss or damage, not exceeding the amount of insurance stated in Schedule A, and costs, attorneys' fee and expenses which the Company may become obligated to pay hereunder, sustained or incurred by said insured by reason of:

1. Title to the estate or interest described in Schedule A being vested other than as stated therein;

2. Any defect in or lien or encumbrance on such title;

3. Unmarketability of such title;

4. Any lack of the ordinary right of any abutting owner for access to at least one physically open street or highway if the land, in fact, abuts upon one or more such street or highway; and in addition, as to an insured lender only:

5. Invalidity of the lien of the insured mortgage upon said estate or interest except to the extent that such invalidity, or claim thereof, arises out of the transaction evidenced by the insured mortgage and is based upon

a. usury, or

b. any consumer credit protection or truth in lending law;

6. Priority of any lien or encumbrance over the lien of the insured mortgage, said mortgage being shown in Schedule B in the order of its priority; or

7. Invalidity of any assignment of the insured mortgage, provided such assignment is shown in Schedule B

IN WITNESS WHEREOF, RIVERFRONT TITLE COMPANY has caused its corporate name and seal to be hereunto affixed by its duly authorizes officers as of the date shown in Schedule A.

Riverfront Commonwealth Title Company

By:_____
President

Attest:_____

GARY BAKER
ABC MORTGAGE
4320 MOUNTAIN RD., #120
ANY CITY, CALIF. 90000

Dated as of March 6, 20xx, at 7:30 AM

In response to the above referenced application for a policy of title insurance,

HOMETOWN TITLE COMPANY

hereby reports that is prepared to issue, or cause to be issued, as of the date hereof, a Policy or Policies of Title Insurance describing the land and the estate or interest therein hereinafter set forth, insuring against loss which may be sustained by reason of any defect, lien or encumbrance not shown or referred to as an Exception in Schedule B or not excluded from coverage pursuant to the printed Schedules, Conditions and Stipulations of said Policy forms.

The printed Exceptions and Exclusions from the coverage of said Policy or Policies are set forth in Exhibit A attached list. Copies of the Policy forms should be read. They are available from the office that issued the report.

Please read the exceptions shown or referred to in Schedule B and the exceptions and exclusions set forth in Exhibit A of this report carefully. The exceptions and exclusions are meant to provide you with notice of matters which are not covered under the terms of the title insurance policy and should be carefully considered.

It is important to note that this preliminary report is not a written representation as to the condition of title and may not list all liens, defects, and encumbrances affecting title to the land.

THIS REPORT (AND ANY SUPPLEMENTS OR AMENDMENTS HERETO) IS ISSUED SOLELY FOR THE PURPOSE OF FACILITATING THE ISSUANCE OF A POLICY OF TITLE INSURANCE AND NO LIABILITY IS ASSUMED HEREBY. IF IT IS DESIRED THAT LIABILITY BE ASSUMED PRIOR TO THE ISSUANCE OF A POLICY OF TITLE INSURANCE, A BINDER OR COMMITMENT SHOULD BE REQUESTED.

This form of policy of title insurance contemplated by this report is:
A.L.T.A. RESIDENTIAL TITLE INSURANCE POLICY
AMERICAN LAND TITLE ASSOCIATION LOAN EXTENDED COVERAGE POLICY

_____
Title Officer

ANY CITY ESCROW, INC.
24321 RIVERFRONT RD., #B
ANY CITY, CALIF. 90000

Dated as of March 6, 20xx, at 7:30 AM

In response to the above referenced application for a policy of title insurance,

HOMETOWN TITLE COMPANY

hereby reports that it is prepared to issue, or cause to be issued, as of the date hereof, a Policy or Policies of Title Insurance describing the land and the estate or interest therein hereinafter set forth, insuring against loss which may be sustained by reason of any defect, lien or encumbrance not shown or referred to as an Exception in Schedule B or not excluded from coverage pursuant to the printed Schedules, Conditions and Stipulations of said Policy forms.

The printed Exceptions and Exclusions from the coverage of said Policy or Policies are set forth in Exhibit A attached list. Copies of the Policy forms should be read. They are available from the office which issued the report.

Please read the exceptions sworn or referred to in Schedule B and the exceptions and exclusions set forth in Exhibit A of this report carefully. The exceptions and exclusions are meant to provide you with notice of matters which are not covered under the terms of the title insurance policy and should be carefully considered.

It is important to note that this preliminary report is not a written representation as to the condition of title and may not list all liens, defects, and encumbrances affecting title to the land.

THIS REPORT (AND ANY SUPPLEMENTS OR AMENDMENTS HERETO) IS ISSUED SOLELY FOR THE PURPOSE OF FACILITATING THE ISSUANCE OF A POLICY OF TITLE INSURANCE AND NO LIABILITY IS ASSUMED HEREBY. IF IT IS DESIRED THAT LIABILITY BE ASSUMED PRIOR TO THE ISSUANCE OF A POLICY OF TITLE INSURANCE, A BINDER OR COMMITMENT SHOULD BE REQUESTED.

The form of policy of title insurance contemplated by this report is:
A.L.T.A RESIDENTIAL TITLE INSURANCE POLICY
AMERICAN LAND TITLE ASSOCIATION LOAN EXTENDED COVERAGE POLICY

_____

Title Officer

SCHEDULE A

Title Order No. 6805790

The estate or interest in the land hereinafter described or referred to covered by this report is:

A FEE AS TO PARCEL 1
AN EASEMENT MORE FULLY DESCRIBED BELOW AS TO PARCEL 2

2. Title to said estate or interest at the date hereof is vested in:

DAN WINTER AND DONNA WINTER, HUSBAND AND WIFE, AS JOINT TENANTS

3. The land referred to in this report is situated in the State of California, County of APPLE and is described as follows:

PARCEL 1:

LOT 6 OF TRACT NO. 13914, IN THE CITY OF ANY CITY, COUNTY OF APPLE, STATE OF CALIFORNIA, AS SHOWN ON A MAP FILED IN BOOK 638, PAGES 45 THROUGH 50, INCLUSIVE OF MISCELLANEOUS MAPS, RECORDS OF APPLE COUNTY, CALIFORNIA.

EXCEPTING THEREFROM ONTO THE GRANTOR, WITH THE RIGHT TO ASSIGN, TRANSFER OR LEASE TO ANY THIRD PARTY, ALL OIL, GAS AND CASINGHEAD GAS, AND OTHER HYDROCARBONS LYING BELOW THE SURFACE OF THE LAND CONVEYED HEREBY, WITHOUT ANY SURFACE ENTRY RIGHTS, AS RESERVED IN THE DEED RECORDED NOVEMBER 1, 20xx, AS INSTRUMENT NO. 90-581069, OFFICIAL RECORDS.

PARCEL 2:

A NON-EXCLUSIVE EASEMENT FOR INGRESS AND EGRESS PURPOSES OVER LOTS L, M AND N (THE PRIVATE STREETS) OF TRACT NO. 14682 AS SHOWN ON A MAP IN BOOK 539, PAGES 45 THROUGH 50, INCLUSIVE OF MISCELLANEOUS MAPS, RECORDS OF APPLE COUNTY, CALIFORNIA.

SCHEDULE B

Title Order No. 6805790

At the date hereof exceptions to coverage in addition to the printed Exceptions and Exclusions in the policy form designated on the face page of this Report would be as follows:

A. 1. PROPERTY TAXES, INCLUDING ANY ASSESSMENTS COLLECTED WITH TAXES, TO BE LEVIED FOR THE FISCAL YEAR 20xx-20xx THAT ARE A LIEN NOT YET DUE.

B. 2. PROPERTY TAXES, INCLUDING ANY PERSONAL PROPERTY TAXES AND ANY ASSESSMENTS COLLECTED WITH TAXES, FOR THE FISCAL YEAR 20xx-20xx

FIRST INSTALLMENT;	$1,749.93 (PAID)
2ND INSTALLMENT;	$1,749.93
PENALTY AND COST;	$184.99 (DUE AFTER APRIL 10)
HOMEOWNERS EXEMPTION;	$7,000.00
CODE AREA	10002
ASSESSMENT NO:	680-561-14

C. 3. AN ASSESSMENT BY THE IMPROVEMENT DISTRICT SHOWN BELOW

ASSESSMENT (OR BOND) NO;	829-73
SERIES;	35-1
DISTRICT;	CITY OF SAN CLEMENTE-10
FOR;	30 AMD 85-1
BOND ISSUED;	FEBRUARY 21, 20xx
ORIGINAL AMOUNT;	$ NOT SET OUT

SAID ASSESSMENT IS COLLECTED WITH THE COUNTY/CITY PROPERTY TAXES.

D. 4. A REPORT ON SAID TAXES AND ASSESSMENTS HAS BEEN ORDERED. WE WILL SEND A TAX SUPPLEMENT WHEN IT IS RECEIVED.

E. 5. AN ASSESSMENT BY THE IMPROVEMENT DISTRICT SHOWN BELOW

ASSESSMENT (OR BOND)	NO: 6628
SERIES	95
DISTRICT	CITY OF SAN CLEMENTE-10
FOR	STREET IMPROVEMENTS
BOND ISSUED	JULY 14, 20xx
ORIGINAL AMOUNT:	$ NOT SET OUT

SAID ASSESSMENT IS COLLECTED WITH THE COUNTY/CITY PROPERTY TAXES.

SCHEDULE B (CONTINUED)

Title Order No. 6805790

F. 6. A REPORT ON SAID TAXES AND ASSESSMENTS HAS BEEN ORDERED.
WE WILL SEND A TAX SUPPLEMENT WHEN IT IS RECEIVED.

G. 7. THE LIEN OF SUPPLEMENTAL OR ESCAPED ASSESSMENTS OF PROPERTY
TAXES, IF ANY, MADE PURSUANT TO THE PROVISIONS OF PART 0.5, CHAPTER 3.5
OR PART 2, CHAPTER 3, ARTICLES 3 AND 4 RESPECTIVELY(COMMENCING WITH
SECTION 75) OF THE REVENUE AND TAXATION CODE OF THE STATE OF
CALIFORNIA AS A RESULT OF THE TRANSFER OF TITLE TO THE VESTEE NAMED
IN SCHEDULE A; OR AS A RESULT OF CHANGES IN OWNERSHIP OR NEW
CONSTRUCTION OCCURRING PRIOR TO DATE OF POLICY.

H. 8. MATTERS IN VARIOUS INSTRUMENTS OF RECORD WHICH CONTAIN
AMONG OTHER THINGS EASEMENTS AND RIGHTS OF WAY IN, ON, OVER AND
UNDER THE COMMON AREA FOR THE PURPOSE OF CONSTRUCTING, ERECTING,
OPERATING OR MAINTAINING THEREON OR THEREUNDER OVERHEAD OR
UNDERGROUND LINES, CABLES, WIRES, CONDUITS, OR OTHER DEVICES FOR
ELECTRICITY, TELEPHONE, STORM WATER DRAINS AND PIPES, WATER
SYSTEMS, SPRINKLING SYSTEMS, WATER, HEATING AND GAS LINES OR PIPES,
AND SIMILAR PUBLIC OR QUASI-PUBLIC IMPROVEMENTS OR FACILITIES.

ALSO THE RIGHT OF USE AND ENJOYMENT IN AND TO AND THROUGHOUT THE
COMMON AREA AS WELL AS THE NON-EXCLUSIVE EASEMENTS AND RIGHTS
FOR INGRESS, EGRESS TO THE OWNER HEREIN DESCRIBED.

REFERENCE IS HEREBY BEING MADE TO VARIOUS DOCUMENTS AND MAPS OF
RECORD FOR FULL AND FURTHER PARTICULARS.

AFFECTS THE COMMON AREA.

I. 9. THE MATTERS SET FORTH IN THE DOCUMENT SHOWN BELOW WHICH,
AMONG OTHER THINGS, CONTAINS OR PROVIDES FOR: CERTAIN EASEMENTS;
LIENS AND THE SUBORDINATION THEREOF; PROVISIONS RELATING TO
PARTITION; RESTRICTIONS ON SEVERABILITY OF COMPONENT PARTS; AND
COVENANTS, CONDITIONS AND RESTRICTIONS, (BUT OMITTING THEREFROM
ANY COVENANT OR RESTRICTION BASED ON RACE, COLOR, RELIGION, SEX,
HANDICAP, FAMILIAL STATUS OR NATIONAL ORIGIN, IF ANY, UNLESS AND
ONLY TO THE EXTENT THAT SAID COVENANT (A) IS EXEMPT UNDER CHAPTER
42, SECTION 3607 OF THE UNITED STATES CODE OR (B) RELATES TO HANDICAP
BUT DOES NOT DISCRIMINATE AGAINST HANDICAPPED PERSONS).

RECORDED: NOVEMBER 28   20xx AS INSTRUMENT NO.89-646298,
OFFICIAL RECORDS

SCHEDULE B (CONTINUED)

Title Order No.6805790

J. 10. SAID COVENANTS, CONDITIONS AND RESTRICTIONS PROVIDE THAT A VIOLATION THEREOF SHALL NOT DEFEAT THE LIEN OF ANY MORTGAGE OR DEED OF TRUST MADE IN GOOD FAITH AND FOR VALUE.

K. 11. THE PROVISIONS OF SAID COVENANTS, CONDITIONS AND RESTRICTIONS WERE EXTENDED TO INCLUDE THE HEREIN DESCRIBED LAND BY AN INSTRUMENT.

RECORDED   JANUARY 25, 20xx AS INSTRUMENT NO: 90-045127, OFFICIAL RECORDS

L. 12. THE MATTERS SET FORTH IN THE DOCUMENT SHOWN BELOW WHICH, AMONG OTHER THINGS, CONTAINS OR PROVIDES FOR: CERTAIN BASEMENTS; LIENS AND THE SUBORDINATION THEREOF; PROVISIONS RELATING TO PARTITION; RESTRICTIONS ON SEVERABILITY OF COMPONENT PARTS; AND COVENANTS, CONDITIONS AND RESTRICTIONS (BUT OMITTING THEREFROM ANY COVENANT OR RESTRICTION BASED ON RACE, COLOR, RELIGION, SEX, HANDICAP, FAMILIAL STATUS OR NATIONAL ORIGIN, IF ANY, UNLESS AND ONLY TOTHE EXTENT THAT SAID COVENANT (A) IS EXEMPT UNDER CHAPTER 42, SECTION 3607 OF THE UNITED STATES CODE OR (B) RELATES TO HANDICAP BUT DOES NOT DISCRIMINATE AGAINST HANDICAPPED PERSONS.)

RECORDED   NOVEMBER 28, 20xx AS INSTRUMENT NO. 89-646299, OFFICIAL RECORDS

M. 13. SAID COVENANTS, CONDITIONS AND RESTRICTIONS PROVIDE THAT A VIOLATION THEREOF SHALL NOT DEFEAT THE LIEN OF ANY MORTGAGE OR DEED OF TRUST MADE IN GOOD FAITH AND FOR VALUE.

N. 14. THE PROVISIONS OF SAID COVENANTS, CONDITIONS AND RESTRICTIONS WERE EXTENDED TO INCLUDE THE HEREIN DESCRIBED LAND BY AN INSTRUMENT.

RECORDED: JANUARY 25, 20xx AS INSTRUMENT NO. 90-045128, OFFICIAL RECORDS

O. 15. AN EASEMENT FOR THE PURPOSE SHOWN BELOW AND RIGHTS INCIDENTAL THERETO AS SET FORTH IN A DOCUMENT

GRANTED TO: XYZ GAS & ELECTRIC
PURPOSE: PUBLIC UTILITIES
RECORDED: DECEMBER 1, 20xx AS INSTRUMENT NO. 89-653629, OFFICIAL RECORDS
AFFECTS: THE NORTHEASTERLY 3 FEET OF PARCEL 1 AND ALL OF PARCEL 2

SCHEDULE B (CONTINUED)

Title order-No. 6805790

P. 16. AN EASEMENT FOR THE PURPOSE SHOWN BELOW AND RIGHTS INCIDENTAL THERETO AS SET FORTH IN A DOCUMENT GRANTED TO:

GRANTED TO:	HILLCREST MASTER ASSOCIATION
PURPOSE:	REASONABLE INGRESS AND EGRESS OVER LOT 16 FOR THE PURPOSES OF MAINTENANCE, REPAIR OR REPLACEMENT OF THE MASONRY WALL, AS SAID WALL IS SHOWN AS "PERIMETER WALL" ON EXHIBIT "A" ATTACHED THERETO AND INCORPORATED THEREIN
RECORDED:	AUGUST 26, 20xx AS INSTRUMENT NO. 92-567937, OFFICIAL RECORDS
AFFECTS:	SAID LAND

Q. 17 A DEED OF TRUST TO SECURE AN INDEBTEDNESS IN THE ORIGINAL AMOUNT SHOWN BELOW:

AMOUNT:	$222,000.00
DATED:	APRIL 21, 20xx
TRUSTOR:	DAN AND DONNA WINTER
TRUSTEE:	FIRST SERVICE CORPORATION
BENEFICIARY:	RIVERFRONT FEDERAL BANK, FSA
RECORDED:	MAY 1, 20xx AS INSTRUMENT NO. 950184380, OFFICIAL RECORDS
ORIGINAL LOAN NUMBER:	0206470049

R. 18. A DEED OF TRUST TO SECURE AN INDEBTEDNESS IN THE ORIGINAL AMOUNT SHOWN BELOW:

AMOUNT:	$225,500.00
DATED:	JULY 20, 20xx
TRUSTOR:	DAN AND DONNA WINTER
TRUSTEE:	XYZ SECURITIES COMPANY
BENEFICIARY:	ANY CITY BANK
RECORDED:	JULY 19,20xx AS INSTRUMENT NO. 95-0030762, OFFICIAL RECORDS
ORIGINAL LOAN NUMBER:	NOT SHOWN

S. 19. THE ABOVE DEED OF TRUST APPEARS TO SECURE A HOME EQUITY TYPE OF LOAN. IF THIS LOAN IS TO PAID OFF AND RECONVEYED THROUGH THIS TRANSACTION, HOMETOWN TITLE WILL REQUIRE A WRITTEN STATEMENT FROM THE BENEFICIARY THAT A FREEZE IS IN EFFECT ON THE ACCOUNT
AND
THE DEMAND FOR PAY OFF MUST PROVIDE THAT A RECONVEYANCE WILL BE ISSUED UPON PAYMENT OF THE AMOUNTS SHOWN THEREIN.

T. 20. **END OF SCHEDULE B**

Title Order-No. 6805790

U. 21. NOTE NO.1: IF A 1970 ALTA OWNER'S OR LENDER'S OR 1975 ALTA
LEASEHOLD OWNER'S OR LENDER'S POLICY FORM HAS BEEN REQUESTED,
WHEN APPROVED FOR ISSUANCE, WILL BE ENDORSED TO ADD THE FOLLOWING
TO THE EXCLUSIONS FROM COVERAGE CONTAINED THEREIN:

LOAN POLICY EXCLUSION:

ANY CLAIM, WHICH ARISES OUT OF THE TRANSACTION CREATING THE
INTEREST OF THE MORTGAGEE INSURED BY THIS POLICY, BY REASON OF THE
OPERATION OF FEDERAL BANKRUPTCY, STATE INSOLVENCY, OR SIMILAR CREDITORS'
RIGHTS LAWS.

OWNER'S POLICY EXCLUSION:

ANY CLAIM WHICH ARISES OUT OF THE TRANSACTION VESTING IN THE
INSURED,THE ESTATE OF INTEREST INSURED BY THIS POLICY, BY REASON OF
THE OPERATION OF FEDERAL BANKRUPTCY, STATE INSOLVENCY OR SIMILAR
CREDITOR'S RIGHTS LAWS.

V. 22. NOTE NO. 2: THE CHARGE FOR A POLICY OF TITLE INSURANCE WHEN
ISSUED THROUGH THIS TITLE ORDER, WILL BE BASED ON THE SHORT-TERM
RATE.

W. 23. NOTE NO. 3: IF THIS COMPANY IS REQUESTED TO DISBURSE FUNDS IN
CONNECTION WITH THIS TRANSACTION, CHAPTER 598, STATUES PF 1989
MANDATES HOLD PERIODS FOR CHECKS DEPOSITED TO ESCROW OR SUB-
ESCROW ACCOUNTS. THE MANDATORY HOLD PERIOD FOR CASHIER'S CHECKS,
CERTIFIED CHECKS AND TELLER'S CHECKS IS ONE BUSINESS DAY AFTER
THEDAY DEPOSITED. OTHER CHECKS REQUIRE A HOLD PERIOD OF FROM TWO
TO FIVE BUSINESS DAYS AFTER THE DAY DEPOSITED. IN THE EVENT THAT THE
PARTIES TO THE CONTEMPLATED TRANSACTION WISH TO RECORD PRIOR TO
THE TIME THAT THE FUNDS ARE AVAILABLE FOR DISBURSEMENT (AND
SUBJECT TO COMPANY APPROVAL), THE COMPANY WILL REQUIRE THE PRIOR

WRITTEN CONSENT OF THE PARTIES. UPON REQUEST, A FORM ACCEPTABLE TO
THE COMPANY AUTHORIZING SAID EARLY RECORDING MAY BE PROVIDED TO
ESCROW FOR EXECUTION.

WIRE TRANSFERS

THERE IS NO MANDATED HOLD PERIOD FOR FUNDS DEPOSITED BY CONFIRMED WIRE
TRANSFER. THE COMPANY MAY DISBURSE SUCH FUNDS THE SAME DAY.

HOMETOWN TITLE WILL DISBURSE BY WIRE (WIRE-OUT) ONLY COLLECTED FUNDS OR
FUNDS RECEIVED BY CONFIRMED WIRE (WIRE-IN). THE FEE FOR EACH WIRE-OUT IS
$25.00. THE COMPANY'S WIRE-IN INSTRUCTIONS ARE:

Title Order-No.6805790

WIRE-IN INSTRUCTIONS FOR BANK OF AMERICA:

BANK: ANY CITY BANK
                                               1200 LAKEFRONT DRIVE
                                               ANY CITY, CA 90000
BANK ABA: 121000359
ACCOUNT NAME: HOMETOWN TITLE COMPANY
title order 6805790   1258972

ACCOUNT NUMBER:

                                               HOMETOWN TITLE COMPANY
FOR CREDIT TO: 189 FRONT STREET
                                               ANY TOWN, CA 90000
FURTHER CREDIT TO: ORDER NO: 01243567

X. NOTE NO. 4: THERE ARE NO CONVEYANCES AFFECTING SAID LAND,
        RECORDED WITHIN SIX (6) MONTHS OF THE DATE OF THIS REPORT.

        Y. NOTE NO.5: NONE OF THE ITEMS SHOWN IN THIS REPORT WILL CAUSE
    THECOMPANY TO DECLINE TO ATTACH CLTA INDORSEMENT FORM100 TO AN
    ALTA LOAN POLICY, WHEN ISSUED.

Z. NOTE NO. 6: THERE IS LOCATED ON SAID LAND A SINGLE-FAMILY
        RESIDENCE KNOWN AS: 987 OCEAN VIEW DRIVE, IN THE CITY OF ANY CITY,
        COUNTY OF APPLE, STATE OF CALIFORNIA

PRINTED EXCEPTIONS AND EXCLUSIONS

CALIFORNIA LAND TITLE ASSOCIATION STANDARD COVERAGE POLICY-20XX

EXCLUSIONS FROM COVERAGE

The following matters are expressly excluded from the coverage of this policy and the Company will not pay loss or damage, costs, attorney's fees or expenses which arise by reason of:

1.

(a) Any law, ordinance or governmental regulation (including but not limited to building and zoning laws, ordinances or regulations) restricting, regulating, prohibiting or relating to the occupancy, use or enjoyment of the land; the character, dimensions or location of any improvement now or hereafter erected on the land; a separation in ownership or a change in the dimensions or area of the land or any parcel of which the land is or was a part; or environment protection, or the effect of any violation of these laws, ordinances or governmental regulations, except to the extent that a notice of the enforcement thereof or a notice of a defect, lien or encumbrance resulting from a violation or alleged violation affecting the land has been recorded in the public records at Date of Policy.

(b) Any governmental police power not excluded by (a) above, except to the extent that a notice of the exercise thereof or a notice of a defect, lien or encumbrance resulting from a violation or alleged violation affecting the land has been recorded in the public records at Date of Policy.

2.

Rights of eminent domain unless notice of the exercise thereof has been recorded in the public records at Date of Policy, but not excluding from coverage any taking which has occurred prior to Date of Policy which would be binding on the rights of a purchaser for value with knowledge,

3.

Defects, liens, encumbrances, adverse claims, or other matters:
(a) whether or not recorded in the public records at Date of Policy, but created, suffered, assumed or agreed to by the insured claimant;
(b) not known to the Company, not recorded in the public records at Date of Policy, but known to the insured claimant and not disclosed.
(c) resulting in no loss or damage to the insured claimant;
(d) attaching or created subsequent to Date of Policy; or
(e) resulting in loss or damage which would not have been sustained if the insured claimant had paid value for the insured mortgage or the estate or interest insured by this policy.

4.

Unenforceability of the lien of the insured mortgage because of the ability or failure of the insured at Date of Policy, or the inability or failure of any subsequent owner of the indebtedness, to comply with applicable doing business laws of the state in which the land is situated.

5.

Invalidity or unenforceability of the lien of the insured mortgage, or claim thereof, which arises out of the transaction evidenced by the insured mortgage and is based upon usury or any consumer credit protection or truth-in-lending law.

6.

Any claim, which arises out of the transaction vesting in the insured the estate or interest insured by this policy or the transaction creating the interest of the insured lender, by reason of the operation of federal bankruptcy, state insolvency or similar creditor' rights laws.

EXCEPTIONS FROM COVERAGE

This policy does not insure against loss or damage (and the Company will not pay cost, attorneys' fees or expenses) which arise by reason of:

1. Taxes or assessments which are not shown as existing liens by the records of any taxing authority that levies taxes or assessments on real property or by the public records.

2. Proceedings by a public agency which may result in taxes or assessments, or notices of such proceedings, whether or not shown by the records of such agency or by the public records.

3. Any facts, rights, interests or claims which are not shown by the public records but which could be ascertained by an inspection of the land or which may be asserted by persons in possession thereof.

4. Easements, liens, or encumbrances, or claims thereof, which are not shown by the public records.

5. Discrepancies, conflicts in boundary lines, shortage in area, encroachments, or any other facts which a correct survey would disclose, and which are not shown by the public records.

6. (a) Unpatented mining claims; (b) reservations or exceptions in patents or in Acts authorizing the issuance thereof; (c) water rights, claims or title to water, whether or not the matters excepted under (a), (b) or (c) are shown by the public records.

AMERICAN LAND TITLE ASSOCIATION
RESIDENTIAL TITLE INSURANCE POLICY

EXCLUSIONS FROM COVERAGE

In addition to the exceptions in Schedule B, you are not insured against loss, costs, attorney's fees and expenses resulting from:

1. Government police power, and the existence or violation of any law or government regulation. This includes building and zoning ordinances and also laws and regulations concerning:

   - land use
   - improvements on the land
   - land division
   - environmental protection

   This exclusion does not apply to the violations or the enforcement of these matters which appear in the public records at Policy Date. This exclusion does not limit the zoning coverage described in Items 12 and 13 of Covered Title Risks.

2. The right to take the land by condemning it, unless:
   - a notice of exercising the right appears in the public records on Policy Date
   - the taking happened prior to the Policy Date and is binding on you if you bought the land without knowing of the taking.

3. Title Risks:
   - that are created, allowed, or agreed to by you
   - that are known to you, but not to us, on the Policy Date unless they appeared in the public records
   - that result in no loss to you
   - that first affect your title after the Policy Date-this does not limit the labor and material lien coverage in item 8 of Covered Title Risks

4. Failure to pay value for your title

5. Lack of a right:
   - to any land outside the area specifically described and referred to item 3 of Schedule A, or
   - in streets, alleys, or waterways that touch your land

This exclusion does not limit the access coverage in Item 5 of Covered Title Risks

EXCEPTIONS FROM COVERAGE

In addition to the Exceptions, you are not insured against loss, costs, attorneys' fees, and expenses resulting from:

1. Someone claiming an interest in your land by reason of:
   A. Easements not shown in the public records
   B. Boundary disputes not shown in the public records
   C. Improvements owned by your neighbor placed on your land

2. If, in addition to a single family residence, your existing structure consists of one or more Additional Dwelling Units, Item 12 of Covered Title Risks does not insure you against loss, costs, attorneys' fees, and expenses resulting from:
   A. The forced removal of any Additional Dwelling Unit, or
   B. The forced conversion of any Additional Dwelling Unit back to its original use.

   If said Additional Dwelling Unit was either constructed or converted to use as a dwelling unit in violation of any law or government regulation

AMERICAN LAND TITLE ASSOCIATION LOAN POLICY WITH ALTA ENDORSEMENT - FORM 1 COVERAGE

and

AMERICAN LAND TITLE ASSOCIATION LEASEHOLD LOAN POLICY WITH ALTA ENDORSEMENT - FORM 1 COVERAGE

EXCLUSIONS FROM COVERAGE

The following matters are expressly excluded from the coverage of this policy and the Company will not pay loss or damage, costs, attorney's fees or expenses which arise by reason of:

1.
(a) Any law, ordinance or governmental regulation (including but not limited to
building and zoning laws, ordinances, or regulations) restricting, regulating, prohibiting or relating to (i) the occupancy, use, or enjoyment of the land; (ii) the character, dimensions or location of any improvement now or hereafter erected on the land; (iii)a separation in ownership or a change in the dimensions or area of the land or any parcel of which the land is or was a part; or (iv) environmental protection, or the effect of any violations of these laws, ordinances or governmental regulations, except to the extent that a notice of the enforcement thereof or a notice of a defect, lien or encumbrance resulting from a violation or alleged violation or alleged violation affecting the land has been recorded in the public records at Date of Policy.

(b) Any governmental police power not excluded by (a) above, except to the extent
that a notice of the exercise thereof or a notice of a defect, lien or encumbrance resulting from a violation or alleged violation affecting the land has been recorded in the public records at Date of Policy.

2. Rights of eminent domain unless notice of the exercise thereof has been recorded
the public records at Date of Policy, but not excluding from coverage any taking which has occurred prior to Date of Policy which would be binding on the rights of a purchaser for value without knowledge.

3. Defects, liens, encumbrances, adverse claims or other matters:
(a) created, suffered, assumed or agreed to by the insured claimant;
(b) not known to the Company, not recorded in the public records at Date of Policy
but known to the insured claimant and not disclosed in writing to the Company by the insured claimant prior to the date the insured claimant became an insured under this policy;
(c) resulting in no loss or damage to the insured claimant;
(d) attaching or created subsequent to Date of Policy (except to the extent that this
policy insures the priority of the lien of the insured mortgage over any statutory lien for services, labor or material or to the extent insurance is afforded herein as to assessments for street improvements under construction or completed at Date of Policy);

(e) resulting in loss or damage which would not have been sustained if the insured claimant had paid value for the insured mortgage

4. Unenforceability of the lien of the insured mortgage because of the inability or failure of the insured at Date of Policy, or the inability or failure of any subsequent owner of the indebtedness, to comply with applicable doing business laws of the state in which the land is situated.

5. Invalidity or unenforceability of the lien of the insured mortgage, or claim thereof, which is based upon usury or any consumer credit protection or truth in lending law.

6. Any statutory lien for services, labor or materials (or priority of any statutory lien for services, labor or materials over the lien of the insured mortgage) arising from an improvement or work related to the land which is contracted for and commenced subsequent to Date of Policy and is not financed in whole or in part by proceeds of the indebtedness secured by the insured mortgage which at Date of Policy the insured has advanced or is obligated to advance.

7. Any claim, which arises out of the transaction creating the interest of the mortgagee insured by this policy, by reason of the operation of federal bankruptcy, state insolvency, or similar creditors' rights laws, that is based on:

(i) the transaction creating the interest of the insured mortgagee being deemed a fraudulent conveyance or fraudulent transfer; or
(ii) the subordination of the interest of the insured mortgagee as a result of the application of the doctrine of equitable subordination; or
(iii) the transaction creating the interest of the insured mortgagee being deemed a referential transfer except where the preferential transfer results from the failure:
(a) to timely record the instrument of transfer; or
(b) of such recordation to impart notice to purchaser for value or a judgment or lien creditor.

The above policy forms be issued to afford either Standard Coverage or Extended Coverage. In addition to the above Exclusions from Coverage, the Exceptions from Coverage in a Standard Coverage policy will also include the following General Exceptions:

EXCEPTIONS FROM COVERAGE

This policy does not insure against loss or damage (and the Company will not pay costs, attorneys' fees or expenses) which arise by reason of:

1. Taxes or assessments which are not shown as existing liens by the records of any taxing authority that levies taxes or assessments on real property or by the public records.

2. Proceedings by a public agency which may result in taxes or assessments, or notices of such proceedings, whether or not shown by the records of such agency or by the public records.

3. Any facts, rights, interests or claims which are not shown by the public records but which could be ascertained by an inspection of the land or by making inquiry of persons in possession thereof.

4. Easements, liens, or encumbrances, or claims thereof, which are not shown by the public records.

5. Discrepancies, conflicts in boundary lines, shortage in area, encroachments, or any other facts which a correct survey would disclose, and which are not shown by public records.

6. (a) Unpatented mining claims; (b) reservations or exceptions in patents or in Acts authorizing the issuance thereof: (c) water rights, claims or title to water, whether or not the matters excepted under (a), (b), or (c) are shown by the public records.

AMERICAN LAND TITLE ASSOCIATION
OWNER'S POLICY
and
AMERICAN LAND TITLE ASSOCIATION LEASEHOLD
OWNER'S POLICY

EXCLUSIONS FROM COVERAGE

The following matters are expressly excluded from the coverage of this policy and the Company will not pay loss or damage, costs, attorney's fees or expenses which arise by reason of:

1.

(a) Any law, ordinance or governmental regulation (including but not limited to building and zoning laws, ordinances or regulations) restricting, regulating, prohibiting or relating to (i) the occupancy, use, or enjoyment of the land; (ii) the character, dimensions or location of any improvement now or hereafter erected on the land; (iii) a separation in ownership or a change in the dimensions or area of the land or any parcel of which the land is or was a part; or (iv) environmental protection, or the effect of any violations of these laws, ordinances or governmental regulations, except to the extent that a notice of the enforcement thereof or a notice of a defect, lien or encumbrance resulting from a violation or alleged violation affecting the land has been recorded in the public records at Date of Policy.

(b) Any governmental police power not excluded by (a) above, except to the extent that a notice of the exercise thereof or a notice of a defect, lien or encumbrance resulting from a violation or alleged violation affecting the land has been recorded in the public records at Date of Policy.

2. Rights of eminent domain unless notice of the exercise thereof has been recorded in the public records at Date of Policy, but not excluding from coverage any taking which has occurred prior to Date of Policy which would be binding on the rights of a purchaser for value without knowledge.

3. Defects, liens, encumbrances, adverse claims or other matters:
    (a) created, suffered, assumed or agreed to by the insured claimant;
    (b) not known to the Company, not recorded in the public records at Date of Policy, but known to the insured claimant and not disclosed in writing to the Company by the insured claimant prior to the date the insured claimant became an insured under this policy.
    (c) resulting in no loss or damage to the insured claimant
    (d) attaching or created subsequent to Date of Policy; or
    (e) resulting in loss or damage which would not have been sustained if the insured claimant had paid value for the estate or interest insured by this policy.

4. Any claim, which arises out of the transaction vesting in the insured the estate or
interest insured by this policy, by reason of the operation of federal bankruptcy, state
insolvency, or similar creditors' rights laws, that is based on:
(i) the transaction creating the estate or interest insured by this policy being deemed
a fraudulent conveyance or fraudulent transfer; or
(ii) the transaction creating the estate or interest insured by this policy being deemed
a preferential transfer except where the preferential transfer results from the failure:
(a) to timely record the instrument of transfer; or
(b) of such recordation to impart notice to a purchaser for value or a
judgment or lien creditor.

**The above policy forms may be issued to afford either Standard Coverage or Extended
Coverage. In addition to the above Exclusions from Coverage, the Exceptions from
Coverage in a Standard Coverage policy will also include the following General
Exceptions:**

EXCEPTIONS FROM COVERAGE

This policy does not insure against loss or damage (and the Company will not pay
costs, attorney's fees or expenses) which arise by reason of:

1. Taxes or assessments which are not shown as existing liens by the records of any
taxing authority that levies taxes or assessments on real property or by the public
records.
Proceedings by a public agency which may result in taxes or assessments, or notices
of such proceedings, whether or not shown by the records of such agency or by the
public records.

2. Any facts, rights, interests or claims which are not shown by the public records but
which could be ascertained by an inspection of the land or by making inquiry of
persons in possession thereof.

3. Easements, liens, or encumbrances, or claims thereof, which are not shown by the
public records.
4. Discrepancies, conflicts in boundary lines, shortage in area, encroachments, or any
other facts which a correct survey would disclose, and which are not shown by the
public records.
5. (a) Unpatented mining claims; (b) reservations or exceptions in patents or in Acts
authorizing the issuance thereof; (c) water rights, claims or title to water, whether or
not the matters excepted under (a), (b) or (c) are shown by the public records.

True-False Quiz

Now that you have read all the material in this chapter, take the following self-test and check your knowledge of title insurance.

True/False

1. _TRUE_ Title insurance is a contract to protect against losses arising through defects in title to real estate.

2. _TRUE_ The foundation of real property ownership is title.

3. _FALSE_ Title officers today are called conveyancers.

4. _FALSE_ Standard coverage insures against matters not of record.

5. _FALSE_ A CLTA policy of title insurance is designed primarily for the lender.

6. _FALSE_ An extended policy of title insurance protects only against matters of record.

7. _TRUE_ A basic policy of title insurance may be expanded or modified by special endorsements.

8. _FALSE_ Title insurance covers defects known by the parties prior to the transfer, even though not disclosed.

9. _TRUE_ The preliminary title report contains all encumbrances against the property in question.

10. _TRUE_ If an untrue statement about the quality of the title to a property is made, the insurance is not valid.

Chapter
12

Computerized Escrow

Learning Objectives

After reading this chapter, you will be able to:

- describe computer tasking using the latest software programs.

- define title insurance.

- explain the process of title examination.

- discuss the automated escrow systems available and what they include.

Introduction

Computer technology, for the most part, has replaced traditional methods of conducting escrows. In addition to software which provides conforming forms, word processing programs allow for quick and accurate input of information. Both escrow and title insurance rely heavily on saved information in computers and on reproduction of data.

Computer Tasking

Efficiency and accuracy of the escrow product have been refined as a byproduct of computer technology. Since the early 1990s, escrow and title officers have learned to use new software capability to create new models for forms and other documents.

Research capabilities also have been extended beyond what was possible before computer memory became available. Word processing software has allowed the timely and consistent storage and retrieval of data as well as faster and more accurate communication between parties to the escrow.

Title Insurance

Computer technology is most often used in the title industry for title searching and title examination. Untold hours have been spent in the past by researchers using archives as their only source to unravel the history of a piece of property. Technology has now supplied those researchers with the tools to make their jobs easier and quicker.

Title Research

The job of a title searcher is mainly to recover information about a specific property or parcel. The researcher uses various systems which classify real property by legal description or assessor's parcel number to find data that might affect the title. The information is accessed from computer storage files.

After the title search has been completed, the documents listed in the chain of title are copied for title examination. Computer communications and graphics may be used for this process.

There are certain items such as divorce, incompetence, parole proceedings, guardianship, probates, bankruptcy filings, judgments, tax liens, or powers of attorney that affect an owner or the property in question. If they cannot be found by legal description of the property in question, the information is gathered using the names of parties involved. These are indexed by grantor and grantee, alphabetically, in computer files.

Unfortunately, all steps necessary to complete a title search do not necessarily lend themselves to automation and the use of technology. Legal opinions still must be sought by the title examiner on matters in the chain of title, such as partition and

quiet title actions, orders confirming sale, attachments and executions, divorces, probates, and other legal matters. Many times documents recorded prior to the transaction in question, or other documents in possession of a third party must be obtained. Commonly, copies of CC&Rs on a property are required for extended coverage insurance or construction of new improvements.

Title Examination

After the title data is collected by the researcher the information gathered is interpreted by a person who specializes in examining chains of title, and a title report is assembled. This information is then entered into a computer and saved for printing the title report and writing the title policy when the title search process is complete.

At the closing, when the title policy is written, the information may be modified if there have been any new documents recorded, such as reconveyances, deeds of trust or liens, since the title search was completed. The final report is then presented to the insured parties.

Data Processing

Word processing supports the entire course of gathering and interpreting title data for the purpose of issuing title insurance. The speed with which information is input, stored, or printed has

allowed the title procedures needed to complete a real estate transaction to be much more efficient than in the past, with fewer mistakes or oversights because of human error.

In transactions where there is an institutional lender of record, the title insurer often is involved in a sub-escrow. The lender will send a demand for payoff of a loan to the title company rather than to the escrow holder, for payment. Also, if a new loan is being funded, the net proceeds are always sent to the title company instead of to the escrow holder.

The complex task of accounting for all payoff funds, checks for payments to the seller or buyer, or any refunds to the escrow holder or other parties is accomplished by computer. Formerly, hours of the escrow holder's time were spent at accounting, tracking, and processing the paperwork.

A special sub-escrow software program may be required to calculate exact figures needed for variations in transactions. Variable interest rate financing, graduated payments and negative amortization, prepayment fees, late charges, or lender fees for producing the demand for pay-off all require special accounting and handling. Computer calculations are essential to the timely and successful closing of these escrows.

A total data processing system will contain applications for the processing of monetary data for financial statements, investments of surplus cash, maintenance, and reconciliations of bank accounts, customer billing, and accounting. In addition, a marketing support system of customer profiles, tracking customer activity, analysis of customer volume, or other customer related activity supports automated escrow and title procedures.

Automated Escrow

Automated systems for an escrow office must be capable of managing a large extent of accounting and document processing. One of the most important charges to an escrow holder is the protection of money that flows through transactions. Suitable apportionment of charges to the responsible parties, as supported by clear escrow instructions, is an application of that duty.

Accounting Procedures

Each escrow office must decide what kind of accounting system it will use. The system must be appropriate to the size of the escrow operation, the number and type of transactions, and the basic management and information requirement of the office.

The escrow office also must decide whether to use manual or automated methods for trust fund accounting and other accounting for which it is responsible.

Manual Accounting

All receipts and disbursements are posted to individual ledger cards by escrow number and then posted and balanced to the office escrow account with the manual bookkeeping method. The main source of information in this process is the ledger card, which is then used to prepare further reports. Manual accounting can be suitable for a small escrow office that keeps a steady but limited volume of business. It is a rare escrow office, however, which manages its accounts without the aid of computerized technology.

Automated Accounting

A small escrow office may use either a small personal computer for accounting or a bank's or title company's server.

The type of information, documents, or reports will be determined by the information put into the computer as well as the adequacy of the accounting software installed for bookkeeping purposes. Each office should assess its accounting needs before making a decision about the extent of automated bookkeeping it will use.

Once an escrow office has committed to using automated accounting rather than the manual method, there are a few basic documents with which to become familiar.

Start Card

The first data for entering a transaction into the system is provided by a start card. Information such as company number, names of the buyer and seller, amount of consideration, date escrow opened, legal description or street address of property, type of escrow, escrow officer assigned, designated title company, and any other useful information about the transaction is entered.

Escrow Receipt

The escrow receipt acts as an audit trail for money being processed through the computer system. When funds are deposited in the escrow account, a receipt for the amount deposited is generated for this purpose by the accounting program.

Adjustment Slip

If a mistake is made when data is entered into the system, an adjustment slip is used to correct the error.

Escrow Checks

As checks are written against deposited funds in the escrow account, data processing accounts for each individual check debit.

Fee Slips

As work is completed on individual escrow files, payment for services is drawn using a fee slip, and the amount earned is transferred to the bank's fee account.

Periodically, the escrow holder transfers funds, as needed, to its operations account.

Other Reports

- Account Control

- Report of new escrow

- Receipt listing and adjustments

- Disbursement activity and adjustments

- Overdraft report

- Fee report

- Status reports

- Master control and summary of activity

- Closed escrow report

- List of missing start cards

- Unprocessed and voided checks

- Peripheral Data

- **Indices:** cross-references by escrow number, buyer, seller, broker, legal description, property address, type of escrow, or other meaningful index for the escrow office.

- **Trial Balance:** monitors escrows open for a prolonged period.

- **Ledger Card:** permanent file record, produced monthly after final file disbursements.

- **Reconciliation:** a report that keeps track of the balance between the trust bank account and the balance shown in the trust account system, making sure they conform with each other.

- **Checks Outstanding:** a list of checks that are unpaid as yet by the bank.

- **Purged Escrow Listing:** a list of the disbursement of all deposited funds, kept as escrows are removed from the system, either through closing or cancellation.

- **Roster of Escrow Officers:** a list of escrow agents conducting each escrow.

- **Roster of Business Sources:** client list.

- **Roster of Title Companies:** sources most used by the escrow holder.

- **Audit Confirmation Letter:** preprinted and addressed audit letters to the parties who deposit money in escrow to confirm the amounts in the trust account.

- **Customer Reports:** a final file accounting with supporting disbursements.

- **Marketing Analysis**

- **Escrow Activity:** all escrows that have been opened, closed or canceled, listed by date and address.

- **Income Analysis by Officer:** a list of fees earned by each escrow officer, thereby indicating strengths and weaknesses in productivity.

- **Income Analysis by Source:** a marketing tool to indicate where market strengths lie.

- **Title Business Placement:** a list of title orders placed by company.

SIMPLE
MORTGAGE
SERVICES

SMS

SMS TITLE WORKS

Revolutionize the title business!

SMS Title Works represents a new concept in the title business - true integration and sharing of information from one department or system to another. This eliminates the need to enter the same information over and over in numerous systems to process a title order.

Imagine entering your new title orders in your computer just once! And having that open order information automatically:

- order your title search
- pull the maps, recorded documents and starter file
- create an "Electronic Title File" with all necessary paperwork
- prepare the preliminary title report or commitment

Your staff could actually do the examination right on the computer and have the preliminary title report or commitment prepared. All available on the same computer screen, with tracking information about each step. No need to make copies, print documents from the reader printer, or pass the paper file from one desk to another.

SMS Title Works is a suite of application systems offered by SMS including *TITLE/ESCROW/CLOSING production, DMS TITLE PLANT, and IMAGE-PRO DOCUMENT IMAGING.* In addition to providing integration between our own systems, we have the ability to interface with competitive products that you may already have in place.

Our goal is to truly automate the process of a title order, from beginning to end. What will this mean to you? Improved productivity, better control, and a competitive advantage that all lead to increased revenue. And the best part... you don't have to radically change the way you currently do business. Simply let SMS Title Works do the work for you!

SMS

COMPANY: NEW
OFFICE: Demo

START CARD

Escrow Number	Opening Date	Officer	Title	Sales Price	Type
1111-Demo	7/8/20xx	JW	Fatco	$950,000.00	Sale

PROPERTY DESCRIPTION	EST. FEE	EST. COE	STATUS
987 Ocean View Drive Any City, CA 90000	$680.00	9/06/20xx	

AGENT   BUYER'S NAME

Dan and Donna Winter

BUYER'S ADDRESS (audit letters)

25892 Mountain Avenue, Any Town CA 90000

AGENT   SELLER'S NAME

Sam and Kate Summers

SELLER'S ADDRESS (audit letters)

987 Ocean View Drive, Any City CA 90000   BAL. FRWD

☐YES ☐NO

COMMENTS   HOLD

Escrow to close concurrently with E#12341   ☐YES ☐NO

FILE COPY

Listing Broker: ABC Realty, Inc.   Agent: Alex Baker
Selling Broker: Sunshine Real Estate   Agent: Teri Paul

Title Company: Any City Title Company
123 Lakeview Pkwy, Any City, CA 90000

Conversation Log

Date: 06-06-20xx   Page No: 1
Escrow: 1111-DEMO

Officer: Kelly Rose   Opened: 4-06-20xx
    Property: 987 Ocean   Closed: 6-06-20xx
    View Drive, Any City,
    CA 90000

Buyer: Seller:
Dan Winter   Sam Summers
Donna Winter   Kate Summers

Entry: 06-06-20xx 2:47 PM By: jjw

This is a sample conversation log, which you would use to type information on this particular escrow, then print a copy and attach in your escrow file.

Escrow No. 1111-Demo

Date Printed: June 6, 20xx
Est. Close Date: June 6, 20xx
Actual Close Date: June 6, 20xx

Page 1

Reference:
987 Ocean View Drive
Any City, CA 90000

SELLER:
Sam Summers
Kate Summers

BUYER:
Dan Winter
Donna Winter

CHECK REGISTER

ISSUE DATE	RECEIPT NUMBER	PAYOR	AMOUNT
6/06/20xx	1234	Deposit: Buyer	2,000.00
6/06/20xx	01000	Deposit: Dan Winter	36,700.00
6/06/20xx	1000	Draft: Fatco	4,311.08

ISSUE DATE	CHECK NUMBER	PAYEE	AMOUNT
6/06/20xx	1000	Sam Summers	26,536.97
6/06/20xx	1001	Dan Winter	359.93
6/06/20xx	1002	ABC Realty, Inc.	2,555.00
6/06/20xx	1003	Alex Baker	2,500.00
6/06/20xx	1004	Sunshine Real Estate	600.00
6/06/20xx	1005	Teri Paul	4,200.00
6/06/20xx	1006	Any Town Insurance Company	460.00
6/06/20xx	1007	Pacific Pest Control	50.00
6/06/20xx	1008	Hillcrest Homeowners' Association	175.00
6/06/20xx	1009	XYZ Property Management	125.00
6/06/20xx	1010	Home Warranty Company	245.00
6/06/20xx	1011	Any City Credit Card	2,345.00
6/06/20xx	1013	Easy Express Services	45.00
6/06/20xx	1014	Sam & Kate Summers	160.27
6/06/20xx	1015	Any City Title Company	1,553.91
6/06/20xx	1012	SMS	1,000.00

Deposits:		38,700.00
Drafts/Wires: +		4,311.08
Checks: -		43,011.08
Funds Held		.00
Balance		.00

Date: 02-20-20xx

Preliminary Disbursement Report

Page 1

Time: 18:30:59   SMS SETTLEMENT SERVICES   User: SMS

Escrow No. 004861   Open Date: 01/24/20xx
Seller/Buyer: Summers/Winter   Closed Date: 02/20/20xx

I. RECEIPTS:
  1. Dan Winter   002381 02/01/20xx $1,750.00.00

                                        $1,750.00

  A. RECEIPTS IN PROCESS:
    Any City Bank   002394 02/20/20xx $80,008.13

    Total receipts in
    process $80,008.13

    Total Receipts $81,758.13

II. DISBURSEMENTS   0.00

  A. DISBURSEMENTS IN PROCESS:

    Total disbursements in process   0.00
                                          0.00
    Total Disbursements

  B. PRELIMINARY DISBURSEMENTS:

    HILLCREST SURVEYING
    4400 SOUTH STREET
    ANY TOWN, CA
    Survey - Buyer   350.00

    Total Checks   350.00

    ABC REALTY, INC.
    2400 RIVERFRONT RD. SUITE B
    ANY CITY, CA
    Commission   5,697.00

    Total Checks   5,697.00

    ANY CITY BANK
    2900 N. OCEAN BLVD.
    ANY CITY, CA
    Interest   450.63
    Principal Balance   67,595.00

    Total Checks   68,045.63

    D.I. GREEN EXTERMINATING CO.
    100 HILL STREET
    ANY TOWN, CA
    Pest Inspection-Buyer   200.00
    Total Checks   200.00

```
Date: 02-20-20xx          Preliminary              Page 2
                          Disbursement
                          Report

Time: 18:30:59        SMS SETTLEMENT SERVICES      User: SMS


Escrow No. 004861              Open Date: 01/24/20xx
Seller/Buyer: Summers/Winter   Closed Date: 02/20/20xx

SUNSHINE REAL ESTATE
20000 HILL STREET
ANY CITY, CA
Commission                       5,697.00
Total Check                                        5,697.00

APPLE COUNTY RECORDER
Recording Fees-Buyer                20.50
Recording Fees-Seller               35.00
Total Check                         55.50

SMS SETTLEMENT SERVICES
Credit line Endorsement             75.00
Escrow Fees-Buyer                  225.00
Escrow Fees-Seller                 175.00
Title Examination-Seller           250.00
Title Insurance-Buyer               50.00
Title Insurance-Seller             813.00
Transfer Fee                        25.00
Total Check                                        1613.00

JONES & SPRING
Attorney's Fees-Seller              85.00
Total Check                                          85.00

CITY CREDIT SERVICE
Credit Report-Buyer                 15.00
Total Check                                          15.00

Total         Preliminary                         81,758.13
Disbursements

Total Disbursements                               81,758.13-

Escrow Balance                                        0.00


Approved by_____


Approved by_____
```

```
┌─────────────────────────────────────────────────────────────────────┐
```

Date: 02-20-20xx			Page 1

Final
Disbursement
Report

Time: 18:33:44	SMS SETTLEMENT SERVICES	User: SMS

Escrow No. 004861   Open Date: 01/24/20xx
Seller/Buyer: Summers/Winter   Closed Date: 02/20/20xx

I. RECEIPTS:

1. Dan Winter	002381 02/01/20xx	$1,750.00.00	
			$1,750.00

A. RECEIPTS IN PROCESS:

Any City Bank	002394 02/20/20xx	$80,008.13	
Total receipts in process			<u>$80,008.13</u>

Total Receipts		$81,758.13

II. DISBURSEMENTS		0.00

A. DISBURSEMENTS IN PROCESS:

1. Hillcrest Surveying	001223 02/20/20xx	350.00
2. ABC Realty, Inc.	001224 02/20/20xx	5,697.00
3. Any City Bank	001225 02/20/20xx	68,045.63
4. D.I. Green Exterminating	001226 02/20/20xx	200.00
5. Sunshine Real Estate	001227 02/20/20xx	5,697.00
6. Apple County Recorder	001228 02/20/20xx	55.50
7. SMS Settlement Services	001229 02/20/20xx	1,613.00
8. Rose & Green	001230 02/20/20xx	85.00
9. Credit Services	001231 02/20/20xx	15.00

Total Disbursements in process		81,758.13
Total Disbursements		81,758.13
Escrow Balance		0.00

Approved by:

Lender Summary

Escrow Number	004859	Page 1
Escrow Officer:	Kelly Rose	User SMS
Borrower Name	Winter, Dan	

Lender Name	Any City Bank
Type of Loan	New Loan

Amount of Loan	24,750.00
Amount withheld	2,428.50
Amount Due From Lender	122,321.50

Items Withheld From Loan

Description	Amount
Loan Origination Fee	180.00
Loan Discount	180.00
Appraisal Fee	350.00
Credit Line	200.00
Documentation Preparation	250.00
Tax Service	68.50
Hazard Insurance Premium	1,200.00

True-False Quiz

Now that you have read all the material in this chapter, take the following self-test and check your knowledge of computerized escrow.

True/False

1. _True_ Traditional methods of conducting escrows have been replaced by computer technology.

2. _False_ The title industry does not use computer technology.

3. _False_ Title research is still done by manual methods.

4. _True_ The job of a title searcher is that of recovery of information about a specific property.

5. _True_ Legal opinions are sought by title examiners on some matters in the chain of title, rather than getting the information by computer search.

6. _True_ Accounting is one of the main uses for computers in escrow offices.

7. _False_ A start card places information in a computer at the end of a transaction.

8. _True_ An audit trail is created with an escrow receipt, which is generated by a computer.

9. _True_ Mistakes made when entering data are corrected with an adjustment slip.

10. _True_ A report that keeps track of the balance between the trust bank account and the balance shown in the trust account system is a reconciliation report.

Chapter

13

Disclosure and Consumer Protection

Learning Objectives

After reading this chapter, you will be able to:

- describe real property disclosures.

- explain disclosures required under the Subdivision Map Act and Subdivided Lands Act.

- define lending disclosures such as RESPA and Reg. Z.

Introduction

As the business of buying and selling real estate gets more complex, so do the required disclosures. What used to be a matter of a buyer's or seller's word, and simple honesty, is now elevated (or reduced, depending on your point of view) to multiple sworn copies of those same statements, with serious penalties for untruths or misrepresentations.

It is true that most of these disclosures are supplied through the real estate agent. The escrow holder is only concerned with carrying out the requirements of the escrow as they apply to the disclosures. The escrow agent, however, ultimately is the tally keeper, and must be aware of each of the requirements for disclosure as the escrow progresses.

Real Property Disclosures

One of your jobs as an escrow agent is to guide the parties through the minefield of disclosure. Most of the disclosures are made by the real estate agent, with a small number made by the escrow holder. However, the practical escrow agent will make sure all disclosures have been made and all documents signed by the proper party.

Required Real Estate Disclosures

- Real Estate Transfer Disclosure Statement (TDS)
- Mello-Roos Disclosure
- Smoke Detector Statement of Compliance
- Lead-Based Paint Disclosure
- State Responsibility Areas Disclosure
- Geological Hazard Disclosure
- Special Studies Zones Disclosure
- Secured Water Heater Disclosure
- Disclosure of Ordnance Location
- Environmental Hazard Disclosures
- Energy Conservation Retrofit Disclosure
- Flood Zone Disclosure
- City and County Ordinance Disclosure

Required Escrow Disclosures

- Foreign Investment in Real Property Tax Act
- Notice and Disclosure to Buyer of State Tax Withholding
- Controlling Documents and Financial Statement (Condo)
- Notice of Advisability of Title Insurance
- Pest Control Inspection Disclosure

Transfer Disclosure Statement (TDS)

Many facts about a residential property could materially affect its value and desirability. In the *Real Estate Transfer Disclosure Statement*, the seller reveals any information that would be important to the buyer regarding condition of the property. The seller states that to his or her knowledge, everything pertinent, or in other words, anything that would significantly affect the value, has been disclosed. The escrow instructions then reflect the buyer and seller's agreement about the disclosures.

Required TDS Disclosures

- Age, condition and any defects or malfunctions of the structural components and/or plumbing, electrical, heating, or other mechanical systems

- Easements, common driveways, or fences

- Room additions, structural alterations, repairs, replacements or other changes, especially those made without required building permits

- Flooding, drainage or soils problems on, near, or in any way affecting the property

- Zoning violations, such as nonconforming uses or insufficient setbacks

- Homeowners' association obligations and deed restrictions or common area problems

- Citations against the property, or lawsuits against the owner or affecting the property

- Location of the property within a known earthquake zone

- Major damage to the property from fire, earthquake, or landslide

California law requires that a seller of one-to-four dwellings deliver to prospective buyers a Transfer Disclosure Statement about the condition of the property. This requirement extends to any transfer: by sale, exchange, installment land sale contract, lease with an option to purchase, any other option to purchase, or ground lease coupled with improvements.

Transfers Exempt from the Transfer Disclosure Statement

- A foreclosure sale

- A court-ordered transfer by a fiduciary in the administration of a probate estate or a testamentary trust

- Dissolution of marriage, legal separation, or property settlement agreement from one spouse to another related person incidental to such a judgment

- Between co-owners

- State controller for unclaimed property

- Tax sale

- Transfer to or from any governmental entity

- The first sale of a residential property within a subdivision

The required disclosure must be made to the prospective buyer, by the real estate agent, as soon as practicable before transfer of title, or in the case of a lease option, sales contract, or ground lease coupled with improvements, before the execution of the contract.

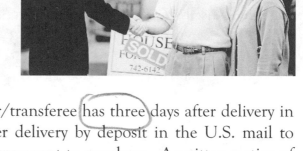

Should any disclosure or amended disclosure be delivered after the required date, the buyer/transferee has three days after delivery in person or five days after delivery by deposit in the U.S. mail to terminate the offer or agreement to purchase. A written notice of termination is the instrument that must reach the seller/transferor or the seller's agent for that purpose.

The obligation to prepare and deliver disclosures is imposed on the seller and the seller's agent and any agent acting in cooperation with them. Should more than one real estate agent be involved in the transaction (unless otherwise instructed by the seller), the agent obtaining the offer is required to deliver the disclosures to the prospective buyer.

Delivery to the prospective buyer of a report or an opinion prepared by a licensed engineer, land surveyor, geologist, structural pest control operator, contractor or other expert (with a specific professional license or expertise) may limit the liability of the seller and the real estate agents when making required disclosures. The overall intention is to provide meaningful disclosures about the condition of the property being transferred. A violation of the law does not invalidate a transfer; however, the seller may be liable for actual damages suffered by the buyer.

For information about the neighborhood or community, a city or county may require use of a Local Option Transfer Disclosure Statement disclosing special local facts.

CALIFORNIA
ASSOCIATION
OF REALTORS®

REAL ESTATE TRANSFER DISCLOSURE STATEMENT
(CALIFORNIA CIVIL CODE §1102, ET SEQ)
(C.A.R. Form TDS, Revised 10/03)

THIS DISCLOSURE STATEMENT CONCERNS THE REAL PROPERTY SITUATED IN THE CITY OF
_____ , COUNTY OF _____ , STATE OF CALIFORNIA,
DESCRIBED AS _____
THIS STATEMENT IS A DISCLOSURE OF THE CONDITION OF THE ABOVE DESCRIBED PROPERTY IN
COMPLIANCE WITH SECTION 1102 OF THE CIVIL CODE AS OF (date) _____ . IT IS NOT A
WARRANTY OF ANY KIND BY THE SELLER(S) OR ANY AGENT(S) REPRESENTING ANY PRINCIPAL(S) IN THIS
TRANSACTION, AND IS NOT A SUBSTITUTE FOR ANY INSPECTIONS OR WARRANTIES THE PRINCIPAL(S) MAY
WISH TO OBTAIN.

I. COORDINATION WITH OTHER DISCLOSURE FORMS

This Real Estate Transfer Disclosure Statement is made pursuant to Section 1102 of the Civil Code. Other statutes require disclosures, depending upon the details of the particular real estate transaction (for example: special study zone and purchase-money liens on residential property).

Substituted Disclosures: The following disclosures and other disclosures required by law, including the Natural Hazard Disclosure Report/Statement that may include airport annoyances, earthquake, fire, flood, or special assessment information, have or will be made in connection with this real estate transfer, and are intended to satisfy the disclosure obligations on this form, where the subject matter is the same:

☐ Inspection reports completed pursuant to the contract of sale or receipt for deposit.
☐ Additional inspection reports or disclosures: _____
_____

II. SELLER'S INFORMATION

The Seller discloses the following information with the knowledge that even though this is not a warranty, prospective Buyers may rely on this information in deciding whether and on what terms to purchase the subject property. Seller hereby authorizes any agent(s) representing any principal(s) in this transaction to provide a copy of this statement to any person or entity in connection with any actual or anticipated sale of the property.

THE FOLLOWING ARE REPRESENTATIONS MADE BY THE SELLER(S) AND ARE NOT THE REPRESENTATIONS OF THE AGENT(S), IF ANY. THIS INFORMATION IS A DISCLOSURE AND IS NOT INTENDED TO BE PART OF ANY CONTRACT BETWEEN THE BUYER AND SELLER.

Seller ☐ is ☐ is not occupying the property.

A. The subject property has the items checked below (read across)

☐ Range	☐ Oven	☐ Microwave
☐ Dishwasher	☐ Trash Compactor	☐ Garbage Disposal
☐ Washer/Dryer Hookups		☐ Rain Gutters
☐ Burglar Alarms	☐ Smoke Detector(s)	☐ Fire Alarm
☐ T.V. Antenna	☐ Satellite Dish	☐ Intercom
☐ Central Heating	☐ Central Air Conditioning	☐ Evaporator Cooler(s)
☐ Wall/Window Air Conditioning	☐ Sprinklers	☐ Public Sewer System
☐ Septic Tank	☐ Sump Pump	☐ Water Softener
☐ Patio/Decking	☐ Built-in Barbecue	☐ Gazebo
☐ Sauna		
☐ Hot Tub ☐ Locking Safety Cover*	☐ Pool ☐ Child Resistant Barrier*	☐ Spa ☐ Locking Safety Cover*
☐ Security Gate(s)	☐ Automatic Garage Door Opener(s)*	☐ Number Remote Controls ____
Garage: ☐ Attached	☐ Not Attached	☐ Carport
Pool/Spa Heater: ☐ Gas	☐ Solar	☐ Electric
Water Heater: ☐ Gas	☐ Water Heater Anchored, Braced, or Strapped*	☐ Private Utility or
Water Supply: ☐ City	☐ Well	Other _____
Gas Supply: ☐ Utility	☐ Bottled	
☐ Window Screens	☐ Window Security Bars ☐ Quick Release Mechanism on Bedroom Windows*	

Exhaust Fan(s) in _____ 220 Volt Wiring in _____ Fireplace(s) in _____
☐ Gas Starter _____ ☐ Roof(s): Type: _____ Age: _____ (approx.)
☐ Other: _____

Are there, to the best of your (Seller's) knowledge, any of the above that are not in operating condition? ☐ Yes ☐ No. If yes, then describe. (Attach additional sheets if necessary): _____
_____

(*see footnote on page 2)

Buyer's Initials (_____)(_____)
Seller's Initials (_____)(_____)
Reviewed by _____ Date _____

EQUAL HOUSING
OPPORTUNITY

TDS REVISED 10/03 (PAGE 1 OF 3)

REAL ESTATE TRANSFER DISCLOSURE STATEMENT (TDS PAGE 1 OF 3)

Agent: _____ Phone: _____ Fax: _____ Prepared using WINForms® software
Broker:

Property Address: _____ Date: _____

B. Are you (Seller) aware of any significant defects/malfunctions in any of the following? ☐ Yes ☐ No. If yes, check appropriate space(s) below.

☐ Interior Walls ☐ Ceilings ☐ Floors ☐ Exterior Walls ☐ Insulation ☐ Roof(s) ☐ Windows ☐ Doors ☐ Foundation ☐ Slab(s)
☐ Driveways ☐ Sidewalks ☐ Walls/Fences ☐ Electrical Systems ☐ Plumbing/Sewers/Septics ☐ Other Structural Components
(Describe: _____

_____

_____)

If any of the above is checked, explain. (Attach additional sheets if necessary): _____

_____

_____

_____

*This garage door opener or child resistant pool barrier may not be in compliance with the safety standards relating to automatic reversing devices as set forth in Chapter 12.5 (commencing with Section 19890) of Part 3 of Division 13 of, or with the pool safety standards of Article 2.5 (commencing with Section 115920) of Chapter 5 of Part 10 of Division 104 of, the Health and Safety Code. The water heater may not be anchored, braced, or strapped in accordance with Section 19211 of the Health and Safety Code. Window security bars may not have quick release mechanisms in compliance with the 1995 Edition of the California Building Standards Code.

C. Are you (Seller) aware of any the following:

1. Substances, materials, or products which may be an environmental hazard such as, but not limited to, asbestos, formaldehyde, radon gas, lead-based paint, mold, fuel or chemical storage tanks, and contaminated soil or water on the subject property .... ☐ Yes ☐ No
2. Features of the property shared in common with adjoining landowners, such as walls, fences, and driveways, whose use or responsibility for maintenance may have an effect on the subject property .... ☐ Yes ☐ No
3. Any encroachments, easements or similar matters that may affect your interest in the subject property .... ☐ Yes ☐ No
4. Room additions, structural modifications, or other alterations or repairs made without necessary permits....... ☐ Yes ☐ No
5. Room additions, structural modifications, or other alterations or repairs not in compliance with building codes.... ☐ Yes ☐ No
6. Fill (compacted or otherwise) on the property or any portion thereof .... ☐ Yes ☐ No
7. Any settling from any cause, or slippage, sliding. or other soil problems .... ☐ Yes ☐ No
8. Flooding, drainage or grading problems .... ☐ Yes ☐ No
9. Major damage to the property or any of the structures from fire, earthquake, floods, or landslides .... ☐ Yes ☐ No
10. Any zoning violations, nonconforming uses, violations of "setback" requirements .... ☐ Yes ☐ No
11. Neighborhood noise problems or other nuisances .... ☐ Yes ☐ No
12. CC&R's or other deed restrictions or obligations .... ☐ Yes ☐ No
13. Homeowners' Association which has any authority over the subject property .... ☐ Yes ☐ No
14. Any "common area" (facilities such as pools, tennis courts, walkways, or other areas co-owned in undivided interest with others) .... ☐ Yes ☐ No
15. Any notices of abatement or citations against the property .... ☐ Yes ☐ No
16. Any lawsuits by or against the seller threatening to or affecting this real property, including any lawsuits alleging a defect or deficiency in this real property or "common areas" (facilities such as pools, tennis courts, walkways, or other areas, co-owned in undivided interest with others) .... ☐ Yes ☐ No

If the answer to any of these is yes, explain. (Attach additional sheets if necessary): _____

_____

_____

_____

_____

Seller certifies that the information herein is true and correct to the best of the Seller's knowledge as of the date signed by the Seller.

Seller _____ Date _____

Seller _____ Date _____

Buyer's Initials (_____)(_____)

Reviewed by _____ Date _____

TDS REVISED 10/03 (PAGE 2 OF 3)

REAL ESTATE TRANSFER DISCLOSURE STATEMENT (TDS PAGE 2 OF 3)

Property Address: _____ Date: _____

III. AGENT'S INSPECTION DISCLOSURE
(To be completed only if the Seller is represented by an agent in this transaction.)

THE UNDERSIGNED, BASED ON THE ABOVE INQUIRY OF THE SELLER(S) AS TO THE CONDITION OF THE PROPERTY AND BASED ON A REASONABLY COMPETENT AND DILIGENT VISUAL INSPECTION OF THE ACCESSIBLE AREAS OF THE PROPERTY IN CONJUNCTION WITH THAT INQUIRY, STATES THE FOLLOWING:

☐ Agent notes no items for disclosure.
☐ Agent notes the following items: _____
_____
_____
_____
_____

Agent (Broker Representing Seller) _____ By _____ Date _____
　　　　　　　　　　　　　　　　　　　(Please Print)　　　　　　　(Associate Licensee or Broker Signature)

IV. AGENT'S INSPECTION DISCLOSURE
(To be completed only if the agent who has obtained the offer is other than the agent above.)

THE UNDERSIGNED, BASED ON A REASONABLY COMPETENT AND DILIGENT VISUAL INSPECTION OF THE ACCESSIBLE AREAS OF THE PROPERTY, STATES THE FOLLOWING:

☐ Agent notes no items for disclosure.
☐ Agent notes the following items: _____
_____
_____
_____

Agent (Broker Obtaining the Offer) _____ By _____ Date _____
　　　　　　　　　　　　　　　　　　(Please Print)　　　　　　　(Associate Licensee or Broker Signature)

V. BUYER(S) AND SELLER(S) MAY WISH TO OBTAIN PROFESSIONAL ADVICE AND/OR INSPECTIONS OF THE PROPERTY AND TO PROVIDE FOR APPROPRIATE PROVISIONS IN A CONTRACT BETWEEN BUYER AND SELLER(S) WITH RESPECT TO ANY ADVICE/INSPECTIONS/DEFECTS.

I/WE ACKNOWLEDGE RECEIPT OF A COPY OF THIS STATEMENT.

Seller _____ Date _____ Buyer _____ Date _____

Seller _____ Date _____ Buyer _____ Date _____

Agent (Broker Representing Seller) _____ By _____ Date _____
　　　　　　　　　　　　　　　　　　　(Please Print)　　　　　　　(Associate Licensee or Broker Signature)

Agent (Broker Obtaining the Offer) _____ By _____ Date _____
　　　　　　　　　　　　　　　　　　(Please Print)　　　　　　　(Associate Licensee or Broker Signature)

SECTION 1102.3 OF THE CIVIL CODE PROVIDES A BUYER WITH THE RIGHT TO RESCIND A PURCHASE CONTRACT FOR AT LEAST THREE DAYS AFTER THE DELIVERY OF THIS DISCLOSURE IF DELIVERY OCCURS AFTER THE SIGNING OF AN OFFER TO PURCHASE. IF YOU WISH TO RESCIND THE CONTRACT, YOU MUST ACT WITHIN THE PRESCRIBED PERIOD.

A REAL ESTATE BROKER IS QUALIFIED TO ADVISE ON REAL ESTATE. IF YOU DESIRE LEGAL ADVICE, CONSULT YOUR ATTORNEY.

SURE TRAC
The System for Success™

Published by the
California Association of REALTORS®

Reviewed by _____ Date _____

EQUAL HOUSING OPPORTUNITY

TDS REVISED 10/03 (PAGE 3 OF 3)

REAL ESTATE TRANSFER DISCLOSURE STATEMENT (TDS PAGE 3 OF 3)　　　T6429805.ZFX

Pest Control Certification

The law does not require that a structural pest control inspection be performed on real property prior to transfer. Should an inspection report and certification be required as a condition of transfer or obtaining financing, however, it must be done as soon as possible. Before transfer of title or before executing a real property sales contract, the seller or the seller's agent (and any agent acting in cooperation) must deliver or have delivered to the buyer a copy of the report. There must also be written certification attesting to the presence or absence of wood-destroying termites in the visible and accessible areas of the property. Such an inspection report and written certification must be prepared and issued by a registered structural pest-control company.

Upon request from the party ordering such a report, the company issuing the report must divide it into two categories: (1) identify the portions of the property where existing damage, infection, or infestation are noted; and (2) point out areas that may have impending damage, infection, or infestation.

Generally, there is more than one real estate agent in the transaction. The agent who obtained the offer is responsible for delivering the report unless the seller has given written directions regarding delivery to another agent involved. Delivery of the required documents may be in person or by mail to the buyer. In reality, the escrow holder in most cases sends the termite report to all parties. The real estate agent responsible for delivery, however, must retain for three years a complete record of the actions taken to effect delivery.

Common Interest Development Documents

The owner (other than a subdivider) of a separate legal share in a common interest development (community apartment project, condominium project, planned development, or stock cooperative) must provide a prospective buyer with the following required disclosures:

- A copy of the governing documents of the development.

- Should there be an age restriction not consistent with the law, a statement that the age restriction is only. enforceable to the extent permitted by law; and applicable provisions of the law.

- A copy of the homeowners association's most recent financial statement.

- A written statement from the association specifying the amount of current regular and special assessments as well as any unpaid assessment, late charges, interest and costs of collection which are or may

  become a lien against the property.

- Information on any approved change in the assessments or fees not yet due and payable as of the disclosure date.

- A preliminary list of construction defects if the association has commenced or plans to commence an action for damages against the developer.

- After resolution, by settlement agreement or otherwise, of a dispute between the association and developer regarding construction defects, a general description of the defects that will be corrected, the association's estimate of when the corrections will be completed, the status of any claims for other defects.

Advisability of Title Insurance

In an escrow for a sale (or exchange) of real property where no title insurance is to be issued, the buyer (or both parties to an exchange) must receive and sign the following notice as a separate document in the escrow:

> Important: In a purchase or exchange of real property, it may be advisable to obtain title insurance in connection with the close of escrow where there may be prior recorded liens and encumbrances that affect your interest in the property being acquired. A new policy of title insurance should be obtained in order to ensure your interest in the property that you are acquiring.

While the law does not expressly assign the duty, it is reasonable to assume that the escrow holder is obligated to deliver the notice. A real estate agent conducting an escrow also would be responsible for delivering the notice.

Geological Hazards

Geologists describe the surface of the earth as always changing. Some of these geological changes are relatively unimportant — not requiring a disclosure. Other changes are apparent by casual inspection of a nature that a potential buyer should be able to judge the impact of the existing geological condition on the intended property's use. In some cases, sellers must disclose the geological condition of their property. This includes potential hazards from earthquakes, flooding, landslides, erosion, and expansive soils. One condition requiring such disclosure is fault creep, caused by stress and/or earthquake shaking.

Geology in the context of the required disclosures refers to the type of soil and how that soil will respond to earthquakes. Soft sediments tend to amplify shaking, whereas bedrock soils tend to lessen the shaking. Generally, the closer in location to the fault, the more intense the shaking will be. However, soils types and conditions may be more important than distance from the epicenter. The state geologist is in the process of identifying areas susceptible to **fault creep,** to be shown on maps prepared by the State Division of Mines and Geology. These maps also identify known historic landslides. The seller or the seller's agent and any agent acting in cooperation with such agent usually may rely on the identification of the special studies zones by the state geologist for disclosure purposes. In some instances, additional investigation may be required. Construction on real property of any structure for human occupancy may be subject to the findings and recommendations of a geologic report prepared by a geologist or soils engineer registered in or licensed by the state of California.

This disclosure must be made on either the Natural Hazard Disclosure Statement (NHDS), the Local Option Real Estate Transfer Disclosure Statement (LORETDS), or in the purchase agreement. The escrow holder is not responsible for this disclosure, but should be aware of the requirement.

In addition, under the California Legislature's authorization, the Seismic Safety Commission developed a *Homeowner's Guide to Earthquake Safety* for distribution to real estate licensees and the general public. The guide includes information on geologic and seismic hazards for all areas, explanations of related structural and nonstructural hazards, and recommendations for mitigating the hazards of an earthquake. The guide states that safety or damage prevention cannot be guaranteed with respect to a major earthquake and that only precautions such as retrofitting can be undertaken to reduce the risk of various types of damage.

If a buyer of real property receives a copy of the *Homeowner's Guide,* neither the seller nor the agent is required to provide additional information regarding geologic and seismic hazards. Sellers and real estate agents must disclose that the property is in a special studies zone, however, and that there are known hazards affecting the real property being transferred.

Delivery of the *Homeowner's Guide to Earthquake Safety* is required in these two transactions.

    (1) Transfer of any real property with a residential dwelling built prior to January 1, 1960, and consisting of one-to-four units, any of which are of conventional light-frame construction

    (2) Transfer of any masonry building with wood-frame floors or roofs built before January 1, 1975

The first transfer item also requires that the following structural deficiencies, and any corrective measures taken that are within the transferor's actual knowledge, are to be disclosed to prospective buyers.

Possible Structural Deficiencies

- Absence of foundation anchor bolts

- Unbraced or inappropriately braced perimeter cripple walls

- Unbraced or inappropriately braced first-story wall(s)

- Unreinforced masonry perimeter foundation

- Unreinforced masonry dwelling walls

- Habitable room or rooms above a garage

- Water heater not anchored, strapped, or braced

Certain exemptions apply to the obligation to deliver the booklet when transferring either a dwelling of one-to-four units or a reinforced masonry building. These exemptions are essentially the same as those that apply to delivery of the Real Estate Transfer Disclosure Statement described earlier in this chapter.

The buyer and/or agent may be responsible for making further inquiries of appropriate governmental agencies. The obligation of the buyer and/or agent to make further inquiry does not eliminate the duty of the seller's agent to: (1) make a diligent inquiry to identify the location of the real property in relationship to a defined special studies zone and (2) determine whether the property is subject to any local ordinance regarding geological and soils conditions. Full and complete disclosure is required of all material facts regarding a special studies zone, local ordinances, or known structural deficiencies affecting the property.

Finally, the state geologist is responsible for the long-term project of mapping California's Seismic Hazard Zones, identifying areas susceptible to strong ground shaking, liquefaction, landslides or other ground failure, and other seismic hazards caused by earthquakes. The seller's duty to disclose that the property is in a special-studies zone or a seismic-hazard zone may be limited by the availability of the maps at locations specified by local county officials.

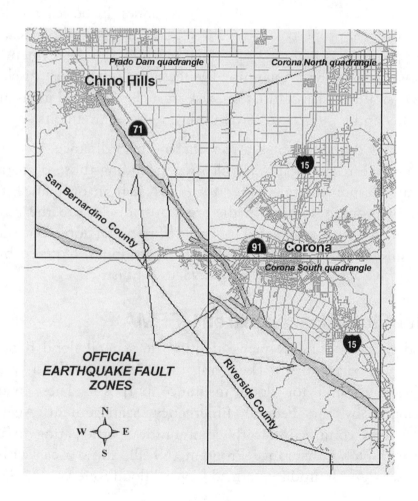

State Responsibility Areas

The Department of Forestry and Fire Protection has produced maps identifying rural lands classified as state responsibility areas. In such areas, the state (as opposed to a local or federal agency) has the primary financial responsibility for the prevention and  extinguishing of fires. Maps of these State Responsibility Areas and any changes (including new maps produced every five years) are to be provided to assessors or planning agencies in the affected counties. If the seller knows his or her real property is located in a State Responsibility Area, or if the property is included on a map given by the department to the county assessor or planning agencies, the seller must disclose the possibility of substantial fire risk in such **wild land areas** and that the land is subject to certain preventive requirements.

With the department's agreement, and by ordinance, a county may assume responsibility for all fires, including those occurring in State Responsibility Areas. If there is such an ordinance, the seller of property located in the area must disclose to the buyer that the state is not obligated to provide fire protection services for any building or structure unless such protection is required by a cooperative agreement with a county, city, or district.

Special Flood Hazard Area - FEMA

Flood hazard boundary maps identify the general flood hazards within a community. They are also used in flood plain management and for flood insurance purposes. These maps, developed by the **Federal Emergency Management Agency (FEMA)** in conjunction with communities participating in the National Flood Insurance Program (NFIP), show areas within **100-year flood boundary**, termed "special flood zone areas". Also, identified are areas between 100 and 500-year levels termed "areas of moderate flood hazards" and the remaining areas above the 500-year level termed "areas of minimal risk".

A seller of property located in a special flood hazard area, or the seller's agent and/or any agent cooperating in the deal, must disclose that fact to the buyer and that federal law requires flood insurance as a condition of obtaining financing on most structures located in a special flood hazard area. Since the cost and extent of flood insurance coverage may vary, the buyer should contact an insurance carrier or the intended lender for further information.

Environmental Hazards

Numerous federal, state, and local laws have been enacted to address the problems created by environmental hazards. Responsible parties, or persons deemed responsible, for the improper disposal of hazardous waste and owners of contaminated property may be held liable for contamination cleanup.

Several disclosure laws relating to the transfer of land affected by hazardous waste contamination also have been enacted. The California Real Estate Transfer Disclosure Statement now requires sellers to disclose whether they are aware of the presence of hazardous substances, materials, or products including—but not limited to—asbestos, formaldehyde, radon gas, lead-based paint, fuel or chemical storage tanks, and contaminated soil or water.

Any owner of nonresidential property who knows or suspects that there has been a release of a hazardous substance, or that it may occur on or beneath the property, must notify a buyer, lessee, or renter of that condition prior to the sale, lease, or rental of that property. Failure to give written notice may subject the owner to actual damages and/or civil penalties.

Under Proposition 65, certain businesses may not knowingly and/or intentionally expose any individual to a cancer-causing chemical or reproductive toxin without first giving clear, reasonable warning to such individuals. Recently, the law also has

imposed extensive asbestos disclosure requirements on owners of commercial buildings constructed prior to January 1, 1979.

The Department of Real Estate and Office of Environmental Health Hazard Assessment have developed a booklet to help educate and inform consumers about environmental hazards that may affect real property. The booklet identifies common environmental hazards, describes the risks involved with each, discusses mitigation techniques, and provides lists of publications and sources from which consumers can obtain more detailed information.

Hazards Discussed in the Environmental Hazard Booklet

- **Asbestos:** A mineral fiber used in construction materials which has been found to cause lung and stomach cancer.

- **Radon:** A colorless gas known to cause cancer. Radon can be detected with a spectrometer.

- **Lead:** A mineral that causes major health problems.

- **Formaldehyde:** A chemical organic compound found in building materials which may be a carcinogen.

- **Hazardous waste:** Materials (chemicals, explosives, radioactive, biological) whose disposal is regulated by the Environmental Protection Agency (EPA).

- **Household hazardous waste:** Consumer products such as paints, cleaners, stains, varnishes, car batteries, motor oil, and pesticides that contain hazardous components.

Once the booklet is provided to a prospective buyer of real property, neither the seller nor a real estate agent involved in the sale has a duty to provide further information on such hazards. If the seller or agent has actual knowledge of environmental hazards on or affecting the subject property, that information must be disclosed.

Lead-Based Paint Hazards

Lead, a highly toxic metal, was used for years in products found in and around homes. Exposure to lead may cause a variety of health effects—from behavioral problems to learning disabilities, seizures, and even death.

The seller or landlord of a property with four or fewer units must give a buyer or tenant a lead-hazard information pamphlet and a form disclosing the presence of any known lead-based paint. This is required by the Residential Lead-Based Paint Hazard Reduction Act of 1992 (Title X). The pamphlet is available at http://www.epa.gov/lead/pubs/leadpdfe.pdf.

This disclosure pertains to residential housing built before 1978 because the Act banned lead based paint for residential use in that year. Some pre-1978 properties, called **target housing**, are exempt from the disclosure. They include housing for the elderly and vacation housing.

The seller, landlord, and real estate agent involved in the sale or rental of pre-1978 housing each have certain obligations under the new law.

Seller/Landlord Obligations

- Give buyers/tenants *Protect Your Family From Lead in Your Home* pamphlet.

- Disclose all known lead-based paint and lead-based paint hazards in the dwelling and provide buyer/tenants with any available reports.

- Include standard warning language as an attachment to the contract or lease.

- Complete and sign statements verifying completion of requirements.

- Retain the signed acknowledgment for three years.

- Give buyers a 10-day opportunity to test for lead (for sale transactions only).

**CALIFORNIA
ASSOCIATION
OF REALTORS®**

LEAD-BASED PAINT AND LEAD-BASED PAINT HAZARDS DISCLOSURE, ACKNOWLEDGMENT AND ADDENDUM
For Pre-1978 Housing Sales, Leases, or Rentals
(C.A.R. Form FLD, Revised 1/03)

The following terms and conditions are hereby incorporated in and made a part of the: ☐ California Residential Purchase Agreement, ☐ Residential Lease or Month-to-Month Rental Agreement, or ☐ other: _____ _____, dated _____ , on property known as: _____ ("Property") in which _____ is referred to as Buyer or Tenant and _____ is referred to as Seller or Landlord.

LEAD WARNING STATEMENT (SALE OR PURCHASE) Every purchaser of any interest in residential real property on which a residential dwelling was built prior to 1978 is notified that such property may present exposure to lead from lead-based paint that may place young children at risk of developing lead poisoning. Lead poisoning in young children may produce permanent neurological damage, including learning disabilities, reduced intelligent quotient, behavioral problems and impaired memory. Lead poisoning also poses a particular risk to pregnant women. The seller of any interest in residential real property is required to provide the buyer with any information on lead-based paint hazards from risk assessments or inspections in the seller's possession and notify the buyer of any known lead-based paint hazards. A risk assessment or inspection for possible lead-based paint hazards is recommended prior to purchase.

LEAD WARNING STATEMENT (LEASE OR RENTAL) Housing built before 1978 may contain lead-based paint. Lead from paint, paint chips and dust can pose health hazards if not managed properly. Lead exposure is especially harmful to young children and pregnant women. Before renting pre-1978 housing, lessors must disclose the presence of lead-based paint and/or lead-based paint hazards in the dwelling. Lessees must also receive federally approved pamphlet on lead poisoning prevention.

1. SELLER'S OR LANDLORD'S DISCLOSURE

I (we) have no knowledge of lead-based paint and/or lead-based paint hazards in the housing other than the following:

_____
_____
_____
_____

I (we) have no reports or records pertaining to lead-based paint and/or lead-based paint hazards in the housing other than the following, which, previously or as an attachment to this addendum have been provided to Buyer or Tenant:

_____
_____
_____

I (we), previously or as an attachment to this addendum, have provided Buyer or Tenant with the pamphlet *"Protect Your Family From Lead In Your Home"* or an equivalent pamphlet approved for use in the State such as *"The Homeowner's Guide to Environmental Hazards and Earthquake Safety."*

For Sales Transactions Only: Buyer has 10 days, unless otherwise agreed in the real estate purchase contract, to conduct a risk assessment or inspection for the presence of lead-based paint and/or lead-based paint hazards.

I (we) have reviewed the information above and certify, to the best of my (our) knowledge, that the information provided is true and correct.

_____   _____
Seller or Landlord   Date

_____   _____
Seller or Landlord   Date

FLD REVISED 1/03 (PAGE 1 OF 2)

Buyer's Initials (_____) (_____)
Seller's Initials (_____) (_____)
Reviewed by _____ Date _____

EQUAL HOUSING OPPORTUNITY

LEAD-BASED PAINT AND LEAD-BASED PAINT HAZARDS DISCLOSURE (FLD-11 PAGE 1 OF 2)

Agent:	Phone:	Fax:	Prepared using WINForms® software
Broker:			

Property Address: _____ Date: _____

2. LISTING AGENT'S ACKNOWLEDGMENT

Agent has informed Seller or Landlord of Seller's or Landlord's obligations under §42 U.S.C. 4852d and is aware of Agent's responsibility to ensure compliance.

I have reviewed the information above and certify, to the best of my knowledge, that the information provided is true and correct.

_____ By _____
Agent (Broker representing Seller) Please Print   Associate-Licensee or Broker Signature   Date

3. BUYER'S OR TENANT'S ACKNOWLEDGMENT

I (we) have received copies of all information listed, if any, in 1 above and the pamphlet *"Protect Your Family From Lead In Your Home"* or an equivalent pamphlet approved for use in the State such as *"The Homeowner's Guide to Environmental Hazards and Earthquake Safety."* **If delivery of any of the disclosures or pamphlet referenced in paragraph 1 above occurs after Acceptance of an offer to purchase, Buyer has a right to cancel pursuant to the purchase contract. If you wish to cancel, you must act within the prescribed period.**

<u>For Sales Transactions Only:</u> Buyer acknowledges the right for 10 days, unless otherwise agreed in the real estate purchase contract, to conduct a risk assessment or inspection for the presence of lead-based paint and/or lead-based paint hazards; OR, (if checked) ☐ Buyer waives the right to conduct a risk assessment or inspection for the presence of lead-based paint and/or lead-based paint hazards.

I (we) have reviewed the information above and certify, to the best of my (our) knowledge, that the information provided is true and correct.

_____   _____
Buyer or Tenant   Date   Buyer or Tenant   Date

4. COOPERATING AGENT'S ACKNOWLEDGMENT

Agent has informed Seller or Landlord, through the Listing Agent if the property is listed, of Seller's or Landlord's obligations under §42 USC 4852d and is aware of Agent's responsibility to ensure compliance.

I have reviewed the information above and certify, to the best of my knowledge, that the information provided is true and correct.

_____ By _____
Agent (Broker obtaining the Offer)   Associate-Licensee or Broker Signature   Date

SURE TRAC
The System for Success™

Published by the
California Association of REALTORS®

Reviewed by _____ Date _____

EQUAL HOUSING
OPPORTUNITY

FLD REVISED 1/03 (PAGE 2 OF 2)

LEAD-BASED PAINT AND LEAD-BASED PAINT HAZARDS DISCLOSURE (FLD-11 PAGE 2 OF 2)

Smoke Detector Statement

Whenever a sale or exchange of a single-family dwelling occurs, the seller must provide the buyer with a written statement representing that the property complies with California law regarding smoke detectors. The state building code mandates that all existing dwelling units must have a smoke detector installed in a central location outside each sleeping area. In a two-story home with bedrooms on both floors, at least two smoke detectors would be required.

Smoke detectors are required for any new construction—additions, alterations, or repairs that exceed $1,000 and require a permit. A smoke detector must be installed in each bedroom, and at a central point in corridors or areas outside the bedrooms. This standard applies for the addition of one or more bedrooms, no matter what the cost.

In new home construction, the smoke detector must be hard-wired, with a battery backup. In existing dwellings, the detector may be only battery operated.

**CALIFORNIA
ASSOCIATION
OF REALTORS®**

SMOKE DETECTOR STATEMENT OF COMPLIANCE
As required by California State Health and Safety Code §13113.8(b)
(C.A.R. Form SDS, Revised 4/05)

Property Address: _____

1. **STATE LAW:** California Law requires that every single-family dwelling and factory built housing unit sold on or after January 1, 1986, must have an operable smoke detector, approved and listed by the State Fire Marshal, installed in accordance with the State Fire Marshal's regulations. (Health and Safety Code §13113.8).

2. **LOCAL REQUIREMENTS:** Some local ordinances impose more stringent smoke detector requirements than does California Law. Therefore, it is important to check with local city or county building and safety departments regarding the applicable smoke detector requirements for your property.

3. **TRANSFEROR'S WRITTEN STATEMENT:** California Health and Safety Code §13113.8(b) requires every transferor of any real property containing a single-family dwelling, whether the transfer is made by sale, exchange, or real property sales contract (installment sales contract), to deliver to the transferee a written statement indicating that the transferor is in compliance with California State Law concerning smoke detectors.

4. **EXCEPTIONS: Exceptions to the State Law are generally the same as the exceptions to the Transfer Disclosure Statement Laws.**

5. **CERTIFICATION:** Seller represents that the Property, as of the Close Of Escrow, will be in compliance with Health and Safety Code §13113.8 by having operable smoke detector(s) approved and listed by the State Fire Marshal installed in accordance with the State Fire Marshal's regulations and in accordance with applicable local ordinance(s).

Seller _____ _____ Date _____
       (Signature)   (Print Name)

Seller _____ _____ Date _____
       (Signature)   (Print Name)

The undersigned hereby acknowledges receipt of a copy of this document.

Buyer _____ _____ Date _____
       (Signature)   (Print Name)

Buyer _____ _____ Date _____
       (Signature)   (Print Name)

SURE TRAC
The System for Success®

Published and Distributed by:
REAL ESTATE BUSINESS SERVICES, INC.
a subsidiary of the CALIFORNIA ASSOCIATION OF REALTORS®
525 South Virgil Avenue, Los Angeles, California 90020

Reviewed by _____ Date _____

EQUAL HOUSING OPPORTUNITY

SDS REVISED 4/05 (PAGE 1 OF 1)

SMOKE DETECTOR STATEMENT OF COMPLIANCE (SDS PAGE 1 OF 1)

Phone: Fax: x.zfx

Produced with ZipForm™ by RE FormsNet, LLC 18025 Fifteen Mile Road, Clinton Township, Michigan 48035, (800) 383-9805 www.zipform.com

Energy Conservation

State law prescribes a minimum energy conservation standard for all new construction, without which a building permit may not be issued. Local governments also have ordinances that impose additional energy conservation measures on new and/or existing homes. Some local ordinances impose energy retrofitting as a condition of selling an existing home. The requirements of the various ordinances, as well as who is responsible for compliance,

may vary among local jurisdictions. The existence and basic requirements of local energy ordinances should be disclosed to a prospective buyer by the seller and/or the seller's agent and any agent cooperating in the deal.

Federal law requires a new home seller to disclose in every sales contract the type, thickness and R-value of the insulation which has been or will be installed in each part of the house, including the ceiling and interior and exterior walls. This law also applies to developers of new home subdivisions.

Military Ordnance Location

Federal and state agencies have identified certain areas once used for military training and which may contain live ammunition as part of the ordnance—or military supplies—from past activity. A seller of residential property located within one mile of such a hazard must give the buyer written notice as soon as possible before transfer of title. This obligation depends upon the seller having actual knowledge of the hazard. The location of military ordnance may be disclosed on the TDS.

Foreign Investment (FIRPTA)

Both federal and state tax laws are affected by the **Foreign Investment in Real Property Tax Act** (FIRPTA). In both cases, the buyer is responsible for making sure either the proper disclosures have been made and/or the proper funds have been set aside. Generally, the broker and escrow agent make sure this is done. All documents must be kept by the broker and the buyer for five years.

Federal FIRPTA Disclosure

Federal law requires that a buyer of real property must withhold and send to the Internal Revenue Service (IRS) 10% of the gross sales price if the seller of the real property is a foreign person.

Primary Grounds for Exemption from this Requirement

- The seller's non-foreign affidavit and U.S. taxpayer identification number

- A qualifying statement obtained through the IRS saying arrangements have been made for the collection of or exemption from the tax

- Sales price does not exceed $300,000

- The buyer intends to reside on the property

Because of the number of exemptions and other requirements relating to this law, it is recommended that the IRS be consulted for more detailed information. Sellers, buyers, and the real estate agents involved who desire further advice should consult an attorney, CPA, or other qualified tax advisor.

California FIRPTA Disclosure

California law requires that if property is sold by a non-citizen of the United States or a resident of another state, the buyer must withhold 3 1/3 % of the total sales price as state income tax and deliver the sum withheld to the State Franchise Tax Board. The escrow holder, in applicable transactions, is required by law to notify the buyer of this responsibility.

A buyer's failure to withhold and deliver the required sum may result in penalties. Should the escrow holder fail to notify the buyer, penalties might be levied against the escrow holder.

Transactions Subject to the Law:

- the seller shows an out-of-state address, or sale proceeds are to be disbursed to the seller's financial intermediary.

- the sales price exceeds $100,000.

- the seller does not certify that he or she is a California resident, or that the property being conveyed is his or her personal residence.

The following transactions are exempt from the law:

- the sales price is $100,000 or less.

- the home is the seller's principal residence.

- the seller signs the Seller's Affidavit of Non-foreign Status and the Buyer's Affidavit of Residency for California.

Remember, both the buyer and the agent are responsible for making sure this law is observed. The paperwork is usually completed through escrow. For further information, contact the Franchise Tax Board at their website, www.ftb.ca.gov.

Mello-Roos

The Mello-Roos Community Facilities Act of 1982 authorizes the formation of community facilities districts, the issuance of bonds, and the levying of special taxes that finance designated public facilities and services. Since July 1, 1993, this Act requires the seller of a property of one-to-four dwelling units (within a Mello-Roos district) to make a good faith effort to obtain and give a disclosure notice of this special tax to any prospective buyer. The transfers listed earlier for the Transfer Disclosure Statement are exempt from this requirement.

ANY CITY, CALIFORNIA

Mello Roos Disclosure Statement
Notice of Special Tax

Community Facilities District 20___-1
ABC Public Facilities Financing Agency
County of _____, State of California

To: The Prospective Purchaser of the Real Property Known as:

Address: Assessors Parcel Number:

_____

THIS IS A NOTIFICATION TO YOU PRIOR TO YOUR PURCHASING THIS
PROPERTY.

1. This property is subject to a special tax, which is in addition to the regular property
taxes and other charges and benefit assessments on the parcel. This special tax may not
be imposed on all parcels within the city or county where the property is located. If you
fail to pay this tax when due each year, the property may be foreclosed upon and sold.
The tax is used to provide public facilities or services that are likely to particularly
benefit the property. **You should take this tax and the benefits from the facilities and
services for which it pays into account in deciding to whether to buy this property.**

2. The maximum annual tax to which this property is subject is $_____ during the
20___ tax year and thereafter. The special tax will be levied each year until all of the
authorized facilities are built and all special tax bonds are repaid.

3. The authorized facilities which are being paid for by the special taxes, and by the
money received from the sale of bonds which are being repaid by the special taxes, are
set forth on Exhibit A attached hereto. These facilities may not yet have all been
constructed or acquired and it is possible that some may never be constructed or acquired.

4. The obligation to pay the special tax, attached to this property, was a condition
required in order to permit this property to be developed. The payment of tax is intended
to insure that there will be adequate capacity in the school district for the children that
may come from this property. However, the payment of the special tax does not
guarantee attendance at any particular school, nor does it guarantee attendance at a newly
constructed school. School attendance boundaries are set by the School Board and are
based on many criteria, only one of which is whether a property pays the special tax.

You may obtain a copy of the resolution of formation which authorized creation of the
community facilities district, and which specifies more precisely how the special tax is
apportioned and how the proceeds of the tax will be used, from the Comptroller of ABC
Public Facilities Financing Agency by telephoning (555) 123-4567. There may be a
charge for this document not to exceed the reasonable cost of providing this document.

I (we) acknowledge that I (we) have read this notice and received a copy of this
notice prior to entering into a contract to purchase or deposit receipt with respect
to the above-references property. I (we) understand that I (we) may terminate the
contract to purchase or deposit receipt within three days after receiving this notice
in person or within five days after it was deposited in the mail by giving written
notice of that termination to the owner, subdivider, or agent selling the property.

Date:

_____

Local Requirements

Residential properties in cities and counties throughout California are typically subject to specific local ordinances on occupancy; zoning and use; building code compliance; fire, health, and safety code regulations; and land subdivision descriptions. The various requirements for compliance as well as who and what is affected thereby should be disclosed to the prospective buyer of the property by the seller or the seller's agent and any agent acting in cooperation with such agent.

Subdivision Disclosures

A subdivision is the division of land into five or more lots for the purpose of sale, lease, or financing. Because of abuses in the early years of development, the division and resale of real property has received significant legislative attention. The escrow officer must be aware of special laws regulating subdivisions and the requirements and time periods involved in the resale of subdivided land.

Subdivision Map Act

This act authorizes city and county governments to enact and carry out subdivision laws according to the regulations set down in the Subdivision Map Act. All division of land into two or more parcels falls under this law.

The main objective of the Subdivision Map Act is to define the rules and procedures for filing maps to create subdivisions. It is directly controlled by local authorities (city and county) and is concerned with the physical aspects of a subdivision—such as building design, streets, and environmental impact.

As a result of the Subdivision Map Act, the direct control of the kind and type of subdivisions to be allowed in each community and the physical improvements to be installed are left to local jurisdictions (city and county) within certain general limits specified in the act.

Subdivision Map Act has two major objectives:

1. to coordinate the subdivision plans and planning, including lot design, street patterns, right-of-way for drainage and sewers, etc., with the community pattern and plan, as laid out by the local planning authorities.

2. to ensure initial proper improvement of areas dedicated for public purposes by filing subdivision maps, including public streets and other public areas, by the subdivider so that these necessities will not become an undue burden in the future for taxpayers in the community.

The Subdivision Map Act requires every city and county to adopt a law to regulate subdivisions for which a tentative and final map, or a parcel map, is required. Also, the act allows cities and counties to adopt laws for subdivisions for which no map is required.

State and local requirements for processing subdivision maps must be acknowledged by the escrow agent while working with the title company that will be principally responsible for map processing and recording.

The approval process for a subdivision starts at the preliminary planning stage, moving along to satisfy the requirements of the state, local government, title company, and lender.

If the transaction includes a map filing, the escrow holder should be practical when calculating the closing time for the escrow. The filing of a parcel map can take six to nine months, and a formal tract map filing process involves 12 to 18 months.

Subdivided Lands Law

In California, the Subdivided Lands Law is administered directly by the Real Estate Commissioner. Its objective is to protect buyers of property in new subdivisions from fraud, misrepresentation, or deceit in the marketing of subdivided lots, parcels, units, and undivided interests.

The Real Estate Commissioner must issue a subdivision public report before any subdivision can be offered for sale in California. This even applies to lands outside the state, if they are being marketed in California. The public report is a document disclosing all-important facts about the marketing and financing of the subdivision.

The public report must show that the subdivider (developer) can complete and maintain all improvements and that the lots or parcels can be used for the purpose for which they are being sold.

Before a developer can sell each lot in the project, he or she must give a copy of the commissioner's final report to the buyer for approval. The buyer signs a receipt for the report stating it has been read. The seller (developer) must keep a copy of the statement for three years. The public report is valid for five years, with any material changes in the development reported to the commissioner, who then can issue an amendment to the original report.

It can take many months for a developer to get project approval, once all the proper paperwork is submitted to the commissioner. During that time, the developer may want to begin marketing the project while waiting for the final report.

By submitting a minimum application filing package the developer can get a preliminary public report which allows taking reservations for the project, but not accepting any non-refundable money or entering into any binding contracts until receiving the final report from the commissioner.

Lending Disclosures

Along with the need for real property disclosures is a need for consumer protection in lending. Borrowers want to know what is the real cost of borrowing money and they demand to be protected from less-than-honest loan brokers. Thus, disclosures regarding loans and consumer credit, and laws governing loan brokers have become part of the rapidly growing consumer protection movement.

Real Estate Settlement Procedures Act

The Real Estate Settlement Procedures Act (RESPA) applies to all federally related mortgage loans. The act requires special disclosures for certain lenders who provide loan funds for transactions involving one-to-four residential units.

Special procedures and forms for settlements (closing costs) must be used for most home mortgage loans, including FHA and VA loans, and those from financial institutions with federally insured deposits.

The lender must furnish a copy of a *Special Information Booklet*, together with a Good Faith Estimate of the amount or range of closing costs to every person from whom the lender receives a written application for any federally related loan.

Every lender is required by the federal Real Estate Settlement Procedures Act to provide the borrower with a good faith estimate of fees due at closing within three days of applying for a loan. These mortgage fees, also called settlement costs, cover every expense associated with home loan: inspections, title insurance, taxes, and other charges. Because closing costs typically amount to between three and five percent of the sale price, it is considered the best practice to make sure the borrower receives this before signing any loan.

Here is a list of some of the items that may be listed on a good faith estimate:

- Loan application and credit report
- Title search and title insurance
- The lender's attorney
- Property appraisal
- Inspection
- Survey
- Document recording
- Transfer taxes
- The buyer's attorney
- Documentary stamps on new note
- Points and origination
- Condominium application
- Escrow account balances/pre-paids

Fees for these items vary, so check with the lender, title, and escrow companies for current charges.

Truth-in-Lending Act

The Truth-in-Lending Act (TILA) became effective July 1, 1969. The main purpose of the law is to promote the informed use of consumer credit by requiring creditors to disclose credit terms so consumers can make comparisons between various credit sources.

To accomplish the objectives of the act, the Board of Governors of the Federal Reserve System issued a directive known as Regulation Z. Under this regulation, a creditor must furnish certain disclosures to the consumer before a contract for a loan is made. A **creditor** includes a lender (person or company) who regularly makes real estate loans, and who extends credit for loans secured by a dwelling. The credit extended is subject to a finance charge or is payable in more than four installments, excluding the down payment.

Disclosure Statement

TILA requires lenders to disclose the important terms and costs of their loans, including the annual percentage rate, finance charge, the payment terms, and information about any variable-rate

feature. The **finance charge** is the dollar amount the credit will cost and is composed of any direct or indirect charge as a condition of obtaining credit. That would include interest, loan fees, finder fees, credit report fees, insurance fees, and mortgage insurance fees (PMI or MMI). In real estate, the finance charge does not include appraisal fees or credit report fees. The **annual percentage rate (APR)** is the relative cost of credit expressed as a yearly rate. It is the relationship of the total finance charge to the total amount financed, expressed as a percentage.

In general, neither the lender nor anyone else may charge a fee until after the borrower has received this information. The borrower usually gets these disclosures when he or she receives an application form and will get additional disclosures before the plan is opened. If any term has changed before the plan is opened (other than a variable-rate feature), and if the borrower decides not to enter into the plan because of a changed term, the lender must return all fees.

Regulation Z requires that creditors disclose the following items for real property secured loans. The first four disclosures must include simple descriptive phrases of explanation similar to those shown in *italics:*

1. **Amount financed**: *The amount of credit (principal amount borrowed less prepaid finance charges includable) provided to you or on your behalf.*

2. **Finance charge**: *The dollar amount the credit will cost you.*

3. **Annual Percentage Rate**: *The cost of your credit expressed as a yearly rate.*

4. **Total of payments**: *The amount you will have paid when you have made all the scheduled payments.*

5. **Payment schedule**: The number, amount, and timing of payments.

6. **Name of the lender**/creditor making the disclosure.

7. Written itemization of the amount financed, or a statement that the consumer has a right to receive a written itemization, and a space in the statement for the consumer to indicate whether the itemization is requested.

8. Variable interest rate and discounted variable rate disclosures, including limitations and effects of a rate increase and an example of payment terms resulting from the increase. This may be accomplished by giving the consumer the *Consumer Handbook on Adjustable Rate Mortgages* or a suitable substitute.

9. In addition to the above-mentioned disclosure, the regulation also requires disclosures regarding due-on-sale clauses, prepayment penalties, late payment charges, description of the property, insurance requirements, and loan assumptions.

Advertising

The Truth-in-Lending Act also establishes disclosure standards for advertisements that refer to certain credit terms. If the annual percentage rate (APR) is disclosed, no more disclosures are required. If the APR is not stated, then all the specifics of all credit terms must be disclosed. An advertisement that discloses the number of payments must also disclose the amount or percentage of down payment, number of payments, amount of any payments, the finance charge, interest rate, property description, etc. In fact, if the interest rate is stated, it must also disclose the APR. Ads that would require complete disclosure would include "No money down" or "100% financing".

Right of Rescission

The right to rescind (cancel) a real estate loan applies to most consumer credit loans (hard money loans) or refinance loans. Loans used for the purchase or construction of the borrower's personal residence (purchase money loans) have no right of rescission. The lender must provide a written rescission disclosure to every borrower who is entitled to rescind. When the right of rescission applies, the borrower has a right to rescind the agreement until midnight of the third business day after the promissory note is signed.

Adjustable Rate Loan Disclosure

A lender offering adjustable rate residential mortgage loans must provide prospective borrowers with a copy of the most recent Federal Reserve Board publication that provides information about adjustable rate loans. The title is *Consumer Handbook on Adjustable Rate Mortgages*. The publication must be given to the prospective borrower when the lender first provides information concerning adjustable rate mortgages, or upon request.

Lenders who have adopted, or are subject to, federal rules may provide the disclosures at the same time and under the same circumstances as when the lender makes the federally required disclosures pursuant to the Truth-in-Lending Act.

Equal Credit Opportunity Act

Credit is used by millions of consumers to finance an education or a house, remodel a home, or get a small business loan. The **Equal Credit Opportunity Act** (ECOA) ensures that all consumers are given an equal chance to obtain credit. This does not mean all consumers who apply for credit get it because factors such as income, expenses, debt, and credit history are considerations for credit-worthiness. The law protects a borrower when dealing with any creditor who regularly extends credit, including banks, small loan and finance companies, retail and department stores, credit card companies, and credit unions. Anyone involved in granting credit, such as real estate brokers who arrange financing, is covered by the law. Businesses applying for credit are protected by the law.

True-False Quiz

Now that you have read all the material in this chapter, take the following self-test and check your knowledge of consumer disclosures.

True/False

1. ___FALSE___ The escrow holder is responsible for making all real estate disclosures.

2. ___FALSE___ The Transfer Disclosure Statement is an optional disclosure.

3. ___TRUE___ Required disclosures must be made to the buyer as soon as practicable.

4. ___TRUE___ The Mello-Roos Community Facilities Act is concerned with levying special taxes to finance public facilities.

5. ___FALSE___ The law requires a structural pest control inspection on all properties in escrow.

6. ___TRUE___ The Foreign Investment in Real Property Tax Act refers to withholding of taxes when the sellers are not citizens.

7. ___TRUE___ In certain California real estate transactions, the buyer must withhold 3 1/3% of the total sales price as state income tax.

8. ___FALSE___ RESPA requires disclosure of good credit practice.

9. ___TRUE___ Truth-in-Lending Act promotes informed use of consumer credit.

10. ___TRUE___ The Equal Credit Opportunity Act (ECOA) ensures that all consumers are given an equal chance to obtain credit.

Chapter
14

Other Types of Escrows

Learning Objectives

After reading this chapter, you will be able to:

- explain the different types of escrows.

- discuss the complexities of mobile home escrow.

- list the escrow responsibilities of a business sale.

- discuss the importance of a 1031 exchange.

Introduction

As you have progressed through this text, the sale escrow has been used as the basic teaching tool for the beginning escrow student. However, every escrow student should be familiar also with other types of escrows.

Each type has its own terminology and special requirements. As you read this chapter, you will learn the many ways escrow serves the real estate industry beyond the more familiar sale escrow.

Many of the other types of escrow that you may encounter in the course of a career in escrow are described in this chapter.

Holding Escrow

The escrow agent, acting in the capacity of a neutral stake-holder, holds money, documents or something else of value until directed to release it upon performance of conditions specified by the principals.

Subdivision Pre-Sale

Reservations on a subdivision may be taken by a developer who has received a Preliminary Public Report from the Real Estate Commissioner. Parcels may be reserved by placing them in an escrow until the developer is issued a final report, at which time a sale escrow can be opened.

Construction Funding

A builder may receive funds from a construction loan, in what is called a **draw.** The lender deposits the proceeds from the loan in an escrow, with instructions about how the funds are to be released to the builder.

Stock Distribution

An escrow is often required when stock that represents a majority interest in a corporation is transferred. An escrow agent must be totally familiar with the needs of the parties and the complexity of the process to be involved in these kinds of transactions. The specialized types of documents, procedures, and government regulations make a stock transfer complicated and critical for the escrow officer.

Loan Escrow

Separate instructions may be prepared for a loan escrow, depending upon the structure of the sale escrow directions. Typically, a loan escrow would be prepared to refinance an existing loan. In some instances, a loan that is connected to a sale transaction may have a separate sub-escrow opened for the loan.

In most cases where there is an open sale escrow, the sale instructions include directions for the escrow officer regarding the financing. Usually, a separate loan escrow is not opened.

If the lender is a private party, the escrow holder is responsible for preparing the loan documents—usually the promissory note and the trust deed. If a transaction requires other types of loan documents, such as a contract of sale or an all-inclusive trust deed (AITD), the principals are encouraged to have an attorney prepare the instruments of finance.

If the transaction calls for a loan to be funded by an institutional lender, the loan documents are prepared by the lender and sent to the escrow holder for signing by the borrower. The promissory note and a copy of the trust deed are then returned to the lender. The original notarized trust deed is held by the escrow officer until the escrow is ready to close. When the title company receives the signed, notarized trust deed from the escrow holder, loan funds are released to the escrow officer for disbursement and closing, and the trust deed is recorded.

SMS - SETTLEMENT SERVICES DIVISION, A CALIFORNIA CORPORATION IS LICENSED AS AN ESCROW AGENT BY THE DEPARTMENT OF CORPORATIONS OF THE STATE OF CALIFORNIA.

LOAN ESCROW INSTRUCTIONS

TO: SMS - Settlement Services Division

Date: **July 8, 20xx**
Escrow Number: DEMOREFI
Escrow Officer: **Kelly Rose**
Page 1 of 5

The undersigned Borrower(s) is obtaining a loan on the property hereinafter described and will cause Lender to hand you the proceeds of a new First Trust Deed in the amount of **$171,000.00**, less Lender's normal costs and charges, which you are authorized to use on or before **September 6, 20xx**, providing upon recordation of the securing Deed of Trust, you obtain an ALTA Lender's Policy of Title insurance, per Lender's requirements covering real property in the County of **Apple**, State of California, as follows:

Lot 123 of Tract 12345, in Any City, County of Apple as per map recorded in Book 324, Page(s) 12-13, of Miscellaneous Maps in the Office of the County Recorder of said County.

COMMONLY KNOWN AS: **987 Ocean View Drive, Any City, CA 90000**

The title policy is to show the title to the property to be vested in:

Dan Winter and Donna Winter, Husband and Wife as Joint Tenants

The policy is to be free of encumbrances except as follows:

(1) Any General and Special Taxes and Special District Levies not due or delinquent; this will include the lien of supplemental taxes, if any, assessed pursuant to Chapter 498, 1983 Statutes of the State of California.
(2) All Taxes, Bonds, and Assessments levied or assessed subsequent to the date of these instructions.
(3) Covenants, conditions, reservations (including exceptions of oil, gas minerals, hydrocarbons, and/or lease without right of surface entry), restrictions, right of way, and easements for public utilities, districts, water companies, alleys, and streets.
(4) First Trust Deed to file, securing a note in the principal amount of **$171,000.00** in favor of **Any City Bank** at the best prevailing rate and terms per lenders instructions to be deposited into escrow.

DEPOSIT OF FUNDS INTO ESCROW: Each of the undersigned acknowledges and understands that pursuant to State of California Assembly Bill ("Good Funds Legislation") which became effective January 1, 1990, funds deposited into escrow and/or deposited with the Title Company for use in this escrow by the Property Owner, Buyer and New Lender in any form other than a wire transfer may cause a delay in the closing of this escrow and/or disbursement of funds at the time of closing. Each of the undersigned hereby indemnifies and holds SMS - Settlement Services Division and its officers and/or Employees harmless with the respect to any delay in closing and/or disbursement of funds due to compliance with the Provisions of "AB512".

NOTICE REGARDING CLOSING FUNDS: In the event Borrower elects to deposit closing funds by Cashier's Check, said funds MUST be deposited not later than 48 hours prior to the anticipated date of close of escrow, pursuant to AB512 Good Funds Law.

CONDITION OF TITLE: Escrow Holder is authorized and instructed to pay any encumbrance necessary to place title in the condition called for herein and Borrower will hand you any instruments and/or funds as required for such purpose.

LOAN ESCROW INSTRUCTIONS

TO: SMS - Settlement Services Division

Date: **July 8, 20xx**
Escrow Number: DEMOREFI
Escrow Officer: **Kelly Rose**
Page 2 of 5

OBTAIN DEMAND: Escrow holder is hereby authorized and instructed to obtain demand from lender(s) of record and to pay for same from Borrower's proceeds at the close of escrow, including prepayment penalties, interest and such other costs, if applicable.

FIRE INSURANCE: Secure for Lender an endorsement on existing insurance policy naming lender as First Trust Deed Holder and providing for replacement cost guarantee, as required by Lender. Charge account of Borrower at close of escrow and pay premiums as may be required for same, per billing to be deposited herein prior to close of escrow.

CLOSING COSTS/CHARGES: Pay escrow charges and proper recording fees, also charges for evidence of title called for above (whether or not this escrow is consummated) and you are authorized to pay off any bonds, assessments and/or taxes, also any encumbrances of record, plus accrued interest, charges and bonus, if any, to show title as called for above and/or necessary to comply with same. Instruct the title company to begin search of title at once.

ADVANCE RELEASE OF DEMAND FEES: In the event the Existing Lienholder(s) requires payment to demand statement fees in advance of issuing their demand statement. Borrower shall deposit sufficient funds as called for by Escrow Holder for payment of same and authorizes Escrow Holder to release said funds to Existing Leinholder(s) prior to close of escrow. Borrower acknowledges and agrees that said funds are NON-REFUNDABLE in the event this escrow is not consummated.

CANCELLATION FEE: Borrower is aware that in the event this escrow is canceled. Borrower shall pay a cancellation fee of $100.00 to Escrow Holder. Said cancellation fee to be deducted from funds on deposit upon written and/or verbal notice of cancellation by Lender or Borrower.

HOLD OPEN FEE: It is agreed that if, for any reason, this escrow is not closed within NINETY (90) days of the established date for closing as shown herein. Escrow Holder may at their option charge a hold-open fee against funds then on deposit in the amount of $25.00 for each month, or fraction thereof, that this escrow remains unclosed.

CLOSE OF ESCROW: The close of escrow shall be the day documents deposited in this escrow are recorded pursuant to these instructions.

EXTENSION OF TIME FOR CLOSING: If the condition of this escrow have not been complied with at the time provided for in these instructions, you are nevertheless to complete this escrow as soon as the conditions (except as to time) have been complied with, unless a written demand for the return of money and/or instruments by a party to his escrow is received by you prior to the recording of any instrument provided for in these instructions.

NECESSITY FOR WRITTEN INSTRUCTIONS: No notice, demand or change or instructions shall be of any effect unless given to you in writing and approved in writing by all parties affected by same.

DEPOSITS AND DISBURSEMENTS: All funds delivered to you by parties to this escrow shall be deposited in any non-interest bearing account designated as a "Trust Account" with any bank or depository authorized by the Federal or State Government, and may be transferred to, and co-mingled with, other such trust accounts. You shall not be obligated to identify or to guarantee the signature of any payee on said checks.

LOAN ESCROW INSTRUCTIONS

TO: SMS - Settlement Services Division

Date: **July 8, 20xx**
Escrow Number: DEMOREFI
Escrow Officer: **Kelly Rose**
Page 3 of 5

SUB-ESCROW AGENTS: As you deem reasonably necessary to the closing of this escrow, you may deposit any funds or documents received by you herein, with any bank, title insurance company, savings and loan association, trust company, industrial loan company, credit union, admitted insurer or licensed escrow agent and any such deposit shall be deemed in accordance herewith. In this regard, you are authorized to utilize the services of one or more sub-escrow agents as defined under the California Financial Code and/or documents prior to close of escrow, if reasonable necessary in your discretion.

ADJUSTMENTS AND PRORATIONS: All adjustments shall be made upon the basis of a thirty day month, including, but not necessarily limited to the following: A. Taxes for the current year, based on tax amounts disclosed on last available tax bill; B. Premiums on fire insurance policies as handed you; C. Interest on loans of record, based on statement from the lender.

RECORDING AND TRANSFER FEES: To facilitate the recording of any documents delivered into or through this escrow, you may pay all required fees; all of the costs of which shall be deemed to constitute an authorized expenditure to be paid or charged to the party responsible therefore.

EFFECT OF CONFLICT: If, before or after recording documents, you receive or become aware of any conflicting demands or claims (hereinafter "conflicts") with respect to this escrow, the rights or obligations of any of the parties of any money or property deposited or affected, you shall have the right to discontinue further performance on your part until the conflict is resolved to your satisfaction. In addition, you shall have the right to commence or defend any action or proceeding you deem necessary for the determination of the conflict. A conflict shall be deemed to include, but is not necessarily limited to, your receipt of unilateral instructions or instructions from some, but not all of the escrow. In the event of a conflict, you shall not be liable to take any action of any kind, but may withhold all moneys, securities, documents or other things deposited into escrow, until such conflict has been determined by agreement of the parties or by legal process.
In the event any action is commenced to determine a conflict or otherwise to enforce or declare the provisions of these instructions or to rescind them, including, but not limited to, a suit in inter pleader (whether or not the action is prosecuted to final judgment, voluntarily dismissed or settled, and irrespective of whether you are the prevailing party in any such action) and it becomes necessary or desirable for you to obtain legal advice with respect to a conflict or on account of any matter or thing arising out of or in any way related to these instructions, whether or not suit is actually commenced, the parties to this escrow jointly and severally agree to pay all of your costs, damages, judgments and expenses, including attorney's fees, incurred by you in connection with the same.

PAYMENT OF FEES AND CHARGES: It is understood that the fees agreed to be paid for your services are for ordinary and usual services only, and should there be any extraordinary or unusual services rendered by you, the undersigned agree to pay reasonable compensation to you for such extraordinary or unusual services, together with any costs and expenses which may be incurred by you in connection with same. Upon the close of the escrow, you may retain, on your own behalf, your charges, costs and fees and charge the same in your accounting against the person responsible therefore.

IT IS UNDERSTOOD THAT, IN THE EVENT THIS ESCROW IS CANCELED OR TERMINATED, YOU WILL RECEIVE COMPENSATION FOR SUCH SERVICES AS YOU HAVE RENDERED IN CONNECTION WITH THIS ESCROW.

LOAN ESCROW INSTRUCTIONS

TO: **SMS - Settlement Services Division**

Date: **July 8, 20xx**
Escrow Number: DEMOREFI
Escrow Officer: **Kelly Rose**
Page 4 of 5

LIMITATIONS ON DUTIES AND LIABILITIES: YOU SHALL NOT, IN ANY MANNER OR UNDER ANY THEORY OF LAW OR EQUITY, HAVE ANY RESPONSIBILITY OR LIABILITY FOR ANY OR ALL OF THE FOLLOWING ACTS, EVENTS, KNOWLEDGE OR CIRCUMSTANCES:

1. Determining the sufficiency, genuineness or validity of any document, instrument or writing deposited with you herein or the form of content, or the identity or authority of the person executing or depositing any of the same;

2. Ascertaining the terms, covenants or conditions of any document, instrument, or writing deposited with you, or to investigate or examine the circumstances under which it was executed and/or delivered to you;

3. The failure to notify any person, including but not limited to the parties herein, of any sale, resale, loan, exchange or other transaction involving the property or rights that are the subject hereof or incidental thereto, or any profit or advantage to any person, firm or corporation, including by not limited to any broker or agent of any party hereto, regardless of the fact that such other transaction(s) may be directly or indirectly handled by you in connection with the within escrow or any other escrow, or come to your knowledge, in any form whatsoever;

4. The payment, examination as to amount, propriety or validity of any tax, including but not limited to personal property, corporate, business or license tax or any description, assessed against, chargeable or payable by either of the parties hereto;

5. Your failure or refusal to comply with any amendments, supplements and/or notation hereof or hereto which are not signed by all parties hereto and actually delivered to you;

6. Your failure or refusal to terminate or cancel the within escrow, without full and complete compliance, to your satisfaction, with the provisions of paragraph "Necessity for Written Instructions" herein;

7. For any liability predicated upon any relationship other than that of an escrow holder, it being specifically irrevocably and conclusively understood, agreed and deemed no other legal relationship is hereby created or shall be implied, assumed or come into being;

8. For failure of any party to this escrow with any of the provisions of any agreement, contract, or other instrument, contract or other instrument filed or referred to in these instructions;

9. Any duties beyond that of an escrow holder, which are expressly limited to the safekeeping of money, instruments, or other document received by escrow holder and for the disposition of them in accordance with the written instructions accepted by you.

10. Your knowledge of matters affecting the property which is the subject hereof shall not, and does not, create any liability or duty in addition to the responsibility of escrow holder under these instructions;

11. You shall not be obligated to make any physical examination of any real or personal property described in any document deposited into this escrow, and the parties agree that you have not made, and will not make, any representations whatsoever regarding said property;

LOAN ESCROW INSTRUCTIONS

TO: SMS - Settlement Services Division

Date: **July 8, 20xx**
Escrow Number: DEMOREFI
Escrow Officer: **Kelly Rose**
Page 5 of 5

12. You shall not be concerned with, nor responsible for, the giving of any disclosures required by Federal or State law, including but not limited to, any disclosures required under Regulation Z, pursuant to the Federal Consumer Credit Protection Act, the effect of any zoning laws, ordinances or regulations affecting any other property described in this escrow. The undersigned jointly and severally agree to indemnify and hold you harmless by reason of any misrepresentation of omission by either party or their respective agents, or the failure of the parties to this escrow to comply with the rules and/or regulations of any governmental agency, state, federal, county, municipal or otherwise. Parties to this escrow have satisfied themselves outside of escrow that this transaction is not in violation of the Subdivision Map Act or any other law relating to land division, and you are relieved of all responsibility and/or liability in connection with same, and are not to be concerned with the enforcement of said laws;

13. Any loss that may occur by reasons of (i) forgeries or false representations; (ii) the exercise of your discretion in any particular manner, (iii) for any act, duty requirement or obligation not expressly required of you hereunder or specifically state herein; or, (iv) for any reason whatsoever except your gross neglect or willful misconduct.

AUTHORITY OF BUSINESS ENTITY: As to any corporation, partnership or other entity which may be a party hereto, it shall be conclusively presumed that any document executed by any officer or general partner of such entity was made upon due, full, legal and complete authority of the governing body of such entity, and you shall have no responsibility to independently investigate or verify such authority.

AUTHORITY TO RELEASE INFORMATION: You are authorized and instructed to furnish information from this escrow to lender and/or brokers as may be requested by them, including, but not limited to copies of all instructions and closing statement(s) in this escrow. You are authorized to accept funds deposited to a party's broker or agent without further authorization.

SUCCESSORS AND ASSIGNS: The provisions hereof shall bind each party hereto and his respective heirs, administrators, executors, assigns, trustees, guardians, conservators, receivers, and successors in interest.

DESTRUCTION OF DOCUMENTS: You are authorized to destroy or otherwise dispose of all documents, instruments or writings received by you herein and accounting or disbursement records pertaining hereto at the expiration of five (5) years from and after the initial date hereof, regardless of any subsequent notations thereto or the date of close of escrow, without liability or further notice to any parties hereto.

EFFECT OF EXECUTION: The signatures of the undersigned hereon and on any document(s) and instrument(s) pertaining to this escrow indicates their unconditional acceptance of the same and constitutes acknowledgment of their receipt or copy of the same.

ESCROW COMPANIES ARE NOT AUTHORIZED TO GIVE LEGAL ADVICE, IF YOU DESIRE LEGAL ADVICE, CONSULT YOUR ATTORNEY BEFORE SIGNING.

We, the undersigned, jointly and severally, acknowledge receipt of a complete copy of the within escrow instructions and by our signature set forth below, acknowledge that we have read, understand and agree to the same in their entirety.

Dan Winter _____   Donna Winter _____

Trust Deed Sale

A loan may be sold many times during its life, whether it was originated by an institutional lender or a private party. A loan can be bought and sold in the secondary mortgage market or privately, and in the course of the sale, go through an escrow.

The primary instrument in the sale of a loan is the trust deed, just as a grant deed is the primary instrument in the sale of real property. Remember, the evidence of the debt is the promissory note, with the deed of trust as collateral or security for the loan.

When the holder of a note secured by a deed of trust wants to sell his or her interest, the instrument of transfer is an assignment of trust deed. The buyer may require an escrow and title insurance to confirm clear title to the indebtedness (the trust deed).

Subdivision Escrow

Some escrow companies specialize exclusively in the business of subdivision escrows.

The subdividing of land parcels by a developer is a time consuming and complex activity. It involves planning and close work between the builder and the escrow holder.

The first step for the builder is to acquire the land and enter into an escrow for the sale of the large parcel that is to be subdivided.

The next required steps are conforming to the regulations of subdivision laws, obtaining approval of a subdivision map, and recording the activity after the builder receives a final public report from the Real Estate Commissioner. Other state or local requirements also may be involved before the developer is allowed to start selling parcels in the subdivision.

At this point, an escrow for the sale of lots in a subdivision involves the basic sale escrow instructions with adaptations to meet specific requirements for the sale of subdivided land.

Leasehold Escrow

An escrow can be required for transactions where fee title is not transferred. In certain instances, a leasehold interest in real property may be transferred from a lessor to a lessee. There are two forms of leases that can be involved in an escrow.

Types of Leaseholds

- Land Lease - A land lease conveys the right to use a certain parcel of land and improvements, for a specified number of years, under the terms and conditions described in the lease.

- Space Lease - A space lease conveys the right to use a certain suite or unit located on the land. Apartment leases, office space, and other commercial uses are common.

Because a large financial investment is usually involved in commercial leasing, title insurance is particularly important. Leases can be very complex, and many factors may determine the validity of a lease. Title insurance is commonly required to protect the investment by assuring the condition of title, and to provide a transfer that meets the wishes of all the parties in the transaction.

Escrows for Manufactured Housing

Manufactured or mobile home escrows can be complicated. There are many regulatory laws and agencies that are involved in the transfer of manufactured or mobile homes. Several questions need to be answered before opening escrow.

What is a manufactured home? What is a mobile home? Is the manufactured or mobile home personal or real property? Is it moveable or permanently attached to a foundation? Is it on an individually owned site or in a mobile home park? If it is on land owned by an association or mobile home park, is that land being leased or rented to the manufactured home owner?

Manufactured and Mobile Homes

Manufactured homes are homes built in a factory after June 15, 1976. They must conform to the federal HUD code regarding Manufactured Home Construction and Safety Standards. These federal standards regulate manufactured housing design and construction, strength and durability, transportability, fire resistance, energy efficiency, and quality. The HUD Code also sets performance standards for the heating, plumbing, air conditioning, thermal, and electrical systems of the home. It is the only federally regulated national building code. Each home or segment of a home is red tagged with the manufacturer's guarantee the home was built to conform to the HUD code. Manufactured homes are built on a non-removable steel chassis and transported to the building site on their own wheels. A **mobile home** is a factory-built home MANUFACTURED prior to June 15, 1976, and constructed on a chassis with wheels.

A manufactured home when semi-attached (mobile or moveable) is considered personal property. A manufactured home is personal property unless it is converted into real property. Real property is immovable. A manufactured home is considered real property upon meeting certain requirements and attaching it to a permanent foundation. After meeting the requirements, the manufactured home is registered with the county recorder and taxed as real property. Determining whether the manufactured home is personal or real property affects how the manufactured home escrow may be conducted.

Review - Requirements to Convert a Manufactured (Mobile) Home to Real Property

- Building permit

- Permanent foundation

- Certificate of occupancy

Mobile Home Parks

A **mobile home park** is any area or tract of land where two or more manufactured (mobile) home lots are rented, leased, or held out for rent or lease to accommodate manufactured homes or mobile homes used for human habitation.

The rental of lots in a mobile home park is regulated by the state Department of Housing and Community Development (HCD). The HCD registers and licenses mobile homes, and must be notified by anyone acquiring or releasing an interest in mobile homes within 10 days after a sale. A copy of the registration will then be provided to all lien holders. Both the buyer and seller must sign a certificate of title. A **certificate of title** transfers ownership of a mobile home owned as personal property. If the mobile home is real property, a **clearance of tax liability** must be signed by the county tax collector. To comply with the law, certain requirements must be met when a manufactured or mobile home is sold in California.

Escrow Requirements to Transfer Ownership in a Manufactured (Mobile) Home

- In most cases, an escrow must be used.

- A notice of escrow opening must be filed with the Housing and Community Development Department.

- The legal owner and any junior lien holders must receive a demand for statements of lien release or assumption.

- A demand for a tax clearance certificate must be sent to the county tax collector.

- If a part of the consideration is for accessories, that part shall not be released until the accessories are actually installed.

- The escrow holder may not be an agency under the Department of Corporations in which the manufactured home dealer or seller holds more than 5% ownership interest.

- If the manufactured home is to be permanently installed on a foundation, it becomes real property. In that case, the registration requirements and other escrow requirements change. A document showing delivery and placement on a foundation must be given to the escrow holder for recording upon close of escrow.

Other Types of Escrows

There are other escrow transactions that may develop, including those for residential properties such as houseboats or time-shares, sale of a business, or a tax-deferred exchange.

Sale of a Business

The sale of a business, or business opportunity as it is known, is another personal property escrow transaction.

This type of transaction is known as a **bulk sale** or bulk transfer, subject to regulations in the Uniform Commercial Code.

The primary reason for the regulation of the sale of a business is to protect creditors of the business, so they can submit unpaid bills for payment before the business is sold to a new owner. When a business is sold and most or all of the inventory, supplies, and other materials are transferred with the sale, public notice must be given.

Twelve business days before the transfer, notice of the sale must be filed with the county recorder, published in a local newspaper in the county where the business is located, and delivered to the county tax collector. The sale must be advertised in local publications to notify creditors and give them time to present a final bill. Any bulk sale that takes place without complying with the requirements of the **bulk transfer law** is considered valid between the buyer and seller, but fraudulent and void against creditors. This means creditors have recourse against the debtor (the seller) because he or she sold the security for the debt without notifying them.

California Gazette Classifieds

Public Notices

NOTICE OF PUBLIC SALE

NOTICE TO CREDITORS OF BULK SALE (SECS. 6104, 6105 U.C.C.) Notice is hereby given to creditors of the within named seller that a bulk sale is about to be made of the assets described below. The names and business addresses of the Seller are ABC INC. 1234 MOUNTAIN AVE., ANY CITY, CA 90000. The location in California of the chief executive office of the seller is: (If "same as above", so state) SAME AS ABOVE As listed by the seller, all other business names and addresses used by the seller within three years before the date such list was sent or delivered to the buyer are: (If "none", so state.) NONE. The names and business addresses of the buyer are TOM BAKER 12354 STATE STREET, ANY TOWN, CA 90000. The assets to be sold are described in general as A BUSINESS INCLUDING FURNITURE, FIXTURE AND EQUIPMENT, GOODWILL, CORPORATION, AND TRADE NAME, LEASE, AND LEASEHOLD IMPROVEMENTS and are located at: 1234 MOUNTAIN AVE., ANY CITY, CA 92800. The business name used by the seller at that location is GOOD BUYS. The anticipated date of the sale/transfer is 12/28/20xx at the office of ABC Escrow, 12345 Elm Street, Any City, CA 90000. This bulk sale IS subject to California Uniform Commercial Code Section 6106.2. If so subject, the name and address of the person with who claims may be filed is Tim Greene. ABC Escrow, 12345 State Street, Any City, CA 92600 and the last date for filing claims shall be 12/27/20xx, which is the business day before the sale date specified above. Dated: 10/27/04 /s/ TOM BAKER Published: Any City News October 29, 20xx.

NOTICE TO CREDITORS OF BULK SALE AND OF INTENTION TO TRANSFER ALCOHOLIC BEVERAGE LICENSE (U.C.C. 6105 et seq. and B & P 24073 et seq.) Notice is hereby given that a bulk sale of assets and a transfer of alcoholic beverage license is about to be made. The names, Social Security or Federal Tax Numbers, and addresses of the Seller/Licensee are DEC INC.,18922 OCEAN AVENUE, ANY CITY, CA 90000. The business is known as OUR PLACE. The names, Social Security or Federal Tax Numbers, and addresses of the Buyer/Transferee are TIM GRENE, 110 HILLCREST BLVD., ANY TOWN, CA 90000, SS#123-00-1960. As listed by the Seller/Licensee, all other business names and addresses used by the Seller/Licensee within three years before the date such list was sent or delivered to the Buyer/Transferee are: (if none, so state.) NONE The Assets to be sold are described in general as: A BUSINESS INCLUDING FURNITURE, FIXTURES AND EQUIPMENT, GOODWILL, TRADE-NAME, LEASE AND LEASEHOLD IMPROVEMENTS and are located at: 18922 SAND AVENUE, HUNTINGTON BEACH, CA 92000. The kind of license to be transferred is: ON-SALE GENERAL EATING PLACE #11-112345 now issued for the premises located at: 18922 HILLCREST AVENUE, ANY TOWN, CA 90000. The anticipated date of the sale/transfer is 12/15/2004 at the office of ABC Escrow, 12345 State Street, Any City, CA 90000. It has been agreed between the Seller/Licensee and the intended Buyer/Transferee, as required by Sec. 24073 of the Business and Professions Code, that the consideration for the transfer of the business and license is to be paid only after the transfer has been approved by the Department of Alcoholic Beverage Control. Dated: 10/15/20xx DEC, INC. BY: PAT SMITH, Published: Beach Wave, November 4, 20xx

BULK ESCROW

Standard Documents

Opening Documents

Instruction: Bulk w/Liquor
Instruction: Bulk Sale
Buyer/Seller Information Form
Exhibit "A": Bulk Sec 24074
Exhibit "A": Bulk Sec 6106.2
Commission Inst.: Bulk Sale
Buyer Open Letter: Bulk Sale
Buyer Information: Bulk Sale
Seller Open Letter: Bulk Sale
Seller Information: Bulk Sale
Inventory Form
Landlord Letter
Statement of Information
Bill of Sale
Demand Request
Demand Note
Demand Note: unsecured
Demand Note: Sec. Agreement
Security Agreement
Security Agreement: Str. Note
Security Agreement: Inst. Note
ABC 226: Consideration
ABC 227: Transfer License
Assignment of Lease
Assumption of Lease
Consent to Lease
Assign of Lease-Collateral
Assumption Agreement
State Board of Equalization
Notice to Creditors
Notice to Creditors/Liquor
Notice to Creditors/Assumption
Notice of Sale Liquor License
Notice Creditor/Auction
Notice Creditor/Liquidation
Notice: Bulk Sale/Capital
Notice: Diss. of Partnership
Statement of Withdrawal
Bulk Instruction Memo
Tenant Estoppel Certificate
Rent Statement
New Lenders Open Letter
Mortgage Broker Open Letter
Private Lender Open Letter

Processing Documents

Amendments
Seller Proc Letter
Seller Misc. Letter: Bulk
Buyer Proc Letter: Bulk
Buyer Misc. Letter: Bulk
New Lender Processing Letter
Mortgage Broker Process Letter
Private Lender Process Letter
Payoff Process Letter-Institution
Payoff Process Letter-Private
Existing Lender Process Letter
Other Disbursement Letter

Closing Documents

Seller Close Letter: Bulk
Buyer Close Letter: Bulk
New Lender Close Letter
Mortgage Broker Close Letter
Listing Broker Close Letter
Selling Broker Close Letter
Private Lender Close Letter
Payoff Close Letter-Institution
Payoff Close Letter-Private
Existing Lender Close Letter
Other Disbursement Letter

1031 Exchanges

Under section 1031 of the Internal Revenue Code, some or all of the profit or gain from the exchange of one property for another may not have to be immediately recognized for tax purposes.

A tax-free exchange is a legal method of deferring capital gains taxes by exchanging one qualified property for another qualified property. When real estate for investment or for production of income is exchanged for like-kind property, and follows strict Internal Revenue Service requirements, a tax-deferred exchange can take place.

In handling a transaction where the properties are involved in a tax-deferred exchange, the escrow holder should be a specialist in exchanges. The law is very precise about whether an exchange qualifies as tax deferred, and the instruments used, the timing of recording and myriad other items must be confronted by the escrow holder in a completely accurate manner. A mistake as small as recording a document out of order could cause the exchange to be disqualified, make all parties more than irritated, and put the escrow holder in great need of legal counsel.

True-False Quiz

Now that you have read all the material in this chapter, take the following self-test and check your knowledge of other types of escrow.

True/False

1. _False_ Only sale escrows may be conducted by private escrow companies.

2. _False_ A loan escrow is used to transfer property that is being sold and funded by a subdivider.

3. _False_ A trust deed is sold whenever property transfers ownership.

4. _True_ An escrow can be required where fee title is not transferred.

5. _True_ Typical leasehold escrows will be a land lease or a space lease.

6. _False_ In commercial leasing, title insurance is never used.

7. _True_ The primary product in a mobile home escrow is considered personal property.

8. _False_ A mobile home never becomes real property.

9. _True_ Bulk transfer refers to the sale of a business.

10. _True_ Capital gains are deferred when a seller completes a 1031 tax-free exchange.

Chapter
15

The Escrow Folder

Learning Objectives

After reading this chapter, you will be able to:

- describe the procedures in conducting an escrow.
- identify and use the various computerized forms.

Introduction

The process of conducting an escrow, while requiring the services of a highly skilled technician, is very simple. As we have seen, it involves three steps: (1) opening the escrow, (2) processing the escrow, and finally (3) closing the escrow.

The three basic requirements, however, involve a considerable amount of detail, knowledge, skill, and basic understanding of all the elements of each unique escrow. No two escrows are the same, and yet, every escrow can be linked to another by its similarities; opening, processing, and closing.

Escrow Checklist

Prepare Escrow Instructions

According to region, bilateral or unilateral instructions, the initial phase of escrow begins with the purchase agreement and introductory documents to open escrow.

Gather Documentation

Grant deeds, trust deeds, quitclaim deeds, notes, bills of sale, security agreements, and Uniform Commercial Code forms (financing statements, information requests, termination statements, assignments) must all be collected and prepared.

Order Title Report

The title report gives the escrow holder information about liens such as existing trust deeds, unpaid taxes, judgments, or tax liens. Generally, the buyer has the right to approve or disapprove the preliminary title report as a contingency of the sale. The preliminary title report gives all the information included in the final title report which is usually insured in favor of the buyer, seller, and/or lender.

A title search begins with escrow completing a form to order title and sending a request to the title company. The original title must be produced and then updated. Then a new title insurance policy is issued. The chart on the following two pages shows the different ways to take title on a property, which is usually determined in escrow. This chart can help people determine the best way to take title without the escrow holder dispensing legal advice.

	Tenancy in Common	Joint Tenancy	Community Property	Community Property w/Right to Survivorship	Partnerships	Trusts	Community Property Trusts
Parties	Any number of persons (includes husband, wife).	Any number of persons (can be husband and wife).	Husband, wife only. Both sign deed to accept special vesting.	Husband, wife only. Both sign deed to accept special vesting.	Any number of persons and/or corporations & partnerships— Must be two parties.	Any individual, group, partnership, corporation. Special restrictions apply.	Husband, wife only.
Division	Ownership can be divided into any number of interests, equal or unequal.	Joint Tenants have one and same interests, but controls interest.	Ownership and management interests are equal.	Ownership and management interests are equal.	Each partner(s) share is personal property in partnership entity.	Ownership is personal property, can be divided into any number of interests.	Property retains character of community property.
Title	Each co-owner has a separate legal title to their undivided interest.	There is only one title to entire property.	Title is in the 'Community'. Each interest is separate but management is not.	Title is in the Community subject to special survivorship right.	Possession by partnership by managing partner(s).	Title held by trustee(s) pursuant to Trust Agreement.	Title held by trustee(s) pursuant to Trust.
Conveyance	Each co-owner's interest may be conveyed separately by the owner.	Conveyance by one severs the Joint Tenancy with other(s) but only regarding that owner(s) interest.	Both co-owners must join in conveyance of real property. Separate interests cannot be conveyed. Requires written consent or actual conveyance by deed, separate interest is divided by will.	Requires both spouses to join for valid conveyance, except for security for attorneys' fees. Estate may be severed as in Joint Tenancy by one spouse conveying to themselves.	Purchaser acquires interest that partnership owned.	Designated parties in Trust instrument authorize trustee to convey real property. Also beneficiary(s) interest may be sold separately (as personal property unless otherwise restricted).	By Trustee pursuant to Trust Agreement.
Possession	Equal right of possession.	Equal right of possession.	Both co-owners have equal control and management.	Both co-owners have equal control and management.	Conveyance must be by designated partners. All limited partners need to consent if sale is 100% of assets.	Provisions of Trust Agreement apply.	Provisions of Trust Agreement apply.
Purchaser's Status	Purchaser becomes a Tenant in Common with the other co-owners.	Purchaser can be Tenant in Common with other(s) according to their 'interest'. Others can remain Joint Tenants.	Purchaser can only acquire 100% of Title. Cannot acquire 'part.' Both spouses required to consent to convey. No co-owners with spouse(s).	Purchaser can only acquire 100% of title. Both spouses must convey and cannot include a co-owner with spouse(s)		Purchaser acquires interest held by Trustee. Beneficiary(s) interest may be conveyed separately (as personal property unless otherwise restricted).	Purchaser acquires interest held by Trustee.

	Tenancy in Common	Joint Tenancy	Community Property	Community Property w/Right to Survivorship	Partnerships	Trusts	Community Property Trusts
Death	On co-owner's death, interest passes by will to his/her heirs subject to administration by the local Superior Court. No survivorship right.	On co-owner's death, the entire tenancy remands to Survivor. Right of Survivorship is primary incident of joint tenancy.	On co-owner's death 1/2 belongs to survivor in servaralty, 1/2 goes by will to decedents' heirs and estate subject to probate administration by the local Superior Court.	On co-owner's death, 1/2 belongs to surviving spouse EXCEPT for no probate administration in courts or expense, thus retaining favorable tax advantage. 1/2 goes to decedent's heirs and estate.			
Successor(s) Status	Devisee(s) or heir(s) become Tenants in Common.	Last survivor owns property in severalty.	If passing by will, tenancy in common between devisee and survivor results.				
Creditor's Rights or 'Purchaser'	Co-owner's interest may be sold on execution sale to satisfy Creditor. Creditor becomes a Tenant in Common.	Co-owner's interest may be sold on execution sale to satisfy creditor. If Joint Tenancy is broken, creditor becomes Tenant in Common.	Co-owner's interest can't be sold separately, the whole property may be sold on execution to satisfy debts of whether husband or wife, depending on debt (consult an attorney with specific questions).				
Presumption	Favored in doubtful cases except husband, wife (see Community Property).	Must be expressly stated and properly formed. Not favored.	Strong presumption that the property acquired by husband, wife is community.				

Joint Escrow Instructions

Escrow instructions are for the purpose of communicating the intentions of the principals in a transaction to the escrow officer. The escrow officer has a stated time period to accomplish all the necessary tasks delegated by the instructions so the escrow will close in a timely manner according to the wishes of the parties. Commissions must be calculated if there is a broker involved, charges must be listed and made to the correct party, and all contingencies must be completed.

Sign Loan Documents

In the presence of a notary public, the borrower agrees to all terms and signs the loan documents.

Prepare to Record

Upon completion of all terms of the agreement between the parties, the escrow officer will authorize the recording of documents necessary to the transfer. All documents, signed instructions and amendments have been deposited and are in the possession of the escrow holder. Good funds have been received and are in the possession of the escrow holder. All conditions of the contract have been satisfied.

Recordation

Upon recordation of grant deed, trust deed or other documents required for the transfer, the sale is complete. The seller gets the money, the broker gets the commission and the buyer gets the property, with the grant deed to follow as soon as it is mailed to him or her by the county recorder. Information about the transfer of ownership is forwarded to the fire insurance company and existing lenders or any other interested parties. A closing statement summarizing the disbursement of funds and costs of the escrow is prepared by the escrow officer and given to each of the parties.

The Escrow Folder

The escrow folder is a legal file containing all the documents pertaining to the escrow. Checklists are printed directly on front, back and inside, to mark incoming and outgoing documents that need to signed, authorized, notarized, certified, and reviewed, and to account for all monies.

They function as general ledger for the critical transfer of money, and as a legal file for the contracts contained in the folder. Essentially, the escrow folder is where all the documents are collated, tacked down, and filed according to type and importance.

The front of the escrow folder divides into two columns for buyer and seller, and then into subsets for lenders, lienholders, insurance agents, so that the escrow holder can look at what documents are outstanding at a glance.

Inside the folder is the escrow status sheet which lists the numerous documents and requirements of the escrow and the date they are ordered, when they are delivered, and if they need signatures or further review.

The back of the escrow folder provides a snapshot of the transaction. It shows the legal description of the property and the vesting of the sellers and buyers. There are several sections used to log and review the total consideration paid for the property and status of any existing or new loans. It lists the contact information for the salesperson and the commissions due the brokers involved in the transaction. The proration checklist helps keep track of impounds and any taxes, interest, association dues, insurance, or rent that may be prorated. Even the agreed-upon date of possession is indicated on the back of the escrow folder.

Like any legal file, escrow folders must be retained for a period of time, often up to seven years, and then warehoused for retrieval in the event of any legal action arising out of the sale of that property. Each office should develop a record retention policy to ensure that records are stored correctly, and readily available. The Statute of Limitations for a claim for breach of contract is six years. Certain documents, such as corporate records, partnership agreements, audit reports, general ledgers, tax returns, and deeds must be kept permanently.

The Escrow Folder – Front Cover

SELLER	REQ'ED	DATE	REC'D	REQ'ED	DATE	REC'D	BUYER
INSTRUCTIONS (_____ Pages)							INSTRUCTIONS (_____ Pages)
PEST CONTROL SUPPLEMENT							PEST CONTROL SUPPLEMENT
STATEMENT OF INFORMATION							STATEMENT OF INFORMATION
COMMISSION AUTHORIZATION							INITIAL DEPOSIT
LOAN INFORMATION FORM							1ST LOAN DOC'S
DEED							2ND LOAN DOC'S
RENT STATEMENT							RENT STATEMENT
30 DAY NOTICE							FIRE INSURANCE POLICY
TITLE REPORT							APPROVE TITLE ITEM
A.L.T.A.							MONEY
DEMAND 1ST							AMEND RE:
DEMAND 2ND							FHA-VA EVALUATION CLAUSE
FHA-VA EVALUATION CLAUSE							
BENE: 1ST							
BENE: 2ND							
PEST CONTROL REPORT							
PEST CONTROL CLEARANCE							
AMEND RE:							

Insurance Company	Lender
	Address — Loan Rep.
Amount $ — Effective	Cert. Inst. Sent — For $
	Appraisal Rec'd — As Req — Low
Policy Number — Term	Requirements
Agent's Name — Phone Number	
Address	Submitted
Date Ordered	Approved on — Points
Premium $ — For — Years	Loan Doc's. Ordered: — Rec'd
	Returned — Ordered Funds

ESCROW NO	
TO CLOSE	
OPENED	DATE
CLOSED	
CANCELLED	DATE
SELLER	
PROPERTY ADDRESS	
DATE SENT	
DATE SENT	
SELLING SALESMAN	
LISTING SALESMAN	
BUYER	
SELLING OFFICE	
LISTING OFFICE	
PHONE NO	
PHONE NO	
COMPANY	
T. OFFICER	
OPENED	
RECORDING ORDERED	
TITLE NO	
DOCS TO TITLE CO.	
DATE RECORDED	
PHONE NO	

SALE ESCROW   Standard Documents

OPENING DOCUMENTS

Instruction: Sale
Instruction: Land contract
Instruction: AITD
CAR Deposit Receipt Phrases
Commission Instruction
Status Sheet: Broker/Lender
Status Sheet: Buyer
Status Sheet: Seller
Seller Open Letter

Buyer Open Letter
Loan Information Sheet
Statement of Information
Fire Insurance Info Form
Cal-FRPTA Notice/Disclosure
California 590-RE Form
PCOR
Vesting Worksheet:
Buyer/Borrower
Vesting Worksheet:
Trust/Corporation
1099 Tax Reporting Form

Listing/Selling Broker Open Letter

New Lender Open Letter

Mortgage Broker Close Letter
Private Beneficiary Open Letter
Beneficiary Statement Request:
Private
Beneficiary Statement Request:
Institutional
Owner's Offset Statement
Rent Statement
Tenant Estoppel Certificate
Third Party Instruction
FRPTA: Notice to Buyer/Seller
FRPTA: Buyer's Exemption1445
FRPTA: Seller's Affidavit
Nonresident Withholding
Statement

PROCESSING DOCUMENTS

Title Open Transmittal
Preliminary title Report Approval
HOA Demand
Demand Request: Institutional
Demand Request: Private
FHA: 30 Day Notice
Instruction Reminder: Seller
Instruction Reminder: Buyer
Trust Certificate: Probate Section
18100.5
Trust Certification
Seller Amendment Letter
Buyer Amendment Letter
Broker Processing Letter
New Lender Processing Letter
Mortgage Broker Process Letter
Private Beneficiary Process Letter
Payoff Lender Process Letter
Fire Insurance Process Letter
Existing Lender Process Letter
Flood Insurance Process Letter
Earthquake Insurance Process
Letter
Pest Company Process Letter
Septic Company Process Letter
Irrevocable Demand: FROM
Escrow
Irrevocable Demand: TO Escrow
Cancel Escrow Instructions

CLOSING DOCUMENTS

Request for Insurance
Title Docs Transmittal
Funding Letter: Mortgage
Funding Letter: New Lender
Wire Instructions
Buyer Close Letter
Buyer Title Policy Transmittal
Seller Close Letter
Broker Close Letter
New Lenders Close Letter
Mortgage Broker Close Letter
Private Beneficiary Close Letter
Payoff Lenders Close Letter
Existing Lender Close Letter
HOA Close Letter
Fire Insurance Close Letter
Earthquake Insurance Close Letter
Pest Company Close Letter
Septic Company Close Letter
Nonresident Withholding
Statement
California 597-A Form
Closing Check List

The Escrow Folder – Status Sheet

ESCROW STATUS SHEET

Escrow Number: _____
Order Number: _____
PROPERTY   :

Escrow Officer

EST. CLOSE: _____

SELLER(s)   :
Address   :
Office Ph.   :   Home: Fax:
ATTN: :

BUYER(s)   :
Address   :
Office Ph.   :   Home: Fax:
ATTN: :

LOAN INFO   :   HOME OWNERS ASSOC.
Address   :
Attn.   :   Attn: :   FAX:
Phone   :   FAX: Phone: :

L-BROKER   :   S-BROKER   :
Agent Name   :   Agent Name   :
Address   :   Address   :
Phone   :   FAX: Phone   :: FAX:

ASSIGNMENT INFO.   FIRE INSURANCE:
Company   Company :
Escrow Officer   Agent   :
Address   Address :
Phone#   FAX: Phone#   :   FAX:

ORDERED	RECEIVED	NEED	- - - S E L L E R - - -	NEED	ORDERED	RECEIVED	- - - B U Y E R - - -
			ESCROW INSTRUCTIONS				ESCROW INSTRUCTIONS
			COMMISSION				INITIAL DEPOSIT
			GRANT DEED				PCOR
			SI/LOAN INFORM.				SI/INSURANCE INFO
			FIRPTSA/CAL FIRPTA				FIRPTA/CAL FIRPTA
			PRELIM ORDERED				VESTING
			PRELIM APPROVAL				PRELIM APPROVAL
			HOA STMT/DOCS ORDERED				
			HOA APPROVED				HOA APPROVED
			TERMITE REPORT REC.				LIEN DEMAND
			TERMITE CLEAR REC.				LIEN DEMAND
			TERMITE APPROVAL				TERMITE APPROVAL
			HOME PROTECTION				SPOUSE DEED/INST.
			ZONE DISCLOS. BILL				POA/INST.
			TRUST CERTIF				TRUST CERTIF
			SPOUSE DEED/INST.				E.I. TO LENDER
			POA/INST.				PRELIM TO LENDER
			DEMAND:				INSURANCE ORDERED
			DEMAND:				
			DEMAND:				
			DEMAND:				
			AMENDMENT:				AMENDMENT
			AMENDMENT:				AMENDMENT
			AMENDMENT:				AMENDMENT
			AMENDMENT:				AMENDMENT
			LIST. COMMISSION				LOAN APPROVED
			SELL. COMMISSION				DOC'S RECEIVED / DOC' SIGN. APPTMNT
							LOAN DOC'S RETUR.
							FUNDING REQUESTED
							B'S CLOSING FUNDS
							SET TO RECORD
							RECORDED

CORRESPONDENCE   ACCOUNTING

The Escrow Folder – Inside Tabs

Typical escrow folders are assembled by tabs

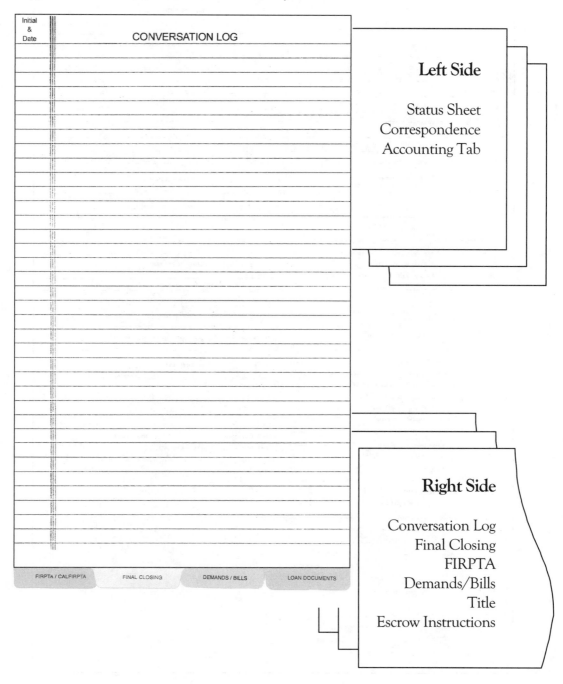

The Escrow Folder – Back Cover

SALESPERSON
_____

PROP. ADDRESS _____ S/S _____ OFF _____
_____ ADDRESS _____ PHONE _____
_____ L/S _____ OFF _____
ESCROW OPENED _____ ESC. # _____ TIME LIMIT _____ ADDRESS _____ PHONE _____

SELLER (Vesting) (MAIL – CALL – BROKER) _____

ADDRESS _____ HOME # _____ BUS # _____

BUYER (Vesting) (MAIL – CALL – BROKER) _____

ADDRESS _____ HOME # _____ BUS # _____

LEGAL DESCRIPTION _____
_____ County _____ BK _____ PG. _____ (Maps)(MR)

CONSIDERATION		COMMISSION	
Initial Cash Deposit	$ _____	(_____%) $ _____	
Balance of Cash	$ _____	$ _____	
1st t/d	$ _____	(_____%) $ _____	
2nd t/d	$ _____	(_____%) $ _____	
	$ _____	Board (_____%) $ _____	
TOTAL _____ $ _____		TOTAL (_____%) $ _____	

EXISTING 1ST LOAN   **PERSONAL PROPERTY**

( ) To remain   ( ) To be paid off   FHA   VA   Conven. _____

Lender _____ Loan # _____ _____

Address _____ _____

Balance due $ _____ Int _____ % Phone _____ _____

Mthly. Pymt. $ _____ Inc. Impounds _____ _____

EXISTING 2ND LOAN   _____

( ) To remain   ( ) To be paid off   _____

Lender _____ Loan # _____

Address _____   **POSSESSION**

Balance due $ _____ Int _____ % Phone ____ ( ) Close of escrow   ( ) ____ days AFTER CLOSE OF ESCROW

Mthly. Pymt. $ _____ DUE DATE _____

ACCELERATION CLAUSE   ( ) Yes   ( ) No   **ADJUSTMENTS AS OF _____**

NEW 1ST LOAN

Points ____   FHA   VA   Conven   ( ) Taxes   ( ) Interest   ( ) Rents

Lender _____   ( ) Existing Insurance   ( ) New Insurance

Address _____ Phone _____   ( ) IMPOUNDS — Refund to seller — Charge Buyer

Loan Amt. $ _____ Int. _____% _____ Yrs. ( ) IMPOUNDS — INSURANCE — ASSIGN TO BUYER — NO REFUND

Mthly. Pymt. $ _____ Inc. Impounds _____   ( ) ASSOCIATION DUES/MAINTENANCE FEES $ _____

WAS CRV ORDERED IN BUYERS NAME ( ) Yes ( ) No   ( ) _____

NEW 2ND LOAN   EQUITY: ( ) Adjust in Cash   ( ) TD to file   ( ) Sales price

Lender _____

Address _____ Phone _____

Amt. $ _____ Int _____% Mthly Pmt. _____

DUE DATE _____ Acceleration Clause: ( ) Yes ( ) No

Request for notice   ( ) Yes ( ) No ( ) Late charge

Pest Control Report   ( ) Yes ( ) No

Title Company _____

Requested By _____

Escrow Taken By _____ Date _____

From _____ By Phone/In Person _____

INFO. SHEET TO COMPUTER _____ BY _____
                          Date   Initial

CALIFORNIA ASSOCIATION OF REALTORS®

CALIFORNIA
RESIDENTIAL PURCHASE AGREEMENT
AND JOINT ESCROW INSTRUCTIONS
For Use With Single Family Residential Property — Attached or Detached
(C.A.R. Form RPA-CA, Revised 1/06)

Date _____ , at _____ , California.
1. **OFFER:**
   A. **THIS IS AN OFFER FROM** _____ ("Buyer").
   B. **THE REAL PROPERTY TO BE ACQUIRED** is described as _____
      _____ , Assessor's Parcel No. _____ , situated in
      _____ , County of _____ , California, ("Property").
   C. **THE PURCHASE PRICE** offered is _____
      _____ Dollars $ _____ .
   D. **CLOSE OF ESCROW** shall occur on _____ (date) (or ☐ _____ **Days** After Acceptance).
2. **FINANCE TERMS:** Obtaining the loans below **is a contingency** of this Agreement unless: **(i)** either 2K or 2L is checked below; or **(ii)** otherwise agreed in writing. Buyer shall act diligently and in good faith to obtain the designated loans. Obtaining deposit, down payment and closing costs **is not a contingency.** Buyer represents that funds will be good when deposited with Escrow Holder.
   A. **INITIAL DEPOSIT:** Buyer has given a deposit in the amount of .... $ _____
      to the agent submitting the offer (or to ☐ _____), by personal check
      (or ☐ _____), made payable to _____ ,
      which shall be held uncashed until Acceptance and then deposited within **3 business days** after Acceptance
      (or ☐ _____), with
      Escrow Holder, (or ☐ into Broker's trust account).
   B. **INCREASED DEPOSIT:** Buyer shall deposit with Escrow Holder an increased deposit in the amount of ..... $ _____
      within _____ **Days** After Acceptance, or ☐ _____ .
   C. **FIRST LOAN IN THE AMOUNT OF** .... $ _____
      (1) NEW First Deed of Trust in favor of lender, encumbering the Property, securing a note payable at maximum
         interest of _____ % fixed rate, or _____ % initial adjustable rate with a maximum interest rate
         of _____ %, balance due in _____ years, amortized over _____ years. Buyer shall
         pay loan fees/points not to exceed _____ . (These terms apply whether the designated loan
         is conventional, FHA or VA.)
      (2) ☐ FHA ☐ VA: (The following terms only apply to the FHA or VA loan that is checked.)
         Seller shall pay _____ % discount points. Seller shall pay other fees not allowed to be paid by Buyer,
         ☐ not to exceed $ _____ . Seller shall pay the cost of lender required Repairs (including
         those for wood destroying pest) not otherwise provided for in this Agreement, ☐ not to exceed
         $ _____ . (Actual loan amount may increase if mortgage insurance premiums, funding
         fees or closing costs are financed.)
   D. **ADDITIONAL FINANCING TERMS:** ☐ Seller financing, (C.A.R. Form SFA); ☐ secondary financing, ... $ _____
      (C.A.R. Form PAA, paragraph 4A); ☐ assumed financing (C.A.R. Form PAA, paragraph 4B)
      _____
      _____
   E. **BALANCE OF PURCHASE PRICE** (not including costs of obtaining loans and other closing costs) in the amount of .. $ _____
      to be deposited with Escrow Holder within sufficient time to close escrow.
   F. **PURCHASE PRICE (TOTAL):** .... $ _____
   G. **LOAN APPLICATIONS:** Within **7** (or ☐ _____) **Days** After Acceptance, Buyer shall provide Seller a letter from lender or mortgage loan broker stating that, based on a review of Buyer's written application and credit report, Buyer is prequalified or preapproved for the NEW loan specified in 2C above.
   H. **VERIFICATION OF DOWN PAYMENT AND CLOSING COSTS:** Buyer (or Buyer's lender or loan broker pursuant to 2G) shall, within **7** (or ☐ _____) **Days** After Acceptance, provide Seller written verification of Buyer's down payment and closing costs.
   I. **LOAN CONTINGENCY REMOVAL:** (i) Within **17** (or ☐ _____) **Days** After Acceptance, Buyer shall, as specified in paragraph 14, remove the loan contingency or cancel this Agreement; **OR** (ii) (if checked) ☐ the loan contingency shall remain in effect until the designated loans are funded.
   J. **APPRAISAL CONTINGENCY AND REMOVAL:** This Agreement is (**OR**, if checked, ☐ is **NOT**) contingent upon the Property appraising at no less than the specified purchase price. If there is a loan contingency, at the time the loan contingency is removed (or, if checked, ☐ within **17** (or _____) **Days** After Acceptance), Buyer shall, as specified in paragraph 14B(3), remove the appraisal contingency or cancel this Agreement. If there is no loan contingency, Buyer shall, as specified in paragraph 14B(3), remove the appraisal contingency within **17** (or _____) **Days** After Acceptance.
   K. ☐ **NO LOAN CONTINGENCY** (If checked): Obtaining any loan in paragraphs 2C, 2D or elsewhere in this Agreement is NOT a contingency of this Agreement. If Buyer does not obtain the loan and as a result Buyer does not purchase the Property, Seller may be entitled to Buyer's deposit or other legal remedies.
   L. ☐ **ALL CASH OFFER** (If checked): No loan is needed to purchase the Property. Buyer shall, within **7** (or ☐ _____) **Days** After Acceptance, provide Seller written verification of sufficient funds to close this transaction.
3. **CLOSING AND OCCUPANCY:**
   A. Buyer intends (or ☐ does not intend) to occupy the Property as Buyer's primary residence.
   B. **Seller-occupied or vacant property:** Occupancy shall be delivered to Buyer at _____ ☐ AM ☐ PM, ☐ on the date of Close Of Escrow; ☐ on _____ ; or ☐ no later than _____ **Days** After Close Of Escrow. (C.A.R. Form PAA, paragraph 2.) If transfer of title and occupancy do not occur at the same time, Buyer and Seller are advised to: (i) enter into a written occupancy agreement; and (ii) consult with their insurance and legal advisors.

Buyer's Initials (_____) (_____)
Seller's Initials (_____) (_____)
Reviewed by _____ Date _____

RPA-CA REVISED 1/06 (PAGE 1 OF 8) CALIFORNIA RESIDENTIAL PURCHASE AGREEMENT (RPA-CA PAGE 1 OF 8)

Agent: _____ Phone: _____ Fax: _____ Prepared using WINForms® software
Broker:

Property Address: _____ Date: _____

C. **Tenant-occupied property: (i) Property shall be vacant** at least **5 (or** ☐ _____ **) Days** Prior to Close Of Escrow, unless otherwise agreed in writing. **Note to Seller: If you are unable to deliver Property vacant in accordance with rent control and other applicable Law, you may be in breach of this Agreement.**

OR **(ii) (if checked)** ☐ **Tenant to remain in possession.** The attached addendum is incorporated into this Agreement (C.A.R. Form PAA, paragraph 3.);

OR **(iii) (if checked)** ☐ **This Agreement is contingent** upon Buyer and Seller entering into a written agreement regarding occupancy of the Property within the time specified in paragraph 14B(1). If no written agreement is reached within this time, either Buyer or Seller may cancel this Agreement in writing.

D. At Close Of Escrow, Seller assigns to Buyer any assignable warranty rights for items included in the sale and shall provide any available Copies of such warranties. Brokers cannot and will not determine the assignability of any warranties.

E. At Close Of Escrow, unless otherwise agreed in writing, Seller shall provide keys and/or means to operate all locks, mailboxes, security systems, alarms and garage door openers. If Property is a condominium or located in a common interest subdivision, Buyer may be required to pay a deposit to the Homeowners' Association ("HOA") to obtain keys to accessible HOA facilities.

4. **ALLOCATION OF COSTS** (If checked): Unless otherwise specified here, this paragraph only determines who is to pay for the report, inspection, test or service mentioned. If not specified here or elsewhere in this Agreement, the determination of who is to pay for any work recommended or identified by any such report, inspection, test or service shall be by the method specified in paragraph 14B(2).

A. **WOOD DESTROYING PEST INSPECTION:**
   (1) ☐ Buyer ☐ Seller shall pay for an inspection and report for wood destroying pests and organisms ("Report") which shall be prepared by _____ , a registered structural pest control company. The Report shall cover the accessible areas of the main building and attached structures and, if checked: ☐ detached garages and carports, ☐ detached decks, ☐ the following other structures or areas _____ . The Report shall not include roof coverings. If Property is a condominium or located in a common interest subdivision, the Report shall include only the separate interest and any exclusive-use areas being transferred and shall not include common areas, unless otherwise agreed. Water tests of shower pans on upper level units may not be performed without consent of the owners of property below the shower.

OR **(2)** ☐ **(If checked)** The attached addendum (C.A.R. Form WPA) regarding wood destroying pest inspection and allocation of cost is incorporated into this Agreement.

B. **OTHER INSPECTIONS AND REPORTS:**
   (1) ☐ Buyer ☐ Seller shall pay to have septic or private sewage disposal systems inspected _____ .
   (2) ☐ Buyer ☐ Seller shall pay to have domestic wells tested for water potability and productivity _____ .
   (3) ☐ Buyer ☐ Seller shall pay for a natural hazard zone disclosure report prepared by _____ .
   (4) ☐ Buyer ☐ Seller shall pay for the following inspection or report _____ .
   (5) ☐ Buyer ☐ Seller shall pay for the following inspection or report _____ .

C. **GOVERNMENT REQUIREMENTS AND RETROFIT:**
   (1) ☐ Buyer ☐ Seller shall pay for smoke detector installation and/or water heater bracing, if required by Law. Prior to Close Of Escrow, Seller shall provide Buyer a written statement of compliance in accordance with state and local Law, unless exempt.
   (2) ☐ Buyer ☐ Seller shall pay the cost of compliance with any other minimum mandatory government retrofit standards, inspections and reports if required as a condition of closing escrow under any Law. _____ .

D. **ESCROW AND TITLE:**
   (1) ☐ Buyer ☐ Seller shall pay escrow fee _____ .
       Escrow Holder shall be _____ .
   (2) ☐ Buyer ☐ Seller shall pay for **owner's** title insurance policy specified in paragraph 12E _____ .
       Owner's title policy to be issued by _____ .
       (Buyer shall pay for any title insurance policy insuring Buyer's **lender**, unless otherwise agreed in writing.)

E. **OTHER COSTS:**
   (1) ☐ Buyer ☐ Seller shall pay County transfer tax or transfer fee _____ .
   (2) ☐ Buyer ☐ Seller shall pay City transfer tax or transfer fee _____ .
   (3) ☐ Buyer ☐ Seller shall pay HOA transfer fee _____ .
   (4) ☐ Buyer ☐ Seller shall pay HOA document preparation fees _____ .
   (5) ☐ Buyer ☐ Seller shall pay the cost, not to exceed $ _____ , of a one-year home warranty plan, issued by _____ , with the following optional coverage: _____ .
   (6) ☐ Buyer ☐ Seller shall pay for _____ .
   (7) ☐ Buyer ☐ Seller shall pay for _____ .

5. **STATUTORY DISCLOSURES (INCLUDING LEAD-BASED PAINT HAZARD DISCLOSURES) AND CANCELLATION RIGHTS:**
   A. (1) Seller shall, within the time specified in paragraph 14A, deliver to Buyer, if required by Law: **(i)** Federal Lead-Based Paint Disclosures and pamphlet ("Lead Disclosures"); and **(ii)** disclosures or notices required by sections 1102 et. seq. and 1103 et. seq. of the California Civil Code ("Statutory Disclosures"). Statutory Disclosures include, but are not limited to, a Real Estate Transfer Disclosure Statement ("TDS"), Natural Hazard Disclosure Statement ("NHD"), notice or actual knowledge of release of illegal controlled substance, notice of special tax and/or assessments (or, if allowed, substantially equivalent notice regarding the Mello-Roos Community Facilities Act and Improvement Bond Act of 1915) and, if Seller has actual knowledge, an industrial use and military ordnance location disclosure (C.A.R. Form SSD).
      (2) Buyer shall, within the time specified in paragraph 14B(1), return Signed Copies of the Statutory and Lead Disclosures to Seller.
      (3) In the event Seller, prior to Close Of Escrow, becomes aware of adverse conditions materially affecting the Property, or any material inaccuracy in disclosures, information or representations previously provided to Buyer of which Buyer is otherwise unaware, Seller shall promptly provide a subsequent or amended disclosure or notice, in writing, covering those items. **However, a subsequent or amended disclosure shall not be required for conditions and material inaccuracies disclosed in reports ordered and paid for by Buyer.**

Buyer's Initials (_____) (_____)
Seller's Initials (_____) (_____)

RPA-CA REVISED 1/06 (PAGE 2 OF 8)

Reviewed by _____ Date _____

CALIFORNIA RESIDENTIAL PURCHASE AGREEMENT (RPA-CA PAGE 2 OF 8)

x.zfx

Property Address: _____ Date: _____

(4) If any disclosure or notice specified in 5A(1), or subsequent or amended disclosure or notice is delivered to Buyer after the offer is Signed, Buyer shall have the right to cancel this Agreement within **3 Days** After delivery in person, or **5 Days** After delivery by deposit in the mail, by giving written notice of cancellation to Seller or Seller's agent. (Lead Disclosures sent by mail must be sent certified mail or better.)

(5) **Note to Buyer and Seller: Waiver of Statutory and Lead Disclosures is prohibited by Law.**

B. **NATURAL AND ENVIRONMENTAL HAZARDS:** Within the time specified in paragraph 14A, Seller shall, if required by Law: (i) deliver to Buyer earthquake guides (and questionnaire) and environmental hazards booklet; (ii) even if exempt from the obligation to provide a NHD, disclose if the Property is located in a Special Flood Hazard Area; Potential Flooding (Inundation) Area; Very High Fire Hazard Zone; State Fire Responsibility Area; Earthquake Fault Zone; Seismic Hazard Zone; and (iii) disclose any other zone as required by Law and provide any other information required for those zones.

C. **DATA BASE DISCLOSURE:** Notice: Pursuant to Section 290.46 of the Penal Code, information about specified registered sex offenders is made available to the public via an Internet Web site maintained by the Department of Justice at www.meganslaw.ca.gov. Depending on an offender's criminal history, this information will include either the address at which the offender resides or the community of residence and ZIP Code in which he or she resides. (Neither Seller nor Brokers are required to check this website. If Buyer wants further information, Broker recommends that Buyer obtain information from this website during Buyer's inspection contingency period. Brokers do not have expertise in this area.)

6. **CONDOMINIUM/PLANNED UNIT DEVELOPMENT DISCLOSURES:**
   A. **SELLER HAS: 7 (or ☐ _____) Days** After Acceptance to disclose to Buyer whether the Property is a condominium, or is located in a planned unit development or other common interest subdivision (C.A.R. Form SSD).
   B. If the Property is a condominium or is located in a planned unit development or other common interest subdivision, Seller has **3 (or ☐ _____) Days** After Acceptance to request from the HOA (C.A.R. Form HOA): (i) Copies of any documents required by Law; (ii) disclosure of any pending or anticipated claim or litigation by or against the HOA; (iii) a statement containing the location and number of designated parking and storage spaces; (iv) Copies of the most recent 12 months of HOA minutes for regular and special meetings; and (v) the names and contact information of all HOAs governing the Property (collectively, "CI Disclosures"). Seller shall itemize and deliver to Buyer all CI Disclosures received from the HOA and any CI Disclosures in Seller's possession. Buyer's approval of CI Disclosures is a contingency of this Agreement as specified in paragraph 14B(3).

7. **CONDITIONS AFFECTING PROPERTY:**
   A. Unless otherwise agreed: (i) the Property is sold **(a)** in its **PRESENT** physical condition as of the date of Acceptance and **(b)** subject to Buyer's Investigation rights; (ii) the Property, including pool, spa, landscaping and grounds, is to be maintained in substantially the same condition as on the date of Acceptance; and (iii) all debris and personal property not included in the sale shall be removed by Close Of Escrow.
   B. **SELLER SHALL,** within the time specified in paragraph 14A, **DISCLOSE KNOWN MATERIAL FACTS AND DEFECTS** affecting the Property, including known insurance claims within the past five years, **AND MAKE OTHER DISCLOSURES REQUIRED BY LAW** (C.A.R. Form SSD).
   C. **NOTE TO BUYER: You are strongly advised to conduct investigations of the entire Property in order to determine its present condition since Seller may not be aware of all defects affecting the Property or other factors that you consider important. Property improvements may not be built according to code, in compliance with current Law, or have had permits issued.**
   D. **NOTE TO SELLER: Buyer has the right to inspect the Property and, as specified in paragraph 14B, based upon information discovered in those inspections: (i) cancel this Agreement; or (ii) request that you make Repairs or take other action.**

8. **ITEMS INCLUDED AND EXCLUDED:**
   A. **NOTE TO BUYER AND SELLER:** Items listed as included or excluded in the MLS, flyers or marketing materials are **not** included in the purchase price or excluded from the sale unless specified in 8B or C.
   B. **ITEMS INCLUDED IN SALE:**
      (1) All EXISTING fixtures and fittings that are attached to the Property;
      (2) Existing electrical, mechanical, lighting, plumbing and heating fixtures, ceiling fans, fireplace inserts, gas logs and grates, solar systems, built-in appliances, window and door screens, awnings, shutters, window coverings, attached floor coverings, television antennas, satellite dishes, private integrated telephone systems, air coolers/conditioners, pool/spa equipment, garage door openers/remote controls, mailbox, in-ground landscaping, trees/shrubs, water softeners, water purifiers, security systems/alarms; and
      (3) The following items: _____
         _____ .
      (4) Seller represents that all items included in the purchase price, unless otherwise specified, are owned by Seller.
      (5) All items included shall be transferred free of liens and without Seller warranty.
   C. **ITEMS EXCLUDED FROM SALE:** _____

9. **BUYER'S INVESTIGATION OF PROPERTY AND MATTERS AFFECTING PROPERTY:**
   A. Buyer's acceptance of the condition of, and any other matter affecting the Property, is a contingency of this Agreement as specified in this paragraph and paragraph 14B. Within the time specified in paragraph 14B(1), Buyer shall have the right, at Buyer's expense unless otherwise agreed, to conduct inspections, investigations, tests, surveys and other studies ("Buyer Investigations"), including, but not limited to, the right to: (i) inspect for lead-based paint and other lead-based paint hazards; (ii) inspect for wood destroying pests and organisms; (iii) review the registered sex offender database; (iv) confirm the insurability of Buyer and the Property; and (v) satisfy Buyer as to any matter specified in the attached Buyer's Inspection Advisory (C.A.R. Form BIA). Without Seller's prior written consent, Buyer shall neither make nor cause to be made: (i) invasive or destructive Buyer Investigations; or (ii) inspections by any governmental building or zoning inspector or government employee, unless required by Law.
   B. Buyer shall complete Buyer Investigations and, as specified in paragraph 14B, remove the contingency or cancel this Agreement. Buyer shall give Seller, at no cost, complete Copies of all Buyer Investigation reports obtained by Buyer. Seller shall make the Property available for all Buyer Investigations. Seller shall have water, gas, electricity and all operable pilot lights on for Buyer's Investigations and through the date possession is made available to Buyer.

Buyer's Initials (_____) (_____)
Seller's Initials (_____) (_____)

RPA-CA REVISED 1/06 (PAGE 3 OF 8)

Reviewed by _____ Date _____

CALIFORNIA RESIDENTIAL PURCHASE AGREEMENT (RPA-CA PAGE 3 OF 8)

EQUAL HOUSING OPPORTUNITY

x.zfx

Property Address: _____ Date: _____

10. REPAIRS: Repairs shall be completed prior to final verification of condition unless otherwise agreed in writing. Repairs to be performed at Seller's expense may be performed by Seller or through others, provided that the work complies with applicable Law, including governmental permit, inspection and approval requirements. Repairs shall be performed in a good, skillful manner with materials of quality and appearance comparable to existing materials. It is understood that exact restoration of appearance or cosmetic items following all Repairs may not be possible. Seller shall: **(i)** obtain receipts for Repairs performed by others; **(ii)** prepare a written statement indicating the Repairs performed by Seller and the date of such Repairs; and **(iii)** provide Copies of receipts and statements to Buyer prior to final verification of condition.

11. BUYER INDEMNITY AND SELLER PROTECTION FOR ENTRY UPON PROPERTY: Buyer shall: **(i)** keep the Property free and clear of liens; **(ii)** Repair all damage arising from Buyer Investigations; and **(iii)** indemnify and hold Seller harmless from all resulting liability, claims, demands, damages and costs. Buyer shall carry, or Buyer shall require anyone acting on Buyer's behalf to carry, policies of liability, workers' compensation and other applicable insurance, defending and protecting Seller from liability for any injuries to persons or property occurring during any Buyer Investigations or work done on the Property at Buyer's direction prior to Close Of Escrow. Seller is advised that certain protections may be afforded Seller by recording a "Notice of Non-responsibility" (C.A.R. Form NNR) for Buyer Investigations and work done on the Property at Buyer's direction. Buyer's obligations under this paragraph shall survive the termination of this Agreement.

12. TITLE AND VESTING:
  A. Within the time specified in paragraph 14, Buyer shall be provided a current preliminary (title) report, which is only an offer by the title insurer to issue a policy of title insurance and may not contain every item affecting title. Buyer's review of the preliminary report and any other matters which may affect title are a contingency of this Agreement as specified in paragraph 14B.
  B. Title is taken in its present condition subject to all encumbrances, easements, covenants, conditions, restrictions, rights and other matters, whether of record or not, as of the date of Acceptance except: **(i)** monetary liens of record unless Buyer is assuming those obligations or taking the Property subject to those obligations; and **(ii)** those matters which Seller has agreed to remove in writing.
  C. Within the time specified in paragraph 14A, Seller has a duty to disclose to Buyer all matters known to Seller affecting title, whether of record or not.
  D. At Close Of Escrow, Buyer shall receive a grant deed conveying title (or, for stock cooperative or long-term lease, an assignment of stock certificate or of Seller's leasehold interest), including oil, mineral and water rights if currently owned by Seller. Title shall vest as designated in Buyer's supplemental escrow instructions. THE MANNER OF TAKING TITLE MAY HAVE SIGNIFICANT LEGAL AND TAX CONSEQUENCES. CONSULT AN APPROPRIATE PROFESSIONAL.
  E. Buyer shall receive a CLTA/ALTA Homeowner's Policy of Title Insurance. A title company, at Buyer's request, can provide information about the availability, desirability, coverage, and cost of various title insurance coverages and endorsements. If Buyer desires title coverage other than that required by this paragraph, Buyer shall instruct Escrow Holder in writing and pay any increase in cost.

13. SALE OF BUYER'S PROPERTY:
  A. This Agreement is NOT contingent upon the sale of any property owned by Buyer.
OR B. ☐ (If checked): The attached addendum (C.A.R. Form COP) regarding the contingency for the sale of property owned by Buyer is incorporated into this Agreement.

14. TIME PERIODS; REMOVAL OF CONTINGENCIES; CANCELLATION RIGHTS: The following time periods may only be extended, altered, modified or changed by mutual written agreement. Any removal of contingencies or cancellation under this paragraph must be in writing (C.A.R. Form CR).
  A. **SELLER HAS: 7 (or ☐ _____) Days** After Acceptance to deliver to Buyer all reports, disclosures and information for which Seller is responsible under paragraphs 4, 5A and B, 6A, 7B and 12.
  B. (1) **BUYER HAS: 17 (or ☐ _____) Days** After Acceptance, unless otherwise agreed in writing, to:
       (i) complete all Buyer Investigations; approve all disclosures, reports and other applicable information, which Buyer receives from Seller; and approve all matters affecting the Property (including lead-based paint and lead-based paint hazards as well as other information specified in paragraph 5 and insurability of Buyer and the Property); and
       (ii) return to Seller Signed Copies of Statutory and Lead Disclosures delivered by Seller in accordance with paragraph 5A.
     (2) Within the time specified in 14B(1), Buyer may request that Seller make repairs or take any other action regarding the Property (C.A.R. Form RR). Seller has no obligation to agree to or respond to Buyer's requests.
     (3) By the end of the time specified in 14B(1) (or 2I for loan contingency or 2J for appraisal contingency), Buyer shall, in writing, remove the applicable contingency (C.A.R. Form CR) or cancel this Agreement. However, if **(i)** government-mandated inspections/ reports required as a condition of closing; or **(ii)** Common Interest Disclosures pursuant to paragraph 6B are not made within the time specified in 14A, then Buyer has **5 (or ☐ _____) Days** After receipt of any such items, or the time specified in 14B(1), whichever is later, to remove the applicable contingency or cancel this Agreement in writing.
  C. **CONTINUATION OF CONTINGENCY OR CONTRACTUAL OBLIGATION; SELLER RIGHT TO CANCEL:**
     (1) **Seller right to Cancel; Buyer Contingencies:** Seller, after first giving Buyer a Notice to Buyer to Perform (as specified below), may cancel this Agreement in writing and authorize return of Buyer's deposit if, by the time specified in this Agreement, Buyer does not remove in writing the applicable contingency or cancel this Agreement. Once all contingencies have been removed, failure of either Buyer or Seller to close escrow on time may be a breach of this Agreement.
     (2) **Continuation of Contingency:** Even after the expiration of the time specified in 14B, Buyer retains the right to make requests to Seller, remove in writing the applicable contingency or cancel this Agreement until Seller cancels pursuant to 14C(1). Once Seller receives Buyer's written removal of all contingencies, Seller may not cancel this Agreement pursuant to 14C(1).
     (3) **Seller right to Cancel; Buyer Contract Obligations:** Seller, after first giving Buyer a Notice to Buyer to Perform (as specified below), may cancel this Agreement in writing and authorize return of Buyer's deposit for any of the following reasons: **(i)** if Buyer fails to deposit funds as required by 2A or 2B; **(ii)** if the funds deposited pursuant to 2A or 2B are not good when deposited; **(iii)** if Buyer fails to provide a letter as required by 2G; **(iv)** if Buyer fails to provide verification as required by 2H or 2L; **(v)** if Seller reasonably disapproves of the verification provided by 2H or 2L; **(vi)** if Buyer fails to return Statutory and Lead Disclosures as required by paragraph 5A(2); or **(vii)** if Buyer fails to sign or initial a separate liquidated damage form for an increased deposit as required by paragraph 16. **Seller is not required to give Buyer a Notice to Perform regarding Close of Escrow.**
     (4) **Notice To Buyer To Perform:** The Notice to Buyer to Perform (C.A.R. Form NBP) shall: **(i)** be in writing; **(ii)** be signed by Seller; and **(iii)** give Buyer at least **24 (or ☐ _____) hours** (or until the time specified in the applicable paragraph, whichever occurs last) to take the applicable action. A Notice to Buyer to Perform may not be given any earlier than **2 Days** Prior to the expiration of the applicable time for Buyer to remove a contingency or cancel this Agreement or meet a 14C(3) obligation.

Buyer's Initials (_____) (_____)
Seller's Initials (_____) (_____)

RPA-CA REVISED 1/06 (PAGE 4 OF 8)

Reviewed by _____ Date _____

CALIFORNIA RESIDENTIAL PURCHASE AGREEMENT (RPA-CA PAGE 4 OF 8)

x.zfx

Property Address: _____ Date: _____

D. EFFECT OF BUYER'S REMOVAL OF CONTINGENCIES: If Buyer removes, in writing, any contingency or cancellation rights, unless otherwise specified in a separate written agreement between Buyer and Seller, Buyer shall conclusively be deemed to have: (i) completed all Buyer Investigations, and review of reports and other applicable information and disclosures pertaining to that contingency or cancellation right; (ii) elected to proceed with the transaction; and (iii) assumed all liability, responsibility and expense for Repairs or corrections pertaining to that contingency or cancellation right, or for inability to obtain financing.

E. EFFECT OF CANCELLATION ON DEPOSITS: If Buyer or Seller gives written notice of cancellation pursuant to rights duly exercised under the terms of this Agreement, Buyer and Seller agree to Sign mutual instructions to cancel the sale and escrow and release deposits to the party entitled to the funds, less fees and costs incurred by that party. Fees and costs may be payable to service providers and vendors for services and products provided during escrow. **Release of funds will require mutual Signed release instructions from Buyer and Seller, judicial decision or arbitration award. A party may be subject to a civil penalty of up to $1,000 for refusal to sign such instructions if no good faith dispute exists as to who is entitled to the deposited funds (Civil Code §1057.3).**

15. **FINAL VERIFICATION OF CONDITION:** Buyer shall have the right to make a final inspection of the Property within 5 (or _____) Days Prior to Close Of Escrow, NOT AS A CONTINGENCY OF THE SALE, but solely to confirm: (i) the Property is maintained pursuant to paragraph 7A; (ii) Repairs have been completed as agreed; and (iii) Seller has complied with Seller's other obligations under this Agreement.

16. **LIQUIDATED DAMAGES: If Buyer fails to complete this purchase because of Buyer's default, Seller shall retain, as liquidated damages, the deposit actually paid. If the Property is a dwelling with no more than four units, one of which Buyer intends to occupy, then the amount retained shall be no more than 3% of the purchase price. Any excess shall be returned to Buyer. Release of funds will require mutual, Signed release instructions from both Buyer and Seller, judicial decision or arbitration award.**
BUYER AND SELLER SHALL SIGN A SEPARATE LIQUIDATED DAMAGES PROVISION FOR ANY INCREASED DEPOSIT. (C.A.R. FORM RID)

Buyer's Initials _____ / _____	Seller's Initials _____ / _____

17. **DISPUTE RESOLUTION:**

A. MEDIATION: Buyer and Seller agree to mediate any dispute or claim arising between them out of this Agreement, or any resulting transaction, before resorting to arbitration or court action. Paragraphs 17B(2) and (3) below apply to mediation whether or not the Arbitration provision is initialed. Mediation fees, if any, shall be divided equally among the parties involved. If, for any dispute or claim to which this paragraph applies, any party commences an action without first attempting to resolve the matter through mediation, or refuses to mediate after a request has been made, then that party shall not be entitled to recover attorney fees, even if they would otherwise be available to that party in any such action. THIS MEDIATION PROVISION APPLIES WHETHER OR NOT THE ARBITRATION PROVISION IS INITIALED.

B. ARBITRATION OF DISPUTES: (1) Buyer and Seller agree that any dispute or claim in Law or equity arising between them out of this Agreement or any resulting transaction, which is not settled through mediation, shall be decided by neutral, binding arbitration, including and subject to paragraphs 17B(2) and (3) below. The arbitrator shall be a retired judge or justice, or an attorney with at least 5 years of residential real estate Law experience, unless the parties mutually agree to a different arbitrator, who shall render an award in accordance with substantive California Law. The parties shall have the right to discovery in accordance with California Code of Civil Procedure §1283.05. In all other respects, the arbitration shall be conducted in accordance with Title 9 of Part III of the California Code of Civil Procedure. Judgment upon the award of the arbitrator(s) may be entered into any court having jurisdiction. Interpretation of this agreement to arbitrate shall be governed by the Federal Arbitration Act.

(2) EXCLUSIONS FROM MEDIATION AND ARBITRATION: The following matters are excluded from mediation and arbitration: (i) a judicial or non-judicial foreclosure or other action or proceeding to enforce a deed of trust, mortgage or installment land sale contract as defined in California Civil Code §2985; (ii) an unlawful detainer action; (iii) the filing or enforcement of a mechanic's lien; and (iv) any matter that is within the jurisdiction of a probate, small claims or bankruptcy court. The filing of a court action to enable the recording of a notice of pending action, for order of attachment, receivership, injunction, or other provisional remedies, shall not constitute a waiver of the mediation and arbitration provisions.

(3) BROKERS: Buyer and Seller agree to mediate and arbitrate disputes or claims involving either or both Brokers, consistent with 17A and B, provided either or both Brokers shall have agreed to such mediation or arbitration prior to, or within a reasonable time after, the dispute or claim is presented to Brokers. Any election by either or both Brokers to participate in mediation or arbitration shall not result in Brokers being deemed parties to the Agreement.

"NOTICE: BY INITIALING IN THE SPACE BELOW YOU ARE AGREEING TO HAVE ANY DISPUTE ARISING OUT OF THE MATTERS INCLUDED IN THE 'ARBITRATION OF DISPUTES' PROVISION DECIDED BY NEUTRAL ARBITRATION AS PROVIDED BY CALIFORNIA LAW AND YOU ARE GIVING UP ANY RIGHTS YOU MIGHT POSSESS TO HAVE THE DISPUTE LITIGATED IN A COURT OR JURY TRIAL. BY INITIALING IN THE SPACE BELOW YOU ARE GIVING UP YOUR JUDICIAL RIGHTS TO DISCOVERY AND APPEAL, UNLESS THOSE RIGHTS ARE SPECIFICALLY INCLUDED IN THE 'ARBITRATION OF DISPUTES' PROVISION. IF YOU REFUSE TO SUBMIT TO ARBITRATION AFTER AGREEING TO THIS PROVISION, YOU MAY BE COMPELLED TO ARBITRATE UNDER THE AUTHORITY OF THE CALIFORNIA CODE OF CIVIL PROCEDURE. YOUR AGREEMENT TO THIS ARBITRATION PROVISION IS VOLUNTARY."

"WE HAVE READ AND UNDERSTAND THE FOREGOING AND AGREE TO SUBMIT DISPUTES ARISING OUT OF THE MATTERS INCLUDED IN THE 'ARBITRATION OF DISPUTES' PROVISION TO NEUTRAL ARBITRATION."

Buyer's Initials _____ / _____	Seller's Initials _____ / _____

RPA-CA REVISED 1/06 (PAGE 5 OF 8)

Buyer's Initials (_____) (_____)
Seller's Initials (_____) (_____)
Reviewed by _____ Date _____

EQUAL HOUSING OPPORTUNITY

CALIFORNIA RESIDENTIAL PURCHASE AGREEMENT (RPA-CA PAGE 5 OF 8)
x.zfx

Property Address: _____ Date: _____

18. **PRORATIONS OF PROPERTY TAXES AND OTHER ITEMS:** Unless otherwise agreed in writing, the following items shall be PAID CURRENT and prorated between Buyer and Seller as of Close Of Escrow: real property taxes and assessments, interest, rents, HOA regular, special, and emergency dues and assessments imposed prior to Close Of Escrow, premiums on insurance assumed by Buyer, payments on bonds and assessments assumed by Buyer, and payments on Mello-Roos and other Special Assessment District bonds and assessments that are now a lien. The following items shall be assumed by Buyer WITHOUT CREDIT toward the purchase price: prorated payments on Mello-Roos and other Special Assessment District bonds and assessments and HOA special assessments that are now a lien but not yet due. Property will be reassessed upon change of ownership. Any supplemental tax bills shall be paid as follows: **(i)** for periods after Close Of Escrow, by Buyer; and **(ii)** for periods prior to Close Of Escrow, by Seller. TAX BILLS ISSUED AFTER CLOSE OF ESCROW SHALL BE HANDLED DIRECTLY BETWEEN BUYER AND SELLER. Prorations shall be made based on a 30-day month.

19. **WITHHOLDING TAXES:** Seller and Buyer agree to execute any instrument, affidavit, statement or instruction reasonably necessary to comply with federal (FIRPTA) and California withholding Law, if required (C.A.R. Forms AS and AB).

20. **MULTIPLE LISTING SERVICE ("MLS"):** Brokers are authorized to report to the MLS a pending sale and, upon Close Of Escrow, the terms of this transaction to be published and disseminated to persons and entities authorized to use the information on terms approved by the MLS.

21. **EQUAL HOUSING OPPORTUNITY:** The Property is sold in compliance with federal, state and local anti-discrimination Laws.

22. **ATTORNEY FEES:** In any action, proceeding, or arbitration between Buyer and Seller arising out of this Agreement, the prevailing Buyer or Seller shall be entitled to reasonable attorney fees and costs from the non-prevailing Buyer or Seller, except as provided in paragraph 17A.

23. **SELECTION OF SERVICE PROVIDERS:** If Brokers refer Buyer or Seller to persons, vendors, or service or product providers ("Providers"), Brokers do not guarantee the performance of any Providers. Buyer and Seller may select ANY Providers of their own choosing.

24. **TIME OF ESSENCE; ENTIRE CONTRACT; CHANGES:** Time is of the essence. All understandings between the parties are incorporated in this Agreement. Its terms are intended by the parties as a final, complete and exclusive expression of their Agreement with respect to its subject matter, and may not be contradicted by evidence of any prior agreement or contemporaneous oral agreement. If any provision of this Agreement is held to be ineffective or invalid, the remaining provisions will nevertheless be given full force and effect. **Neither this Agreement nor any provision in it may be extended, amended, modified, altered or changed, except in writing Signed by Buyer and Seller.**

25. **OTHER TERMS AND CONDITIONS,** including attached supplements:
    A. ☑ Buyer's Inspection Advisory (C.A.R. Form BIA) _____
    B. ☐ Purchase Agreement Addendum (C.A.R. Form PAA paragraph numbers: _____) _____
    C. ☐ Statewide Buyer and Seller Advisory (C.A.R. Form SBSA) _____
    D. _____

26. **DEFINITIONS:** As used in this Agreement:
    A. **"Acceptance"** means the time the offer or final counter offer is accepted in writing by a party and is delivered to and personally received by the other party or that party's authorized agent in accordance with the terms of this offer or a final counter offer.
    B. **"Agreement"** means the terms and conditions of this accepted California Residential Purchase Agreement and any accepted counter offers and addenda.
    C. **"C.A.R. Form"** means the specific form referenced or another comparable form agreed to by the parties.
    D. **"Close Of Escrow"** means the date the grant deed, or other evidence of transfer of title, is recorded. If the scheduled close of escrow falls on a Saturday, Sunday or legal holiday, then close of escrow shall be the next business day after the scheduled close of escrow date.
    E. **"Copy"** means copy by any means including photocopy, NCR, facsimile and electronic.
    F. **"Days"** means calendar days, unless otherwise required by Law.
    G. **"Days After"** means the specified number of calendar days after the occurrence of the event specified, not counting the calendar date on which the specified event occurs, and ending at 11:59PM on the final day.
    H. **"Days Prior"** means the specified number of calendar days before the occurrence of the event specified, not counting the calendar date on which the specified event is scheduled to occur.
    I. **"Electronic Copy"** or **"Electronic Signature"** means, as applicable, an electronic copy or signature complying with California Law. Buyer and Seller agree that electronic means will not be used by either party to modify or alter the content or integrity of this Agreement without the knowledge and consent of the other.
    J. **"Law"** means any law, code, statute, ordinance, regulation, rule or order, which is adopted by a controlling city, county, state or federal legislative, judicial or executive body or agency.
    K. **"Notice to Buyer to Perform"** means a document (C.A.R. Form NBP), which shall be in writing and Signed by Seller and shall give Buyer at least 24 hours **(or as otherwise specified in paragraph 14C(4))** to remove a contingency or perform as applicable.
    L. **"Repairs"** means any repairs (including pest control), alterations, replacements, modifications or retrofitting of the Property provided for under this Agreement.
    M. **"Signed"** means either a handwritten or electronic signature on an original document, Copy or any counterpart.
    N. **Singular and Plural** terms each include the other, when appropriate.

Buyer's Initials (_____) (_____)
Seller's Initials (_____) (_____)

RPA-CA REVISED 1/06 (PAGE 6 OF 8)

Reviewed by _____ Date _____

CALIFORNIA RESIDENTIAL PURCHASE AGREEMENT (RPA-CA PAGE 6 OF 8)

x.zfx

Property Address: _____ Date: _____

27. AGENCY:

A. DISCLOSURE: Buyer and Seller each acknowledge prior receipt of C.A.R. Form AD "Disclosure Regarding Real Estate Agency Relationships."

B. POTENTIALLY COMPETING BUYERS AND SELLERS: Buyer and Seller each acknowledge receipt of a disclosure of the possibility of multiple representation by the Broker representing that principal. This disclosure may be part of a listing agreement, buyer-broker agreement or separate document (C.A.R. Form DA). Buyer understands that Broker representing Buyer may also represent other potential buyers, who may consider, make offers on or ultimately acquire the Property. Seller understands that Broker representing Seller may also represent other sellers with competing properties of interest to this Buyer.

C. CONFIRMATION: The following agency relationships are hereby confirmed for this transaction:
Listing Agent _____ (Print Firm Name) is the agent of (check one): ☐ the Seller exclusively; or ☐ both the Buyer and Seller.
Selling Agent _____ (Print Firm Name) (if not same as Listing Agent) is the agent of (check one): ☐ the Buyer exclusively; or ☐ the Seller exclusively; or ☐ both the Buyer and Seller. Real Estate Brokers are not parties to the Agreement between Buyer and Seller.

28. JOINT ESCROW INSTRUCTIONS TO ESCROW HOLDER:

A. **The following paragraphs, or applicable portions thereof, of this Agreement constitute the joint escrow instructions of Buyer and Seller to Escrow Holder,** which Escrow Holder is to use along with any related counter offers and addenda, and any additional mutual instructions to close the escrow: 1, 2, 4, 12, 13B, 14E, 18, 19, 24, 25B and 25D, 26, 28, 29, 32A, 33 and paragraph D of the section titled Real Estate Brokers on page 8. If a Copy of the separate compensation agreement(s) provided for in paragraph 29 or 32A, or paragraph D of the section titled Real Estate Brokers on page 8 is deposited with Escrow Holder by Broker, Escrow Holder shall accept such agreement(s) and pay out from Buyer's or Seller's funds, or both, as applicable, the Broker's compensation provided for in such agreement(s). The terms and conditions of this Agreement not set forth in the specified paragraphs are additional matters for the information of Escrow Holder, but about which Escrow Holder need not be concerned. Buyer and Seller will receive Escrow Holder's general provisions directly from Escrow Holder and will execute such provisions upon Escrow Holder's request. To the extent the general provisions are inconsistent or conflict with this Agreement, the general provisions will control as to the duties and obligations of Escrow Holder only. Buyer and Seller will execute additional instructions, documents and forms provided by Escrow Holder that are reasonably necessary to close the escrow.

B. A Copy of this Agreement shall be delivered to Escrow Holder within **3** business days after Acceptance (or ☐ _____). Buyer and Seller authorize Escrow Holder to accept and rely on Copies and Signatures as defined in this Agreement as originals, to open escrow and for other purposes of escrow. The validity of this Agreement as between Buyer and Seller is not affected by whether or when Escrow Holder Signs this Agreement.

C. Brokers are a party to the escrow for the sole purpose of compensation pursuant to paragraphs 29, 32A and paragraph D of the section titled Real Estate Brokers on page 8. Buyer and Seller irrevocably assign to Brokers compensation specified in paragraphs 29 and 32A, respectively, and irrevocably instruct Escrow Holder to disburse those funds to Brokers at Close Of Escrow or pursuant to any other mutually executed cancellation agreement. Compensation instructions can be amended or revoked only with the written consent of Brokers. Escrow Holder shall immediately notify Brokers: **(i)** if Buyer's initial or any additional deposit is not made pursuant to this Agreement, or is not good at time of deposit with Escrow Holder; or **(ii)** if Buyer and Seller instruct Escrow Holder to cancel escrow.

D. A Copy of any amendment that affects any paragraph of this Agreement for which Escrow Holder is responsible shall be delivered to Escrow Holder within **2** business days after mutual execution of the amendment.

29. BROKER COMPENSATION FROM BUYER: If applicable, upon Close Of Escrow, **Buyer** agrees to pay compensation to Broker as specified in a separate written agreement between Buyer and Broker.

30. TERMS AND CONDITIONS OF OFFER:

This is an offer to purchase the Property on the above terms and conditions. All paragraphs with spaces for initials by Buyer and Seller are incorporated in this Agreement only if initialed by all parties. If at least one but not all parties initial, a counter offer is required until agreement is reached. Seller has the right to continue to offer the Property for sale and to accept any other offer at any time prior to notification of Acceptance. Buyer has read and acknowledges receipt of a Copy of the offer and agrees to the above confirmation of agency relationships. If this offer is accepted and Buyer subsequently defaults, Buyer may be responsible for payment of Brokers' compensation. This Agreement and any supplement, addendum or modification, including any Copy, may be Signed in two or more counterparts, all of which shall constitute one and the same writing.

RPA-CA REVISED 1/06 (PAGE 7 OF 8)

Buyer's Initials (_____) (_____)
Seller's Initials (_____) (_____)

Reviewed by _____ Date _____

EQUAL HOUSING OPPORTUNITY

CALIFORNIA RESIDENTIAL PURCHASE AGREEMENT (RPA-CA PAGE 7 OF 8)

x.zfx

Property Address: _____ Date: _____

31. EXPIRATION OF OFFER: This offer shall be deemed revoked and the deposit shall be returned unless the offer is Signed by Seller and a Copy of the Signed offer is personally received by Buyer, or by _____ , who is authorized to receive it by 5:00 PM on the third Day after this offer is signed by Buyer (or, if checked, ☐ by _____ (date), at _____ ☐ AM ☐ PM).

Date _____   Date _____
BUYER _____   BUYER _____

(Print name) _____   (Print name) _____

(Address)

32. BROKER COMPENSATION FROM SELLER:
   A. Upon Close Of Escrow, **Seller** agrees to pay compensation to Broker as specified in a separate written agreement between Seller and Broker.
   B. If escrow does not close, compensation is payable as specified in that separate written agreement.

33. ACCEPTANCE OF OFFER: Seller warrants that Seller is the owner of the Property, or has the authority to execute this Agreement. Seller accepts the above offer, agrees to sell the Property on the above terms and conditions, and agrees to the above confirmation of agency relationships. Seller has read and acknowledges receipt of a Copy of this Agreement, and authorizes Broker to deliver a Signed Copy to Buyer.
   ☐ (If checked) **SUBJECT TO ATTACHED COUNTER OFFER, DATED** _____ .

Date _____   Date _____
SELLER _____   SELLER _____

(Print name) _____   (Print name) _____

(Address)

(_____ / _____)   **CONFIRMATION OF ACCEPTANCE:** A Copy of Signed Acceptance was personally received by Buyer or Buyer's authorized
(Initials)   agent on (date) _____ at _____ ☐ AM ☐ PM. **A binding Agreement is created when a Copy of Signed Acceptance is personally received by Buyer or Buyer's authorized agent whether or not confirmed in this document. Completion of this confirmation is not legally required in order to create a binding Agreement; it is solely intended to evidence the date that Confirmation of Acceptance has occurred.**

REAL ESTATE BROKERS:
A. Real Estate Brokers are not parties to the Agreement between Buyer and Seller.
B. Agency relationships are confirmed as stated in paragraph 27.
C. If specified in paragraph 2A, Agent who submitted the offer for Buyer acknowledges receipt of deposit.
D. **COOPERATING BROKER COMPENSATION:** Listing Broker agrees to pay Cooperating Broker **(Selling Firm)** and Cooperating Broker agrees to accept, out of Listing Broker's proceeds in escrow: **(i)** the amount specified in the MLS, provided Cooperating Broker is a Participant of the MLS in which the Property is offered for sale or a reciprocal MLS; or **(ii)** ☐ (if checked) the amount specified in a separate written agreement (C.A.R. Form CBC) between Listing Broker and Cooperating Broker.

Real Estate Broker (Selling Firm) _____ DRE Lic. # _____
By _____ DRE Lic. # _____ Date _____
Address _____ City _____ State _____ Zip _____
Telephone _____ Fax _____ E-mail _____

Real Estate Broker (Listing Firm) _____ DRE Lic. # _____
By _____ DRE Lic. # _____ Date _____
Address _____ City _____ State _____ Zip _____
Telephone _____ Fax _____ E-mail _____

ESCROW HOLDER ACKNOWLEDGMENT:
Escrow Holder acknowledges receipt of a Copy of this Agreement, (if checked, ☐ a deposit in the amount of $ _____), counter offer numbers _____ and _____ , and agrees to act as Escrow Holder subject to paragraph 28 of this Agreement, any supplemental escrow instructions and the terms of Escrow Holder's general provisions.

Escrow Holder is advised that the date of Confirmation of Acceptance of the Agreement as between Buyer and Seller is _____

Escrow Holder _____ Escrow # _____
By _____ Date _____
Address _____
Phone/Fax/E-mail _____
Escrow Holder is licensed by the California Department of ☐ Corporations, ☐ Insurance, ☐ Real Estate. License # _____

(_____ / _____)   **REJECTION OF OFFER:** No counter offer is being made. This offer was reviewed and rejected by Seller on
(Seller's Initials) _____ (Date)

THIS FORM HAS BEEN APPROVED BY THE CALIFORNIA ASSOCIATION OF REALTORS® (C.A.R.). NO REPRESENTATION IS MADE AS TO THE LEGAL VALIDITY OR ADEQUACY OF ANY PROVISION IN ANY SPECIFIC TRANSACTION. A REAL ESTATE BROKER IS THE PERSON QUALIFIED TO ADVISE ON REAL ESTATE TRANSACTIONS. IF YOU DESIRE LEGAL OR TAX ADVICE, CONSULT AN APPROPRIATE PROFESSIONAL.
This form is available for use by the entire real estate industry. It is not intended to identify the user as a REALTOR®. REALTOR® is a registered collective membership mark which may be used only by members of the NATIONAL ASSOCIATION OF REALTORS® who subscribe to its Code of Ethics.

Published and Distributed by:
REAL ESTATE BUSINESS SERVICES, INC.
a subsidiary of the California Association of REALTORS®
525 South Virgil Avenue, Los Angeles, California 90020

Reviewed by _____ Date _____

RPA-CA REVISED 1/06 (PAGE 8 OF 8)
CALIFORNIA RESIDENTIAL PURCHASE AGREEMENT (RPA-CA PAGE 8 OF 8)
x.zfx

REAL ESTATE TRANSFER DISCLOSURE STATEMENT
(CALIFORNIA CIVIL CODE §1102, ET SEQ)
(C.A.R. Form TDS, Revised 10/03)

THIS DISCLOSURE STATEMENT CONCERNS THE REAL PROPERTY SITUATED IN THE CITY OF
_____ , COUNTY OF _____ , STATE OF CALIFORNIA,
DESCRIBED AS _____
THIS STATEMENT IS A DISCLOSURE OF THE CONDITION OF THE ABOVE DESCRIBED PROPERTY IN
COMPLIANCE WITH SECTION 1102 OF THE CIVIL CODE AS OF (date) _____ . IT IS NOT A
WARRANTY OF ANY KIND BY THE SELLER(S) OR ANY AGENT(S) REPRESENTING ANY PRINCIPAL(S) IN THIS
TRANSACTION, AND IS NOT A SUBSTITUTE FOR ANY INSPECTIONS OR WARRANTIES THE PRINCIPAL(S) MAY
WISH TO OBTAIN.

I. COORDINATION WITH OTHER DISCLOSURE FORMS

This Real Estate Transfer Disclosure Statement is made pursuant to Section 1102 of the Civil Code. Other statutes require disclosures, depending upon the details of the particular real estate transaction (for example: special study zone and purchase-money liens on residential property).

Substituted Disclosures: The following disclosures and other disclosures required by law, including the Natural Hazard Disclosure Report/Statement that may include airport annoyances, earthquake, fire, flood, or special assessment information, have or will be made in connection with this real estate transfer, and are intended to satisfy the disclosure obligations on this form, where the subject matter is the same:

☐ Inspection reports completed pursuant to the contract of sale or receipt for deposit.
☐ Additional inspection reports or disclosures: _____
_____

II. SELLER'S INFORMATION

The Seller discloses the following information with the knowledge that even though this is not a warranty, prospective Buyers may rely on this information in deciding whether and on what terms to purchase the subject property. Seller hereby authorizes any agent(s) representing any principal(s) in this transaction to provide a copy of this statement to any person or entity in connection with any actual or anticipated sale of the property.

THE FOLLOWING ARE REPRESENTATIONS MADE BY THE SELLER(S) AND ARE NOT THE REPRESENTATIONS OF THE AGENT(S), IF ANY. THIS INFORMATION IS A DISCLOSURE AND IS NOT INTENDED TO BE PART OF ANY CONTRACT BETWEEN THE BUYER AND SELLER.

Seller ☐ is ☐ is not occupying the property.

A. The subject property has the items checked below (read across)

☐ Range	☐ Oven	☐ Microwave
☐ Dishwasher	☐ Trash Compactor	☐ Garbage Disposal
☐ Washer/Dryer Hookups		☐ Rain Gutters
☐ Burglar Alarms	☐ Smoke Detector(s)	☐ Fire Alarm
☐ T.V. Antenna	☐ Satellite Dish	☐ Intercom
☐ Central Heating	☐ Central Air Conditioning	☐ Evaporator Cooler(s)
☐ Wall/Window Air Conditioning	☐ Sprinklers	☐ Public Sewer System
☐ Septic Tank	☐ Sump Pump	☐ Water Softener
☐ Patio/Decking	☐ Built-in Barbecue	☐ Gazebo
☐ Sauna		
☐ Hot Tub ☐ Locking Safety Cover*	☐ Pool ☐ Child Resistant Barrier*	☐ Spa ☐ Locking Safety Cover*
☐ Security Gate(s)	☐ Automatic Garage Door Opener(s)*	☐ Number Remote Controls _____
Garage: ☐ Attached	☐ Not Attached	☐ Carport
Pool/Spa Heater: ☐ Gas	☐ Solar	☐ Electric
Water Heater: ☐ Gas	☐ Water Heater Anchored, Braced, or Strapped*	☐ Private Utility or
Water Supply: ☐ City	☐ Well	Other _____
Gas Supply: ☐ Utility	☐ Bottled	
☐ Window Screens	☐ Window Security Bars ☐ Quick Release Mechanism on Bedroom Windows*	

Exhaust Fan(s) in _____ 220 Volt Wiring in _____ Fireplace(s) in _____
☐ Gas Starter _____ ☐ Roof(s): Type: _____ Age: _____ (approx.)
☐ Other: _____
Are there, to the best of your (Seller's) knowledge, any of the above that are not in operating condition? ☐ Yes ☐ No. If yes, then describe. (Attach additional sheets if necessary): _____
_____

(*see footnote on page 2)

Buyer's Initials (_____) (_____)
Seller's Initials (_____) (_____)

Reviewed by _____ Date _____

EQUAL HOUSING OPPORTUNITY

TDS REVISED 10/03 (PAGE 1 OF 3)

REAL ESTATE TRANSFER DISCLOSURE STATEMENT (TDS PAGE 1 OF 3)

Agent:	Phone:	Fax:	Prepared using WINForms® software
Broker:			

Property Address: _____ Date: _____

B. Are you (Seller) aware of any significant defects/malfunctions in any of the following? ☐ Yes ☐ No. If yes, check appropriate space(s) below.

☐ Interior Walls ☐ Ceilings ☐ Floors ☐ Exterior Walls ☐ Insulation ☐ Roof(s) ☐ Windows ☐ Doors ☐ Foundation ☐ Slab(s)
☐ Driveways ☐ Sidewalks ☐ Walls/Fences ☐ Electrical Systems ☐ Plumbing/Sewers/Septics ☐ Other Structural Components
(Describe: _____

_____

_____)

If any of the above is checked, explain. (Attach additional sheets if necessary): _____

_____

_____

_____

*This garage door opener or child resistant pool barrier may not be in compliance with the safety standards relating to automatic reversing devices as set forth in Chapter 12.5 (commencing with Section 19890) of Part 3 of Division 13 of, or with the pool safety standards of Article 2.5 (commencing with Section 115920) of Chapter 5 of Part 10 of Division 104 of, the Health and Safety Code. The water heater may not be anchored, braced, or strapped in accordance with Section 19211 of the Health and Safety Code. Window security bars may not have quick release mechanisms in compliance with the 1995 Edition of the California Building Standards Code.

C. Are you (Seller) aware of any the following:

1. Substances, materials, or products which may be an environmental hazard such as, but not limited to, asbestos, formaldehyde, radon gas, lead-based paint, mold, fuel or chemical storage tanks, and contaminated soil or water on the subject property .... ☐ Yes ☐ No
2. Features of the property shared in common with adjoining landowners, such as walls, fences, and driveways, whose use or responsibility for maintenance may have an effect on the subject property .... ☐ Yes ☐ No
3. Any encroachments, easements or similar matters that may affect your interest in the subject property .... ☐ Yes ☐ No
4. Room additions, structural modifications, or other alterations or repairs made without necessary permits. ...... ☐ Yes ☐ No
5. Room additions, structural modifications, or other alterations or repairs not in compliance with building codes. ... ☐ Yes ☐ No
6. Fill (compacted or otherwise) on the property or any portion thereof .... ☐ Yes ☐ No
7. Any settling from any cause, or slippage, sliding. or other soil problems .... ☐ Yes ☐ No
8. Flooding, drainage or grading problems .... ☐ Yes ☐ No
9. Major damage to the property or any of the structures from fire, earthquake, floods, or landslides .... ☐ Yes ☐ No
10. Any zoning violations, nonconforming uses, violations of "setback" requirements .... ☐ Yes ☐ No
11. Neighborhood noise problems or other nuisances .... ☐ Yes ☐ No
12. CC&R's or other deed restrictions or obligations .... ☐ Yes ☐ No
13. Homeowners' Association which has any authority over the subject property .... ☐ Yes ☐ No
14. Any "common area" (facilities such as pools, tennis courts, walkways, or other areas co-owned in undivided interest with others) .... ☐ Yes ☐ No
15. Any notices of abatement or citations against the property .... ☐ Yes ☐ No
16. Any lawsuits by or against the seller threatening to or affecting this real property, including any lawsuits alleging a defect or deficiency in this real property or "common areas" (facilities such as pools, tennis courts, walkways, or other areas, co-owned in undivided interest with others) .... ☐ Yes ☐ No

If the answer to any of these is yes, explain. (Attach additional sheets if necessary): _____

_____

_____

_____

_____

Seller certifies that the information herein is true and correct to the best of the Seller's knowledge as of the date signed by the Seller.

Seller _____ Date _____

Seller _____ Date _____

Buyer's Initials (_____)(_____)

Reviewed by _____ Date _____

TDS REVISED 10/03 (PAGE 2 OF 3)

REAL ESTATE TRANSFER DISCLOSURE STATEMENT (TDS PAGE 2 OF 3)

Property Address: _____ Date: _____

III. AGENT'S INSPECTION DISCLOSURE
(To be completed only if the Seller is represented by an agent in this transaction.)

THE UNDERSIGNED, BASED ON THE ABOVE INQUIRY OF THE SELLER(S) AS TO THE CONDITION OF THE PROPERTY AND BASED ON A REASONABLY COMPETENT AND DILIGENT VISUAL INSPECTION OF THE ACCESSIBLE AREAS OF THE PROPERTY IN CONJUNCTION WITH THAT INQUIRY, STATES THE FOLLOWING:

☐ Agent notes no items for disclosure.
☐ Agent notes the following items: _____
_____
_____
_____

Agent (Broker Representing Seller) _____ By _____ Date _____
                   (Please Print)   (Associate Licensee or Broker Signature)

IV. AGENT'S INSPECTION DISCLOSURE
(To be completed only if the agent who has obtained the offer is other than the agent above.)

THE UNDERSIGNED, BASED ON A REASONABLY COMPETENT AND DILIGENT VISUAL INSPECTION OF THE ACCESSIBLE AREAS OF THE PROPERTY, STATES THE FOLLOWING:

☐ Agent notes no items for disclosure.
☐ Agent notes the following items: _____
_____
_____
_____

Agent (Broker Obtaining the Offer) _____ By _____ Date _____
                   (Please Print)   (Associate Licensee or Broker Signature)

V. BUYER(S) AND SELLER(S) MAY WISH TO OBTAIN PROFESSIONAL ADVICE AND/OR INSPECTIONS OF THE PROPERTY AND TO PROVIDE FOR APPROPRIATE PROVISIONS IN A CONTRACT BETWEEN BUYER AND SELLER(S) WITH RESPECT TO ANY ADVICE/INSPECTIONS/DEFECTS.

I/WE ACKNOWLEDGE RECEIPT OF A COPY OF THIS STATEMENT.

Seller _____ Date _____   Buyer _____ Date _____

Seller _____ Date _____   Buyer _____ Date _____

Agent (Broker Representing Seller) _____ By _____ Date _____
                   (Please Print)   (Associate Licensee or Broker Signature)

Agent (Broker Obtaining the Offer) _____ By _____ Date _____
                   (Please Print)   (Associate Licensee or Broker Signature)

SECTION 1102.3 OF THE CIVIL CODE PROVIDES A BUYER WITH THE RIGHT TO RESCIND A PURCHASE CONTRACT FOR AT LEAST THREE DAYS AFTER THE DELIVERY OF THIS DISCLOSURE IF DELIVERY OCCURS AFTER THE SIGNING OF AN OFFER TO PURCHASE. IF YOU WISH TO RESCIND THE CONTRACT, YOU MUST ACT WITHIN THE PRESCRIBED PERIOD.

A REAL ESTATE BROKER IS QUALIFIED TO ADVISE ON REAL ESTATE. IF YOU DESIRE LEGAL ADVICE, CONSULT YOUR ATTORNEY.

SURE TRAC
The System for Success™

Published by the
California Association of REALTORS®

Reviewed by _____ Date _____

EQUAL HOUSING OPPORTUNITY

TDS REVISED 10/03 (PAGE 3 OF 3)

REAL ESTATE TRANSFER DISCLOSURE STATEMENT (TDS PAGE 3 OF 3)   T6429805.ZFX

Sam Summers   Date: June 6, 20xx
Kate Summers   Escrow No: 1111-DEMO
987 Ocean View Drive
Any City, CA 90000

Re: **987 Ocean View Drive, Any City, CA**

Dear Mr. & Mrs. Summers:

Thank you for selecting SMS to process your escrow. The enclosed items are required in your escrow, please review and comply as noted below and return to us as soon as possible.

SIGN AND RETURN the enclosed items, retain the copy for your records:
Escrow Instructions
Commission Instructions
Misc. sign & return enclosure

COMPLETE IN FULL, SIGN AND RETURN the enclosed items:
CAL-FIRPTA 590 Form and/or Certificate
Statement of Information
Loan Information Sheet
IRS 1099 Reporting Form
Misc. complete, sign & return enclosure

SIGN AND ACKNOWLEDGE BEFORE A NOTARY PUBLIC <u>EXACTLY</u> as your name(s) appear on the enclosed items:
Grant Deed
Misc. sign before a notary enclosure

Please Furnish the Following:
Misc. furnish us with enclosure

All documents should be signed EXACTLY as your name(s) appear. Should your name(s) be misspelled, sign them correctly and advise us in writing when you return these papers.

We appreciate the opportunity to be of service to you in this transaction. Should you have any questions, please call us at the telephone number(s) referenced above.

SMS

Kelly Rose
Escrow Officer

jjw

Escrow No: 004860
Date: April 24, 20xx

SALE ESCROW INSTRUCTIONS

INITIAL DEPOSIT	5,000.00
NEW FIRST TRUST DEED TO FILE	180,000.00
ADDIITIONAL CASH THROUGH ESCROW	8,980.17
TOTAL CONSIDERATION	$193,980.17

I/We will hand you the sum of **$8,980.17**, of which the sum of **$5,000.00** shall be handed escrow as the initial deposit upon opening of this escrow. I/We will further hand you any and all sufficient funds for closing costs, expenses and prorations between Buyer and Seller, prior to the close of this escrow.

I/We will deliver to you any executed instruments and or funds required to enable you to comply with these instructions, all of which you are authorized to use, provided that on or before **01/01/20xx** you are in a position to order a standard policy of title insurance with the usual title company exceptions, provided that said policy has a liability of at least the amount of the above total consideration, covering the property described as follows:

All that tract and parcel of land located on the northwest corner of the subdivision more commonly known as Rainbow Ridge and being more fully described in Deed Book 123, page 891.

Commonly known as:
987 Ocean View Drive, Any City, CA 90000 (not verified by escrow holder)

Showing title vested in: **Dan Winter and Donna Winter**

FREE FROM ENCUMBRANCES EXCEPT:
1. First installment(s) of the General and Special County, and City (if any) Taxes for the current fiscal year, not delinquent, and taxes for the ensuing year, if any, a lien not yet payable.
2. All taxes, bonds and assessments levied or assessed subsequent to the date of these instructions.
3. Covenants, conditions, restrictions, reservations, rights, rights of way, easements and the exception or reservation of water, oil, gas, minerals, carbons, hydrocarbons or kindred substances on or under said land, now of record, if any, or in the Deed to file.

SMS SETTLEMENT SERVICES IS LICENSED BY THE DEPARTMENT OF CORPORATIONS, STATE OF CALIFORNIA.

PRORATE OR ADJUST THE FOLLOWING ITEMS AS OF DATE OF CLOSE OF ESCROW:

Taxes (based on latest tax bill)   Homeowners Association Dues

Each party signing these instructions has read the additional escrow conditions, general provisions and instructions on the reverse side hereof and approves, accepts and agrees to be bound thereby as though the reverse side hereof appeared over their signatures.

SELLER: BUYER:

_____   _____
Sam Summers   Dan Winter

_____   _____
Kate Summers   Donna Winter

Escrow Officer: **Kelly Rose**
Date: **April 24, 20xx**

Escrow No: **004860**
Page 2

THE CLOSING OF THIS ESCROW IS CONTINGENT UPON:

A. Buyer and property qualifying for new loan set out above. Buyer's execution of loan documents shall constitute Buyer's approval of all terms and conditions contained therein and a satisfaction of this condition.

B. Buyer's approval of a preliminary title report covering the subject property together with any and all exceptions referred to therein, within 5 business days of Buyer's receipt of copies of same from Escrow does not deposit his written disapproval within time limit specified said preliminary title report shall be deemed approved.

INSTRUCTIONS:

1. A new hazard insurance policy to comply with lender's requirements will be delivered to escrow by buyer's agent. The buyer will deposit into his escrow sufficient funds to enable you to pay the premium at close of escrow.

AS A MEMORANDUM AGREEMENT ONLY WITH WHICH ESCROW HOLDER IS NOT TO BE CONCERNED AND/OR LIABLE.

2. All plumbing, electrical, heating and related systems and equipment are to be in working order at the close of escrow.

3. All carpets, drapes, window coverings, attached fixtures and appliances, except any which may be reserved herein, are to remain with subject property at the close of the escrow.

4. Seller herein agrees to maintain subject property in its present condition until possession of subject property is delivered to buyer.

5. Buyers to walk through subject property 7 days prior to close of escrow.

EACH PARTY SIGNING THESE INSTRUCTIONS HAS READ THE ADDITIONAL ESCROW CONDITIONS, GENERAL PROVISIONS AND INSTRUCTIONS ON THE REVERSE SIDE HEREOF AND APPROVES, ACCEPTS AND AGREES TO BE BOUND THEREBY AS THOUGH THE REVERSE SIDE HEREOF APPEARED OVER THEIR SIGNATURES.

SELLER: BUYER:

_____   _____
Sam Summers   Dan Winter

_____   _____
Kate Summers   Donna Winter

Escrow Officer: **Kelly Rose**
Date: **April 24, 20xx**

Escrow No: **004860**

page 3

BUYER:

SET OUT ON THE FINAL PAGE OF THESE INSTRUCTIONS ARE UNDERSTOOD AND APPROVED IN THEIR ENTIRETY BY EACH OF THE UNDERSIGNED. I AGREE TO PAY ON DEMAND BUYER'S CUSTOMARY COSTS AND CHARGES INCURRED HEREIN, INCLUDING BUT NOT LIMITED TO, RECORDING FEES, DOCUMENT PREPARATION FEES, ONE HALF OF YOUR ESCROW FEE, ANY COSTS INCURRED BY REASON OF ANY FINANCING OBTAINED OR ASSUMED BY ME, ONE-HALF OF ANY TRANSFER FEE CHARGED BY ANY ASSOCIATION COVERING THE SUBJECT PROPERTY, AND ANY OTHER CHARGE INCURRED FOR MY BENEFIT.

SELLER:

THE FOREGOING TERMS, CONDITIONS, PROVISIONS AND INSTRUCTIONS, TOGETHER WITH THE GENERAL PROVISIONS SET OUT ON THE FINAL PAGE OF THESE INSTRUCTIONS ARE UNDERSTOOD, APPROVED AND ACCEPTED IN THEIR ENTIRETY BY EACH OF THE UNDERSIGNED. I WILL HAND YOU MY EXECUTED GRANT DEED AND/OR OTHER DOCUMENTS OR INSTRUMENTS REQUIRED FROM ME TO CAUSE TITLE TO BE AS SHOWN ABOVE, WHICH YOU ARE AUTHORIZED TO USE AND OR DELIVER WHEN YOU CAN COMPLY WITH THESE INSTRUCTIONS AND WHEN YOU CAN HOLD FOR MY ACCOUNT THE TOTAL CONSIDERATION AS SET FORTH ABOVE (LESS ANY AMOUNT TO BE DEBITED TO MY ACCOUNT SET FORTH BELOW), TOGETHER WITH ANY DOCUMENT(S) EXECUTED IN MY FAVOR.

FROM THE TOTAL CONSIDERATION DUE TO MY ACCOUNT AT THE CLOSE OF ESCROW, YOU ARE AUTHORIZED AND INSTRUCTED TO DEDUCT THE AMOUNT OF ANY REAL ESTATE BROKER'S COMMISSION TO BE PAID BY ME IN ACCORDANCE WITH SEPARATE INSTRUCTIONS, THE AMOUNT OF ANY FUNDS PAID TO ME OUTSIDE OF ESCROW, THE AMOUNT OWING UNDER ANY LIEN OR ENCUMBRANCE TO REMAIN OF RECORD AFTER CLOSE OF ESCROW, THE DEMAND OF ANY LIEN OR ENCUMBRANCE, REQUIRED TO BE PAID TO PLACE TITLE IN THE CONDITION AS CALLED FOR HEREIN, AND SELLER'S CUSTOMARY COSTS AND CHARGES INCURRED HEREIN, INCLUDING, BUT NOT LIMITED TO, THE PREMIUM FOR THE C.L.T.A. OWNER'S POLICY OF TITLE INSURANCE TO BE PROVIDED TO THE BUYER, THE AMOUNT OF ANY DOCUMENTARY TRANSFER TAX OWING ON THE DEED, ONE-HALF OF YOUR ESCROW FEE, RECORDING FEES FOR DOCUMENTS, INSTRUMENTS RECORDED FOR MY BENEFIT, ONE HALF OF ANY TRANSFER FEE CHARGED BY ANY ASSOCIATION COVERING THE SUBJECT PROPERTY, THE COST OF OBTAINING ANY STATEMENT(S) OR DEMAND CONCERNING ANY LIEN OR ENCUMBRANCE OF RECORD, AND ANY OTHER COST OR CHARGE INCURRED FOR MY BENEFIT.

EACH PARTY SIGNING THESE INSTRUCTIONS HAS READ THE ADDITIONAL ESCROW CONDITIONS, GENERAL PROVISIONS AND INSTRUCTIONS ON THE REVERSE SIDE HEREOF AND APPROVES, ACCEPTS AND AGREES TO BE BOUND THEREBY AS THOUGH THE REVERSE SIDE HEREOF APPEARED OVER THEIR SIGNATURES.

SELLER:

BUYER:

Sam Summers

Dan Winter

Kate Summers

Donna Winter

435

Seller Tax Options
Request for Taxpayer ID Number

SMS

AMENDMENT TO ESCROW INSTRUCTIONS

Date: January 18, 20xx   Escrow No: 000020

RE: 987 Ocean View Drive, Any City, CA 90000

TO: Simple Mortgage Services

My previous escrow instructions in the above numbered escrow are hereby amended and/or supplemented in the following particulars only:

Type Verbiage or Insert Amendment Clause Here

All other items and conditions shall remain the same.

EACH OF THE UNDERSIGNED STATES THAT EACH HAS READ THE FOREGOING INSTRUCTIONS, UNDERSTANDS THEM, AND ACKNOWLEDGES RECEIPT OF A COPY OF THESE INSTRUCTIONS.

_____   _____
Sam Summers   Dan Winter

_____   _____
Kate Summers   Donna Winter

SMS

Statement of Information

FILL OUT COMPLETELY AND RETURN TO SIMPLE MORTGAGE SERVICES

ESCROW # 00020-SMS   TRACT#   LOT#

Name_____   Social Security #_____   Driver's License#_____

Date of Birth_____   Place of Birth_____   Bus. Phone_____   Home Phone_____

Resided in USA since_____   Resided in California since_____

If you are married, please complete the following: Date Married_____at_____

Name of Spouse_____   Social Security #_____Driver's License #_____

Resided in USA since_____   Resided in California since_____

Previous Marriage or Marriages (if no previous marriage, write "None"):
Name of former spouse_____   Deceased___Divorced_____Where_____When____
Name of former spouse_____   Deceased___Divorced_____Where_____When____

Children by current or previous Marriages:
Name_____   Born_____   Name_____   Born_____
Name_____   Born_____   Name_____   Born_____

Information covering past 10 years:

Residence: _____
              Number/Street   City   From   To

              _____
              Number/Street   City   From   To

Employment   _____
              Firm Name   Location

              _____
              Firm Name   Location

Spouse Employment: _____
                      Firm Name   Location

                      _____
                      Firm Name   Location

Have you or your spouse owned or operated a business?
☐Yes   ☐No   If so please list names_____

I have never been adjudged, bankrupt, nor are there any unsatisfied judgments or other matters pending against me which might affect my title to this property except as follow:

Escrow Officer: Kelly Rose

SMS

LOAN INFORMATION SHEET

January 18, 20xx   Escrow No: 000020

RE: 987 Ocean View Drive, Any City, CA 90000

In order to proceed with the above referenced escrow, we need the following information about your property. **PLEASE COMPLETE, SIGN, AND RETURN** this form to our office as soon as possible.

FIRST   Name of Lender _____
LOAN: Address _____
          Loan Number _____ Approximate unpaid balance _____

SECOND Name of Lender _____
LOAN: Address _____
          Loan Number _____ Approximate unpaid balance _____

ADDITIONAL ENCUMBRANCE

Third Trust Deed ☐   Pool Loan ☐   Home Improvement Loan ☐   Lien ☐

Lienholder Name _____
Address _____
Account No _____ Approximate unpaid balance _____

If your property is affected by a Community Association please complete the following:

Name of Association _____
Name of Management Company _____
Address _____
Account No _____

If you have shares of Water Stock please complete the following:

Name of Water Company _____
Address: _____

FORWARDING ADDRESS AFTER CLOSE OF ESCROW:

_____
_____

INSURANCE INFORMATION

Name of Insurance Company _____

Agent's name _____ Phone No. _____
Address _____
Policy Number _____ Expiration Date _____

We, the undersigned, certify that the above information is true and correct to the best of our knowledge.

_____   _____
Dan Winter   Donna Winter

**CALIFORNIA
ASSOCIATION
OF REALTORS®**

**SELLER'S AFFIDAVIT OF NONFOREIGN STATUS
AND/OR CALIFORNIA WITHHOLDING EXEMPTION**
FOREIGN INVESTMENT IN REAL PROPERTY TAX ACT (FIRPTA)
AND CALIFORNIA WITHHOLDING LAW
(Use a separate form for each Transferor)
(C.A.R. Form AS, Revised 11/06)

Internal Revenue Code ("IRC") Section 1445 provides that a transferee of a U.S. real property interest must withhold tax if the transferor is a "foreign person." California Revenue and Taxation Code Section 18662 provides that a transferee of a California real property interest must withhold tax unless an exemption applies.

I understand that this affidavit may be disclosed to the Internal Revenue Service and to the California Franchise Tax Board by the transferee, and that any false statement I have made herein may result in a fine, imprisonment or both.

1. **PROPERTY ADDRESS** (property being transferred): _____ ("Property")
2. **TRANSFEROR'S INFORMATION:**
   Full Name _____ ("Transferor")
   Telephone Number _____
   Address _____
   (Use HOME address for individual transferors. Use OFFICE address for an "Entity" i.e.: corporations, partnerships, limited liability companies, trusts and estates.)
   Social Security No., Federal Employer Identification No. or California Corporation No. _____
   Note: In order to avoid withholding by providing this affidavit, IRC Section 1445 (b) (2) requires a Seller to provide the Buyer with the Seller's taxpayer identification number ("TIN").
3. **AUTHORITY TO SIGN:** If this document is signed on behalf of an Entity Transferor, THE UNDERSIGNED INDIVIDUAL DECLARES THAT HE/SHE HAS AUTHORITY TO SIGN THIS DOCUMENT ON BEHALF OF THE TRANSFEROR.
4. **FEDERAL LAW:** I, the undersigned, declare under penalty of perjury that, for the reason checked below, if any, I am exempt (or if signed on behalf of an Entity Transferor, the Entity is exempt) from the federal withholding law (FIRPTA):
   ☐ (For individual Transferors) I am not a nonresident alien for purposes of U.S. income taxation.
   ☐ (For corporation, partnership, limited liability company, trust and estate Transferors) The Transferor is not a foreign corporation, foreign partnership, foreign limited liability company, foreign trust or foreign estate, as those terms are defined in the Internal Revenue Code and Income Tax Regulations.
5. **CALIFORNIA LAW:** I, the undersigned, declare under penalty of perjury that, for the reason checked below, if any, I am exempt (or if signed on behalf of an Entity Transferor, the Entity is exempt) from the California withholding law.
   Certifications which fully exempt the sale from withholding:
   ☐ The total sales price for the Property is $100,000 or less.
   ☐ The Property qualifies as my principal residence (or the decedent's, if being sold by the decedent's estate) within the meaning of IRC Section 121 (owned and occupied as such for two of the last five years).
   ☐ The Property was last used as my principal residence (or the decedent's, if being sold by the decedent's estate) within the meaning of IRC Section 121 without regard to the two-year time period.
   ☐ The transaction will result in a loss or zero gain for California income tax purposes. (Complete FTB Form 593-L.)
   ☐ The Property has been compulsorily or involuntarily converted (within the meaning of IRC Section 1033) and Transferor intends to acquire property similar or related in service or use to be eligible for non-recognition of gain for California income tax purposes under IRC Section 1033.
   ☐ Transferor is a corporation (or an LLC classified as a corporation) that is either qualified through the California Secretary of State or has a permanent place of business in California.
   ☐ Transferor is a partnership (or an LLC that is not a disregarded single member LLC, classified as a partnership) and recorded title to the Property is in the name of the partnership or LLC. If so, the partnership or LLC must withhold from nonresident partners or members as required.
   ☐ Transferor is exempt from tax under California or federal law.
   ☐ Transferor is an insurance company, qualified pension/profit sharing plan, IRA or charitable remainder trust.
   Certifications which may partially or fully exempt the sale from withholding:
   ☐ The Property is being, or will be, exchanged for property of like kind within the meaning of IRC Section 1031.
   ☐ The Property is subject to an installment sale, that Transferor will report as such, and Buyer has agreed to withhold on each principal payment instead of withholding the full amount at the time of transfer.
   ☐ As a result of the sale of the Property, Seller's tax liability, calculated at the maximum tax rate regardless of Seller's actual rate, will be less than the 3 1/3% withholding otherwise required. Seller will be required to sign a certification, under penalty of perjury, specifying the amount to be withheld. **(Not to be used for sales closing prior to January 1, 2007)**

By _____ Date _____
(Transferor's Signature) (Indicate if you are signing as the grantor of a revocable/grantor trust.)

Typed or printed name _____ Title (If signed on behalf of Entity Transferor) _____

Buyer's unauthorized use or disclosure of Seller's TIN could result in civil or criminal liability.

Buyer _____ Date _____
(Buyer acknowledges receipt of a Copy of this Seller's Affidavit)

Buyer _____ Date _____
(Buyer acknowledges receipt of a Copy of this Seller's Affidavit)

SURE TRAC
The System for Success™

Published and Distributed by:
REAL ESTATE BUSINESS SERVICES, INC.
a subsidiary of the California Association of REALTORS®
525 South Virgil Avenue, Los Angeles, California 90020

Reviewed by _____ Date _____   EQUAL HOUSING OPPORTUNITY

AS REVISED 11/06 (PAGE 1 OF 2)

SELLER'S AFFIDAVIT OF NONFOREIGN STATUS AND/OR CALIFORNIA WITHOLDING EXEMPTION (AS PAGE 1 OF 2)

Agent:	Phone:	Fax:	Prepared using WINForms® software
Broker:			

IMPORTANT NOTICE: An Affidavit should be signed by each individual or entity Transferor to whom or to which it applies. Before you sign, any questions relating to the legal sufficiency of this form, or to whether it applies to you or to a particular transaction, or about the definition of any of the terms used, should be referred to an attorney, certified public accountant, or other professional tax advisor, the Internal Revenue Service, or the California Franchise Tax Board. For further information on federal guidelines, see C.A.R. Legal Q & A *"Federal Withholding: The Foreign Investment in Real Property Tax Act,"* and/or IRS Publication 515 or 519. For further information on state guidelines, see C.A.R. Legal Q & A *"California Nonresident Withholding,"* and/or California FTB Pub. 1016.

FEDERAL GUIDELINES

FOREIGN PERSONS DEFINED. The following general information is provided to assist sellers in determining whether they are "foreign persons" for purposes of the Foreign Investment in Real Property Tax Act (FIRPTA), IRC §1445. FIRPTA requires a buyer to withhold and send to the Internal Revenue Service 10% of the gross sales price of a United States (U.S.) real property interest if the seller is a foreign person. No withholding is required for a seller who is a U.S. person (that is, not a foreign person). In order for an individual to be a U.S. person, he/she must be either a U.S. citizen or a U.S. resident alien. The test must be applied separately to each seller in transactions involving more than one seller. Even if the seller is a foreign person, withholding will not be required in every circumstance.

NONRESIDENT ALIEN INDIVIDUAL. An individual whose residence is not within the U.S. **and** who is not a U.S. citizen is a nonresident alien. The term includes a nonresident alien fiduciary. An alien actually present in the U.S. who is not just staying temporarily (i.e., not a mere transient or sojourner), is a U.S. resident for income tax purposes. An alien is considered a U.S. resident and not subject to withholding under FIRPTA if the alien meets either the **green card test** or the **substantial presence test** for the calendar year.

GREEN CARD TEST. An alien is a U.S. resident if the individual was a lawful permanent resident of the U.S. at any time during the calendar year. This is known as the "green card test."

SUBSTANTIAL PRESENCE TEST. An alien is considered a U.S. resident if the individual meets the substantial presence test for the calendar year. Under this test, the individual must be physically present in the U.S. on at least: (1) 31 days during the current calendar year; and (2) 183 days during the current year and the two preceding years, counting all the days of physical presence in the current year but only 1/3 the number of days present in the first preceding year, and 1/6 the number of days present in the second preceding year.

DAYS OF PRESENCE IN THE U.S. TEST. Generally, a person is treated as physically present in the country at any time during the day. However, if a person regularly commutes to work in the U.S. from a residence in Canada or Mexico, or is in transit between two points outside the U.S. and is physically present in the country for less than 24 hours, he/she is not treated as present in the U.S. on any day during the transit or commute. In addition, the individual is not treated as present in the U.S. on any day during which he/she is unable to leave the U.S. because of a medical condition which arose while in the U.S.

EXEMPT INDIVIDUAL. For the substantial presence test, do not count days for which a person is an exempt individual. An exempt individual is anyone in the following categories:

(1) An individual temporarily present in the U.S. because of (a) full-time diplomatic or consular status, (b) full-time employment with an international organization or (c) an immediate family member of a person described in (a) or (b).

(2) A teacher or trainee temporarily present in the U.S. under a "J" visa (other than as a student) who substantially complies with the requirements of the visa. An individual will not be exempt under this category for a calendar year if he/she was exempt as a teacher or trainee or as a student for any two calendar years during the preceding six calendar years.

(3) A student temporarily present in the U.S. under an "F" or "J" visa who substantially complies with the requirements of the visa. Generally, a person will not be exempt as a student for any calendar year after the fifth calendar year for which he/she was exempt as a student, teacher or trainee. However, the individual may continue to be exempt as a student beyond the fifth year if he/she is in compliance with the terms of the student visa and does not intend to permanently reside in the U.S.

CLOSER CONNECTION TO A FOREIGN COUNTRY. Even if an individual would otherwise meet the substantial presence test, that person is not treated as meeting the test for the current calendar year if he/she:

(1) Is present in the U.S. on fewer than 183 days during the current year, and

(2) Has a tax home in a foreign country and has a closer connection to that country than to the U.S.

SPECIAL RULES. It is possible to be both a nonresident alien and a resident alien during the same tax year. Usually this occurs for the year a person arrives in or departs from the U.S. Other special provisions apply to individuals who were U.S. residents for at least three years, cease to be U.S. residents, and then become U.S. residents again.

NONRESIDENT ALIEN INDIVIDUALS MARRIED TO U.S. CITIZENS OR RESIDENT ALIENS may choose to be treated as resident aliens for most income tax purposes. However, these individuals are considered **nonresidents** for purposes of withholding taxes.

A FOREIGN PERSON OR PARTNERSHIP is one that does not fit the definition of a domestic corporation or partnership. A domestic corporation or partnership is one that was created or organized in the U.S., or under the laws of the U.S., or of any U.S. state or territory.

GUAM AND U.S. VIRGIN ISLANDS CORPORATIONS. A corporation created or organized in or under the laws of Guam or the U.S. Virgin Islands is not considered a foreign corporation for the purpose of withholding tax for the tax year if:

(1) at all times during the tax year, less than 25% in value of the corporation's stock is owned, directly or indirectly, by foreign persons, and

(2) at least 20% of the corporation's gross income is derived from sources within Guam or at least 65% of the corporation's income is effectively connected with the conduct of a trade or business in the U.S. Virgin Islands or the U.S. for the 3-year period ending with the close of the preceding tax year of the corporation, or the period the corporation has been in existence, if less.

A NONRESIDENT ALIEN TRUSTEE, ADMINISTRATOR OR EXECUTOR of a trust or an estate is treated as a nonresident alien, even though all the beneficiaries of the trust or estate are citizens or residents of the U.S.

Buyer's Initials (_____) (_____)
Seller's Initials (_____) (_____)

Reviewed by _____ Date _____

EQUAL HOUSING OPPORTUNITY

AS REVISED 11/06 (PAGE 2 OF 2)

SELLER'S AFFIDAVIT OF NONFOREIGN STATUS AND/OR CALIFORNIA WITHOLDING EXEMPTION (AS PAGE 2 OF 2)

x.zfx

YEAR
CALIFORNIA FORM

Withholding Exemption Certificate

20xx (For use by Individuals, corporations, partnerships and estates)

590

File this form with your withholding agent.

Name: Dan Winter and Donna Winter

Address (number and street)
25892 Mountain Avenue

Telephone number

City
Any Town, CA 90000

State

ZIP code

Complete the appropriate line: Individuals - Social security no. _____ ☐ Married ☐ Single
Corporations - California corporation no. _____ (Issued by Secretary of State)
Partnerships and - F.E.I.N. _____

To _____
(Withholding Agent or Payer)

Individuals:

Certificate of Residency
I hereby declare under penalty perjury that I am a resident of California and that I reside at the address shown above.

Signature _____ Date_____

Certificate of Residency of Deceased Person
I hereby certify under penalty of perjury, as executor of the above named person's estate that decedent was a California resident at the time of death.

Name of Executor (type or print)_____ Date_____

Signature _____

Certificate of Principal Residence (Real estate sales only)
I hereby certify under penalty of perjury that the California real property located at __25892 Mountain Avenue, Any Town__ __CA, 90000__ was my principal residence within the meaning of IRC Section 1034.

Signature _____ Date_____

Corporations:
I hereby certify the above-named corporation has a permanent place of business in California at the address shown above or is qualified to do business in California.

Signature _____ Date_____

Title of corporate officer_____

Tax Exempt Entities and Non Profit Organizations:
I hereby certify, under penalty of perjury, that the above-named entity is exempt from tax under California or Federal law.

Name and Title _____

Signature _____ Date_____

Trusts:

I hereby certify, under penalty of perjury, that at least one trustee of the above-named trust is a California resident.

Name and Title _____

Signature _____ Date_____

1099-S INPUT

IMPORTANT

All areas and data fields
with numbers must be completed
before submissions to SMS.

COMPANY NUMBER	OFFICE NUMBER	TYPE	ORDER/ESCROW FILE NO.	ACTUAL CLOSING DATE
(1)Co#244	(2)Off#1	(3)	(4)5072-J	(5)

SUBJECT PROPERTY INFORMATION

Street Address or Brief Form of Legal Description for vacant land, use APN, county, state:

_____

City	State	Zip Code

TRANSACTION DATA

CONTRACT SALES PRICE (line 401 HUD-1 form. If this is an exchange, provide total dollar value of cash, notes and debt relief received by exchanger.	NO. OF 1099S forms required for the sale of this property.	2 OR MORE 1099S FORMS If 2 or more 1099-S forms are required, record the dollar amount for this seller based on the seller's declaration.	BUYERS PART OF REAL ESTATE TAX Show any real estate tax, on a residence, charged to the buyer at settlement.	CONTINGENT TRANSACTION Is this a contingent transaction wherein gross proceeds cannot be determined with certainty at time of closing?	EXCHANGE Was (or will there be) other property or services received?
$321,000.00				yes	yes

SELLER INFORMATION-PLEASE PRINT CLEARLY

Seller's Last Name   Seller's First Name   M.I.

Seller's Forwarding Street Address

City   State   Zip Code (or country if not USA)

Seller's Social Security Number   or   Seller's Tax Identification Number

You are required by law to provide your closing agent with your correct Taxpayer Identification Number. If you do not provide your correct Taxpayer Identification Number, you may be subject to civil or criminal penalties imposed by law.

Under penalties of perjury, I certify that the number shown above is my correct Taxpayer Identification Number.

_____

Seller's Signature

RECORDING REQUESTED BY
Any City Title Company
AND WHEN RECORDED MAIL TO:

Name: Sam and Kate Summers
Street Address: 987 Ocean View Drive
City, State: Any City, CA 90000
Zip

REC
RCF
MICRO
RTCF
LIEN
SMPF
PCOR

Order No. 56748932-SMS

_____

Space Above This Line for Recorder's Use

GRANT DEED

THE UNDERSIGNED GRANTOR(S) DECLARE(S)
City of: <u>Any City</u>

Conveyance tax is $_____
Parcel No. 123-45-6789

DOCUMENTARY TRANSFER TAX $_____

☐Computed on full value of interest of property conveyed

☐Full value less value of liens or encumbrances remaining at the time of sale

FOR A VALUABLE CONSIDERATION, receipt of which is hereby acknowledged, Sam Summers and Kate Summers Husband and Wife as Joint Tenants do (does) hereby GRANTS to Dan Winter and Donna Winter Husband and Wife as Joint Tenants

the following real property in the city of Any City county of Apple, state of California

Lot 12 in Tract 2316 as recorded in Book 42 pages 5-10 inclusive of Miscellaneous Maps in the office of the County Recorder of the County of Apple, State of California and described as follows: commencing at a point on the Southerly line thereof 450.8 feet West of the Southeast corner thereof, thence North 68 degrees 58 minutes West 100 fee, thence North 23 degrees 02 minutes East 60 feet, thence South 66 degrees 58 minutes East one hundred feet, thence South 23 degrees 02 minutes West 60 feet to the point of beginning..

Dated:_____

STATE OF CALIFORNIA
COUNTY OF_____

On_____before me.

a Notary Public in and for said County and State, personally appeared:
_____

_____

Personally known to me (or provided to me on the basis of satisfactory evidence whose name(s) is/are subscribed to the within instrument and acknowledged to me that he/she/they executed the same in his/her/their authorized capacity(ies) and that by his/her/their signature(s) on the instrument the person(s) or the entity upon behalf of which the person(s) acted, executed the instrument.

WITNESS my hand and official seal.

Signature_____

_____
Sam Summers

_____
Kate Summers

(This area for official notorial seal)

RECORDING REQUESTED BY
Any City Title Company
AND WHEN RECORDED MAIL TO:

REC	
RCF	
MICRO	
RTCF	
LIEN	
SMPF	
PCOR	

Name: Sam & Kate Summers
Street Address: 987 Ocean View Drive
City, State: Any City, CA 90000
Zip

Order No. 56748932-SMS

Space Above This Line for Recorder's Use

QUITCLAIM DEED

THE UNDERSIGNED GRANTOR(S) DECLARE(S)
City of: <u>Any City</u>
Conveyance tax is $_____
Parcel No. 123-45-6789

DOCUMENTARY TRANSFER TAX $_____ .
▯ Computed on full value of interest of property conveyed
▯ Full value less value of liens or encumbrances remaining at the time of sale

FOR A VALUABLE CONSIDERATION, receipt of which is hereby acknowledged, Sam Summers and Kate Summers, Husband and Wife as Joint Tenants do (does) hereby REMISE, RELEASE AND FOREVER QUITCLAIM to Dan Winter and Donna Winter, Husband and Wife as Joint Tenants

the following real property in the city of Any City county of Apple, state of California

Lot 12 in Tract 2316 as recorded in Book 42 pages 5-10 inclusive of Miscellaneous Maps in the office of the County Recorder of the County of Apple, State of California and described as follows: commencing at a point on the Southerly line thereof 450.8 feet West of the Southeast corner thereof, thence North 68 degrees 58 minutes West 100 fee, thence North 23 degrees 02 minutes East 60 feet, thence South 66 degrees 58 minutes East one hundred feet, thence South 23 degrees 02 minutes West 60 feet to the point of beginning..

Dated:_____

STATE OF CALIFORNIA
COUNTY OF_____

On_____ before me.

a Notary Public in and for said County and State, personally appeared:

_____

_____

Personally known to me (or provided to me on the basis of satisfactory evidence whose name(s) is/are subscribed to the within instrument and acknowledged to me that he/she/they executed the same in his/her/their authorized capacity(ies) and that by his/her/their signature(s) on the instrument the person(s) or the entity upon behalf of which the person(s) acted, executed the instrument.

Signature_____

_____
Sam Summers

_____
Kate Summers

(This area for official notorial seal)

INSTALLMENT NOTE
(INTEREST INCLUDED)
(THIS NOTE CONTAINS AN ACCELERATION CLAUSE)

$189,000   Any City   ,California,   1/1/20xx

In installments and at the times hereinafter stated, for value received, Dan Winter and Donna Winter

promise to pay to   Sam Summers and Kate Summers

_____ , or order

at   987 Ocean View Drive, Any City, CA 90000

the principal sum of One Hundred Eighty Thousand   dollars

with interest from January 1, 20xx   on the amounts of

principal remaining from time to time unpaid, until said principal sum is paid, at the rate of 8.9   percent

per annum. Principal and interest due in monthly installments of One Thousand Five Hundred Dollars, $1,500, or more on the 15th day of each and every month, beginning on the 15th day of February, 20xx. And continuing until said principal sum has been fully paid. AT ANY TIME, THE PRIVILEGE IS RESERVED TO PAY MORE THAN THE SUM DUE. Should the interest not be so paid, it shall be added to the principal and thereafter bear like interest as the principal, but such unpaid interest so compounded shall not exceed an amount equal to simple interest on the unpaid principal at the maximum rate permitted by law. Should default be made in the payment of any of said installments when due, then the whole sum of principal and interest shall become immediately due and payable at the option of the holder of this note.

If the trustor shall sell, convey, or alienate said property, or any part thereof, or any interest therein, or shall be divested of his title or any interest therein in may manner or way, whether voluntarily or involuntarily, without the written consent of the beneficiary being first had and obtained, beneficiary shall have the right, at its option, to declare any indebtedness or obligations secured hereby, irrespective of the maturity date specified in any note evidencing the same, immediately due and payable.

Should suit be commenced to collect this note or any portion thereof, such sum as the Court may deem reasonable shall be added hereto as attorney's fees. Principal and interest payable for lawful money of the United States of America. This note is secured by a certain DEED OF TRUST to the SMS SETTLEMENT SERVICES, a California corporation, as TRUSTEE.

_____   _____
Dan Winter   Donna Winter

RECORDING REQUESTED BY
SMS SETTLEMENT SERVICES
AND WHEN RECORDED MAIL TO:

Name: Dan & Donna Winter
Street Address: 25892 Mountain Ave.
City, State: Any Town, CA
Zip: 90000

| REC |
| RCF |
| MICRO |
| RTCF |
| LIEN |
| SMPF |
| PCOR |

Order No. 004860-DW

Space Above This Line for Recorder's Use

DEED OF TRUST WITH ASSIGNMENT OF RENTS

This DEED OF TRUST, made **January 1, 20xx**, between **Dan Winter and Donna Winter** herein called TRUSTOR, whose address is:
25892 Mountain Avenue, Any Town, CA

SMS SETTLEMENT SERVICES, a California Corporation, herein called TRUSTEE and **Sam Summers and Kate Summers**, herein called BENEFICIARY, Trustor irrevocably grants, transfers and assigns to Trustee in Trust, with Power of Sale, that property in City of **Any City**, County of **Apple**, California, described as:

All that tract and parcel of land located on the northwest corner of the subdivision more commonly known as Hillcrest and being more fully described in Deed Book 123, page 891.

Together with the rents, issues and profits thereof, subject, however, to the right, power and authority hereinafter given to and conferred upon Beneficiary to collect and apply such rents, issues and profits.

For the Purpose of Securing (1) payment of the sum of $180,000.00 with interest thereon according to the terms of a promissory note or notes of even date herewith made by Trustor, payable to order of Benficiary, and extensions or renewals thereof; (2) the performance of each agreement of Trustor incorporated by reference or contained herein or reciting it is so secured; (3) Payment of additional sums and interest thereon which may hereafter be loaned to Trustor, or his successors or assigns, when evidenced by a promissory note or notes reciting that they are secured by this Deed of Trust.

To protect the security of this Deed of Trust, and with respect to the property above described, Trustor expressly makes each and all of the agreements, and adopts and agrees to perform and be bound by each and all of the terms and provisions set forth in subdivision A of that certain Fictitious Deed of Trust reference herein, and it is mutually agreed that all of the provisions set forth in subdivision B of that certain Fictitious Deed of Trust recorded in the book and page of Official Records in the office of the county recorder of the county where said property is located, noted below opposite the name of such county:

Said agreements, terms and provisions contained in said Subdivision A and B, (identical in all counties are printed on the reverse side hereof) are by the within reference thereto, incorporated herein and made a part of this Deed of Trust for all purposes as fully as if set forth at length herein and Beneficiary may charge for a statement regarding the obligation secured hereby, provided the charge therefore does not exceed the maximum allowed by laws.

The foregoing assignment of rents is absolute unless initiated here, in which case, the assignment serves as additional security.

The undersigned Trustor, requests that a copy of any notice of default and any notice of sale hereunder be mailed to him at this address hereinbefore set forth.

Dated: __January 1, 20xx__

STATE OF CALIFORNIA
COUNTY OF_____

Dan Winter
_____

Donna Winter
_____

On_____before me.

a Notary Public in and for said County and State, personally appeared:

_____

_____

Personally known to me (or proved to me on the basis of satisfactory evidence whose name(s) is/are subscribed to the within instrument and acknowledged to me that he/she/they executed the same in his/her/their authorized capacity(ies) and that by his/her/their signature(s) on the instrument the person(s) or the entity upon behalf of which the person(s) acted, executed the instrument.

WITNESS my hand and official seal.

Signature_____   (This area for official notorial seal)

Federal Truth-In-Lending Disclosure Statement

Borrower:

Creditor:
ANY CITY MORTGAGE CORP.
535 LAKEVIEW DRIVE, SUITE 100
ANY CITY, CA 90000

Loan Number: 2-0111-2457

4/19/20xx

ANNUAL PERCENTAGE RATE	FINANCE CHARGE	AMOUNT FINANCED	TOTAL OF PAYMENTS
The cost of your credit as a yearly rate.	The dollar amount the credit will cost you.	The amount of credit provided to you or on your behalf.	The amount you will have paid after you have made all payments as scheduled
9.2730%	$229,540.84	$115,848.97	$345,389.81

Your payment schedule will be:

No. of Pmts.	Amt. of Pmts.	Monthly Pmts. Begin	No. of Pmts.	Amt. of Pmts.	Monthly Pmts. Begin	No. of Pmts.	Amt. of Pmts.	Monthly Pmts. Begin
359	959.42	7/01/20xx						
1	958.03	6/01/20xx						

INSURANCE: The following insurance is required to obtain credit: *Property
You may obtain the insurance from anyone that is acceptable to creditor.

SECURITY: You are giving a security interest in the real property being purchased.
Property Address: 987 Ocean View Drive, Any City, CA 90000

FILING FEES: $50.00

LATE CHARGE: If a payment is more than 15 days late, you will be charged 5% of the payment.

PREPAYMENT: If you pay off your loan early, you will not have to pay a penalty. You will not be entitled to a refund of part of the finance charge.

ASSUMPTION: Someone buying your property cannot assume the remainder of your loan on the original terms.

All dates and numerical disclosures except the late payment disclosures are estimates.

See your contract documents for any additional information about nonpayment, default, any required repayment in full before the scheduled ate, and prepayment refunds and penalties.

Name   Date   Name   Date

GOOD FAITH ESTIMATE OF SETTLEMENT CHARGES

Borrower:

Creditor:
Any City Mortgage Corp.
535 Lakeview Drive, Suite 500
Any City, CA 90000

Loan Number: Date:

The information provided below reflects estimates of the charges which you are likely to incur at the settlement of your loan. The fees listed are estimates-the actual charges may be more or less. Your transaction may not involve a fee for every item listed.

The numbers listed beside the estimates generally correspond to the numbered lines contained in the HUD-1 settlement statement which you will be receiving at settlement. The HUD-1 settlement statement will show you the actual cost for items paid at settlement.

LOAN AMOUNT: $ 118,750.00

ITEMIZATION OF PREPAID FINANCE CHARGES:
801	Loan Origination Fee 1.25%(Lender)	$ 1,484.38
810	Tax Services	75.00
811	Processing Fee	200.00
813	UNDERWRITING	375.00
814	TAX SERVICE	75.00
901	Prepaid Interest (5/14/99-6/01/20xx)	489.78
1002	Mortgage Insurance Reserves	

TOTAL PREPAID FINANCE CHARGE $ 2,901.03
AMOUNT FINANCED   115,848.97

OTHER SETTLEMENT CHARGES:

AMOUNTS PAID TO OTHERS ON YOUR BEHALF
BY CREDITOR
803	Appraisal Fee to ABC Appraisal Company	295.00
804	Credit Report Fee	55.00
903	Property Insurance to Insurance Co.	400.00
1001	Property Insurance Reserves (2 mo.)	66.68
1004	County Tax Reserves (4 mo.)	520.00
1101	Settlement or Closing Fee	400.00
1106	Notary Fees to ESCROW COMPANY	10.00
1108	Title Insurance to TITLE COMPANY	300.00
1201	Recording Fees	50.00

TOTAL OTHER SETTLEMENT CHARGES   2,097.52
LOAN PROCEEDS $ 113,751.45

These estimates are provided pursuant to the Real Estate Settlement Procedures Act of 1974 (RESPA). Additional information can be found in the HUD Special Information booklet, which is to be provided to you by your mortgage broker or lender.

I (WE) HEREBY ACKNOWLEDGE RECEIVING AND READING A COMPLETEDS COPY OF THIS DISCLOSURE.

_____   _____
Date   Date

SMS

REQUEST FOR DEMAND

December 29, 20xx   Escrow No: 004860

Attn: Payoff Department
Any City Mortgage
1212 N. Main Street
Santa Ana, CA 92705

RE: **LOAN NUMBER: 1022290-09**
   BORROWER: Dan Winter and Donna Winter

An escrow has been opened with our company by the above reference borrowers and provides for the payment in full of the loan number referenced above. Your loan encumbers the real property described as:

See Exhibit A attached hereto and made a part hereof.

The property is commonly known as **987 Ocean View Drive**

We hereby request that you forward your **ORIGINAL DEMAND,** together with either (1) the original Note, Deed of Trust securing same and your executed Request for Full Reconveyance, or (2) your executed Full Reconveyance, to the following title company:

Any City Title Company
ATTN: Tom Baker
10229 Main Street
Any City, CA 90000
RE: TITLE ORDER No: 4860

Please fax a copy of your DEMAND to our office at (714) 549-0684 with an additional copy in the mail.

We wish to thank you for your cooperation and assistance. Please be sure to call our office if you have any questions concerning this matter.

Sincerely,

Kelly Rose
Escrow Officer

TITLE ORDER

December 29, 20xx

ESCROW No.: 004860

ATTN: Tom Baker
Any City Title Company
10229 Main Street
Any City, CA 90000

RE: TITLE ORDER No.: 4860

PLEASE ACCEPT THIS AS OUR REQUEST FOR THE FOLLOWING POLICY(IES):
CLTA $ 189,900.00   JOINT PROTECTION   ALTA $ 80,000.00

on property described as follows:

All that tract and parcel of land located on the northwest corner of the subdivision more commonly known as Rainbow Ridge and being more fully described in Deed Book 123, page 891.

Subject Property is commonly known as: 987 Ocean View Drive, Any City, CA 90000

Present Owner's Name: Sam Summers

WE ENCLOSE THE FOLLOWING:
1. Statements of information from Dan Winter, Donna Winter, Sam Summers, Kate Summers
2. Grant Deed from Sam Summers and Kate Summers to Dan Winter and Donna Winter
3. First Deed of Trust to record in favor of Any City Bank, in the amount of $180,000.00
4. Note/Deed of Trust

UPON FURTHER AUTHORIZATION you are to record all instruments without collection when you can issue said form of Policy showing Title vesting in:
        Dan Winter and Donna Winter

FREE FROM ENCUMBRANCES EXCEPT:
1. ALL general and Special Taxes for the Fiscal Year 20xx
2. Covenants, Conditions, Restrictions, Easements and Rights of Way of record.
3. Bonds and assessments not delinquent.
4. Deeds of Trust now of record in the amount of $89,000.90
5. New First Deed of Trust to record in favor of Any City Bank

PLEASE ABSTRACT ALL DOCUMENTS AND ADVISE US IMMEDIATELY IF ANY CORRECTIONS ARE NEEDED

Please send the original policy(ies) and/or copies as appropriate to:

Any City Bank
24591 Mountain Street
Any City, CA 90000

SMS SETTLEMENT SERVICES
3021 Hillcrest Avenue
Any Town, CA 90000

If you have questions, please do not hesitate to contact our office.
Thank you.

Kelly Rose
ESCROW OFFICER

PRELIMINARY CHANGE OF OWNERSHIP REPORT

To be completed by transferee (buyer) prior to transfer of subject property in accordance with Section 480.03 of the Revenue and Taxation Code. A Preliminary Change of Ownership Report must be filed with each conveyance in the County Recorder's office for the county where the property is located; this particular form may be used in all 58 counties of California.
THIS REPORT IS NOT A PUBLIC DOCUMENT

FOR RECORDER'S USE ONLY

SELLER/TRANSFEROR: **Sam Summers and Kate Summers**
BUYER/TRANSFEREE: **Dan Winter and Donna Winter**
ASSESSOR'S PARCEL NUMBER(S) 123-45-6789
PROPERTY ADDRESS OR LOCATION: **987 Ocean View Drive**
Any City, CA 90000

MAIL TAX INFORMATION TO:
Name **Dan Winter**
Address **25892 Mountain Avenue**
Any Town, CA 90000

NOTICE: A lien for property taxes applies to your property on March 1 of each year for the taxes owing in the following fiscal year, July 1 through June 30. One-half of these taxes is due November 1, and one-half is due February 1. The first installment becomes delinquent on December 10, and the second installment becomes delinquent on April 10. One tax bill is mailed before November 1 to the owner of record. **IF THIS TRANSFER OCCURS AFTER MARCH 1 AND ON OR BEFORE DECEMBER 31, YOU MAY BE RESPONSIBLE FOR THE SECOND INSTALLMENT OF TAXES DUE FEBRUARY 1.**
The property which you acquired may be subject to a supplemental assessment in an amount to be determined by the Apple County Assessor. For further information on your supplemental roll obligation, please call the Apple County Assessor

---

PART I: TRANSFER INFORMATION   Please answer all questions.

YES	NO		
☐	☑	A.	Is this transfer solely between husband and wife (Addition of a spouse, death of a spouse, divorce settlement, etc.)?
☐	☑	B.	Is this transaction only a correction of the name(s) of the person(s) holding title to the property (For example, a name change upon marriage)?
☐	☑	C.	Is this document recorded to create, terminate, or reconvey a lender's interest in the property?
☐	☑	D.	Is this transaction recorded only to create, terminate, or reconvey a security interest (e.g. cosigner)?
☐	☑	E.	Is this document recorded to substitute a trustee under a deed of trust, mortgage, or other similar document?
☐	☑	F.	Did this transfer result in the creation of a joint tenancy in which the seller (transferor) remains as one of the joint tenants?
☐	☑	G.	Does this transfer return property to the person who created the joint tenancy (original transferor)?
		H.	Is this transfer of property:
☐	☑		1. to a trust for the benefit of the grantor, or grantor's spouse?
☐	☑		2. to a trust revocable by the transferor?
☐	☑		3. to a trust from which the property reverts to the grantor within 12 years?
☐	☑	I.	If this property is subject to a lease, is the remaining lease term 35 years or more including written options?
☐	☑	J.	Is this a transfer from parents to children or from children to parents?
☐	☑	K.	Is this transaction to replace a principal residence by a person 55 years of age or older?
☐	☑	L.	Is this transaction to replace a principal residence by a person who is severely disabled as defined by Revenue and Code Section 69.5?

If you checked yes to J, K, or L, an applicable claim form must be filed with the County Assessor.
Please provide any other information that would help the Assessors to understand the nature of the transfer.

IF YOU HAVE ANSWERED "YES" TO ANY OF THE ABOVE QUESTIONS EXCEPT J, K, OR L, PLEASE SIGN AND DATE, OTHERWISE COMPLETE BALANCE OF THE FORM.

PART II: OTHER TRANSFER INFORMATION
A. Date of transfer if other than recording date _____.
B. Type of transfer. Please check appropriate box.
☑ Purchase   ☐ Foreclosure   ☐ Gift   ☐ Trade or Exchange   ☐ Merger, Stock, or Partnership Acquisition
☐ Contract of Sale - Date of Contract _____
☐ Inheritance - Date of Death _____   ☐ Other: Please explain: _____
☐ Creation of Lease   ☐ Assignment of a Lease   ☐ Termination of a Lease
Date lease began _____
Original term in years (including written options) _____
Remaining term in years (including written options) _____
C. Was only a partial interest in the property transferred? ☐ Yes ☑ No   If yes, indicate the percentage transferred _____%

A. Settlement Statement

U.S. Department of Housing and Urban Development

OMB Approval No. 2502-0265

B. Type of Loan

1. ☐ FHA	2. ☐ FmHA	3. ☐ Conv. Unins.	6. File Number:	7. Loan Number:	8. Mortgage Insurance Case Number:
4. ☐ VA	5. ☐ Conv. Ins.				

C. Note: This form is furnished to give you a statement of actual settlement costs. Amounts paid to and by the settlement agent are shown. Items marked "(p.o.c.)" were paid outside the closing; they are shown here for informational purposes and are not included in the totals.

D. Name & Address of Borrower:	E. Name & Address of Seller:	F. Name & Address of Lender:

G. Property Location:	H. Settlement Agent:	
	Place of Settlement:	I. Settlement Date:

J. Summary of Borrower's Transaction

100. Gross Amount Due From Borrower		
101. Contract sales price		
102. Personal property		
103. Settlement charges to borrower (line 1400)		
104.		
105.		
Adjustments for items paid by seller in advance		
106. City/town taxes	to	
107. County taxes	to	
108. Assessments	to	
109.		
110.		
111.		
112.		
120. Gross Amount Due From Borrower		
200. Amounts Paid By Or In Behalf Of Borrower		
201. Deposit or earnest money		
202. Principal amount of new loan(s)		
203. Existing loan(s) taken subject to		
204.		
205.		
206.		
207.		
208.		
209.		
Adjustments for items unpaid by seller		
210. City/town taxes	to	
211. County taxes	to	
212. Assessments	to	
213.		
214.		
215.		
216.		
217.		
218.		
219.		
220. Total Paid By/For Borrower		
300. Cash At Settlement From/To Borrower		
301. Gross Amount due from borrower (line 120)		
302. Less amounts paid by/for borrower (line 220)	(	)
303. Cash ☐ From ☐ To Borrower		

K. Summary of Seller's Transaction

400. Gross Amount Due To Seller		
401. Contract sales price		
402. Personal property		
403.		
404.		
405.		
Adjustments for items paid by seller in advance		
406. City/town taxes	to	
407. County taxes	to	
408. Assessments	to	
409.		
410.		
411.		
412.		
420. Gross Amount Due To Seller		
500. Reductions In Amount Due To Seller		
501. Excess deposit (see instructions)		
502. Settlement charges to seller (line 1400)		
503. Existing loan(s) taken subject to		
504. Payoff of first mortgage loan		
505. Payoff of second mortgage loan		
506.		
507.		
508.		
509.		
Adjustments for items unpaid by seller		
510. City/town taxes	to	
511. County taxes	to	
512. Assessments	to	
513.		
514.		
515.		
516.		
517.		
518.		
519.		
520. Total Reduction Amount Due Seller		
600. Cash At Settlement To/From Seller		
601. Gross amount due to seller (line 420)		
602. Less reductions in amt. due seller (line 520)	(	)
603. Cash ☐ To ☐ From Seller		

Section 5 of the Real Estate Settlement Procedures Act (RESPA) requires the following: • HUD must develop a Special Information Booklet to help persons borrowing money to finance the purchase of residential real estate to better understand the nature and costs of real estate settlement services; • Each lender must provide the booklet to all applicants from whom it receives or for whom it prepares a written application to borrow money to finance the purchase of residential real estate; • Lenders must prepare and distribute with the Booklet a Good Faith Estimate of the settle likely to incur in connection with the settler manadatory.

Section 4(a) of RESPA mandates that HUD develop and prescribe this standard form to be used at the time of loan settlement to provide full disclosure of all charges imposed upon the borrower and seller. These are third party disclosures that are designed to provide the borrower with pertinent information during the settlement process in order to be a better shopper.

The Public Reporting Burden for this collection of information is estimated to ... nstructions, ... ta needed.

This agency may not collect this information, and you are not required to complete this form, unless it displays a currently valid OMB control number. The information requested does not lend itself to confidentiality.

form HUD-1 (3/86)

L. Settlement Charges

			Paid From Borrowers Funds at Settlement	Paid From Seller's Funds at Settlement
700.	Total Sales/Broker's Commission based on price $ @ % =			
	Division of Commission (line 700) as follows:			
701.	$ to			
702.	$ to			
703.	Commission paid at Settlement			
704.				
800.	**Items Payable In Connection With Loan**			
801.	Loan Origination Fee %			
802.	Loan Discount %			
803.	Appraisal Fee to			
804.	Credit Report to			
805.	Lender's Inspection Fee			
806.	Mortgage Insurance Application Fee to			
807.	Assumption Fee			
808.				
809.				
810.				
811.				
900.	**Items Required By Lender To Be Paid In Advance**			
901.	Interest from to @$ /day			
902.	Mortgage Insurance Premium for months to			
903.	Hazard Insurance Premium for years to			
904.	years to			
905.				
1000.	**Reserves Deposited With Lender**			
1001.	Hazard insurance months@$ per month			
1002.	Mortgage insurance months@$ per month			
1003.	City property taxes months@$ per month			
1004.	County property taxes months@$ per month			
1005.	Annual assessments months@$ per month			
1006.	months@$ per month			
1007.	months@$ per month			
1008.	months@$ per month			
1100.	**Title Charges**			
1101.	Settlement or closing fee to			
1102.	Abstract or title search to			
1103.	Title examination to			
1104.	Title insurance binder to			
1105.	Document preparation to			
1106.	Notary fees to			
1107.	Attorney's fees to			
	(includes above items numbers:)			
1108.	Title insurance to			
	(includes above items numbers:)			
1109.	Lender's coverage $			
1110.	Owner's coverage $			
1111.				
1112.				
1113.				
1200.	**Government Recording and Transfer Charges**			
1201.	Recording fees: Deed $; Mortgage $; Releases $			
1202.	City/county tax/stamps: Deed $; Mortgage $			
1203.	State tax/stamps: Deed $; Mortgage $			
1204.				
1205.				
1300.	**Additional Settlement Charges**			
1301.	Survey to			
1302.	Pest inspection to			
1303.				
1304.				
1305.				
1400.	**Total Settlement Charges (enter on lines 103, Section J and 502, Section K)**			

References and Links

- http://www.payoffassist.com. Use this web site to contact Mortgage Lenders and Loan Services.

- LANE GUIDE   (http://www.laneguide.com)

Since 1957, the Lane Guide has been the leading creditors directory used by the industry to locate information concerning payoffs, ratings, verifications, bank/lender mergers, acquisition references, and other types of financial information.

The Lane Guide offers a complete reference on all banks, savings banks, finance companies, mortgage lenders, loan services, credit unions, and other major creditors. With the Guide, you get instant access to loan service centers, main offices, loan departments, specialized departments, and branch offices.

True-False Quiz

Now that you have read all the material in this chapter, take the following self-test and check your knowledge of the escrow folder.

True/False

1. _FALSE_ The initial phase of escrow begins with the loan application.

2. _FALSE_ There is only one kind of escrow.

3. _TRUE_ In opening an escrow, the names of the parties, legal description, and selling price, among other information, are collected by the escrow holder.

4. _TRUE_ Escrow instructions are prepared to direct the escrow holder.

5. _FALSE_ Escrow instructions need to be signed only by the seller to make an escrow valid.

6. _FALSE_ The escrow holder never prepares a note and trust deed.

7. _FALSE_ Closing costs are calculated before the escrow is opened.

8. _TRUE_ The borrower agrees to all terms and signs the loan documents in the presence of a notary public.

9. _TRUE_ Once a deed is recorded along with a trust deed or other documents required for the transfer, the sale is complete.

10. _TRUE_ Escrow instructions are commonly generated by computer.

ANSWERS TO QUIZZES

Chapter 1		Chapter 2		Chapter 3		Chapter 4	
1.	T	1.	T	1.	T	1.	F
2.	F	2.	T	2.	T	2.	T
3.	T	3.	T	3.	F	3.	T
4.	F	4.	F	4.	F	4.	T
5.	F	5.	F	5.	T	5.	F
6.	T	6.	T	6.	T	6.	T
7.	T	7.	F	7.	T	7.	T
8.	F	8.	F	8.	F	8.	T
9.	T	9.	T	9.	T	9.	F
10.	F	10.	T	10.	T	10.	F

Chapter 5		Chapter 6		Chapter 7		Chapter 8	
1.	T	1.	F	1.	T	1.	T
2.	F	2.	T	2.	T	2.	T
3.	T	3.	T	3.	F	3.	F
4.	F	4.	F	4.	F	4.	T
5.	F	5.	F	5.	T	5.	T
6.	F	6.	T	6.	F	6.	F
7.	F	7.	T	7.	T	7.	F
8.	T	8.	F	8.	F	8.	T
9.	F	9.	F	9.	F	9.	F
10.	T	10.	F	10.	T	10.	T

ANSWERS TO
QUIZZES continued

Chapter 9		Chapter 10		Chapter 11		Chapter 12	
1.	F	1.	F	1.	T	1.	T
2.	T	2.	T	2.	T	2.	F
3.	T	3.	T	3.	F	3.	F
4.	T	4.	F	4.	F	4.	T
5.	T	5.	F	5.	F	5.	T
6.	T	6.	T	6.	F	6.	T
7.	T	7.	F	7.	T	7.	F
8.	F	8.	F	8.	F	8.	T
9.	F	9.	T	9.	T	9.	T
10.	F	10.	T	10.	T	10.	T

Chapter 13		Chapter 14		Chapter 15	
1.	F	1.	F	1.	F
2.	F	2.	F	2.	F
3.	T	3.	F	3.	T
4.	T	4.	T	4.	T
5.	F	5.	T	5.	F
6.	T	6.	F	6.	F
7.	T	7.	T	7.	F
8.	F	8.	F	8.	T
9.	T	9.	T	9.	T
10.	T	10.	T	10.	T

A

A.L.T.A. owner's policy
An owner's extended title insurance policy.

A.L.T.A. title policy
A type of title insurance policy issued by title insurance companies. It expands the risks normally insured against under the standard type policy to include unrecorded mechanic's liens; unrecorded physical easements; facts a physical survey would not show; water and mineral rights; and rights of parties in possession, such as tenants and buyers under unrecorded instruments.

abstract of judgment
A summary of a court decision.

abstract of title
Written summary of all useful documents discovered in a title search.

acceleration clause
Clause in a loan document describing events causing entire loan to come due.

acceptance
Unqualified agreement to the terms of an offer.

acknowledgment
A signed statement, made before a notary public, by a named person confirming the signature on a document and that it was made of free will.

actual notice
A fact, such as seeing the grant deed, or knowing a person was willed or inherited a property.

adjustable rate mortgage
A note whose interest rate is tied to a movable economic index.

administrator
A person appointed by the probate court to administer the estate of a deceased person. Duties include making an asset inventory, managing the property, paying the debts and expenses, filing required reports and tax returns, and distributing the assets as ordered by the probate court.

affidavit of title/ownership
A written statement made under oath by seller or grantor, acknowledged before a Notary Public. In it the sellers/affiants identify themselves and indicate marital status; certify by examination of title on contract that there are no judgments, bankruptcies, or divorces, no unrecorded deeds, contracts, unpaid repair, or improvements, or defects of title known to seller; and that seller possesses the property.

after-acquired title
Any benefits that come to a property after a sale must follow the sale and accrue to the new owner.

agency
A legal relationship in which a principal authorizes an agent to act as the principal's representative when dealing with third parties.

agency relationship
A special relationship of trust by which one person (agent) is authorized to conduct business, sign papers, or otherwise act on behalf of another person (principal).

agreement
A mutual exchange of promises (either written or oral). Although often used as synonymous with contract, technically it denotes mutual promises that fail as a contract for lack of consideration.

agreement of sale
A contract for the sale of real property where the seller gives up possession, but retains the title until the purchase price is paid in full. Also called contract for sale or land contract.

agricultural property
Property zoned for use in farming, including the raising of crops and livestock.

air rights
Rights in real property to the reasonable use of the air space above the land surface.

airspace
The interior area which an apartment, office or condominium occupies. Airspace is considered real property to a reasonable height. For example, an owner or developer of condominiums may sell the airspace as real property.

alienate
To transfer, convey, or sell property to another. The act of transferring ownership, title, or interest.

alienation clause
A clause in a loan document allowing lender to call the balance of the loan due upon the sale of the property. Also called the **due-on-sale** clause.

all-inclusive trust deed (A.I.T.D.)
A purchase money deed of trust subordinate to—but still including—the original loan.

amendment
Change to escrow instructions. Any changes must be made by mutual agreement between buyer and seller. The escrow agent does not have the authority to make changes in the contract upon the direction of either the buyer or seller, unless both agree to the change, in the form of an amendment. A change to an existing contract by mutual agreement of the parties.

amortization
The liquidation of a financial obligation on an installment basis.

amortized loan
A loan, interest and principal, to be repaid by a series of regular payments that are equal or nearly equal, without any special balloon payment prior to maturity. Also called a Level Payments Loan.

annual percentage rate
The relationship of the total finance charge to the total amount to be financed as required under the Truth-in-Lending Act.

appraisal
An unbiased estimate or opinion of the property value on a given date.

appraisal report
A written statement where an appraiser gives his or her opinion of value.

arm's length transaction
A transaction, such as a sale of property, in which all parties involved are acting in their own self-interest and are under no undue influence or pressure from other parties.

assessed value
Value placed on property by a public tax assessor as a basis for taxation.

assessor's parcel number (APN)
The official identification number for a specific property. The assessor, who has the responsibility of determining assessed values, to determine property tax. Also referred to as account, folio or UPC number, and appears in legal property descriptions.

assignment
The transfer of entire leasehold estate to a new person.

assignment of rents clause
A clause in a deed of trust or mortgage, providing that in the event of default, all rents and income from the secured property will be paid to the lender to help reduce the outstanding loan balance.

assumption clause
A clause in a document that allows a buyer to take over existing loan and agree to be liable for the repayment of the loan.

attachment
The process by which the court holds the property of a defendant pending outcome of a lawsuit.

attachment lien
When the court holds the real or personal property of a defendant as security for a judgment pending the outcome of a lawsuit. Also known as a writ of attachment.

attorney-in-fact
The person holding the power of attorney. A competent and disinterested person who is authorized by another person to act in his or her place in legal matters.

B

balloon payment
Under an installment loan, a final payment that is substantially larger than any other payment and repays the debt in full.

bare legal title
The title to real property passes to a third party called a trustee who holds the bare legal title, and forecloses in event of default. Also called naked legal title. The trustee has bare title and the owner has equitable ownership or possession.

beneficiary
The lender under a deed of trust.

beneficiary statement
A statement of the unpaid balance of a loan and describes the condition of the debt.

bequest
A gift of personal property by will.

bilateral contract
An agreement in which each person promises to perform an act in exchange for another person's promise to perform.

bill of sale
A written agreement used to transfer ownership in personal property.

blanket loan
A loan secured by several properties. The security instrument used can be a blanket deed of trust or a blanket mortgage.

boot
Extra cash or non like-kind property put into an exchange.

breach of contract
A failure to perform on part or all of the terms and conditions of a contract.

bridge loan
A loan to bridge the gap between the termination of one mortgage and the beginning of another, such as when a borrower purchases a new home before receiving cash proceeds from the sale of a prior home, aka 'swing loan.'

bulk transfer law
The law concerning any transfer in bulk (not a sale in the ordinary course of the seller's business).

bundle of rights
An ownership concept describing all the legal rights that attach to the ownership of real property.

business opportunity
Any type of business that is for lease or sale.

buydown
A cash payment, usually measured in points, to a lender in order to reduce the interest rate a borrower must pay. The seller may increase the sales price to cover the cost of the buy down.

C

CC&Rs (See *covenants, conditions and restrictions*)

C.L.T.A. standard policy
A policy of title insurance covering only matters of record.

California Land Title Association
A trade organization of the state's title companies.

CAL-VET Program
A program administered by the State Department of Veterans Affairs for the direct financing of farm and home purchases by eligible California veterans of the armed forces.

capital assets
Assets of a permanent nature used in producing an income (land, buildings, machinery and equipment).

capital gain
At resale of a capital item, the amount by which the net sale proceeds exceed the adjusted cost basis (book value). Used for income tax computations. Gains are called short or long term based upon length of holding period after acquisition. Usually taxed at lower rates than ordinary income.

carryback financing
Financing by a seller who takes back a note for part of the purchase price.

cashout refinance
A loan that refinances a prior mortgage and that provides additional cash to the borrower. Funds, usually to pay off debts, or renovate.

certificate of eligibility
Issued by Department of Veterans Affairs – evidence of individual's eligibility to obtain VA loan.

certificate of occupancy
A certificate issued by local building authorities that indicates new construction is in compliance with codes and may be occupied.

certificate of reasonable value
The Federal VA appraisal commitment of property value.

certificate of taxes due
A written statement or guaranty of the condition of the taxes on a certain property made by the County Treasurer of the county wherein the property is located. Any loss resulting to any person from an error in a tax certificate shall be paid by the county which such treasurer represents.

certificate of title
A written opinion by an attorney that ownership of the particular parcel of land is as stated in the certificate.

chain of title
A chronological history of property's ownership. Also, sequential record of changes in ownership showing the connection from one owner to the next. A complete chain of title is desirable whenever property is transferred and required by title insurance companies if they are writing a policy on a property.

chattel
Personal property.

chattel real
An item of personal property connected to real estate; for example, a lease.

closing
Process by which all the parties to a real estate transaction conclude the details of a sale or mortgage. The process includes the signing and transfer of documents and distribution of funds.

closing costs
The miscellaneous expenses buyers and sellers normally incur in the transfer of ownership of real property over and above the cost of the property. A general term to describe the fees that a borrower will pay at closing. Sometimes called settlement fees.

closing statement
An accounting of funds made to the buyer and seller separately. Required by law to be made at the completion of every real estate transaction.

cloud on title
Any condition that affects the clear title of real property or minor defect in the chain of title which needs to be removed.

co-borrower
One who is individually and jointly obligated to repay a mortgage loan and shares ownership of the property with one or more borrowers.

Code of Civil Procedure
One of the 25 California codes that contain the statutes passed by the state legislature. It contains most of the procedural requirements for enforcing rights granted by other codes, including the procedures for evictions, foreclosures, and lawsuits.

Code of Ethics
A set of rules and principles expressing a standard of accepted conduct for a professional group and governing the relationship of members to each other and to the organization.

codicil
A change in a will before the maker's death.

collateral
Something of value given as security for a debt.

commission
A fee for services rendered usually based on a certain percentage of the sales price of a property.

commission split
The previously agreed upon division of money between a broker and sales-associate when the brokerage has been paid a commission from a sale made by the associate.

common area
An entire common interest subdivision except the separate interests therein.

common interest subdivision
Individuals owning a separate lot or unit, with an interest in the common areas of the entire project. The common areas are usually governed by a homeowner's association.

community property
All property acquired by a husband and wife during a valid marriage (excluding certain separate property).

community property with right of survivorship
A law allowed a husband and wife to hold title to their property.

complete escrow
All terms of the escrow instructions have been met.

compound interest
Interest paid on original principal and also on the accrued and unpaid interest which has accumulated as the debt matures.

concurrent ownership
When property is owned by two or more persons or entities at the same time. Also known as co-ownership.

condition
Similar to a covenant, a promise to do or not to do something. The penalty for breaking a condition is return of the property to the grantor Also, Conditions, Covenants and Restrictions-CC&Rs found in Homeowners Associations master deed.

condition precedent
A condition which requires something to occur before a transaction becomes absolute and enforceable; for example, a sale that is contingent on the buyer obtaining financing.

condition subsequent
A condition which, if it occurs at some point in the future, can cause a property to revert to the grantor; for example, a requirement in a grant deed that a buyer must never use the property for anything other than a private residence.

conditional use permit
Allows a land use that may be incompatible with other uses existing in the zone.

condominium
A housing unit consisting of a separate fee interest in a particular specific space, plus an undivided interest in all common or public areas of the development. Each unit owner has a deed, separate financing and pays the property taxes for their unit.

condominium declaration
The document which establishes a condominium and describes the property rights of the unit owners.

conforming loans
Loans which conform to Fannie Mae guidelines, which sets loan limits to a certain amount.

consideration
Something of value—such as money, a promise, property, or personal services.

construction loan
A loan made to finance actual construction or improvement on land. Funds are usually disbursed in increments as the construction progresses.

constructive eviction
Conduct by a landlord that impairs tenant's possession of the premises making occupancy hazardous.

constructive notice
Notice given by recording a document, or taking physical possession of the property.

Consumer Credit Protection Act
A federal law that includes the Truth-in-Lending Law.

contingent
Conditional, uncertain, conditioned upon the occurrence or nonoccurrence of some uncertain future event.

contract
A legally enforceable agreement made by competent parties, to perform or not perform a certain act.

contract date
The date the contract is created. The contract is created when the final acceptance was communicated back to the offeror.

contract of sale
A contract for the sale of real property where the seller gives up possession but retains title until the total of the purchase price is paid off. Also called installment sales contract, a contract of sale, an agreement of sale, a conditional sales contract, or a land sales contract.

contractual intent
An intention to be bound by an agreement; thereby, thus preventing jokes and jests from becoming valid contracts.

covenant
A promise to do or not do certain things.

conventional loan
Any loan made by lenders without any governmental guarantees.

convey
To transfer ownership or title.

conveyance
The transfer of title to land by use of a written instrument.

cooperative
Ownership of an apartment unit in which the owner has purchased shares in the corporation that holds title to the entire building. A residential multifamily building.

co-signer
A second party who signs a promissory note together with the primary borrower.

co-tenancy
Ownership of an interest in a particular parcel of land by more than one person; e.g., tenancy in common, joint tenancy, partnership.

covenants, conditions and restrictions (CC&Rs)
Restrictions are placed on certain types of real property and limit the activities of owners. Covenants and conditions are promises to do or not to do certain things. Consequence for breaking those promises may either be money damages in the case of covenants, or the return of the property to the grantor, in the case of conditions.

credit report
Report generated by a credit reporting agency (such as TransUnion, Experion®, or Equifax). Shows history of on-time and late payments on mortgages, credit cards, rent, utilities, and other debts. Credit reports are used with other information to generate a credit score to reflect credit risk.

credit score
Number showing the lender how likely a person will repay a loan - whether they are a good or poor credit risk. This score can be a very big factor in determining whether a person gets a loan, from whom, and what interest rate and fees they will be charged for the loan. The score is generated by a mathematical formula that considers the credit reports and other factors. It may also be referred to as **FICO**® score or Beacon score or some other name-These are companies that create credit scores.

D

damages
The indemnity recoverable by a person who has sustained an injury, either in his or her person, property, or relative rights, through the act or default of another. Loss sustained or harm done to a person or property.

Declaration of Homestead
The recorded document that protects a homeowner from foreclosure by certain judgment creditors.

Declaration of Restrictions
A written legal document which lists covenants, conditions and restrictions (CC&Rs). This document gives each owner the right to enforce the CC&Rs.

deed
A formal transfer by a party.

deed in lieu of foreclosure
A deed to real property accepted by a lender from a defaulting borrower to avoid the necessity of foreclosure proceedings by the lender.

deed of trust
In some states loans are secured by means of a document called a deed of trust, instead of a mortgage document. (See *Trust Deed*)

deed restrictions
Limitations in the deed to a property that dictate certain uses that may or may not be made of the property.

default
Failure to pay a debt or on a contract.

default judgment
A judgment entered in favor of the plaintiff when the defendant fails to appear in court.

defeasance clause
The clause in a mortgage that gives the mortgagor the right to redeem mortgagor's property upon the payment of mortgagor's obligations to the mortgagee.

deficiency judgment
A judgment against a borrower for the balance of a debt owed when the security or the loan is not sufficient enough to pay the debt.

delivery (of a deed)
The unconditional, irrevocable intent of a grantor immediately to divest (give up) an interest in real estate by a deed or other instrument.

deposit receipt
Contract that acts as the receipt for earnest money given by the buyer to secure an offer, as well as being the basic agreement, between the buyer and seller.

devise
A gift of real property by will.

disclosure statement
The statement required by the Truth-in-Lending Law whereby a creditor must give a debtor a statement showing the finance charge, annual percentage rate, and other required information.

discount points
The amount of money the borrower or seller must pay the lender to get a mortgage at a stated interest rate, the amount is equal to the difference between the principal balance on the note and the lesser amount which a purchaser of the note would pay the original lender for it under market conditions. A point equals one percent of the loan.

discount rate
The interest rate that is charged by the Federal Reserve Bank to its member banks for loans.

discounting a note
Selling a note for less than the face amount or the current balance.

document preparation fee
An amount of money charged for the preparation of mortgage loan documents. This charge will be shown on the HUD-1 Settlement Statement and is part of closing costs.

documentary transfer tax
A state enabling act allowing a county to adopt a documentary transfer tax to apply on all transfers of real property located in the county. Notice of payment is entered on face of the deed or on a separate paper filed with the deed.

due-on-sale clause
An acceleration clause granting the lender the right to demand full payment of the mortgage upon a sale of the property.

E

earthquake insurance
A special policy or endorsement that provides coverage for a building and its contents because standard homeowners' and most business insurance policies do not cover earthquakes. The special policy or endorsement usually carries a large deductible.

earnest money
Down payment made by a purchaser of real estate as evidence of good faith. A deposit or partial payment.

easement
The right to use another's land for a specified purpose, sometimes known as a right-of-way. The right to enter or use someone else's land for a specified purpose.

EFT
Electronic Funds Transfer, also known as a wire transfer. Banks routinely wire monies from account to account via EFT so as to avoid any accrual of interest.

electronic signature
A method (an electronic sound, symbol, or process) of signing an electronic message that identifies and authenticates a particular person as the source of the electronic message, and indicates such person's approval of the information contained in the electronic message.

emancipated minor
Someone who is legally set free from parental control or supervision.

encroachment
The unauthorized placement of permanent improvements that intrude on adjacent property owned by another.

encumbrance
An interest in real property that is held by someone who is not the owner.

Environmental Impact Report
A study of how a development will affect the ecology of its surroundings. Also known as EIR.

Equal Credit Opportunity Act
Federal act to ensure that all consumers are given an equal chance to obtain credit.

equitable title
The interest held by the trustor under a trust deed. Selling a note for less than the face amount or the current balance.

equity
The difference between the appraised value and the loan. Also, dollar amount of a home that is paid for. Calculate equity by taking the market value of the home and subtracting debt. Ex.: A house worth $150,000 with $65,000 owed on a first mortgage and $15,000 owed on a home equity line of credit. Take $150,000 - $80,000 (65,000 + 15,000) to arrive at $90,000 or the equity of the home.

escalator clause
A clause in a contract providing for the upward or downward adjustment of certain items to cover specified contingencies, usually tied to some index or event. Often used in long term leases to provide for rent adjustments, to cover tax and maintenance increases.

escrow
A small and short-lived trust arrangement. Escrow Money, property, a deed, or a bond put into the custody of a third party for delivery to a grantee only after the fulfillment of the conditions specified.

escrow agent
The neutral third party holding funds or something of value in trust for another.

escrow holder
Acts as a neutral agent of both buyer and seller. An independent third party legally bound to carry out the written provisions of an escrow agreement; a neutral, bonded third party who is a dual agent for the principals; sometimes called an escrow agent.

escrow instructions
Written directions, signed by a buyer and seller, detailing the procedures necessary to close a transaction and directing the escrow agent how to proceed.

estate
The ownership interest or claim a person has in real property. A legal interest in land; defines the nature, degree, extent and duration of a person's ownership in land.

estate for life
A possessory, freehold estate in land held by a person only for the duration of his or her life or the life or lives of another.

evidence of title
Proof of property ownership.

exchange
A means of trading equities in two or more properties, treated as a single transaction through a single escrow.

execute/ executed contract
To perform or complete; to sign. An indication that all parties have performed completely.

executor/executrix
A person named in a will to handle affairs of the deceased.

executory contract
A contract in which obligation to perform exists on one or both sides.

express contract
Parties declare the terms and put their intentions in words, either oral or written.

extended policy An extended title insurance policy.

F

Federal Housing Administration (FHA)
A federal government agency that insures private mortgage loans for financing of homes and home repairs.

Federal National Mortgage Association
Fannie Mae a quasi-public agency converted into a private corporation whose primary function is to buy and sell FHA and VA mortgages in the secondary market.

fees
Money paid or is charged up front to get a mortgage loan. Fees are paid in cash or financed as part of the loan. If financed, loan balance increases equity is reduced. The fees appear on the Good Faith Estimate and HUD-1 Settlement Statement. Many of these fees are negotiated. (See *Up Front Fees, finance charge, underwriting, warehousing fees*)

fee simple
The greatest possible interest a person can have in real estate.

fee simple absolute
The largest, most complete ownership recognized by law. An estate in fee with no restrictions on its use. Property transferred or sold with no conditions or limitations on its use.

fee simple estate
The most complete form of ownership.

fee simple qualified/defeasible
An estate in which the holder has a fee simple title, subject to return to the grantor if a specified condition occurs. Also known as fee simple defeasible.

FICO®
Credit scores calculated by Fair Isaac Company are often referred to as FICO®. Normally an average of credit scores taken by three national credit bureaus. (See *Credit Score*)

fictitious business name
A business name other than the name of the person who has registered the business. Also known as assumed name. A name that does not include the last name of the owner in the name of the business, and known as DBA or doing business as.

fiduciary
A relationship that implies a position of trust or confidence.

fiduciary duty
That duty owned by an agent to act in the highest good faith toward the principal and not to obtain any advantage over the latter by the slightest misrepresentation, concealment, duress of pressure.

fiduciary relationship
A relationship that implies a position of trust or confidence.

finance charge
The dollar amount the credit will cost and is composed of any direct or indirect charge as a condition of obtaining credit. Also, disclosure that appears on the Truth-in-Lending Act Disclosure Statement, intended to show cost of loan as a dollar amount. Includes: interest that will be charged over the life of the loan, and some upfront fees (prepaid finance charges).

financing statement
A written notice filed with the county recorder by a creditor who has extended credit for the purchase of personal property; establishes the creditor's interests in the personal property which is security for the debt. A document used to record debt.

fire insurance
Coverage protecting property against losses caused by a fire or lightning that is usually included in homeowners or commercial multiple peril policies.

first mortgage
A mortgage superior to any other mortgages.

first trust deed
A legal document pledging collateral for a loan that has first priority over all other claims against the property except taxes and bonded indebtedness. That trust deed is superior to any other. (See *trust deed*)

fiscal year
Starts on July 1 and runs through June 30 of the following year; used for real property tax purposes.

fixed rate fully amortized loan
A loan with two distinct features. First, the interest rate remains fixed for the life of the loan. Second, the payments remain level for the life of the loan and are structured to repay the loan at the end of the loan term.

fixed rate loan
The most common type of loan. The principal and interest are calculated for the term of the loan. Payments are determined by dividing the total by the number of payments in the term of the loan. Regular payments of fixed amounts, to include both interest and principal are made. This payment pays off the debt completely by the end of the term.

fixture
Personal property that has become affixed to real estate.

flood certification fee
Fee charged to determine if the property lies in a flood zone and flood insurance is required.

forbearance
Forgiving a debt or obligation.

fraud
An act meant to deceive in order to get someone to part with something of value.

freehold estate
An estate in real property which continues for an indefinite period of time.

foreclosure
A legal procedure by which mortgaged property in which there has been default on the part of the borrower is sold to satisfy the debt.

fully amortized loan
A loan that is fully repaid at maturity. The borrower makes periodic payments of the principal and interest.

G

general lien
A lien on all the property of a debtor.

gift deed
Used to make a gift of property to a grantee, usually a close friend or relative.

gift tax
Tax that can be due when you give property or other assets to someone.

goodwill
An intangible, salable asset arising from the reputation of a business; the expectation of continued public patronage.

Good Faith Estimate (GFE)
Lenders are required to give borrowers a good faith estimate of all fees due at closing within three days of applying for a loan. These fees, also called settlement costs, cover expenses associated with home loans: inspections, title insurance, taxes, and other charges. Costs average between 3 and 5 percent of the sale price.

Government National Mortgage Association
An agency of HUD, which functions in the secondary mortgage market, primarily in social housing programs. Also known as Ginnie Mae.

government survey
A method of specifying the location of parcel of land using prime meridians, base lines, standard parallels, guide meridians, townships, and sections.

graduated payment adjustable mortgage
A loan in which the monthly payment graduates by a certain percentage each year for a specific number of years, then levels off for the remaining term of the loan.

grant
A technical legal term in a deed of conveyance bestowing an interest in real property on another. The words convey and transfer have the same effect.

grant deed
A type of deed in which the grantor warrants that he or she has not previously conveyed the property being granted, has not encumbered the property except as disclosed, and will convey to the grantee any title to the property acquired later.

grantee
The person receiving the property, or the one to whom it is being conveyed.

grantor
The person conveying, or transferring, the property.

granting clause
The clause in a deed or mortgage that conveys the property and usually states "To grant and release" from grantor to grantee.

gross income
Total income from property before any expenses are deducted.

ground lease
A lease for only the land.

guarantee of title
An assurance of clear title.

H

habendum clause
The "to have and to hold" clause which may be found in a deed.

hard money loan
Any loan made on real property in exchange for cash.

hazard insurance
A property insurance policy that protects the owner and lender against physical hazards to property such as fire and windstorm damage.

hold harmless clause
Protects the broker from incorrect information.

holder
The party to whom a promissory note is made payable.

holder in due course
A person who buys an existing negotiable instrument (promissory note, check) in the ordinary course of business before it is due. It is obtained in good faith and for value, without knowledge that it has been previously dishonored and without notice of any defect or setoff.

home equity loan
A cash loan made against the equity in the borrower's home.

homeowners' association
A group of property owners in a condominium or other subdivision neighborhood, who manage common areas, collect dues, and establish property standards.

homeowners' exemption
A $7,000 tax exemption available to all owner-occupied dwellings.

homeowners' insurance
Policy providing coverage for the house, garage, and other structures on the property, and personal possessions inside the house such as furniture, appliances, and clothing, from losses due to wind, storms, fire, and theft. Living expenses, or Loss of Use, are also covered in the event of a disaster. Accidents that happen to third parties and/or their property while on or in the premises are covered under the liability section of the insurance policy. Insurance coverage for flood and earthquake damage is excluded and must be purchased separately.

homestead
A piece of land that is owned and occupied as a family home.

HUD/Hud 1
U.S. Department of Housing and Urban Development form settlement (closing) statement of all costs and fees in closing escrow.

hypothecation
A process which allows a borrower to remain in possession of the property while using it to secure a loan.

I

intestate
Dying without leaving a will.

implied contract
An agreement shown by acts and conduct rather than written words.

impound account
A trust account set up for funds set aside for future costs relating to a property.

improvements
Valuable additions made to property to enhance value or extend useful remaining life.

injunction
A court order forcing a person to do or not do an act.

installment note
A note which provides for a series of periodic payments of principal and interest, until amount borrowed is paid in full. This periodic reduction of principal amortizes the loan.

instrument
A formal legal document such as a contract, deed or will.

interest
The charge for the use of money.

interest rate
The percentage charged for the use of money.

interpleader action
A court proceeding initiated by the stakeholder of property who claims no proprietary interest in it for the purpose of deciding who among claimants is legally entitled to the property.

involuntary lien
When the owner does not pay taxes or the debt owed, a lien may be placed against his or her property without permission. Created by operation of law, such as real property tax lien, judgment lien, or mechanic's lien.

J

joint tenancy
When two or more parties own real property as co-owners, with the right of survivorship.

judgment
The final legal decision of a judge in a court of law regarding the legal rights of parties in a dispute.

judgment lien
The final determination of the rights of parties in a lawsuit by the court.

judicial foreclosure
Foreclosure by court action.

jumbo loans
Loans which exceed the Fannie Mae guidelines for loan size and amount. Jumbo loans may have different guidelines from a conforming loan.

junior mortgage
A second mortgage; one that is subordinate or has an inferior priority to the first mortgage.

junior trust deed
Any trust deed that is recorded after a first trust deed, whose priority is less than that first trust deed.

L

land contract
A contract for the sale of real property where the seller gives up possession, but retains the title until the purchase price is paid in full. Also known as a contract of sale or agreement of sale.

leasehold
An agreement, written or unwritten, transferring the right to exclusive possession and use of real estate for a definite period of time. Also known as a rental agreement or lease.

leasehold estate
A tenant's right to occupy real estate during the term of the lease. This is personal property interest.

legacy
A gift of personal property by will.

legal description
A land description recognized by law; a description by which property can be definitely located by reference to government surveys or approved recorded maps.

legal title
Title that is complete and perfect regarding right of ownership.

lender
A company or person that makes mortgage loans, such as a mortgage banker, credit union, bank, or savings and loan. Lender's name will appear on the promissory note.

lessee
Tenant. Renter.

lessor
Landlord, property owner, and/or the person who owns the property and signs the lease to give possession and use to the tenant.

less-than-freehold estate
The lessee's interest. An estate owned by a tenant who rents real property.

lien
A claim on the property of another for the payment of a debt. A legal obligation to pay.

life estate
An estate that is limited in duration to the life of its owner or the life of another designed person.

limited partnership
A partnership of at least one general partner and one limited partner.

liquidated damages clause
Clause in a contract that allows parties to the contract to decide in advance the amount of damages to be paid, should either party breach the contract.

listing agreement
A written contract by which a principal, or seller, employs a broker to sell real estate.

loan application
The loan application is a source of information on which the lender bases a decision to make the loan; defines the terms of the loan contract, gives the name of the borrower, place of employment, salary, bank accounts, and credit references, and describes the real estate that is to be mortgaged. It states the amount of loan being applied for and repayment terms. (Also known as a *1003*)

loan assumption
A buyer assumes the exiting loan when a property is sold. The buyer takes over primary liability for the loan, with the original borrower secondarily liable if there is a default.

loan closing
When all conditions have been met, the loan officer authorizes the recording of the trust deed or mortgage. The disbursal procedure of funds is similar to the closing of a real estate sales escrow. The borrower can expect to receive less than the amount of the loan, as title, recording, service, and other fees may be withheld, or can expect to deposit the cost of these items into the loan escrow. This process is sometimes called funding the loan.

loan commitment
Lender's contractual commitment to make a loan based on the appraisal and underwriting.

loan term
Length of time until loan is due and payable.

loan-to-value ratio
The percentage of appraised value to the loan. (Also known as LTV)

lot, block, and tract system
A process where developers divide parcels of land into lots. Each lot in a subdivision is identified by number, as is the block in which it is located; each lot and block is in a referenced tract. This process is required by the California Subdivision Map Act.

M

maker
The borrower who executes a promissory note and becomes primarily liable for payment to the lender.

manufactured home
A home built in a factory after June 15, 1976. It must conform to the U.S. government's Manufactured Home Construction and Safety Standards.

marketable title
Good or clear saleable title reasonably free from risk of litigation over possible defects.

material fact
Any fact that would seem likely to affect the judgment of the principal in giving consent to the agent to enter into the particular transaction on the specified terms.

mechanic's lien
A lien placed against a property by anyone who supplies labor, services, or materials used for improvements on real property and who did not receive payment for the improvements.

Mello-Roos Act
Allows developers to make improvements (roads, parks, schools, fire stations) while making each homeowner pay for the improvements. These improvements are listed in the property taxes.

meridian
A survey line running north and south, used as a reference when mapping land.

metes and bounds
Land description that delineates boundaries and measures distances between landmarks to identify property.

mineral rights
The legal interest in the valuable items found below the surface of a property (i.e., gold and coal).

minor
A person under 18 years of age.

misrepresentation
Making a false statement or concealing a material fact. Any action that conveys a false message.

mobile home
A factory-built home manufactured prior to June 15, 1976, constructed on a chassis and wheels, and designed for permanent or semi-attachment to land.

money encumbrance
An encumbrance that affects the title.

monument
A fixed landmark used in a metes and bounds land description.

mortgage
A legal document used as security for a debt. Also known as a Trust Deed (TD). A promise in which the principal agrees to put up one's home as security for a loan. The mortgage is the instrument which secures the Promissory Note, in which the buyer or borrower promises to repay the loan by a certain date. This document allows the lender to force a sale of the home (foreclosure), if the principal fails to make payments, to pay property taxes or insurance, or to keep other promises. In some states the mortgage document is called a Deed of Trust.

mortgage banker
A person whose principal business is the originating, financing, closing, selling, and servicing of loans secured by real property for institutional lenders on a contractual basis.

mortgage broker
A person or company that obtains a mortgage loan for the borrower from another lender. A mortgage broker will not always be representing the borrower and will not necessarily be looking after the borrower's best interests.

mortgage insurance
Insurance that may be required when a loan is greater than 80% of the value of the home. This insurance protects the lender in the event a borrower fails to make his or her loan payments. The borrower ordinarily pays the cost of MI or PMI, in the form of monthly premiums added to the mortgage payments. Also known as PMI or MI.

mortgage yield
The amount received or returned from an investment expressed as a percentage.

mortgagee
The lender under a mortgage.

mortgagor
The borrower, or one who gives a mortgage as security for a debt.

mutual assent
An agreement between the parties in a contract. The offer and acceptance of a contract.

mutual consent
The offer by one party and acceptance by another party. Also known as mutual assent or meeting of the minds.

mutual mortgage insurance (MMI)
A fee for an insurance policy charged the borrower to protect lender under an FHA loan, in the event of foreclosure on the property.

N

naked legal title
Title lacking the rights and privileges commonly associated with ownership may be held by trustee under a trust deed. Also called bare legal title.

negative amortization
Occurs when monthly installment payments are insufficient to pay the interest, so any unpaid interest is added to the principal due.

negligence
The failure to act as a reasonable person. The performance of an act that would not be done by a reasonable person.

negotiable instrument
Any written instrument that may be transferred by endorsement or delivery.

net lease
The tenant pays an agreed-upon sum as rent, plus certain agreed-upon expenses per month (i.e., taxes, insurance, and repairs).

neutral depository
An escrow business conducted by someone who is a licensed escrow holder.

nominal interest rates
The interest rate that is named or stated in loan documents.

notary public
A licensed public officer who takes or witnesses the acknowledgement.

note
An evidence of a debt.

notice of completion
A notice filed by the owner or general contractor after completion of work on improvements, limiting the time in which mechanic's liens can be filed against the property.

notice of default
A notice to a defaulting party that there has been a nonpayment of a debt.

notice of non-responsibility
When an owner discovers unauthorized work on the property, he or she must file a notice. This is a notice that must be recorded and posted on the property to be valid, stating the owner is not responsible for work being done. This notice releases the owner from the liability for work done without permission.

notice of right to cancel
Under federal law, a borrower or buyer may be permitted to cancel or rescind a mortgage loan within a specified time (usually three days), after signing loan documents in a refinance, second mortgage, or other mortgage loan that does not involve the purchase of a home. The lender is required to give the borrower notice in writing of this right to cancel or rescind, and the deadline in which to cancel. (See *Right of Rescission*)

O

1 month/1 year
For escrow purposes, 30 days=1 month / for escrow and proration purposes 1 year = 12 months, 52 weeks.

1031 exchange
A method of deferring tax liability. Also known as a tax-free exchange.

obligor
One who is bound by a legal obligation. A person, delinquent in paying child support, whose name is listed by the Child Support Services.

offer
A presentation or proposal for acceptance to form a contract.

option
A contract to keep open, for a set period of time, an offer to purchase or lease property.

or more clause
A clause in a mortgage or trust deed that allows a borrower to pay it off early with no penalty.

ownership
The right of one or more persons to possess and use property to the exclusion of all others. A collection of rights to the use and enjoyment of property.

ownership in severalty
Property owned by one person or entity.

P

paramount title
Title which is superior or foremost to all others.

parcel map
Map showing a parcel of land that will be subdivided into less than five parcels or units, and shows land boundaries, streets, and parcel numbers.

partial reconveyance
A clause in a trust deed or mortgage permitting the release of a parcel or part of a parcel from the lien of that security instrument. The release usually occurs upon the payment of a specified sum of money.

partially amortized note
A promissory note with a repayment schedule that is not sufficient to amortize the loan over its term.

partition action
A court action to divide a property held by co-owners.

partnership
A form of business in which two or more persons join their money and skills in conducting the business.

personal property
Anything movable that is not real property.

plaintiff
In a court action, the one who sues; the complainant.

planned development
A planning and zoning term describing land not subject to conventional zoning to permit clustering of residences or other characteristics of the project which differ from normal zoning. Sometimes called a planned unit development (PUD).

points
Charges levied by the lender based on the loan amount. Each point equals one percent of the loan amount; for example, two points on a $100,000 mortgage is $2,000. Discount points are used to buy down the interest rate. Points can also include a loan origination fee, which is usually one point. See *Discount Points*.

power of attorney
A legal document that gives another person the legal authority to act on his or her behalf.

power of sale
A clause in a trust deed or mortgage that gives the holder the right to sell the property in the event of default by the borrower.

preliminary title report
An offer to issue a policy of title insurance in the future for a specific fee.

prepaid items of expense
Prorations of prepaid items of expense which are credited to the seller in the closing escrow statement.

prepayment clause
A clause in a trust deed that allows a lender to collect a certain percentage of a loan as a penalty for an early payoff.

prepayment penalty
Penalty for the payment of a note before it actually becomes due. A fee or charge imposed upon a debtor who desires to pay off their loan before its maturity.

principal
In a real estate transaction, the one (seller) who hires the broker to represent him or her in the sale of the property. The amount of money borrowed.

principal note
The promissory note which is secured by the mortgage or trust deed.

priority
The order in which deeds are recorded.

private grant
The granting of private property to other private persons.

private mortgage insurance
Mortgage guarantee insurance available to conventional lenders on the first part of a high risk loan.

private restrictions
Created at the time of sale or in the general plan of a subdivision.

pro rata
In proportion; according to a certain percentage or proportion of a whole.

probate
The legal process to prove a will is valid.

probate sale
A court-approved sale of the property of a deceased person.

procuring cause
A broker who produces a buyer "ready, willing and able" to purchase the property for the price and on the terms specified by the seller, regardless of whether the sale is completed.

promissory note
The evidence of the debt.

property taxes
Taxes used to operate the government in general.

prorate
The division and distribution of expenses and/or income between the buyer and seller of property as of the date of closing or settlement. The process of making a fair distribution of expenses, through escrow, at the close of the sale.

purchase money mortgage or trust deed

A trust deed or mortgage given as part or all of the purchase consideration for real property. In some states the purchase money mortgage or trust deed loan can be made by a seller who extends credit to the buyer of property or by a third party lender (typically a financial institution) that makes a loan to the buyer of real property for a portion of the purchase price to be paid for the property. In many states there are legal limitations upon mortgages and trust deed beneficiaries collecting deficiency judgments against the purchase money borrower after the collateral hypothecated under such security instruments has been sold through the foreclosure process.

Q

quiet title action

A court proceeding to clear a cloud on the title of real property. Also known as action to quiet title.

quitclaim deed

Transfers any interest the grantor may have at the time the deed is signed with no warranties of clear title.

R

radon

Colorless, odorless, gas that is a carcinogen detected by a spectrometer.

range lines

Government survey imaginary vertical lines six miles east and west of the meridian to form columns.

rate

The percentage of interest charged on the principal.

rate and term

The note rate (percentage) and the period of time during which loan payments are made must be specified on the promissory note to be binding.

rate lock

Locks in the interest rate. Refers to the agreement between the borrower and the lender or broker that as long as the loan is closed within a certain period of time (for example, 30 or 60 days), the interest rate on the loan will be set (locked) at an agreed-upon rate.

ratification

The approval of a previously authorized act, performed on behalf of a person, which makes the act valid and legally binding.

Real Estate Settlement Procedures ACT (RESPA)

A federal law requiring disclosure to borrowers of settlement (closing) procedures and costs by means of a pamphlet and forms prescribed by the United States Department of Housing and Urban Development.

Real Estate Transfer Disclosure Statement

A document that the seller must provide to any buyer of residential property (one-to-four units).

real property

Land (air, surface, mineral, water rights), appurtenances and anything attached, and immovable by law. Also included in real property are the interests, benefits and rights inherent in owning real estate, i.e., the bundle of rights. Current usage makes the term real property synonymous with real estate.

reconveyance deed

Conveys title to property from a trustee back to the borrower (trustor) upon payment in full of the debt secured by the trust deed.

recording

The process of placing a document on file with a designated public official for public notice. This public official is usually a county officer known as the County Recorder who designates the fact that a document has been presented for recording by placing a recording stamp upon it indicating the time of day and the date when it was officially placed on file.

recording fees

Fees charged by the local government to record loan documents (for example, the mortgage). These fees will be charged to the borrower and shown on the Settlement Statement (HUD-1).

red flag

Something that alerts a reasonably observant person of a potential problem.

redemption period

A period of time established by state law during which a property owner has the right to recover real estate after a foreclosure or tax sale by paying the sales price plus interest and costs.

refinancing
The payoff of an existing obligation and assuming a new obligation in its place. To finance anew, or extend or renew existing financing.

release clause
A provision found in many blanket mortgage or trust deeds enabling the borrower to obtain partial release from the loan of specific parcels.

request for notice
A notice that is sent, upon request, to any parties interested in a trust deed, informing them of a default.

rescission
Legal action taken to repeal a contract either by mutual consent of the parties or by one party when the other party has breached a contract.

Right of Rescission
The right of a consumer to nullify a contract within three business days of signing it without paying a penalty or down payment. Federal law allows for cooling-off period when obtaining a home equity loan or line of credit, or refinance with another lender. Allows borrower to rescind, or cancel some types of home loans and walk away without losing money. The right of rescission provides a three-day period when borrower can back out of the loan before getting the borrowed money, no questions asked. Within 20 days, the lender must give up its claim to the property as collateral and must refund any fees paid. This provision is included in the Truth-in-Lending Act (TILA).

restriction
A limitation placed on the use of property and may be placed by a private owner, a developer or the government. It is usually placed on property to assure that land use is consistent and uniform within a certain area.

revocation
The canceling of an offer to contract by the person making the original offer.

right of survivorship
The right of a surviving tenant or tenants succeeds to the entire interest of the deceased tenant; the distinguishing feature of a joint tenancy.

rollover mortgage
A loan that allows the rewriting of a new loan at the termination of a prior loan.

S corporation
A corporation that operates like a corporation but is treated like a partnership for tax purposes.

sales contract
A contract by which buyer and seller agree to terms of a sale.

sales tax
Collected as a percentage of the retailing sales of a product, by a retailer, and forwarded to the State Board of Equalization.

satisfaction
Discharge of a mortgage or trust deed from the records upon payment of the debt.

section
An area of land, one square mile, or 640 acres; 1/36 of a township.

security
Evidence of obligations to pay money.

security agreement
A document commonly used to secure a loan on personal property.

security deposit
Money given to a landlord to prepay for any damage other than just normal wear and tear.

security interest
The interest of a creditor (lender) in the property of a debtor (borrower).

Settlement Statement
A mortgage loan closing form required by HUD that is often called a HUD-1. It provides details of all charges and payments made in connection with your loan, and shows to whom they are distributed.

severalty
Ownership of real property by one person or entity.

shared appreciation mortgage (SAM)
Lender and borrower agree to share a certain percentage of the appreciation in market value of the property.

sheriff's deed
A deed given to a buyer when property is sold through court action in order to satisfy a judgment for money or foreclosure of a mortgage.

simple interest
Interest computed on the principal amount of a loan only as distinguished from compound interest.

sole proprietorship
A business owned and operated by one person.

special assessments
Taxes used for specific local purposes.

special warranty deed
A deed in which the grantor warrants or guarantees the title only against defects arising during grantor's ownership of the property and not against defects existing before the time of grantor's ownership.

specific lien
A lien placed against a certain property, such as a mechanic's lien, trust deed, attachment, property tax lien, or lis pendens.

specific performance
An action brought in a court to compel a party to carry out the terms of a contract.

standard policy
A policy of title insurance covering only matters of record.

Statute of Frauds
A state law which requires that certain contracts must be in writing to prevent fraud in the sale of land or an interest in land.

Statute of Limitations
The period of time limited by statute within which certain court actions may be brought by one party against another.

straight note
A promissory note in which payments of interest only are made periodically during the term of the note, with the principal payment due in one lump sum upon maturity; may also be a note with no payments on either principal or interest until the entire sum is due.

subject to clause
A buyer takes over the existing loan payments, without notifying the lender. The buyer assumes no personal liability for the loan.

subordination clause
A clause in which the holder of a trust deed permits a subsequent loan to take priority.

subrogation
Replacing one person with another in regard to a legal right or obligation. The substitution of another person in place of the creditor, to whose rights he or she succeeds in relation to the debt. The doctrine is used very often where one person agrees to stand surety for the performance of a contract by another person.

succession
The legal transfer of a person's interest in real and personal property under the laws of descent.

T

tax deed
A deed given to a successful bidder at a tax auction.

tax-deferred exchange
The trade or exchange of one real property for another without the need to pay income taxes on the gain at the time of trade. Also call a tax-free exchange.

tax delinquent property
Property that has unpaid taxes.

tax lien
When income or property taxes are not paid.

tax sale
Sale of property after a period of non-payment of taxes.

tenancy
The interest of a person holding property by any right or title. A mode or method of ownership or holding title to property.

tenancy in common
When two or more persons, whose interests are not necessarily equal, are owners of undivided interests in a single estate.

tenancy in partnership
Ownership by two or more persons who form a partnership for business purposes.

tenant
A renter.

tenants by the entirety
Under certain state laws, ownership of property acquired by a husband and wife during marriage, which property is jointly and equally owned. Upon death of one spouse it becomes the property of the survivor.

term
The period of time during which loan payments are made. At the end of the loan term, the loan must be paid in full. (See *Rate and Term*)

testate
A person who dies leaving a valid will.

testator / testatrix
A person who has made a will.

third party
A person who may be affected by the terms of an agreement but who is not a party to the agreement.

timely manner
An act must be performed within certain time limits described in a contract.

time is of the essence clause
A clause in a contract that emphasizes punctual performance as an essential requirement of the contract.

title
Evidence that the owner of land is in lawful possession.

title company
A company that performs a title search on the property and issue a title policy for the lender and the purchaser. It ensures that there is a valid mortgage lien against the property and title is clear.

title insurance
An insurance policy that protects the named insured against loss or damage due to defect in the property's title.

title plant
The storage facility of a title company in which it has accumulated complete title records of properties in its area.

title report
A report which discloses condition of the title, made by a title company preliminary to issuance of title insurance policy.

title theory
Mortgage arrangement whereby title to mortgaged real property vests in the lender. Some states give greater protection to mortgage lenders and assume lenders have title interest. Distinguished from Lien Theory States.

to let, to demise
These phrases mean the same as to rent.

trade fixture
An item of personal property, such as a shelf, cash register, room partition or wall mirror, used to conduct a business.

transfer fee
A charge made by a lending institution holding or collecting on a real estate mortgage to change its records to reflect a different ownership. A government tax or charge usually based on a percentage of the property value or loan amount and imposed by state or local law. Also called Transfer Tax or Charge

transferability
The title must be marketable with an unclouded title.

trust account
An account separate and apart, and physically segregated from broker's own funds; an account in which a broker is required by law to deposit all funds collected for clients.

trust deed
A security instrument that conveys naked legal title of real property.

trust funds
Money or other things of value received from people by a broker to be used in real estate transactions.

trustee
Holds naked legal title to property as a neutral third party where there is a deed of trust.

trustee's deed
A deed given to a buyer of real property at a trustee's sale.

trustee's sale
The forced sale of real property, by a lender, to satisfy a debt.

trustor
The borrower under a deed of trust.

Truth in Lending Act (TILA)
A federal law that requires borrowers to be informed about the cost of borrowing money. Also known as Regulation Z. (See *Right of Rescission*)

Truth-in-Lending Disclosure Statement
Federal law requires for this document for all consumer loans. It provides key information to enable borrowers to shop around and compare loan terms from various lenders.

U

underwriting
The process of evaluating a borrower's risk factors before the lender will make a loan.

underwriting fee
A fee charged by lender to evaluate whether the borrower qualifies for a mortgage loan.

undivided interest
The buyer receives an undivided interest in a parcel of land as a tenant in common with all the other owners.

undue influence
Using unfair advantage to get agreement in accepting a contract.

unenforceable contract
A contract that was valid when made but either cannot be proved or will not be enforced by a court.

Uniform Commercial Code
A code that establishes a unified and comprehensive method for regulation of security transactions in personal property.

unilateral contract
A contract where a party promises to perform without expectation of performance by the other party.

unilateral rescission
Legal action taken to repeal a contract by one party when the other party has breached a contract.

unity
Equal right of possession or undivided interest. For example, each tenant has the right to use the whole property. None of the owners may exclude any co-owner from the property, nor claim any portion of the property for exclusive use.

Up Front Costs
Costs or fees charged to the borrower at or before closing a loan, such as application fees, appraisal fees, points, broker fees, credit report fees, real estate taxes, etc. They can be paid in several ways: they can be paid by the borrower in cash; or they can be added to the loan amount and financed over the life of the loan.

usury
The act of charging a rate of interest in excess of that permitted by law.

V

VA loan
A loan made to qualified veterans for the purchase of real property wherein the Department of Veteran's Affairs guarantees the lender payment of the mortgage.

valid
Legally binding.

valid contract
A binding and enforceable contract; a document that has all the basic elements required by law.

valuable consideration
Money, or other items of value, that is given by one party in exchange for the performance of another party, usually in support of a contract.

valuation
The process of estimating market value.

value
The present and future anticipated enjoyment or profit from the ownership of property. Also known as worth.

variable-rate mortgage (VRM)
A mortgage where the interest rate varies according to an agreed-upon index, thus resulting in a change in the borrower's monthly payments. Mortgages used prior to 1982 replaced by ARMs.

variance
An exception granted to existing zoning regulations for special reasons.

vendee
The buyer under a contract of sale (land contract).

vendor
The seller under a contract of sale (land contract).

verification
Sworn statement before a duly qualified officer to correctness of contents of an instrument.

vested/ vesting
Owned by. The way title will be taken.

Veteran's Exemption
Entitles a resident of California who has been in the military during wartime to take a $4,000 real estate tax emption.

void / void contract
An agreement which is totally absent of legal effect. Contract that has no legal effect due to incapacity or illegal subject matter.

voidable
An agreement which is valid and enforceable on its face, but may be rejected by one or more of the parties.

voluntary lien
When an owner chooses to borrow money, using the property as security for the loan.

W

waiver
The relinquishment or refusal to accept a right.

warehousing
The process of assembling into one package a number of mortgage loans, prior to selling them to an investor.

warehousing fees
Charges included in home loans on the settlement statement or closing costs.

warranty deed
No longer used in California; a deed used to transfer title to property, guaranteeing that the title is clear and the grantor has the right to transfer it.

will
A written instrument whereby a person makes a disposition of his or her property to take effect after their death.

writ of execution
A legal document issued by a court forcing the sale of a property to satisfy a judgment.

writ of possession
A legal action granted by the court to the landlord if the tenant does not move out or answer a lawsuit.

Z

zone
Area set off by authorities for specific use; subject to certain restrictions or restraints.

zoning
The regulation of structures and uses of property within selected districts.

zoning ordinance
Regulates land use for individual projects.